Silk, Slaves, and Stupas

The publisher and the University of California Press Foundation gratefully acknowledge the generous support of the Constance and William Withey Endowment Fund in History and Music.

Silk, Slaves, and Stupas

MATERIAL CULTURE OF THE SILK ROAD

Susan Whitfield

UNIVERSITY OF CALIFORNIA PRESS

University of California Press, one of the most distinguished university presses in the United States, enriches lives around the world by advancing scholarship in the humanities, social sciences, and natural sciences. Its activities are supported by the UC Press Foundation and by philanthropic contributions from individuals and institutions. For more information, visit www.ucpress.edu.

University of California Press
Oakland, California

Library of Congress Cataloging-in-Publication Data

Names: Whitfield, Susan, 1960–   author.
Title: Silk, slaves, and stupas : material culture of the Silk Road / Susan Whitfiel.
Description: Oakland, California : University of California Press, [2018] | Includes bibliographical references and index. |
Identifiers: LCCN 2018001196 (print) | LCCN 2018002111 (ebook) | ISBN 9780520957664 (e-edition) | ISBN 9780520281776 (cloth : alk. paper) | ISBN 9780520281783 (pbk. : alk. paper)
Subjects: LCSH: Silk Road—History. | Asia—Antiquities. | Material culture—Silk Road.
Classification: LCC DS33.1 (ebook) | LCC DS33.1 .W46 2018 (print) | DDC 950.1—dc23
LC record available at https://lccn.loc.gov/2018001196

27   26   25   24   23   22   21   20   19   18
10   9   8   7   6   5   4   3   2   1

CONTENTS

ILLUSTRATIONS

PLATES
follow page 52

MAPS
follow page 148

FIGURES

ACKNOWLEDGMENTS

This book is a distillation of decades of working with Silk Road objects and landscapes. I could not even start to list all the people who have helped with its gestation since the idea took shape many years ago, let alone to remember or name all the people who helped me reach that point, often unwittingly. These latter include a long tradition of scholars, travelers, photographers, curators, conservators, scientists, archaeologists, and others, many from previous centuries, whose works have informed and inspired me. There are also the many people I have encountered in Silk Road travels—drivers, guides, and others, such as local families offering hospitality. It would be invidious to make a selection, and instead I take this opportunity to acknowledge and thank them all.

Many people have helped specifically and most recently by reading individual chapters in their areas of expertise and pointing out my worse mistakes and omissions. I acknowledge their role at the start of each chapter and thank them for their time and scholarly generosity. All remaining errors are my own. Of course, I must thank friends and colleagues who have been supportive during the inevitable up and downs of writing. And I must also thank the team at University of California Press, including the freelance staff, for all their work, most especially in helping me to chase up those elusive missing footnotes.

Finally I must acknowledge the many other—nonhuman—material objects that have played a part in the inspiration for this book; some of them get lead roles here, some bit parts, but many more are the supporting cast, hidden behind the scenes but vital nevertheless.

NOTE ON TRANSLITERATION AND NAMES

If there is one point I would hope readers might take away from this book, it is the commonality of human experience among great diversity. That diversity includes languages and scripts, and thus the names of peoples, things, and places. The roman script is very much in the minority along the Silk Road, and the transliteration of languages into the roman script—romanization—while necessary for a book written in English and intended for many readers, can obscure this diversity. Except where words are in common English usage, I have deliberately retained diacritics/accents for languages that cannot be transcribed using the meager twenty-six letters of the Latin alphabet in order to try to impart something of the richness of the languages of the Silk Road.

For many scripts there are accepted romanization systems and I have used these for Chinese, Sanskrit, and Tibetan (pinyin, the IAST/ISO 15919 convention, and the Wylie system respectively). There is no standard transliteration for Turkic, and I have followed the advice of colleagues as to accepted current practice or common usage. For Arabic and Persian I have followed the systems used by the online versions of the *Encyclopedia of Islam* (http://referenceworks.brillonline.com/browse/encyclopaedia-of-islam-2) and the *Encyclopaedia Iranica* (www.iranicaonline.org/) respectively. I am not a linguist and I apologize for the mistakes that are certain to have crept in despite my—and my editor's—best efforts.

Consistency is difficult for the names of archaeological sites, towns, regions, countries, and political entities. I use contemporary names where possible or meaningful, but in some case historical accuracy has been sacrificed to clarity and then names are necessarily anachronistic.

Introduction

> We are surrounded by things, and we are surrounded by history.
> But too seldom do we use the artifacts that make up our envi-
> ronment to understand the past. Too seldom do we try to read
> objects as we read books—to understand the people and times
> that created them, used them, and discarded them.
>
> —STEVEN LUBAR AND W. DAVID KINGER,
> *History from Things: Essays on Material Culture*

THIS IS A BOOK ABOUT THINGS ON THE SILK ROAD.[1] Things or
objects speak to us, in the sense of causing us to create a narrative. The narrative, however simple—"This is a receptacle made to hold my tea"—is dependent not only on the object's qualities and context but on our qualities and
context. This is a dialogue. The initial narrative might be one of many pro-
voked by the object for one individual, let alone across individuals with different experiences, knowledge, beliefs, and cultural backgrounds. A drinking receptacle might be recognized as such across individuals, although some
might see it as a cup for drinking wine, others as a cup for water. Outside
its initial context—outside the space and time in which it was created—the
object might no longer invoke the narrative intended by its creator. Such is
often the case with objects created for religious or ritual purposes. Historians
and archaeologists seek to understand more about the context in order to try
to recreate the narrative of the object, its biography or history: How, why,
when, and by whom was it made? Where, how, and by whom was it used, and
for what purposes? Did it travel? Was it adapted, changed, broken, repaired?
Without direct access to the original context, we have to accept that at times
we might get the answers to these questions spectacularly wrong.[2]

1. I use the terms *objects* and *things* interchangeably here. See below for my explanation
of their scope.
2. The South African film *The Gods Must Be Crazy* used this scenario to good effect. A
tribe living in the Kalahari Desert are perplexed by a Coca-Cola bottle that lands in their
village after having been thrown from a small plane. In this new context, the object, which

Telling history through objects rather than people or events is not a new approach, but over the past two decades it has become more central in teaching and in popularizing world history.[3] Particularly successful has been the history of commodities.[4] This approach has increasingly been adopted by academic institutions, especially for modern history.[5] Seeking alternative sources for history is not, however, restricted to commodities, and new textbooks in this area range across the mundane, the ornamental, the useful, and the built.[6]

This book focuses on made rather than raw materials but takes a broad view of objects or things—including commodities; "natural" and animate things such as people, horses, and camels; and complex created things, such as jewelry, glass, paintings, and buildings. I do not exclude texts. Instead of arguing that texts are distinct from other things—that texts are "not neutral epistles . . . like other products of human creativity" but are "active in the production, negotiation and transformation of social relationships"[7]—I view the nontextual objects of human creativity also to be active in the production, negotiation, and transformation of these relationships. This book therefore takes the approach of historical archaeology, described by John Moreland as recognizing "that people *in* the past conducted their social practice, and construed their identities, through the Object, the Voice and the Word in specific historical circumstances."[8]

For some historiographers, the seduction of a key object is similar that of a "great man," whereas others look at the humble but plentiful potsherds to understand the past. This book attempts to take a middle line, concentrating most chapters around a single object but considering its context by looking at related objects—including people. The objects selected have complex stories

---

they see as a gift from the gods, is bestowed with all sorts of meaning completely unrelated to its original function. It should be noted that even access to the culture does not guarantee that an outsider will correctly interpret the situation, as some anthropological reports have shown.

3. Most notably with MacGregor (2011).

4. See, e.g., Mintz (1985); Kurlansky (2002).

5. Such as the project "Commodities in World History, 1450–1950," carried out by the University of California Santa Cruz's Center for World History.

6. See, for example, Harvey (2009) and Hicks and Beaudry (2010).

7. Moreland (2001: 31).

8. Moreland (1991: 119).

to be told, and this book aims to give this "thick description," a close-grained analysis of each object in its times and places.[9]

Movement of objects—including people—is essential to the concept of the Silk Road, and most of the objects chosen here have journeyed along the Silk Road. But the vast majority of such objects—everyday or luxury, traded or not—have long disappeared: food, wine, and medicines were consumed; slaves, elephants, and horses died; textiles, wood, and ivory decayed; glass and pottery were broken.[10] Only in rare cases did objects survive by design or accident, as in hoards of metal or glass, or in burials when objects were sufficiently valued to be interred with corpses, as in the case of three of the objects discussed here (chapters 1, 2, and 5). Texts are often the only evidence for the existence of other objects, but both the archaeology and the texts are extremely fragmentary.

Objects are not neutral and inert in this story: they change and also effect change. This is where a material culture approach is especially relevant to the Silk Road. In the interaction of the objects with the cultures they encountered—those that made them, carried them, received them, used them, sold them, discarded them—we can gain new perspectives on those cultures at those times. This book seeks to take account of more recent discussions of "things" to include their interactions with humans (themselves "things"), the usual approach to material culture, but also the interdependence of things and humans—their entanglement.[11]

This is a book set in a period and places characterized by such entanglement. Most of the objects selected here have more than one cultural context and find themselves entangled with things—including people—of different cultures and times. I do not restrict discussion to the object in its original setting but in many cases bring the story to the present, looking at a range of very different relationships—the entanglement of the object and the conservator, the curator, the scholar, the collector, the looter, and others.

Several of the objects I discuss are luxury or monumental objects—the

9. "Culture is not a power, something to which social events, behaviours, institutions, or processes can be casually attributed; it is a context, something within which they can be intelligibly—that is, thickly—described" (Geertz 1973: 316).

10. "Transport of horses and elephants from India both to Sri Lanka and southeast Asia" (Ray 1994: 39).

11. For a recent and detailed discussion of the entanglement of humans and things, see Hodder (2012).

earrings, ewer, silk, Qur'an, and stupa. The pair of earrings (chapter 1), were discovered in a tomb in the territories of the Xiongnu Empire and show characteristics and materials from a variety of cultures subsumed under the imperial labels of "Xiongnu" and "Chinese."[12] The presentation of their story often tends to veer to the dichotomous—steppe and settled, nomad and agriculturalist, barbarian and civilized—and I very much hope to avoid that here, as I believe it to be crude and unhelpful.[13] The discussion is intended to challenge the use of binary labels or any such hard distinctions. These include those sometimes made between trade and tribute and between government and private trade. One intention of this book is to show that the issues are more complex than sometimes presented, to sow uncertainty and to give references for further reading.

The environment is an essential part of the stories of all the things discussed in this book. It provided materials, conditions, and impetus for the development of technologies, the exploitation and manufacture of items, and the movement of peoples.[14] The changing environment, for example, is a catalyst in the story of the earrings: some scholars have argued that the Xiongnu peoples originated in the Altai but were forced out by changes in climate in the fourth century BC, thus moving south into Central Asia and the borders of China, where we encounter them in chapter 1.[15] In turn, it is argued, this movement forced the existing population, the Yuezhi, to move west, where they established the Hephthalite Empire, possibly the makers of the Bactrian ewer discussed in chapter 5.

Another similarly complex issue raised in this first chapter is the question of where, by whom, and for whom things were made. Technologies, materials, fashions, and craftsmen all traveled—I would argue this is an important characteristic of the Silk Road—and we have at best tentative hypotheses about where these earrings were made. We have to accept that these might be

12. The steppe (and sea) routes links across Eurasia were included under the "Silk Road" rubric in a 1957 report on Japanese scholarship on the Silk Road (Japanese National Commission 1957 and Whitfield 2018).

13. Whitfield (2008).

14. For the relationship between objects, people, and the environment, see Ryan and Durning (1997).

15. Schlütz and Lehmkuhl (2007: 114). They might also have spread to the borders of Europe, if we accept that these are the peoples subsumed under the term *Huns* in the literature of the settled. For a critique of this assumption, see Kim (2016: 141) and chapter 1.

challenged by future finds. In other words, in many cases, when dealing with the material culture of the Silk Road, we are on shaky ground.

The earrings survived, as they were buried in a tomb, and this is the case with another two objects discussed here: the Hellenistic glass bowl (chapter 2) and the Bactrian ewer (chapter 5). These were found in elite tombs, and it is possible that such objects were considered to be "foreign" or "exotic" and that their inclusion in the tombs was intended to heighten the status and cosmopolitanism of the owner. This would assume, in turn, that cosmopolitanism was considered positively in the owners' societies.

The chapter on the Bactrian ewer raises the important and often overlooked role of the transmission of intangible cultural heritage on the Silk Road. Like the material object itself, which has antecedents in Roman and then Sasanian vessels but which has developed its own characteristics, the story depicted on the vessel, most probably part of the Trojan War cycle, has developed its own characteristics. Not least among these is the depiction of Paris holding two fruits, little resembling apples. Of course, we have no evidence to suggest that there was any direct knowledge of Roman ewers or the Trojan War epic, and the craftsmen who made this object and the original owner might well have seen it as an entirely local production representing a local story. However, as it moved eastwards into China, it would certainly have been viewed as foreign—as coming from the "west" even if that west was Central Asia and not the borders of Europe.

Glass and glass technology, discussed in chapter 2 on the Hellenistic glass bowl, present an interesting comparison and contrast to sericulture on the Silk Road (see chapter 8). The raw materials for glass were readily available throughout much of Eurasia. The techniques were also present, at least the firing of raw materials to transform them and the use of flux to reduce the firing temperatures. The technology was invented or diffused across Eurasia from at least the first millennium BC. But whereas silk started in the East, for glass the technology was refined in West Asia on the fringes of Europe—and spread east into Sasanian Persia and to China and Korea. The South Asia tradition might have developed independently but was certainly informed by objects arriving from West Asia. And, also unlike silk technology and its products, which were mastered and valued in all the major cultures across the Silk Road, glass technology had a stuttering progress in China. Perhaps this is because other materials—jade and increasingly fine ceramics—filled the aesthetic need for a translucent but hard material that glass filled in other cultures where ceramic technology was far less developed. But glass was clearly valued by some, as shown by the existence of items in elite tombs, the importance of glass in Buddhism, and the adoption of and experimentation with the technology at different times in China.

Silk is an ongoing and central part of this story, and in chapter 8 I have chosen a piece to discuss that comes from fairly late, from the eighth to tenth centuries, so that I can explore the spread of silk technologies—moriculture, sericulture, weaving—from their origins in China. While silk was not always the major trade item over the whole period or even the major item across some of the networks, it certainly remained significant. The raw and finished materials continued to be valued and traded throughout the period. We also see the development of new weaves as the materials and technologies spread outside China.

Silk—and glass—were both part of the story of Buddhism, playing an important role in the practice of the faith. Buddhism is explored further in the discussion of the main stupa at Amluk Dara Stupa in chapter 4. As an architectural object, this stupa has not moved along the Silk Road, but it reflects the movement of Buddhism and the changing landscape—environmental, cultural, religious, political—of a place, in this case the Swat valley. It also brings into discussion the complex logistics involved in the transmission of architectural forms.

The wooden plaque, discussed in chapter 6, also belongs to the story of Buddhism, but I chose it because of the other narratives it tells, especially about the importance of the horse and the role of smaller and often forgotten Silk Road cultures: in this case, that of the Khotanese. It also exemplifies how far we have to travel yet as scholars to understand the Silk Road: it depicts iconography that is commonly found throughout Khotan but that we are still struggling to interpret.

The three textual objects in this book are selected because in each the text has a different context. Chapter 3 looks at a hoard of coins from the Kushan Empire. Coins fall on the cusp of text and object, and it is therefore perhaps not surprising that numismatics is a discipline that straddles both history and archaeology. In many cultures coins confirm other sources about the chronology and names of rulers and sometimes complete gaps. For the Kushan Empire, coins are the main source for reconstructing this chronology. Their inscriptions enable historians to reconstruct a time line of rulers, even though there has been considerable dispute about where to place the start of this time line.[16] Few other extant written records have been found that are produced by the Kushans themselves, and the names of rulers in the annals of neighboring empires, such as the Chinese Later Han dynasty, are difficult to reconstruct. Therefore archaeology plays a much greater role in our understanding of Kushan history than in many other literate cultures. The cache of coins considered here have a further story to tell, as they were discovered, not in Kushan or a neighboring country that was a trading partner, but thousands of miles away in a Christian monastery in what is now Ethiopia. The reason for their journey is not certain, although we can hypothesize, but the fact of their making it is indicative of long-distance routes across sea and land at this time.

The second text considered here (chapter 9) is from a culture (China) where evidence from text and evidence from archaeology are both plentiful and have sometimes supported each other—notably, for example, in the case of the Shang rulers. In China, there are numerous texts, including detailed political histories. And Chinese history has given primacy to the word over the archaeological and other evidence, though as Charles Holcombe has pointed out, "Three subjects that mainstream traditional Chinese historians seldom addressed were trade, Buddhism and foreigners."[17] The transmitted texts are very much the voice of the literate and official elite. But the textual fragment here comes from an archaeological context, not subject to the same selection, and thus gives voice to another part of the culture. It is a fragment of a printed almanac, a popular but proscribed text at the time. This chapter considers the role of texts in largely illiterate or semiliterate societies, arguing that they also "spoke" to these groups.

The third text is a sacred object, a folio from the "Blue Qur'an" (chapter 7) that was produced by the elite. This copy of the Islamic text was written in Arabic using gold and silver on indigo-colored parchment. Its provenance and inspiration are both uncertain and have been subject to much debate. Possible links to similar texts being produced thousands of miles away in Buddhist East Asia have been suggested.

Although I have tried to cover a wide range of topics, some have inevitably been neglected. I would like to have discussed music, medicine, and foodstuffs, and I have not included a specifically military item. My decision to

16. On Kushan chronology, see Falk (2014a).

17. Holcombe (1999: 285). See also chapter 1 for tensions between the Chinese historical records and archaeology regarding the peoples of the Xiongnu alliance and others on China's borders.

include a slave, though, was very deliberate. Slaves are found across the Silk Road, regardless of period or culture, and they undoubtedly formed a major part of Silk Road trade. Despite this, they often appear only in passing in histories of the Silk Road.

I have worked with Silk Road things for over three decades, but I remain surprised that, when I come to ask more about the objects, I encounter a lack of understanding of—or interest in—their materiality. In some cases this is because what they are made of or how they are made is not certain: we have lost techniques mastered by past craftsmen and struggle to replicate methods and, sometimes, materials. But often it seems to be a matter of a lack of interest, either to find out or to question assumptions made without any evidence.

This leads to numerous cases in which the material descriptions of the object are at best imprecise and at worst inaccurate. An example of the former is the designation in many catalogs of Western medieval manuscripts of the medium as "vellum." This tells us only that the parchment is finely made and does not specify the animal skin from which it is made (see chapter 7). The same can be said for the use of the terms *hemp* and *mulberry* to describe the paper of East Asian medieval manuscripts. These are also imprecise terms, usually denoting quality of paper rather than its main fiber, and as such are often misunderstood. While centuries of work have been done on identifying texts, much less effort has been spent on identifying the parchment or paper.[18]

A striking case of inaccuracy is found in descriptions of most glass excavated in China, dating from around Han-period contexts and deemed to be foreign. Such glass has usually been labeled "Roman"—even though some pieces are certainly Hellenistic and some were probably locally produced.[19]

In an exhibition I curated in 2009, I assumed that the description given in the institutional records of the glass bowl discussed in chapter 5 as "Roman" was correct. But when I started to study glass in more detail my misjudgment became clear, and, as at so many other times in my scholarly career, I had to question what I thought I had learned. This book is a part of this process: an attempt to accept the many uncertainties of Silk Road history and material culture while trying, by listening to the many "things" of the Silk Road, to find some small areas of firm ground on which to base further research and knowledge.

18. This is not to undervalue the contributions of people who have worked in this area and asked these questions.

19. See chapter 5. Also see Watt et al. (2004) and Whitfield (2009) for acceptance of this description.

ONE

A Pair of Steppe Earrings

THE EARRINGS SHOWN IN PLATE 1A were buried with a woman who died in the second century BC.[1] She was a member of the elite in one of the cultures possibly belonging to the Xiongnu political alliance, which, at its greatest extent, controlled a large empire to the north of China.[2] Made of worked gold with inlays of semiprecious stones and oval pieces of openwork carved jade, the earrings showcase the arts and aesthetics of the many cultures of the empires of both the Xiongnu and the Chinese. The relationship between the Xiongnu and the Chinese, long neighbors in East Asia, is central to understanding the early history of the eastern Silk Road but is often simply characterized as one of conflict. These earrings tell a more complex story—of diplomatic endeavors, trade, intermarriages, and technical and cultural dialogues. They come from a time when these cultures were renegotiating their interrelationships and territories. That process was one of the catalysts for the expansion of long-distance Eurasian trade, the Silk Road. The earrings also reflect the story of the encounter between the peoples—and other objects or "things"—along the ecological boundary of Inner and Outer Eurasia, stretching across the length of the Silk Road.[3] But we must not for-

---

For places mentioned in this chapter see Map 2 in the color maps insert.

1. I am greatly indebted to Sergey Miniaev for his detailed comments on this chapter and for so generously sharing his extensive knowledge. Thanks are also owing to Karen Rubinson, whose perceptive suggestions have helped me greatly. All mistakes, misunderstandings, and omissions are my own.

2. For sake of brevity I will use *Xiongnu* hereafter, but to designate the political alliance rather than a homogeneous culture. I use the term *Chinese* in the same way; see discussion and references below.

3. A boundary that David Christian describes as "the dynamo of Inner Eurasian history" (1998: xxi).

get that the earrings were possibly also the valued possession of an individual. Seeing them through her eyes is not possible, but as historians of material culture we strive to understand something of the world in which she lived, a world that shaped her perceptions of and reactions to the objects around her.

THE XIONGNU AND THE STEPPE

Most of the largely nomadic pastoralists who lived in northern Eurasia had no need for a written culture.[4] Their histories were therefore told by their largely settled neighbors to their south: outsiders to their society, who tended to interpret it by the norms of their own.[5] There were no professional anthropologists in these early societies trying to understand other peoples from their own viewpoint.[6] Moreover, the pastoralists often make an appearance in these histories at times that they are seen as a threat to the settled. Archaeology is thus very important for providing an alternative viewpoint to understand such cultures and their complexities. It has, for example, disproved the long-propounded idea that early pastoralists did not practice agriculture: the discovery of domesticated wheat and millet at the site of Begash in Kazakhstan, for example, has led Michael Frachetti to conclude that "pastoralists of the steppe had access to domesticated grains already by 2300 BC" and that "they were likely essential to the diffusion of wheat into China, as well as millet into SW Asia and Europe in the mid-third millennium BC."[7] It has also uncovered cities: not all the occupants of the steppe lived in tents, nor did any spend their lives constantly on the move. In other words, this land was home to a great range of cultures and lifestyles, but ones that were necessarily shaped by their environment.

4. I use these terms advisedly—there was no simple dichotomy between the settled and the nomadic (peoples sometimes characterized as the civilized and the barbaric). The range of lifestyles, very much dictated by ecology for much of history, was on a continuum, with pastoralist cultures practicing agriculture to a greater or lesser degree. For an example, see Chang et al. (2003).

5. As Paul Goldin points out on the Chinese view of the Xiongnu, "The Chinese conceived of their northern neighbours as mutatis mutandis, identical to themselves ... greedy and primitive only because they had not benefitted from the transformative influence of sage teachers" (2011: 220).

6. Although individuals may have attempted it.

7. Frachetti (2011). On the spread of millet, see N. Miller, Spengler, and Frachetti (2016); Frachetti et al. (2010).

There is evidence that from the earliest times the cultures that occupied the lands of China had contacts with and were influenced by the steppe. This is seen in religion, as in the adoption of oracle bone divination, as well as in the introduction of domesticated wheat, the use of horse-drawn chariots as found in late Shang (Yin)-period (ca. 1600–ca. 1046 BC) burials, animal-head daggers with looped handles, and bronze mirrors. Jessica Rawson has noted the presence in early China of carnelian beads produced in Mesopotamia and has suggested they were transported by steppe peoples.[8] As Gideon Shelach-Lavi concludes, "We should not underestimate the role of the steppe peoples in the transmission of cultural influences to the 'Chinese' societies," which "selectively endorsed those features that suited the elites as well as the 'Chinese' societies' sedentary way of life."[9]

However, this situation was to change in the second half of the first millennium BC, when a dichotomy started to emerge in Chinese writings between what the histories characterized as a settled, civilized "Chinese" culture and that of their steppe neighbors. Largely on the basis of archaeological sources, Nicola Di Cosmo and others argue that, before the rise of the Xiongnu as a nomadic force of mounted warriors in the late first millennium BC, the Chinese had not encountered such a threat.[10] Their northern neighbors up to then had largely been agriculturalists with written language who fought on foot. Others have countered this view, pointing out that the cultures of China must have encountered some semipastoralist and seminomadic peoples.[11] But the confederation of tribes known as the Xiongnu possibly changed the perception of the elite in the various states that ruled central China at the time. Previously that elite seems to have held that all men under heaven were of a nature capable of being civilized, if subjected to civilizing forces. We see a change to a more dichotomous view, in which the Xiongnu became "the other," a people with a "heaven-endowed nature" essentially different from that of the Chinese.[12]

8. Rawson (2010).

9. Shelach-Lavi (2014: 23–26). The point that both the transmitters and the receivers of culture and technology played a role is discussed further below. The receivers have to be receptive to the new culture and technology, but their receptiveness can be encouraged in various ways by the transmitters. This also has parallels with the point in chapter 7 about Western collectors of Islamic manuscripts in the twentieth century and the roles played by the booksellers of the Muslim world.

10. Di Cosmo (2002). For dating, see notes below.

11. Shelach–Lavi (2014). See also Chang (2008).

12. To quote Sima Qian, discussed in Goldin (2011: 228–29).

Chinese histories show an escalation in this view of the "other," undoubtedly promoted by the need to demonize peoples who had become a major threat but also, as Paul Goldin points out, in response to the concept of "Chinese" formulated by the Qin Empire (221–206 BC)—the first rulers of a united China: "As there is no Self without an Other, calling oneself Chinese meant calling someone else non-Chinese; the new China had to invent an irreconcilable opponent, and the Xiongnu were in the right place at the right time."[13] As Sergey Miniaev notes, the early histories use a variety of names for their northern neighbors, and the first mention of the Xiongnu in the *Shiji*, the first history of China, by Sima Qian, of an encounter in 318 BC is probably a later interpolation or was being used "as a collective designation, common in this time, for stock-breeding tribes, being devoid of a particular ethnocultural meaning."[14] Tamara Chin notes that Sima Qian avoids "anthropological rhetoric" and does not embed the Chinese conquest "in a narrative of cultural or moral superiority."[15] That rhetoric, she argues, came post-Qin with the expansion of China under the Han emperor Wu (r. 141–87 BC). By the time of the next history, *Hanshu*, composed in the first century AD, it was firmly embedded.[16]

Other settled cultures also have to name or label the "other" to tell their story, and we inevitably learn more about the settled cultures from these histories than about the "other." The fifth-century BC historian Herodotus used the term *Scythian*; the Achaemenids in Iran termed their steppe neighbors the Saka. Early Chinese histories use several terms for the peoples the Chinese encountered to their north. This has given rise to numerous discussions about the origins and ethnicity of the peoples so labeled. In the case of the Xiongnu, these have especially concentrated on a possible identification with the peoples that historians and archaeologists have called the Huns.[17]

13. Goldin (2011: 235). As he and others (Pines 2012a: 34) also point out, this characterization of the other is exemplified more concretely with the attempts to build walls to demarcate the boundary between the two, the so-called "Great Wall."

14. Vasil'ev (1961); Miniaev (2015: 323).

15. Chin (2010: 320).

16. See chapter 10 on the Chinese labeling of peoples on their southwestern borders as "other" and their exploitation of these peoples as slaves.

17. For an early and influential discussion identifying the Xiongnu with the Huns, see Bernshtam (1951), and see Frumkin (1970) for a summary of scholarship based on archaeology in the Soviet period. For a more recent summary, see La Vaissière (2014), who, like Bernshtam, argues for an identification of the Xiongnu with the Huns—as well as with the Hephthalites (see chapter 5). For a recent history of the "Huns" that concurs with this view,

However, many scholars remain skeptical; as Goldin notes, "The semantic domain of the term 'Xiongnu' was political: there is no reason to assume that it ever denoted a specific ethnic group—and, indeed, plenty of reason not to. . . . Excavations in areas that came to be dominated by the Xiongnu have uncovered a wealth of distinct cultures."[18]

The Chinese histories tell of settled and pastoralist peoples and mounted warriors living both northeast of and within the area enclosed by the great northward curve of the Yellow River, known now as the Ordos.[19] Many scholars have proposed that it was the encounter with these peoples in the late fourth century that led a ruler of the Zhao (403–222 BC)—a kingdom in what is now northern China that bordered their territory—to change his army from an infantry to a cavalry force.[20] The horse up until then had been used to pull chariots or as a pack animal. Despite breeding programs, central China never succeeded in raising sufficient stock to equip its armies.[21] The adoption of horseback riding also necessitated a change in clothing and weaponry. Over the next millennium the horse became an essential part of life in northern China, not just for the military, and was celebrated in art and literature (see chapter 6).

The Zhao was the last kingdom of what is now known as the Warring States period (ca. 475–221 BC) to succumb to the army of the Qin, who declared a united empire of China in 221 BC. Chinese histories tell how around 209 BC, following the Qin's successful expansion into the northern and western Ordos, the various pastoralist tribes on the borders of China were united under a leader called Modu; the histories refer to these tribes as the Xiongnu.[22] Under Modu's alliance they expanded, bringing other tribes to the north—in what is now Mongolia—into their confederation.

---

see Kim (2016). But some scholars strongly disagree with the identification of the Xiongnu as Huns: Miniaev, for example, argues that "written sources and archaeological data contradict this" (pers. comm., October 8, 2017; see also his 2015 article).

18. Goldin (2011: 227) and Di Cosmo (1994). The same can be said for the Huns.

19. Ordos is a later Mongolian name. The area now lies within the provinces of Ningxia, Gansu, and Shaanxi and the Inner Mongolia Autonomous Regions in China.

20. Di Cosmo (2002: 134–37) discusses the 307 BC debate at the Zhao court and argues against this view.

21. For references to early programs of breeding in China, see Erkes (1940). The dependency on the steppe for the supply of military ponies continued; see chapter 6. India had similar issues; see chapter 3.

22. Di Cosmo (1999: 892–93); Kim (2016: 20–23). Miniaev takes issue with the oft-cited interpretation that the Xiongnu moved into the Ordos at this time, arguing that the area was still occupied by "tribes of Loufang and Baiyang" (2015: 326).

They moved westwards toward the Tarim, pushing out the peoples whom the Chinese called the Yuezhi and asserting their rule in some of the oasis kingdoms of the Tarim.[23] To the south they had easy victories over the forces of the newly founded Chinese Han dynasty (206 BC–AD 220), expelling them from territories the Qin had previously taken.[24] The Han responded with an envoy sent to broker a peace treaty. Like many such treaties from this time onwards between the Chinese and their neighbors, this included a marriage alliance (*heqin*) between a Chinese princess and the foreign ruler.[25] Both sides accepted the equal status of their respective empires and a border in part demarcated by the walls built by the Han and their predecessors; further, the Chinese agreed to provide the alliance with regular gifts of goods, including silk and grain. The Chinese historians record the words of the Xiongnu ruler: "According to former treaties Han emperors always sent a princess, provided agreed quantities of silks, coarse silk wadding and foodstuffs, thus establishing harmony and a close relationship [i.e., *heqin*]. For our part, we refrained from making trouble on the border."[26] Hyun Jin Kim characterizes this as Han China becoming a tributary state of the Xiongnu alliance.[27]

The balance turned again with the Han emperor Wu, who embarked on a successful expansion policy northeastward into what is now Korea, westward into the Tarim basin, and southward to defeat the Nan Yue kingdom (see chapter 2). His plan to defeat the Xiongnu alliance was to find allies among the Yuezhi—themselves previously displaced from the Tarim according to the Chinese histories. The strategy was that the Yuezhi would attack from the west, while Chinese forces would attack from the southeast. However, the envoy sent to negotiate this, Zhang Qian, was singularly unsuccessful (although, having been captured by a member of the Xiongnu alliance on his way out and having been resident there with a local wife, he must have gained very useful intelligence).[28] The Han went ahead anyway, and although

23. On the Yuezhi as both farmers and herders, see Chang et al. (2003).

24. The battle took place at Baideng—to the east of the Ordos. The Chinese forces were led by the emperor Gaozu (r. 202–195), who only narrowly escaped capture.

25. For discussion of the *heqin*, see Psarras (2003: 132–42). Many of the so-called princesses sent in such marriage alliances were not in the direct imperial line. The system continued in later periods. For an account of marriages that did involve genuine imperial princesses sent to marry Turkic Uygur *kaghan*s in the Tang period, see "The Princess's Tale" in Whitfield (2015b).

26. Quoted in Kroll (2010: 113).

27. See Kim (2016: 22) and his map on 26.

28. The intelligence on goods and potential markets gained by Zhang Qian is usually

they were successful the battles were costly and ultimately of limited value, as it was not possible to hold onto the steppe land. This was accepted by both sides in 54/3 BC in another peace treaty between one ruler of the now-divided Xiongnu and the Chinese, precipitated by the breakdown in the Xiongnu alliance. The positions of power were now reversed, with the southern Xiongnu ruler accepting the lower status. Yuri Pines argues that this encounter, because of the pastoralists' strength and refusal to accept the settled way of life in China, "became the single most significant event in the political, cultural and ethnic history of the Chinese."[29]

Across Eurasia and during the Silk Road period, this encounter was by no means unique to the Xiongnu and the Chinese. Nor was there a single model of interaction. The nature of the relationships was complex, although often simplified by the historians of the settled into one of dichotomy and conflict. The Romans themselves struggled with incursions along their borders and, like the Chinese, built a network of defensive walls and forts.[30] In Greek histories the northern equestrian nomads were the archetype of the "other." Labeled as Scythians, their image as other continued to be perpetuated from Herodotus into Byzantine histories.[31] Further east, the Persian Achaemenids (550–330 BC) were to be defeated by a group of pastoralists moving from their northeast who established the Parthian Empire (247 BC–AD 224). The Parthians successfully adopted a new settled lifestyle while retaining their military prowess, threatening even the borders of Rome.[32]

So are these earrings Xiongnu or Chinese, or does it even make sense to try to label them in this way? To answer this, we need to explore some of the complexity hidden by the labels *Xiongnu* and *Chinese* and the aspects of their

---

given as a factor in the Han expansion west and the growth of trade—one of the factors in the start of the Silk Road (but certainly not the only one—see chapter 2).

29. Pines (2012b: 34).

30. Under the Roman emperor Hadrian (r. 117–38), walls were built throughout the empire, including northern Europe. Edward Luttwak discusses the point of such defenses and challenges the arguments that their regular breaching by enemy forces proves their failure, arguing instead that "they were intended to serve not as total barriers but rather as the one fixed element in a mobile strategy of imperial defense" (1976: 63). For an insightful discussion of the Chinese "Great Wall," see Waldron (1990).

31. And beyond: Reynolds quotes the 1483 work of the chronicler Jacobo Filippo Foresti da Bergamo: "The Bactrians and Parthians descended from the Scythians, as did Attila the Great. . . . Our Lombards, Hungarians, Castellani, and Goths are all descended from the Scythians. . . . The Turks too . . . came from Scythia. Indeed the nation of Scythians traces its origins back to Magog" (2012: 53).

32. For Parthian history, see Colledge (1986).

relationship that are revealed by the tombs—at Xigoupan—in which the earrings were found.

THE XIGOUPAN TOMBS

Xigoupan lies at the northeastern edge of the Ordos, where the Yellow River starts to turn south. It is roughly at the same latitude as Beijing to its east.[33] The tombs were excavated in 1979. Unfortunately, the archaeological reports are not detailed, and drawings of most of the graves and details of the inventory are missing. The tombs are dispersed, suggesting they might belong to different burial grounds and have widely varying dates. The earliest tombs excavated here date to around 300 BC or possibly earlier, but later tombs and a settlement have also been discovered that date from the second century BC, the period of the Xiongnu confederation.[34] The archaeologists date to the second century nine of the tombs, four of which have not been robbed.[35] Among these, tomb M4 stands out because of the richness of its grave goods. The earrings are associated with this tomb.

M4 lies in the south of the site less than a kilometer away from a site possibly identified as a settlement.[36] Tomb drawings are missing, but it is described as a pit burial with a single supine female corpse with her head to the northeast. Gold objects were the most plentiful among the grave goods, but goods also included ornaments made of silver, bronze, jade, stone, and glass, among them necklaces of amber, agate, crystal, and lapis; dancers, tigers, and dragons fashioned from stone; bronze three-winged arrowheads; and bronze horses. The earrings themselves form part of a more elaborate head decoration placed on the head of the corpse (figure 1).[37]

33. Although the capital of China for most of its history from the Qin onwards was located much further south along the Yellow River (Chang'an [Xian] and Luoyang).

34. Miniaev (2015) points out issues with the archaeology records and the dating of these tombs. He argues that M3 is earlier and M9 much later and that these tombs belonged to separate graveyards.

35. Xigoupan (1980: 7: 1–10) and Tian and Guo (1986).

36. As Psarras (2003: 77) points out, the published literature makes this claim on the presence of surface finds including pottery shards, an ax, a hoe, an awl, knives, fragments of armor, and stone beads. This is hardly conclusive as evidence of a settlement.

37. For the headdress, see Tian and Guo (1986: pl. 4) and A. Kessler (1993: 62).

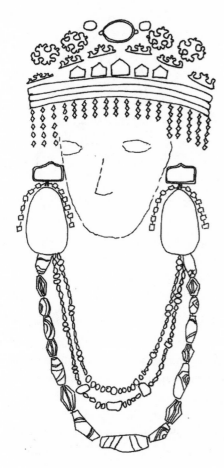

FIGURE 1. A reconstruction of the head-dress that includes the steppe earrings. After Tian and Guo (1986: pl. 4).

The earrings were made from two ovoid openwork carved jade plaques.[38] The plaques are not mirror images of each other, but both show sinuous creatures, one with its head in profile and the other face on (figure 2).[39] They are enclosed within a thin gold border decorated with granulation. A loop on the top attaches them to gold plaques, also with granulation around their borders and with inlaid stone moose. Sets of inlaid gold squares joined with fine

38. The earrings are shown in A. Kessler (1993: 62, fig. 35), So and Bunker (1995: 24), and Whitfield (2009: 57, cat. 27). They are not always shown in the same combination.
39. They are usually both identified as dragons. See discussion below.

FIGURE 2. The designs on the jade plaques from which the steppe earrings were made. After A. Kessler (1993: 62, fig. 35).

chains hang to either side. Most of the inlays are lost, but those that have been found include mother-of-pearl, quartz, agate, amber, and glass.[40]

The gold for the inlaid stones and the moose has been hammered into shape and decorated with beads of gold. Hammering is the simplest method of working gold and is found in both steppe and settled populations well before this time. Granulation—whereby beads of gold are joined onto a surface for decoration—is a more developed technique but is also found along the steppe and in the bordering settled cultures, such as those of the Greeks and the Chinese, well before this period.[41] Zhixin Sun has suggested a possible route into China through maritime links with South Asia, based on gold decorative items with granulation found in the tomb of King Zhao Mo (r. 137–122 BC) of Nan Yue, a kingdom on the coast of what is now southern China and northern Vietnam.[42] There is evidence of Nan Yue's maritime links with South Asia—and further west (see chapter 2). However, granu-

40. As far as I know, the origin of the glass has not been explored; see chapter 2.

41. True granulation does not use metallic solders but either heats the gold surface and the granule sufficiently to enable bonding or uses nonmetallic solders, such as copper salts. Granulation is found on earrings dating from the third millennium BC found in a grave at Ashur on the Tigris (P. Harper 1995: 55).

42. Bunker, Watt, and Sun (2002: 114). Sun's argument suggests that granulation is found in the Harappan culture of the Indus, but there is no evidence of this. See Wolters (1998) for the history and variations of the technique.

FIGURE 3. The design on the belt plaque from grave M2.

lation was used in ancient cultures of Egypt and Mesopotamia and is also found on the steppe before this period, so there are many possible routes of diffusion.[43]

M2, like M4, contained gold and silver objects, including a belt plaque (see figure 3) and remains of a horse, a sheep, and a dog skull. The other second-century tombs at the site are not so richly endowed. Their grave goods consist of weapons, tools, and horse tack and decorations, along with animal bones. The presence of surface finds and agricultural implements might suggest a settlement and thus indicate a seminomadic society that also practiced agriculture. The richness of the grave goods in M2 and M4 indicates elite graves, while the lack of such riches in other graves suggests sharp social differentiation.[44] As Di Cosmo notes, "The complexity of this later nomadic society is nowhere more visible than at [this] site."[45] The form, materials, and motifs on these earrings and other tomb objects are part of this complexity.

43. For Akkadian-period (2334–2154 BC) earrings with granulation found in Ashur on the Tigris, see P. Harper (1995: cat. 35a–d).

44. Although, as Linduff (2008: 181–82) points out, the data from twelve tombs can hardly been taken as representative.

45. Di Cosmo (2002: 85). Although note his comments about the weakness of the evidence for a settlement.

MIRRORS AND BELT PLAQUES:
TRADE AND EXCHANGE

The state of scholarship in the field of interactions between and identities of the cultures of the steppe and China is well illustrated by a brief consideration of two types of object found in tombs across the ecological divide—the mirror and the belt plaque. The former has long been associated with the Chinese and the latter with the steppe, but this has recently been challenged, and more complex models have been proposed.

Mirrors were long assumed by most to have arisen independently in the central China Shang (Yin) culture. This assumption has been subjected to careful research, and many scholars now argue that the mirror came to China from Central Asia.[46] In this revised scenario, Li Zhang (Jaang) has proposed two early and consecutive routes of influence between the steppe and central China.[47] The first had its intermediary in the Qijia culture (ca. 2200–1700 BC) of the Hexi corridor in present-day Northwest China—an important section on the later "Silk Road." Mirrors arrived here from the Bactrian-Margiana Archaeological Complex (BMAC) in northern Central Asia, going north to the Altai and then south along the Ejin River or Etsingol to its source in the Qilian Mountains, which form the southern border of the Hexi corridor. From here the fashion and technology were transferred to the Erlitou culture (ca. 1900–1500 BC), which thrived around present-day Luoyang, just south of the Yellow River in central China.

A new route of influence emerged around the middle or end of the Erlitou culture, which, Li argues, was to supplant the Ejin River route and is called the Northern Zone. This comprised the Ordos region and surrounding areas to the east and south. It was separated from the Ejin River route by a mountain range, the Helan, and Li Zhang further argues that connections between central China and the Hexi corridor, home of the cultures that later gave rise to the Zhou (1046–256 BC), were not very active at this time.[48] She sees interaction with central China from across the length of the steppe through the

---

46. "The problem of the geographical-cultural origin of the form of the 'Chinese' mirror must remained unsolved for the present, but it clearly lies outside of or on the peripheral areas of China" (Rubinson 1985: 48). See also Juliano (1985).

47. Li Jaang (2011).

48. She cites a scientific analysis of the many jades found in the tomb of the Yin elite woman and general Fu Hao (Jing et al. 2007), which concludes that the jade was possibly not sourced from Khotan, as was long assumed. Khotan was reached through the Hexi corridor,

Northern Zone. This interaction is shown by objects that appeared in tombs in this area but also by objects found in central China—namely the bronzes of the Shang. Shang burials, meanwhile, also held objects from the steppe. Mirrors, however, disappeared from central China, only reappearing—but in a different style and again probably introduced from the steppe—in the eleventh century in the Zhou culture that was to succeed the Shang. So we see, not a single transmission, or one route, but changing spheres of influence and diffusion. If we accept this, we also see clear cultural importation from the steppe into central China.

The belt plaque found in tomb M2 is a typical accouterment found in graves across the steppe from the Black Sea to the Ordos and the subject of much continuing scholarly debate (figure 3). The belt made of plaques was particular to no one people of the steppe and, as well as being a practical item of clothing, was widely used as an indicator of social status and much more besides.[49] The plaque in M2 is gold and shows a design of a beast of prey attacking another animal, in this case a tiger attacking a wild boar. This theme of animal predation is found in the Scythic-Siberian culture, which spread across the steppe and thrived into the first millennium AD.[50] It is usually wrought in gold belt plaques, sword scabbards, buckles, and other portable objects.[51] But animal predation is not a theme unique to the steppe. It appears in Egypt in the late fourth millennium BC and then in West Asia a millennium later; the lid of a silver cosmetic box from the Royal Cemetery at Ur (ca. 2650–2550 BC) (present-day southern Iraq) shows a lion savaging a ram.[52] From the first millennium BC it is depicted by the empires bordering the steppe in a variety of settings and media: for example, shown in the ninth century BC on an obelisk at the Assyrian city of Nimrud; in gold and silver among the Ziwiye treasure from around 700 BC, on the border of present-day Iran and Iraq; in stone reliefs at the Achaemenid capital of Persepolis

passing through the proto-Zhou culture, and she suggests that such a route was not likely at the time (Li Jaang 2011: 42). For the Northern Zone, see Di Cosmo (1999: 885, 893).

49. Pohl (2002); Schopphoff (2009)—as a sign of power, rank, adulthood, spiritual status, etc. Brosseder (2011: 350, see fig. 1 for a distribution map). Also see chapter 2 for belt plaques found in Nan Yue in South China.

50. Miniaev (2016) dates this as the first to second century AD on the basis of analysis of bronzes from Dyrestuy cemetery.

51. Jacobson (1995: 25), who also groups the Yuezhi under this Scythic-Siberian culture (see chapter 2).

52. University of Pennsylvania Museum of Archaeology and Anthropology, B16744a/b. See A. Cohen (2010: 108, fig. 48).

from the sixth century BC; and in the fourth century BC on a mosaic at the House of Dionysus, in Pella, Greece, painted in Macedonian tombs, and carved on an Etruscan sarcophagus.[53] To see a simple line of transmission is all too tempting. As Ada Cohen notes in her discussion of this theme in the art of Alexander the Great (r. 336–323 BC), "There is an unavoidable impulse to postulate intercultural influence in order to explain its presence in the Greek world."[54] But as Cohen also notes, writers from the time of the French essayist Michel de Montaigne (1533–92) have noticed the universality of the appeal of this theme in human societies, and it could be argued with equal force that it emerged in different places at different times.[55] What might be more interesting, she suggests, would be to explore the meanings and depictions of the theme in different cultures and see if and how they overlapped.[56]

How much the Xiongnu were influenced by the Scythic-Siberian culture that stretched across the steppe to their west is uncertain. Some scholars see the Xiongnu as the continuation of this culture, while others see the Xiongnu as distinct, albeit having absorbed some influences.[57] Whatever the case, the Xiongnu also used belt plaques, as shown by those in the Xigoupan and many other tombs. They were part of steppe attire, used both to hold the short upper tunic of the horseman—or woman—in place and as portable storage, to hold daggers and other essential implements. In classical China, the traditional dress was a long gown, unsuitable for riding and not needing such a belt.[58] Yet we see steppe-style belt plaques in central China from this time, as in the grave of the king of the Chu state, Liu Wu (r. 174–154 BC), at Shizhishan near Xuzhou in eastern China, and in the tomb of King Zhao

53. See A. Cohen (2010: 93–101) for examples.

54. See A. Cohen (2010: 108, 93–118) for discussion of the theme.

55. See A. Cohen (2010: 110) for Montaigne. She also notes Jacobson's argument that the direction of influence was the other way, citing the Hellenistic elements in a fourth-century winged griffin (A. Cohen 2010: 319, 160n; Jacobson 1999: 62–3).

56. A. Cohen (2010) also discusses the theme of the hunt, in tandem with the animal predation theme. See chapter 8 for further discussion. For an insightful discussion about possible diffusion of a very distinctive representation of the animal predation theme, see Nathalie Monnet's presentation at the Symposium "Cave Temples of Dunhuang: History, Art, and Materiality," May 20, 2016, session 2, "Dunhuang: East and West," https://www. youtube.com/watch?v=RBNgfAeJy6E.

57. Pulleybank (2000a: 53). Also see A. Cohen (2010: 17–18) for a discussion of similarities in their political systems.

58. Some centuries later, the so-called foreigner's dress of a short tunic secured with a belt over baggy trousers became a fashion statement among both men and women in China. See Shen Congwen (2012) for a history of Chinese dress.

Mo of Nan Yue in southern China (see chapter 2). Those in the tomb of Liu Wu are in gold. They are identical to gilded bronze pieces found in a burial in Pokrovka 2 cemetery on the Ural River, north of the Caspian in Russia; to belt plaques from a Han-period tomb outside Xian in central China; and to two others in gilded bronze now in a New York collection.[59] Emma Bunker discusses these and suggests a possible origin in North China. She further argues that the design has been adapted to fit Chinese taste in that "the vigor of the attack scene is almost lost in the manipulation of shapes into pleasing patterns."[60]

The belt plaques found in Liu Wu's tomb near Xuzhou and those from Xigoupan have Chinese characters engraved on the back, giving their weight and details of their subject matter. This supports the argument that they were produced in Chinese workshops or at least by Chinese craftsmen.[61] In addition, the reverse of a Xigoupan M2 plaque shows the impression of a textile, suggesting that it was made by the lost-wax lost-textile technique.[62] In her study of these objects, Katheryn Linduff suggests that this "was a Chinese invention that was aimed particularly at the efficient production of objects for the foreign [steppe] market."[63] Other items from these tombs of the Xiongnu period show mercury gilding, and Bunker concludes that these were also made in Chinese workshops.[64] If this is indeed the case, then we see a steppe object and motif—the belt plaque with the motif of animal predation—being adopted within central China and also adapted for production for a market outside China. Evidence suggests that the production of artifacts for the steppe market probably began in the kingdoms of fourth- to

59. Discussed in Bunker, Watt, and Sun (2002: 101) and Brosseder (2011).

60. Bunker, Watt, and Sun (2002: 101). But see comments from the Russian archaeologists of Xiongnu sites at Noin-Ula on the Xiongnu "schematization" of Scythic-Siberian animal subjects to geometric compositions (Davydova and Miniaev 2008: 22).

61. Di Cosmo (2002: 85). For images, see Brosseder (2011: 357) and Linduff (2008: 176). However, Psarras (2003: 104) has challenged this argument, suggesting the possibility of a different form of casting for the belt plaques and pointing out that the Chinese characters were added after casting.

62. On discussion of the M2 plaque and this technique, see Bunker, Watt, and Sun (2002: 20, 27–28 and figs. 42, 43) and Bunker (1988).

63. Linduff (2009: 94).

64. Bunker (1988: 29) notes that there is no evidence that the Xiongnu knew the technique of mercury gilding (also referred to as fire or chemical gilding) but that it was developed in China in the fourth century BC by alchemists seeking to make gold. It was also found to be used in Greece around the same time.

third-century China, before its unification.[65] Other finds demonstrate the further movement of these items, whether by trade, gift, or plunder.

The discovery of these belt plaques shows not only that artisans in the kingdoms of China were producing items for the steppe market but that some Chinese had also acquired a taste for these items, even if in some cases the theme was modified.[66] Their lavishness and their presence in elite tombs, as instanced by the gold and glass plaques of the king of Nan Yue (see chapter 2) and the massive gold plaques of the king of Chu, suggests they were a mark of wealth and power. Military leadership undoubtedly remained a mark of the Xiongnu elite, but this elite was now also involved in trade as an alternative form of wealth and status.[67] In Di Cosmo's words:

> The emphatic accumulation of precious objects reflects a "network mode" of elite representation. Nomadic elites became increasingly involved in long-distance contacts, and drew legitimacy and power from their connections with other elites. Exchange of prestige items, as well as trade and tribute, became the source of stored wealth that demonstrated and consolidated a lineage's enduring power. Foreign connections and representations of one's elite status in terms that would be readily recognized outside one's community marked a transition, among certain groups, to a symbolic system resembling the "network" rather than the "corporate" mode.[68]

The Xiongnu did not acquire objects only from their Chinese neighbors. Textiles from burials in Noin-Ula, another Xiongnu-period site in southern Mongolia, included Chinese and locally made felts but also other textiles that were almost certainly made in Central or West Asia.[69] A Greek silver medallion was also discovered in Noin-Ula, recycled as a platera, and a Roman glass bowl in Gol Mod 2, also in the Xiongnu area in what is now Mongolia.[70] These are generally dated later than the Ordos tombs, from the late first century BC to the first century AD. They are different from the pit

---

65. Proposed by Bunker (1983), and discussed further by Linduff (2009), in relation to ceramic molds for belt plaques found in tombs in Xian.

66. Of course, it is possible that the people in central China with a taste for these had steppe ancestry and that some peoples in southern China developed a taste for this "foreign" style. It can be argued that *Chinese* is as much a term denoting a political alliance as is *Xiongnu* and that it incorporates as much, if not more, diversity.

67. Di Cosmo (2002: 85). See also Di Cosmo (2013).

68. Di Cosmo (2013: 43).

69. See chapter 8 for reference to the Chinese silk.

70. Erdenebaatar et al. (2011: 311–13).

burials at Xigoupan and other Ordos sites in that they consist of a deeply buried wooden burial chamber accessed by a ramp. They include peripheral burial pits that belong to people who followed the elite occupant of the main chamber into death.[71]

The earrings are part of this story: they might also have been made in Chinese or steppe workshops. Alternatively, the jade plaques could have been fashioned by Chinese artisans well accustomed to working with this material—either in China or on the steppe—and then sold or given as gifts to the Xiongnu, whose craftsmen then incorporated them into this elaborate headdress. Jade and dragons are both often associated with the cultures of central China, but, as with most subjects in this book, the story is not a simple one.

JADE AND DRAGONS

Several different minerals are often termed *yu* (玉), the Chinese word for jade, the most valued in early China being nephrite found locally in the Yangzi River delta in eastern China.[72] But some pieces identified as "jade" are not nephrite but serpentine and marble.[73] The stone was worked from Neolithic times into copies of weapons and tools but also into forms that clearly had a ritual meaning and are found in a mortuary context. These included the *bi*, a flat disc with a circular hole in the center.[74] Few of the jades found in burials had any wear, supporting this ritual use. However, since little jade survives outside burials, we cannot be certain how much was produced for other contexts and has long been lost.[75]

Jade is a hard stone and has to be worked by abrading with sand.[76] The fine

71. Possible reasons for this development are discussed in Di Cosmo (2013: 44–45). Brosseder (2011: 247–80) suggests that the cause is the split of the Northern and Southern Xiongnu in AD 49.

72. Nephrite is a dense form of actinolite or, sometimes, tremolite. The other jade mineral, jadeite, was later sourced from Southwest China and present-day Myanmar.

73. Glass was also used, possibly to emulate jade—see the belt plaques of the king of Nan Yue, chapter 2.

74. The *bi* is also sometimes made of glass (see chapter 2).

75. Rawson (1992: 61) points out the paucity of ritual jades listed in classical texts and found in burials, suggesting that it might not have been considered appropriate to bury them. She notes the presence in tombs of jade pendant sets, belt ornaments, and body shrouds in addition to the ritual objects.

76. It is 6 (nephrite) or 6.5 (jadeite) on the Moh scale.

work of these early jades attests to high levels of skill and investment of time: these were expensive and valued objects. There is still considerable uncertainty about the sources of jade used in China, but for nephrite they certainly might have included Lake Baikal in Siberia and Khotan in the Tarim basin in eastern Central Asia (see below and chapter 6). It is possible, therefore, that some jade was imported two thousand miles from Khotan.[77] This, and the skill and time required to work it, probably made it as valuable to the early kings in China as lapis was to the Egyptian pharaohs. Jade ranges in color from white to black, with the lightest jade having translucent qualities. The aesthetic appreciation of different colored jades is reflected by the vocabulary developed to describe them: mutton fat, chicken bone, orange peel, nightingale, egg, ivory, duck bone, antelope, fish belly, shrimp, chrysanthemum, rose madder, and many more.[78]

Nephrite jades also include a dark green stone found in Mongolia and eastern Siberia near Lake Baikal. Bunker discusses an openwork plaque, probably carved using stone from eastern Siberia, and argues that this piece was probably created on the steppe.[79] The most likely method of creating jade ornaments, because of the stone's hardness, was abrasion with quartz sand, crushed sandstone, or crushed loess, the main part of which is quartz.[80] Metal tools started to be used before the time our piece was made. The design of the dark-green plaque is almost identical to that on bronze belt plaques discovered in Ivolga (near Ulan-Ude) and eastern Siberia. It also resembles gold plaques, inlaid rather than openwork, excavated from a tomb in Sidorovka, near Omsk in western Siberia. This last site is dated to the late third to second century BC, whereas the bronze and nephrite objects are slightly later. Communities of Chinese craftsmen were known to have worked at Ivolga, so it is also possible that this dark-green plaque was made by them.[81]

One of the sinuous animals on the nephrite, bronze, and gold belt plaques is of a type now often associated with the Xiongnu, described as a dragon with a horned lupine head and proposed as an antecedent to the elongated dragon found in Han-period China.[82] The dragon is seen in the arts of Central Asia

77. See Wang Binghua (1993: 167).
78. The use of food terminology perhaps also reflects the importance of cuisine in the culture.
79. Bunker, Watt, and Sun (2002: 134, cat. 106).
80. Ward (2008: 304).
81. Bunker, Watt, and Sun (2002: 134, cat. 106).
82. Bunker, Watt, and Sun (2002: 133).

from the late third/early second millennium, but it is, as Sara Kuehn points out in her study of the dragon in eastern Christian and Islamic contexts, "one of the most ancient iconographies of mankind."[83] She argues that, as well as being used in Xiongnu-period art, it is a motif of the Yuezhi who founded the Kushan Empire (see chapter 3). The dragon in profile on the earrings (figure 2) shows some features of the lupine style, with its long nose and horn. In the jade, the carving, and the depiction of the dragon the piece is also similar to a piece found in the Xiongnu graves of Noin-Ula, considerably further north on the Selenga River in present-day Mongolia.[84] The identity of the animal on the second plaque—shown face on—is less clearly a dragon: the small ears are more tiger-like (figure 2). Dragons and tigers are often found together, as in the Ivolga belt plaque, mentioned above, but sometimes an animal with a long sinuous body and such a head is described as a dragon with a tiger head or, in Bunker's terminology, a "feline dragon."[85] The tiger shown on the belt plaque from tomb 2 at Xigoupan (figure 3) shows something of this sinuousness, with its body twisted around in almost a full circle.

Little scientific testing on the jades has been carried out, and most identifications of its source are based on the style. But this is always open to revision. Some scholars, for example, have long concurred that many of the 755 "jade" carvings in the twelfth-century BC tomb of Fu Hao on the Yellow River near Anyang are made from nephrite from Khotan.[86] Fu Hao was a woman in the Shang elite, married to the king and buried around 1200 BC. But scientific testing on the "jades" in her tomb suggests that a variety of jade-like stones were used, such as a marble-type nephrite "Anyang jade," sassurite mined in the mountains of Henan in central China. There are few nephrite pieces, and their origin is uncertain.[87] This would seem to be supported by the argument, mentioned above in relation to the diffusion of mirrors, that the Hexi corridor route between the steppe and China was not very active at this time, having been replaced by the Northern Zone route. However, it must be said that jade from Khotan could also have traveled

83. Kuehn (2011: 4).

84. Illustrated in Borovka (1928: 72C) and with a line drawing in Yetts (1926: 181).

85. Bunker, Watt, and Sun (2002: 135). She describes a similar motif used on a different piece as a "coiled feline" (25, fig. 24). Such pieces could as validly be described as representing "tigers with a dragon-like body." We do not know how, if at all, they were labeled in their time.

86. Wang Binghua (1993: 167).

87. Jing Zhichun et al. (1997: 376–81).

north, on routes across the Taklamakan and the Tianshan to the steppe and then to China.

A few centuries later, an early Chinese text, *Guanzi*, attributed to Guan Zhong (ca. 720–645 BC), refers to the Yuezhi as a people who supplied jade to the Chinese. The Yuezhi lived in the Hexi corridor and would have been ideally placed to control the trade. This suggests that the route had opened up again. By the time of our earrings, however, the Yuezhi had been driven out by the Xiongnu, thus giving the Xiongnu control of this important route—and of the jade supply into China. This was a good reason for the Chinese Qin and then the Han to try to seize control of the route. After the Han successes, it seems there was a plentiful supply of Khotan jade in China, exemplified by Han burial suits.[88] The Han also protected the routes by building walls to the north of the Ordos and from Wuwei to the northwest of Dunhuang—the Hexi corridor.[89]

WOMEN ON THE STEPPE

The fact that the most richly endowed tomb excavated so far in the Xigoupan complex is that of a woman calls for comment. The comparable treatment of men and women in death is not unique to Xigoupan. Kathryn Linduff discusses the cemetery at Daodunzi in the southwestern Ordos. On the basis of Chinese coin finds, it can be dated from the end of the second century to the first century BC, and twenty-seven graves have been excavated here, nine of which are of women and seven of men. The tombs include pit burials, as at Xigoupan with supine bodies facing northwest, but also catacomb tombs, and the female burials include chambers for the remains of sacrificed animals: cattle, sheep, and horses. Belt plaques, knives, coins, and cowrie shells are found in both male and female burials, whereas beads and gold earrings are only in female tombs. None are as richly endowed as Xigoupan, and Linduff concludes that these were intercultural families, less powerful than those represented at Xigoupan, but where men and women were treated equally in death. She concludes that "no essentialized view of the

88. For a Han burial suit from Nan Yue in southern China, see J. Lin (2012).

89. It has been suggested that one of the primary functions of defensive walls—from Rome to China—was to defend roads. This was the view taken by Aurel Stein (1921: 18) when he surveyed the Chinese Han walls at Dunhuang, a point noted by Psarras (2003: 63).

Xiongnu is, therefore, adequate, to explain the complex nature of their identity as expressed in burial customs found even at the one site of Daodunzi. Although the Chinese records give us a single view, archaeological research gives us a rich and more nuanced view of the Xiongnu, or whoever these peoples were, including a window on how one's age and sex affected the solemn ritual of burial."[90]

In fact, richly endowed tombs for women are found elsewhere from the second millennium. The tomb of Fu Hao, mentioned above, is an obvious example. The fact that she is buried with many steppe accouterments has led some to argue that she was from the steppe herself: marriage is always part of the exchange that goes on between neighboring peoples, whether formally for diplomatic purposes, as in the Xiongnu-Chinese *heqin* treaties; as part of the plunder of war, with captured women becoming sexual partners, free or otherwise (see chapter 10); or just as a result of the intermixing of neighboring populations.[91]

Another female burial that has led to discussion about the role of women on the steppe is at Tillya Tepe, on the borders of present-day Afghanistan and Turkmenistan and dating to the middle of the first century AD. Scholars have argued that these are burials of Yuezhi peoples. A battle-ax and Siberian daggers were found in this woman's grave, and she has been described as a "woman warrior." Karen Rubinson offers an interesting discussion of this attribution in her article on gender and cultural identity. She briefly traces the discussion on the status of women on the steppe and points out that military equipment is found in many female tombs. However, she follows others in making an important point, quoting Feldore McHugh's study of mortuary practices—namely that a "danger lies in attempting to make a direct connection between particular objects placed in the grave and a function that they might have performed during life as used by the deceased."[92] McHugh gives an example of a culture where a spear and a battle-ax in the grave represent the status of an unmarried male rather than a warrior. Rubinson follows this to argue that some of the objects in the Tillya Tepe burials were intended to indicate cultural identity rather than the role of the tomb occupant—an

90. Linduff (2008: 194).
91. Sergey Miniaev (2015) argues that the steppe accouterments belonged to her attendants.
92. Rubinson (2008: 53), quoting McHugh (1999: 14).

identity that displayed the transition by the Yuezhi in their pastoralist role to a more settled lifestyle.[93]

Tomb objects, apart from indicating the actual wealth and status of the occupant in his or her lifetime, might also reflect aspirations, just like the possessions of a living person. Of course, there is the question of whether the deceased had any choice in the objects or whether this was decided by others on the occupant's death. Then there is the inclusion of what might be considered "exotic" or "foreign" objects in tombs, such as the Hellenistic glass bowl discussed in chapter 2 or the Bactrian ewer discussed in chapter 5.

Many unanswered questions remain about these earrings. Was their original recipient the woman buried in tomb M4 at Xigoupan, or had they been passed from one owner to another and finally put in her tomb as a sign of her status? When were they worn, if at all? Where were they made and by whom? We can say that they were almost certainly made for possession by an elite woman living on the northern steppe borders of what is now China. And we can also say that, whether made by Chinese or steppe craftsmen—or both— they represent elements of both of these cultures and their rich interaction during this period.

So where does this leave us? What we can assume, given the earrings' materials and their complexity, is that they were an indication of wealth and status. But apart from this, as with many archaeological artifacts, we are in a state of uncertainty. We cannot be certain where they were made or who made them, and whether they were made as a whole or in parts. We do not know whether they were made for trade, gift, or ritual and whether they were acquired by purchase, plunder, or some other means. Nor do we know whether the peoples of the Xigoupan burials saw these artifacts as part of their own culture or considered them somehow foreign.

RECENT HISTORY

The earrings remained buried until their discovery in 1979 and were then discussed in the 1980 excavation report. The burial site is in modern-day China: they were excavated by a Chinese archaeological team and became part of the

93. She identifies some objects, such as glass in one of the graves, as "represent[ing] the exotic and the rare" and thus as reflecting the elite status of the individual (Rubinson 2008: 57).

cultural collections of China. There are no peoples claiming descent from the Xigoupan, or even the Xiongnu, who might argue that these objects belong to their cultural patrimony. Across the border, Russian archaeologists similarly excavate and take ownership of steppe objects that are found in modern-day Russia.

The earrings became part of the collections of the Ordos Museum, although on display in the Inner Mongolian Provincial Museum, established in Hohhot in 1957. They became part of the growing number of objects sent by China to exhibitions abroad from the 1980s. As Chinese museums were reopened following the Cultural Revolution, foreign curators were able to gain access to many objects excavated since the 1950s but previously not very accessible. They took full advantage. The earrings were first loaned abroad to an exhibition on objects from Inner Mongolia that opened in Los Angeles in March 1994.[94] They traveled with the exhibition to New York, Nashville, and Victoria until September 1995 and then to Alberta in 1997.[95] The exhibition was headlined as "Genghis Khan," presumably as a means of attracting visitors by a familiar name. Although the authors were clear about the very varied provenance and dating of the objects included, it is inevitable that the complexities of the many cultures represented by these objects and their tenuous links to Genghis Khan would not be noticed by many visitors. But the exhibition provided an opportunity for scholars to see a range of objects, previously unexhibited in North America, that reflected this complexity and, most especially, the influence of steppe cultures on China.

The art of the steppe, which had been richly represented in museums and in scholarship under the USSR, started to receive more attention in North America around this time.[96] New York's Asia Society Gallery 1970 exhibition displayed material that came from Siberia but was held in US collections. This was followed by a loan exhibition from USSR museums in

94. A. Kessler (1993: 62). *Genghis Khan: Treasures from Inner Mongolia*, exhibited at the Natural History Museum of Los Angeles County (March 6–August 14, 1994). I have not been able to find any prior exhibition history.

95. The exhibition then traveled to the American Museum of Natural History, New York (September 10–November 27, 1994), the Tennessee State Museum, Nashville (December 17, 1994–March 5, 1995), the Royal British Columbia Museum, Victoria (March 25–September 10, 1995), and the Royal Alberta Museum (March 22–July 6, 1997). See A. Kessler (1993).

96. See Jacobson (1995) for a summary of the interest in and scholarship on Scythian art (20–26).

1975 held at the Metropolitan Museum of Art.[97] Two more exhibitions concentrating on these collections were held in 1999–2000. The first, *Scythian Gold: Treasures from Ancient Ukraine*, toured North America and then went to Paris. The second, *The Golden Deer of Eurasia: Scythian and Sarmatian Treasures from the Russian Steppes*, opened at the Metropolitan Museum in 2000.[98] By this time the USSR had broken up, and many of the museums it had previously represented were no longer under Russian control. The former exhibition concentrated on items from one former Soviet state, Ukraine, independent since 1990. The latter, organized with the Russians, showcased items in Russian museums.[99]

While these exhibitions concentrated on the western Eurasian steppe, attention also turned to the eastern lands with a major catalog and an exhibition at the Metropolitan Museum, both showcasing private collections in North America rather than collections held in China.[100] However, while Scythian culture was the focus of the earlier exhibitions, the cultures of the Xiongnu have yet to be the named focus of a major exhibition in North America.[101]

Between 2002 and 2012 all of the provincial museums in China were

97. Bunker, Chatwin, and Farkas (1970); Piotrovsky (1973–74); P. Harper et al. (1975).

98. Reeder and Jacobson (1999); Aruz et al. (2000).

99. Some of these items had been excavated in lands, such as Ukraine, that were by now independent, and this did not go without notice. An article in the *Ukrainian Weekly,* for example, criticized the MMA show as being driven by politics rather than scholarship: "It seems that the only purpose of the Russian-inspired show at the Metropolitan Museum of Art was to take the shine off the Ukrainian exhibition at the Brooklyn Museum of Art. It is a sad example of an august museum fawning to the interests of a fading political star" (Fedorko 2000). The tension continues: in late 2016 a Dutch court ruled on objects still being held in Amsterdam following the takeover of Crimea by Russia during the course of a 2014 exhibition, *Crimea: Gold and Secrets from the Black Sea*, organized with Ukraine. The court held that the objects belonged to Ukraine and not to the loaning museums in Crimea (Allard Pierson Museum, "The Crimea Exhibition," press release, August 20, 2014, www.allardpiersonmuseum.nl/en/press/press.html).

100. The Arthur M. Sackler Collection and the Eugene V. Thaw Collection respectively: the latter was gifted to the Metropolitan Museum (Bunker 1997; Bunker, Watt, and Sun 2002).

101. The Beijing World Art Museum had an exhibition, *Huns and the Central Plains: Collision and Mergence of the Two Civilizations*, in 2010. An exhibition in Korea, *Xiongnu, the Great Empire of the Steppes* (National Museum of Korea, 2013), concentrated on recent archaeological finds from one site in Mongolia. A small exhibition *The Huns* was organized as part of the 2005 Europalia festival in Belgium, showcasing finds from Russian collections (Nikolaev 2005).

rebuilt, with vast modern buildings replacing the old sites.[102] The new Inner Mongolian Provincial Museum, opened in 2007, is ten times the size of the original. The earrings are on display. By this time the cultures of the steppe from the late first millennium BC were starting to be incorporated into the "Silk Road" label.[103] The earrings duly traveled to Brussels in 2008 for an exhibition on the Silk Road, which included this steppe element.[104]

Excavations and scholarship on the Xiongnu continue to reveal new evidence and findings about the complexity of cultures under their empire, but it remains to be seen whether these earrings will be displayed as part of any future exhibitions showcasing this complexity or whether they will continue to occupy a cultural hinterland.

102. Gledhill and Donner (2017: 120). As the authors also show, this has been accompanied by an enormous growth in museums, including private ones: from 14 in 1949 to 1,215 in 2005 to 4,510 in 2015 (119).

103. Routes across the steppe had been included as part of the 1988 UNESCO project "Integral Study of the Silk Roads: Roads of Dialogue," probably in part as a result of the 1957 report of the Japanese National Commission to UNESCO (Japanese National Commission 1957; Whitfield 2018b).

104. Whitfield (2009: 57, cat. 27).

TWO

A Hellenistic Glass Bowl

A PHOTOGRAPH DOES NOT DO JUSTICE to the object shown in plate 1b.[1] Although its outside is roughened by weathering, the inside still shows the original rich deep blue of the glass. The dating, its shape, and the groove under the rim suggest it was a late Hellenistic piece, probably made in the Levant. We have to imagine it fresh from the workshop, over two thousand years ago, smooth and unblemished. But it was not admired for long. A century or less after its casting, it was interred, with two similar bowls, in a tomb at Hengzhigang in South China. Here it remained until the tomb was excavated in 1954. Most of its short life was probably spent in the bowels of one or more ships, making their way across the Indian Ocean and the South China Sea with a cargo of trade. Was it once one of many—hundreds, possibly thousands—as seen in ships dispatched in the opposite direction from China with their loads of ceramics? Was it made for trade? And why was it placed in the tomb? Before addressing these questions, let us start with how and where it was made.

The origin of this and the other two bowls is far from certain. In the original Chinese archaeological report they were simply designated as coming from outside China, and such glass of this early period was typically labeled "Roman" by Chinese archaeologists. This is the designation that came with the vessel when it was displayed in Brussels in 2009.[2] *Roman* was simply a

For places mentioned in this chapter see Map 3 in the color maps insert.

1. I am indebted to many scholars for this chapter, but especially Julian Henderson of Nottingham University. The work and comments of Cecilia Braghnin and Shen Hsueh-man have also been invaluable. All mistakes, misunderstandings, and omissions are my own.
2. Whitfield (2009: cat. 48). An Jiayao (2004: 58) also described it as Roman.

catch-all for anything Western. On the basis of its date, its shape, the groove under its rim, and the weathering, Julian Henderson has suggested that it is late Hellenistic, made in the Levant and similar to many other pieces excavated there. This is plausible, as there is other evidence that late Hellenistic or early Roman bowls were being imported into China.[3] However, there was also a glass industry in China at this time, and Brigitte Borell, who has studied it, suggests that the bowl might rather be a product of an industry local to Southwest China and Vietnam.[4] Working with objects from the past often involves accepting uncertainty, and while new analytical techniques such as isotopic analysis may promise to answer some of our questions they are unlikely to resolve them all.

THE ORIGINS OF GLASS

Glass is produced from materials occurring naturally that need only heat to transform them, such as silica, found in sand, and alkaline plant ash, the latter used as a flux to reduce the melting temperature of the silica. Volcanic eruptions, nuclear explosions, asteroids, and even mundane events such as burning haystacks can produce glass if the raw materials are present.[5] Before humans started producing glass they worked obsidian, volcanic glass naturally created when lava flow—rich in silica—cools rapidly. The presence of iron and aluminum makes the resulting brittle and shiny substance dark. It is found worked by humans from 700,000 BC, fractured like flint to create sharp blades and arrowheads. It continues to be used today by some surgeons for their scalpels, producing a sharper and smoother cutting edge than steel.[6] Naturally occurring glass was also used for decorations: it has been suggested that the carved scarab found in the breastplate of King Tutankhamun (d. 1323 BC) might be from a piece of glass formed by a meteorite crashing into the Egyptian desert.[7]

Most manmade glass is made from silica and a flux, but the process means

3. See below, note 76. Conventionally the Roman period begins in 27 BC. *Late Hellenistic* refers to the period preceding this.

4. Borell (2011).

5. As Henderson points out, "Glassy slags can be produced in virtually any high-temperature environment" (2013: 6).

6. Buck (1982).

7. See Henderson (2013: 5–6) and "Tut's Gem Hints at Space Impact," BBC News, July

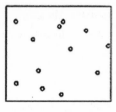 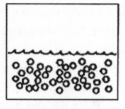 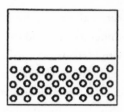

gaseous state   liquid state   crystalline state

FIGURE 4. Structure of crystalline solid, liquid, and amorphous materials. After Corning Museum of Glass, "What Is Glass?" December 2, 2011, www.cmog.org/article/what-is-glass.

these are not arranged in any regular way like the lattices of solid materials. The bridges between the atoms of the silica and oxides are broken, and other atoms, such as sodium and calcium, are distributed fairly randomly. It is therefore termed an amorphous material—not like a usual crystalline solid or like a liquid (figure 4). Plastic is another amorphous material.

Glassmaking was the last to be developed of three main nonorganic human technologies (the other two being pottery and metalworking). Before glass the same materials and technologies were developed for the production of vitreous materials such as faience and Egyptian blue. Faience is a hard, highly colored glazed material often reflecting the light and is made from the same materials as glass—silica and plant ash—although fired at a temperature about two hundred degrees Centigrade lower than that required to produce glass. It also is produced on one firing, whereas glass requires two: one to produce the raw glass and then a second to work it into beads and other objects. Faience is found in Mesopotamia from around 4000 BC, in Egypt in the fourth millennium, and at an Early Harappan site in South Asia around 2700 BC.[8]

Egyptian blue, considered to be the earliest synthetic pigment, was made by repeated high firings from silica, copper alloy filings or crushed ore, calcium oxide, and a fluxing material. It was probably developed to imitate lapis lazuli, a stone imported to Egypt over three thousand miles from the mines in present-day eastern Afghanistan.[9] It appears from around 2500 BC, and

---

19, 2006, http://news.bbc.co.uk/1/hi/sci/tech/5196362.stm. Manmade glass is also extensively used in Tutankhamun's tomb.

8. Hodges (1992: 125); McCarthy (2008: 915). For a discussion of faience and glass, see Henderson (2013: 14–16).

9. Its name in Egyptian means "artificial lapis" (Pagès-Camagna 1998). On the trade, see Tosi (1974).

later examples show that it was also being made in Ugarit in present-day Syria. It continued in use until around AD 400.[10]

The first known manmade glass—in the form of beads—is found in northern Mesopotamia and dates to about 2500 BC.[11] The raw glass—known as soda-lime glass—was made from silica and plant ash fused together in crucibles in small quantities. Silica by itself has a melting temperature of over 1700°C, but when it is mixed with an alkali, such as soda, this can be reduced to about 1000°C. The alkali is called a flux. The resulting glass slag was then fired again and fashioned into beads by various means, such as winding the molten glass around a clay-coated wire. Glass beads came to be produced in various colors, the glass colored and made opaque with the addition of raw materials. Some of the resulting beads resembled semiprecious stones such as turquoise and lapis lazuli.[12] Raw glass from Eridu in present-day Iraq, dating from around 2300 BC, is made from silica and plant ash, combined with a cobalt-rich material to produce this blue coloring.[13]

Tutankhamun's death mask contains lapis lazuli along with locally made deep-blue glass. Presumably the substitutions were made because of the cost and rarity of lapis. By this time glass technology had spread into Egypt, possibly taken there by Mesopotamian craftsmen. Beads of the same composition as those on Tutankhamun's mask are found in northern France and Scandinavia, evidence of early trading in glass.[14] Some scholars argue that glass technology was also developed in the Indus valley and that some beads previously classified as stone are in fact weathered glass. The evidence is uncertain, but given the production of siliceous faience there by around 2700 BC, the development of glass would not be unexpected.[15] Firm evidence for glass production across the Indian subcontinent is datable to around 1450–

10. In 1824, the Societé d'Encouragement in France offered a prize of F 6,000 to anyone who could produce a synthetic variety of lapis lazuli pigment at a price not to exceed F 300 per kilo. The prize was not awarded for four years. Finally, in 1828, it was awarded to Jean-Baptiste Guimet. Guimet's ultramarine was sold for F 400 per pound (lapis lazuli cost between F 3,000 to F 5,000 per pound at that time). For preliminary observations on the economics of lapis as a pigment on the eastern Silk Road, see Whitfield (2016).

11. Moorey (1994).

12. For a history of beads, see Dubin (2009).

13. Henderson (2013: 134).

14. Also glass from Mesopotamia that has been found in northern France.

15. Basu, Basu, and Lele (1974); McCarthy and Vandiver (1991). For example, faience bangles from Gola Dhora are discussed in "Gola Dhoro (Bagasra)," n.d., accessed September 14, 2017, www.harappa.com/goladhoro/faiencemaking.html.

1200 BC, and there was contact between the Harappan cultures in the Indus valley and those in Mesopotamia by land and sea.[16]

The first glass vessels, rather than beads, were also found in northern Mesopotamia and date from around 1500 BC, probably produced under the Hurrian kingdom of the Mitanni.[17] They were core formed and made from silica and plant ash.[18] Making vessels in this way required the fusion of large volumes of glass inside furnaces that could reach approximately 1150 to 1200°C. The molten glass was used to coat a core of dung and clay that had been shaped around a rod. Trailed-on glass provided surface decoration. Colored glass started to be produced systematically, with the addition of antimony leading to opaque white, yellow, and turquoise, and the addition of cobalt to produce the deep blue. These required further technological innovations: the glass had to be heat treated, so that crystals of the antimony or other substance would form, and then had to be cooled slowly to develop the opacifiers. This resulted in a stronger glass. Sources and supply of the raw materials were also required, not all available locally. This period also sees the appearance of mosaic glass vessels produced in molds and decoration using marbling, further technological innovations.

As well as the export of beads and, later on, finished vessels, unworked glass—raw furnace glass or ingots—was exported as neighboring cultures developed glass technology and were able to work glass into local products. The discovery of a fourteenth-century BC shipwreck off the coast of southwestern Turkey near Kas gives us a glimpse into the network of trade and exchange of this pre–Silk Road time across western Eurasia and Africa.[19] The wreck contained, among many other items, amber from the Baltic, ostrich eggs, ebony and ivory from Africa, an Egyptian gold scarab inscribed with the name of Nefertiti, Cypriot pottery, Canaanite jewelry, pomegranates, cumin, and almonds (and a stowaway house mouse). Copper ore for the 345 ingots (each weighing twenty-three kilograms) came from Cyprus. It was probably a merchant ship of the Syro-Palestinian peoples who lived on the

16. Lal (1987). The trade in lapis and in other semiprecious stones such as carnelian is material evidence of these links (During Caspers 1979), but whether there was any transfer of glass technology from Mesopotamia to the Indus valley is more difficult to establish.

17. Henderson (2013: 134–45).

18. Moorey (2001: 4) argues that the technology was developed earlier and refined under the Mitanni.

19. Pulak (1998). For a brief description of the ship and for a general introduction to ships across the Silk Road, see McGrail (2001: 123–25).

eastern coast of the Mediterranean, and was on its regular circular voyage from Syro-Palestine northwest to Cyprus, thence to the Aegean, and occasionally as far west as Sardinia, then back home via North Africa and Egypt.[20] The ship's cargo included about 175 translucent cobalt-blue and turquoise glass ingots, about fifteen centimeters in diameter. These are known from textual sources to be called *mekku*-stone, and analysis has shown them to be identical to Egyptian and Mycenaean glass.[21] Around 9,500 glass beads and 75,000 faience beads, along with others in carnelian and other semiprecious stones, were also found. Many of these would have been items for trade, but others were probably the personal possession of crew members.[22] Scholars have also suggested that the one ton of tin found in the Mediterranean shipwreck might also have come from mines in Central Asia.[23]

Glass technology developed in different cultures across West Asia and Europe in the following millennium. Glass started being worked in Greece around the thirteenth to twelfth centuries BC; it was fused in northern Italy around the eleventh to tenth centuries BC; and thereafter the technology moved across Europe.[24] From about 800 BC there was a significant development in the composition of glass made in western Eurasia with the use of the sodium-rich minerals natron or trona largely replacing plant ash as the alkali. Natron is found on the edge of the desert northwest of Cairo at a place called Wadi el Natrun (Natron valley). Natron was a purer and denser source of the alkali required for glassmaking and, unlike plant ash, did not need prior preparation. It had been used for embalming bodies in Egypt as early as about 2000 BC, but it was relatively rare. However, it became the main source of the alkali in glass in the Levant and Europe for one and a half millennia. The Roman scholar Pliny the Elder (ca. AD 23–79) recorded one account of the start of glassmaking near the Belus River: "A ship of [Phoenician] natron merchants came to shore and when the men were scattered all along the beach preparing their meal, since there were no stones to support their kettles, they put pieces of natron from their ship under them. When these had caught on fire and the sand of the shore mixed with them, there flowed transparent streams of a new substance, and this was the origin of glass."[25]

20. Bass (1987: 699; Cline 1994: 100).
21. Jackson and Nicholson (2010).
22. Ingram (2005).
23. Pulak (1998); Muhly (2011); Hauptmann, Madding, and Prange (2002).
24. Although there is no firm evidence that it was fused in Europe.
25. Trowbridge (1930: 95–96).

The Greek historian Strabo (64/63 BC–ca. AD 24) also wrote of glassmaking in the region, identifying another source of sand further north along the Mediterranean coast near Sidon. Excavations over the past two decades in Beirut have given evidence of both glassmaking and glass working, and thousands of glass vessels have been uncovered.[26] These date from the late Hellenistic period onwards and include the type seen in the bowl under discussion, namely a blue monochrome hemispherical bowl with a decoration of a single groove below the rim. They were made by casting, that is by either pouring the molten glass into or over a mold or heating the raw glass inside the mold.[27] Although plain bowls are found, ones with a grooved decoration are most common, the groove probably being cut by a wheel and not formed by the mold.[28] Large assemblages have been found of such bowls in this region at every type of settlement.[29] Ruth Jackson-Tal suggests that this shows they "were available to most classes of society," were stored by being stacked upside down, and were predominantly used for drinking.[30] Glass vessels became the choice for tableware, preferred over gold and silver as they did not give off an odor.[31] They were also cheaper, a mark of the transition that took place around this time from the production of "small numbers of luxury core-formed cosmetic vessels to the mass production of simpler cast drinking vessels."[32] As Henderson observes, since silica, in the form of sand, was readily available, economies were dependent on the supply of fuel for the furnaces and the supply of natron, still the principal alkali flux, but also on the development of sagging. This method of casting bowls by placing a flat disk over a mold meant that the mold could be reused and was a quick and cheap method of production.[33]

The glass for our bowl could have been produced in one of the tank furnaces uncovered in Beirut or in one of the other glass production centers in the Levant or North Africa. It was not necessarily the case that the vessel was produced in the same center as the glass, but given the ubiquity of this form of vessel in the Levant at this time we can assume it was probably made

26. Kowatli et al. (2008) and Jennings (2000). For a discussion of the tank furnaces discovered in Beirut, see Henderson (2013: 215–22).
27. Jennings (2000) distinguishes between slumping, slagging, and casting.
28. Jackson-Tal (2004: 19).
29. Jackson-Tal (2004: 19n22, 22–23 for a list).
30. Jackson-Tal (2004: 17, 27).
31. Henderson (2013: 207), quoting from Petronius's *Satyricon*.
32. Jackson-Tal (2004: 27).
33. Henderson (2013: 212). There was an additional major development in the next century in glass production, the invention of glassblowing.

there along with hundreds or thousands of other similar items. Although many questions about this piece may never be answered, the composition and source of the material for its production could be confirmed using scientific analysis.

The chemical composition of ancient glass is complex, with many different compounds found in many different combinations. A variety of oxides are formed from the primary components, such as the sand, quartz, and various alkali fluxes, as well as in the colorant and opacifying materials. In addition, other oxides associated with the impurities are found with the various minerals used for coloring. Up to the 1960s, various analytical techniques were in use to identify these components, but from this time more efficient techniques became available. These include X-ray fluorescence (XRF), scanning-electron microscopy (SEM), particle-induced X-ray emission (PIXE), and various methods of spectroscopy. Each technique provides slightly different kinds of analytical information, and often several techniques are used to cross-check or add to results.[34] In isolation, the chemical analysis of a piece of glass will not necessarily add greatly to our understanding. Data need to be collated from a variety of sources in order to build a picture of glass production in different regions at different times. Material found at production sites is a key part of this, as is a knowledge of trade patterns.

Analysis over the past half century has resulted in a much greater understanding of glass: for example, identifying that natron starts to be used from around 800 BC and that glass produced in central China from around 500 BC—discussed below—uses barium oxide and lead with potassium as the flux and is not of the soda-lime type found across western Eurasia and North Africa. These methods would, for example, confirm whether or not the glass for this bowl was made in the Hellenistic or Chinese worlds. Qualitative XRF analysis has been carried out on one of the bowls discovered in the tomb. Such analysis indicates all the elements present in the glass, without providing information on the quantities. This analysis showed the presence of potash, lead and barium, along with silica and various alkalis.[35]

34. Henderson (2013a). For his introduction to the various techniques, see 8–23.
35. Fan and Zhou (1991).

Two decades ago Henderson noted that "glasses made at two different areas using the same technological tradition but with slightly different raw materials will probably contain recognizably different trace elements and will possibly have different stable isotope signatures."[36] Since then, techniques of isotopic analysis have been developed that have the potential to enhance further our understanding of glass and other material.[37] The relative levels of strontium and neodymium in Hellenistic glass have distinguished two different sand sources used in making such glass.[38] As Henderson points out, there might be a compositional and isotopic distinction between the sands found on the beach at the Belus River and those at Sidon, indicating the two sources and providing a means of distinguishing glass melted in the two areas.[39] An analysis of these sands awaits. Trace element analysis has already provided evidence for more than one production area for Middle Hellenistic glass, one of them possibly in Italy.[40] This is just the start of a potentially very rich methodology for mapping and understanding in much greater detail the sources of glassmaking, glass production, and glass trade.

In the case of our bowl, however, we are still reliant on its style, form, and dating, along with the basic information provided by the XRF analysis. The former points strongly to this being a late Hellenistic bowl produced in the Levant. The latter introduces an element of doubt into this hypothesis. Without further information the results are inconclusive but certainly leave open the possibility, as Borell points out, that this bowl was produced in China.

GLASS PRODUCTION IN ASIA

In South Asia, as noted above, faience is found in Indus valley cultures, and there are signs of glass production there in the early second millennium BC.[41] The evidence remains fragmentary through the first millennium. Glass

36. Henderson (1995: 62).
37. For a simple introduction, see Hirst (2017).
38. Henderson (2013: 238–40).
39. See Henderson (2013: 240, 326–34) for the importance of the environmental approach in isotopic analysis.
40. A. Oikonomou et al. (2016).
41. Kenoyer (1998: 176)—although the finds are very weathered and there has been discussion about whether they are glass.

with a high aluminum content is found at Rupar in the Punjab from the beginning of the first millennium BC and a high-potassium (potash) glass from Hastinapura in Uttar Pradesh around the middle of the first millennium BC.[42] From about 400 BC potash glass is also found in Southeast Asia, though the production sites of the Indian and Southeast Asian glass are still uncertain for this period. But by around 200 BC, production sites on the southeastern coast of India were producing glass beads. These, now known as Indo-Pacific beads, were traded to Southeast and East Asia as well as to Africa.[43] "The Indo-Pacific bead industry produced one of the, if not the, most widespread and ubiquitous trade item of all time."[44] This glass is distinguished by its high aluminum and low lime content.

Potash glass continued to be produced in Southeast Asia, including at sites around the Tonkin Gulf in what are now Northeast Vietnam and Southwest China. A detailed analysis of the potash glass from South and Southeast Asia of this period distinguished several subgroups, suggesting different production sites, possibly including one in Southwest China.[45]

Elsewhere in Asia, glass beads are found in tombs in the Tarim basin, in present-day Chinese Central Asia, dating from around 1000 BC, and in central China from around the fifth century BC.[46] Scientific analysis shows that most are soda-lime glass, which suggests that they were imports from West Asia, but the crudeness of some of the beads and the presence of lead and magnesium has led some scholars to suggest the possibility of the start of local glass production in Central Asia at this time.[47] Glass from other Tarim sites dating from the fifth century BC onwards shows more sophistication and is of various compositions, including soda-lime. But other examples show significant levels of barium oxide and lead with potassium as the principal

42. Brill (1999, XIII 335, sample 443).

43. "From Mali to Bali," in the words of Peter Francis. See M. Wood (2016) for an update on Francis's conclusions about trade to Africa.

44. Francis (2002: 41).

45. Lankton and Dussubieux (2006). See Borell (2011) for the argument about the Southwest China production site.

46. Gan (2009b: 56–57) and Wang Bo and Lu (2009). Faience is also found further east from around the same period, and since there is no evidence of faience production in this region and the find-site this also suggests that they came by land routes from regions further west (Brill 1995: 270). Soda-lime glass eye beads have been discovered in the Xu Jialing Tomb, Xichuan County, Henan Province, in central China. For images and analysis, see Gan, Cheng, et al. (2009).

47. Li Qinghui et al. (2009: 343); Q. Li et al. (2014).

alkali. This glass seems to have been imported from China, as we see evidence of glass technology with these materials in central China from this time. No other place is known to have produced glass of this composition.

Both the relatively late appearance of glass in China and the use of barium oxide are features worthy of comment. By the end of the second millennium BC, potters in China were using furnaces to fire pots with ash glazes at temperatures of about one thousand degrees Centigrade and at higher temperatures within the early first millennium. Glazes are vitreous substances, and it has been suggested that the technology for glazing ceramics in Mesopotamia evolved from the glass industry.[48] In China, the use of glazes seems, however, to have preceded glass.[49] The ceramic technology in the Chinese region continued to develop, and by the end of the first millennium semivitreous glazed stonewares were produced that were both hard and able to hold hot liquids. This led to the production of porcelain, which, being vitreous and semiopaque, even more closely replicated some of the qualities of jade. The materials used for stonewares in southern China contained virtually no clay but instead consisted of fine mica or hydromicas. These were 6 to 10 percent potassium oxide, which, when fired, melted some of the silica in the clay body into a stiff glass and toughened the resulting stoneware.[50] So the technology was available for making glass.

Possibly as early as 1000 BC the Chinese produced a synthetic pigment, called Han blue or purple, that was used for about a thousand years. It was similar in composition to Egyptian blue but was synthesized at a higher temperature. Elisabeth West FitzHugh and Lynda Zycherman have tentatively suggested that the discovery of Han blue—made from barium copper silicate—may have been a serendipitous accident of glassmaking. However, there is currently no firm evidence for glassmaking in China by 1000 BC.[51] The earliest finds are potash-lime glass beads made in central China from about 800

48. Paynter (2009).

49. Kerr, Needham, and Wood (2004: 464) note the "puzzling example" of a high-potassium glaze found on a Chinese vessel from the second or first century BC and point out the affinity with high-potassium glassmaking in South and Southeast Asia, the latter including South China.

50. Kerr, Needham, and Wood (2004: 59–60).

51. West FitzHugh and Zycherman (1992). A fourth-century textual source records the probably much older legend of the goddess Nuwa, who "smelted stones of all five colours to patch up the flaws" in the sky when it had been damaged by the collapse of a supporting pillar. This is often cited as a reference to an earlier glassmaking tradition. The "five" or various colors becomes a common motif for glass; see Shen Hsueh-man (2002).

BC. They are replaced from the fifth century along the central Yangzi valley by lead-barium and potash glass.[52] Han purple is seen used to decorate glass beads found in burials from the second half of the first millennium.[53]

Lead-barium glass remained the predominant glass in central China up to the early first millennium AD and is found throughout China, north and northwest into the steppe and Central Asia, and south to the sea. Brill and others have suggested that the turbidity that barium produced resulted in a glass resembling jade and that this glass was produced as a jade substitute.[54] The lead made the glass more brilliant and reduced its melting temperature.[55] As Gan Fuxi observes, it was natural for the Chinese to use lead as a flux, as they had long experience of using it in bronze working. In addition, both lead and barium ores are found in large quantities along the Yangzi River valley.[56] The use of saltpeter or potash as an alternative flux to make potash-lime glass is also not surprising given a long history of use in China.[57] Glass vessels were mold-made, again utilizing a technique well honed from bronze technology.

The evidence therefore points to glass production starting in China around 800 BC but adapting local techniques. Does this suggest that Chinese artisans experimented using familiar technology to emulate this foreign product? But why would they wish to produce it? As discussed above, we see glass being produced for aesthetic and economic reasons. There is no reason to think that glass would have been cheaper to produce than the high-fired stoneware in China, although there might be an economic argument for producing it as a substitute for jade. The argument that technologies develop from aesthetics is an interesting one, made in a structuralist context by Cyril Smith, and might lead us to conclude that the human desire that was met by glass in Mesopotamia, Europe, and Egypt, for example, was largely satisfied in China by high-fired pottery.[58]

52. Gan (2009a: 8).
53. Easthaugh et al. (2007: 36).
54. Brill, Tong, and Dohrenwend (1991: 34).
55. The preference in Chinese culture for hot drinks—in terms of both temperature and their effect upon the body—is well evidenced from a later period, although is not clear in this early period. A thousand years later, Islamic glass was praised by the Chinese for being able to contain hot liquids (Shen Hsueh-man 2002).
56. Gan (2009a: 20).
57. Gan (2009a: 21).
58. "The discovery of the materials, processes, and structures that comprise technology almost always arose out of aesthetic curiosity, out of the desire for decorative objects and not, as the popular phrase would have it, out of preconceived necessity" (Smith 1981: 347).

Why was glass produced? What set it apart from other available materials? Perhaps, as Smith suggests, it was "the desire for decorative objects" that led to the discovery of the materials, processes, and structures of faience and then glass technology.[59] The invention of Egyptian blue was driven by an aesthetic desire for the deep blue pigment but possibly also by economic need. The aesthetic appetite had been whetted by the introduction of lapis but could never be satisfied given that the logistics and cost of importing the material from thousands of miles away ensured it would always be relatively scarce and expensive. Blue glass could substitute for the rare stone. Later in Southeast Asia translucent prismatic-cut glass beads appear resembling the beryl crystals found in South India.[60] Beryl is often used in Buddhist relic chambers, representing one of the seven treasures of Buddhism, but glass is also found, possibly as a crystal substitute (see chapter 4).

In the early cultures of what is now China, jade became the most valued stone, representing imperial and religious power (see chapter 1).[61] It was worked from Neolithic times into copies of weapons and tools, but also into forms that clearly had a ritual meaning. It is probable that much jade was imported two thousand miles from Khotan.[62] This, and the skill and time required to work it, probably made it as valuable to the Chinese emperors as lapis was to the Egyptian pharaohs.

It is therefore not surprising that some of the early glass objects discovered in China, such as glass *bi*, seem to be emulating jade.[63] Given the value but also the expense of jade, it might be expected that other materials that could simulate it would be sought. But while glass has some of the same qualities

59. Smith (1981: 347).

60. For example, at Ban Don Ta Phet (Reade 2013; Glover 2004: 75).

61. For a discussion of the role of jade in Chinese culture, see chapter 1. Also see Rawson (2002).

62. This trade might have started by the end of the second millennium BC, since jades from the tomb of Fu Hao (ca. 1200 BC) have been identified by some as from Khotan (Di Cosmo 1996: 90). However, see chapter 1 for doubts expressed by some scholars on Khotan as an early source.

63. For example, a bead necklace unearthed in Suzhou (Gan 2009a: 3, photo 1.2). Shen Hsueh-man has pointed out, however, that this does not mean that the glass *bi* was considered a cheaper alternative. As she notes, glass was probably as difficult to work as jade, and making a traditional shape in this material might add to its value (pers. comm., January 16, 2016).

that were valued in jade, such as a certain translucency and hardness (glass is 5.5 and jade is 6 on the Moh scale of hardness), it is more brittle, and, perhaps more importantly for an aesthetic argument, has a different feel. Glass, as an amorphous substance, is warm to the touch, whereas jade, as a crystalline material, is initially cold but then slowly warms in the hand. The jade collectors of Khotan waded barefoot through the river, since they were said to be able to identify jade from its feel on their feet.[64]

As Hsueh-man Shen has observed, early Chinese cultures did not know where to fit glass in their taxonomy. This divided "stuff" into the elements of metal, wood, water, fire, and earth. The elements of pottery were apparent: it was made from earth and transformed by fire. But the elements of glass were unclear to the Chinese for many centuries. Comparisons were made with pottery but also with metal, precious stones (particularly jade), and even water.[65] This ambiguity is reflected in the terminology, with words adopted from outside. The term *liuli* 琉璃 came in during the Han period and was used to refer to glazes as well as to opaque glass and gemstones. Both Chinese characters making up *liuli* contain an element or radical for jade (玉). It possibly derives from the Sanskrit word *vaiḍūrya*, referring to blue and green stones, including lapis lazuli, as does the Chinese term *boli* 玻璃, which became the primary term for translucent glass.[66] Its possible Sanskrit origin—*sphaṭika*—also referred to a crystal or quartz.[67] Both terms almost certainly came in with Buddhism. We do not know what terms were used to refer to glass products prior to this.

Cecilia Braghin argues that glass technology remained a "marginal tradition in China" and that production "appears to have been encouraged by contacts with imported glass artefacts."[68] Was this also because the tradition, developed early in the cultures of China, for jade and ceramics covered the aesthetic range offered by glass, so that as a material it was seen to offer nothing new? Jade and ceramics were relatively plentiful, and the technology had been honed over thousands of years by the time glass was introduced into

64. "The Art of Feeling Jade," *Gemmologist*, July 1962, 131–33.
65. Shen Hsueh-man (2002: 72–73). See chapter 4 for further discussion of this.
66. Note that *liuli* and *boli* are the modern pronunciations.
67. For a discussion of the names used for glass, see Schafer (1963: 235–36) and Brill (1991–92).
68. Braghin (2002: xi). This became one of the seven treasures of Buddhism. However, Francis asserts that "China was one of the great glass beadmaking and trading nations of the world" (2002: 54).

China. In Braghin's scenario, the original impetus for glassmaking in China came from glass beads from West Asia. It was then revived by the arrival of Hellenistic vessels, as found in central China and, as in this piece, in a tomb on the southern coast. This is supported by the two references to glass in the histories of the Han period (206 BC–AD 220), which mention the emperor importing it from Central Asia and from the kingdoms in what is now southern China (see below). The third- to fourth-century alchemical text *Baopuzi Neibian* (Book of the master who embraces simplicity, inner chapters) also notes the process of glassmaking in the South while acknowledging that it was not invented in China and was also imported. Ascribing glassmaking to foreign craftsmen is found in the Chinese histories. For example, the *Beishi* (History of the Northern Dynasties; 386–581) notes the visit of a merchant from Central Asia in the mid-fifth century.[69] The *Suishu* (History of the Sui dynasty; 581–618) contains a reference to a man called He Chou (540–620), described as a descendant of a Sogdian family who were specialists in technology of the region. He is credited with reviving glass technology in China at this time.[70] Its appearance in tombs of the elite shows that, even if glassmaking never became central to the culture, glass objects were nevertheless valued.[71]

TOMBS OF THE SOUTH

The tomb where our bowl was found is in present-day Guangzhou in the far south of China and is dated to the Former Han (206 BC–AD 9). This area has an interesting history. Qin Shihuangdi (r. 246–210 BC), the "first emperor" of China, was originally ruler of one of the so-called Warring States who managed to conquer the other kingdoms and set himself up as the emperor of a united China in 221 BC. He expanded Qin rule southwards, into what was home to very different cultures from the agricultural heartland or the steppe to the northwest, collectively known by the Chinese as the Yue peoples. The region to the south of the Nanling Mountains was called the Southern Yue—

69. Quoted by Kinoshita (2009: 255)—he suggests the merchant was from Kushan, but this was probably post-Kushan.

70. Quoted by Kinoshita (2009: 256).

71. For example, Lullo argues that glass replicas prepared for tomb objects held more value than other substitutes, partly because of their association with "foreign exotica" (2004: 17, 22). See also chapter 5 for a discussion of "exotica" in tombs.

or Nan Yue (Nanyue) in Chinese.[72] The military commander of this region for the Qin was named Zhao Tuo, and at the end of the Qin dynasty (221–206 BC) he declared Nan Yue a separate kingdom (in Vietnam—Yue nan—it is called the Triệu dynasty). The kingdom included a belt of land along the sea extending into present-day Vietnam, as well as modern China's Guangxi and Guangdong provinces. The capital was in Panyu, modern-day Guangzhou, where royal tombs have been excavated.[73] Zhao Tuo, his grandson Zhao Mo, and their three successors largely retained the kingdom's autonomy until 111 BC, when an army sent by the Chinese Han dynasty managed to impose their rule. Although there were a number of uprisings—most famously that of the Trưng sisters in AD 40—these were unsuccessful, and the region remained under Han Chinese authority.

The brief published archaeological report on the 1954 excavation of this tomb dates it to the later part of the Former Han period, suggesting that it probably dates from after the fall of Nan Yue, but a legacy would have remained especially given the diverse population of the region. When the tomb of Zhao Mo, the second ruler of Nan Yue (d. 122 BC), was excavated nearby, the tomb objects showed influences from the cultures of the steppe, West Asia, Vietnam, and central China. There was a spectacular collection of jade, and, most notably, the corpse was dressed in a jade suit. This was a tradition developed in China and reserved for emperors and their families; it was believed to confer immortality. Zhao Mo's jade suit was composed of 2,291 plaques, many of them reworked from other objects. But the tomb also contained glass beads and twenty-two blue glass plaques with gilt bronze frames, measuring ten by five centimeters. Five pairs had been wrapped and placed face to face in a bamboo container for burial. Two were discovered in the burial chamber of the wives, but six were in the main burial chamber. The glass is lead-barium as made in central China, but the plaques, in their shape, size, and position around the middle of the corpse, seem to be belt plaques, as commonly found on the steppe. Chinese gentlemen wore long robes, while the horsemen of the steppe wore short robes—more suitable for riding—and hung their dagger and other accouterments from a belt. Zhao Mo's family came from northern China where the steppe met the settled, and Lukas Nickel suggests that he might have had mixed ancestry, which "made him appreciate a drinking horn, robes in nomadic fashion and a box with foreign-

72. Brindley (2015). (The name Vietnam is a transposition of this—Yue nan.)
73. Lin (2012: 233–44).

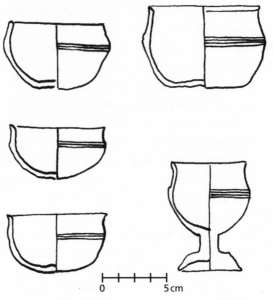

FIGURE 5. Form of glass bowls found in Hepu and Guixian, South China. After Borell (2011: fig. 3.1).

inspired decoration," all objects buried with him.[74] This would explain the belt plaques, although the use of glass remains unusual. Glass beads, necklaces, and a glass *bi* were also found in the burial.

Over two thousand other tombs from the same period have been excavated, some near Hepu and Guixian, also part of the Nan Yue kingdom and nearer the Vietnamese border. While many contained glass beads, only eleven contained glass vessels—one or two ribbed glass bowls (figure 5).[75] These, along with another bluish-green bowl found in a tomb in central China, were originally identified as Roman.[76] The latter is still believed to be

74. Nickel (2012: 105).

75. Eleven tombs out of the approximately two thousand excavated.

76. The broad dating of the tombs near Hepu and Guixian to the Han period, i.e., 206 BC–AD 220, does not help in the identification of the glass bowls as either late Hellenistic or early Roman. However, fragments of a bowl made of ribbed mosaic glass from the same region are in a tomb dated to AD 67, and, as Borell (2011: 61) points out, its pattern seems to be emulating a stone—murrhine—that Pliny mentions as being introduced from Parthia in the first century BC. Such bowls were produced in the eastern Mediterranean and exported widely throughout the Roman Empire (27 BC–AD 1453).

early Roman—showing that some glass vessels did indeed make their way to China at this time.[77]

Borell concludes that these were tombs of those who held a status just below the top rank. The mold-made shape of the bowls is distinctive, unlike anything Roman or Hellenistic, and analysis has shown them to be potash glass with a low magnesium level, which suggests a mineral source for the potash, possibly saltpeter. Borell has argued convincingly that these were products of a local industry and that such glass was exported from this region by the maritime routes: similar pieces have been found in Arikamedu in southeastern India. She places the dating of the start of this industry to the middle or late Former Han, that is, after Nan Yue. The use of glass imported from central China in the Nan Yue royal tomb suggests that the material was valued and might have prompted the start of this local industry. But the industry could also have been influenced by glassware coming from central China, from elsewhere in South or Southeast Asia, or from further afield.

The preliminary scientific analysis of one of the bowls found with the one under consideration here from the Hengzhigang burial has shown some presence of potash, and given this Borell suggests it might also be a product of a local workshop. However, the presence of some potash is not in itself inconsistent with the bowls being Hellenistic, and without further evidence the shape, color, weathering, and design still point toward a Hellenistic origin. If we accept this—allowing some element of uncertainty—then the question remains how these bowls came to Guangzhou.

Analysis of the many beads found in the other burials shows that they are of four different types, including the local potash and the Chinese lead-barium glass. Borell concludes that this is evidence for "a complex network of interregional exchange."[78] A large part of this exchange was almost certainly by sea.

MARITIME TRADE ROUTES

Maritime trade routes connected Africa and Eurasia from earliest times, with trade relations, for example, between the Harappan civilization of the Indus

77. Analysis has shown it to be natron-based soda-lime glass (Borell 2010: 128).
78. Borell (2011: 59).

valley and Mesopotamia in the third millennium BC.[79] By the second half of the first millennium, spices from India were reaching Greece via the ports of southern Arabia.[80] Within a few centuries, sailors were making use of the monsoon winds: the Greek historian Strabo (64/63 BC–ca. AD 24) tells of a man called Eudoxus of Cyzicus who made the return journey twice, setting sail from the Egyptian Red Sea in the time of Ptolemy VIII Euergetes II (r. 145–116 BC).[81] This use of monsoon winds opened up easier access to ports in southern India and, from there, to Southeast Asia.

At Arikamedu near Pondicherry in southeastern India, excavations have shown the port developing from the mid-third century BC with a distinctive type of pottery produced in the Hellenistic Mediterranean, rouletted ware, being imitated in Arikamedu from the mid-second century.[82] The presence of unfinished agate pendants in a Southeast style were, as Bérénice Bellina points out, probably also imitations intended for export to Southeast Asia, where Indian imports are common.[83] The site also contained numerous locally produced glass and stone beads that were also widely exported.[84] Imported glass vessels discovered here, although not in great numbers, include soda-lime Hellenistic and South China potash glass.[85]

The southwestern coast of China and the coast of northern Vietnam bordered the Tonkin Gulf, protected from the ocean by the island of Hainan. Petroglyphs found along the coast suggest the Yue people were accustomed to traveling by sea. In 1975 the excavation at Zhongshansilu to the east revealed a shipyard dating from the third century BC. It is estimated that this could have been used to build ships twenty-nine meters long and three to six meters

---

79. "A great amount of evidence testifies to the lively trade relations in the Gulf and the Arabian Sea in the late third millennium. It was both direct and transit trade. The main stations were the Sumerian ports in Southern Mesopotamia, then Dilmun, Makan, and Meluḫḫa, or with modern names, Bahrain, Oman with Eastern Iran and the ports of the Harappan civilization" (Karttunen 1989: 330).

80. For an introduction to ships from this time, see McGrail (2001).

81. Thiel (1966); Salles (1996).

82. The chronology of Arikamedu is based on that proposed by Begely (1983), which, as Salles (1996: 262–63) points out, suggests direct or indirect contact between the Hellenistic world and Southeast India by the second century BC.

83. Bellina (1997); Bellina and Glover (2004). Southeast Asia has a long history of maritime activity, but there is more sustained evidence from the second half of the first millennium BC.

84. Francis (2002: 27–30).

85. Borell (2010: 136–37).

PLATE 1A. *(top)* A pair of steppe earrings (chapter 1).
Ordos Museum, China.

PLATE 1B. *(bottom)* A Hellenistic glass bowl (chapter 2).
National Museum of China, Beijing.

PLATE 2. View showing Dabra Damo in 2011 (chapter 3).
Photograph by Fabian Lambeck.

PLATE 3. The sacred area and main stupa of Amluk Dara (chapter 4), June 15, 2012. Courtesy of Italian Archaeological Mission/ACT Project. Photograph by Edoardo Loliva (ACT/ISCR).

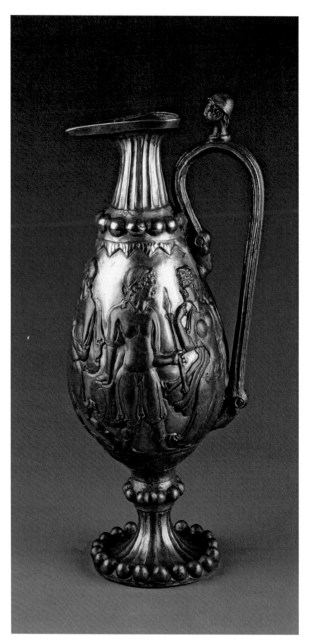

PLATE 4. A Bactrian ewer (chapter 5).
Guyuan Museum, China.

PLATE 5. A Khotanese plaque (chapter 6).
British Museum, London, 1907,1111.70, D.VII.5.
Trustees of the British Museum.

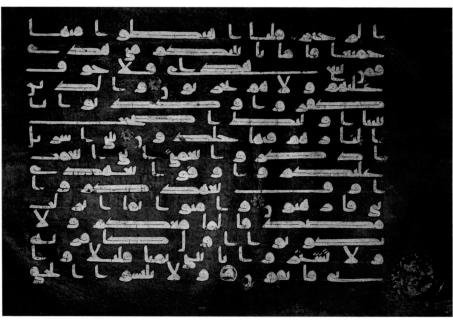

PLATE 6. A folio of the Blue Qur'an (chapter 7).
Doha, Museum of Islamic Art MS.8.2006.

PLATE 7. A Byzantine hunter silk (chapter 8).
Lyon, Musée des Tissus MT 27386. Lyon MTMAD.
Photograph by Pierre Verrier.

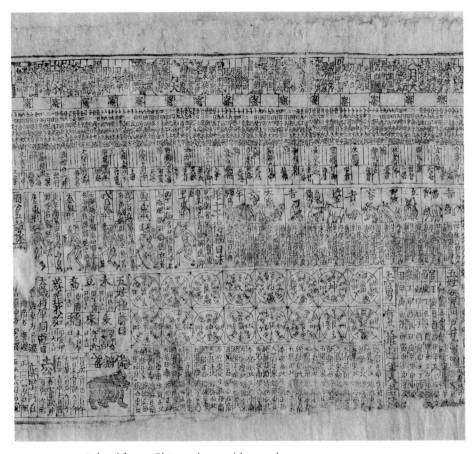

PLATE 8. A detail from a Chinese almanac (chapter 9).
London, British Library Or.8210/P.6. British Library Board.

FIGURE 6. A line engraving on a bucket from the tomb of the king of Nan Yue (ca. 122 BC), Guangzhou, showing a wooden boat. After Erickson, Yi, and Nylan (2010: 166).

wide that could carry a cargo of twenty-five to thirty tons.[86] The Chinese official history of the Han dynasty describes a route from near Hue, in present-day Vietnam, to what is now the island of Sri Lanka via the Malay Peninsula, several stops in Myanmar, and Chennai on the east coast of India.[87] The Chinese were said to have carried silk and gold to trade for pearls, precious stones, and other items—including one named *biliuli* in Chinese, which could mean glass.[88] A poem from a later period shows the continuing importance of this region for trade, including slaves (see chapter 10): "Argosies laden with slaves from the sea—rings in their ears; / Elephants laden with girls of the Man—bodies bound with bunting."[89]

A design on a vessel in Zhao Mo's tomb is a depiction of four ships, clearly showing a rudder that would have been essential for such navigation (figure 6).[90] Clay and wooden models of both river and seafaring ships have been found in other Han-period tombs.

The transport by sea of this glass bowl and its two companions at this

86. Ting (2006: 46). For other excavations of ships in China, see McGrail (2001: 360–78).

87. *Hanshu*, trans. Needham, Wang and Lu (1971: 444)—see also Borell (2010: 136).

88. Loewe (2004: 75–77).

89. Schafer (1967: 76), citing Du Xunhe (846–904). *Man* was a Chinese term meaning "southern heathens" and was used by this period indiscriminately for all the different peoples of the Southwest; see chapter 10 for a brief discussion of the "other" in Chinese and other cultures.

90. Erickson, Yi, and Nylan (2010: 166).

time from a Red Sea or Gulf port via India and possibly several other land-falls to South China in this period is therefore certainly possible. We can tentatively date the production of the glass bowl to the late second century or early first century BC and its burial in the tomb to the first century BC. We do not know whether it was exported directly after production, possibly taking a year or more to reach its final destination. Given that it was found with two other similar bowls, we might hypothesize that they were part of a much larger glass cargo. How did they come into the possession of the buried man, or his family? What was their significance? Were they even used before being buried with him, or were they acquired solely for burial?

These, and many more questions, will probably always remain without definite answers. However, because the elements used to make glass have a distinctive geographical signature based on their isotopes, refined methods of isotopic analysis combined with trace element analysis developed in the past few decades have enabled tests that will confirm the geographical source of the materials and therefore suggest the probable production area. Such isotopic analysis of this piece would provide support—or otherwise—for our hypothesis: that it was Hellenistic and made in the Levant. Discoveries of other pieces, in tombs, in shipwrecks, or elsewhere, might also add support or suggest other stories we can tell about this piece. This story is not yet finished.

If this is confirmed as a Hellenistic piece, then it was one of many such items made as an everyday drinking cup and not as a luxury item. But far away in South China it was rarer and almost certainly considered as both exotic and a luxury: it might never have been used for its original purpose. A possibly analogous situation is seen in the Chinese ceramics exported by sea to Europe from the fourteenth century. These were usually everyday items or pieces made for the export market and were far from being considered luxuries in China. But once they reached Europe they acquired a new and much higher status.[91] The status of the glass vessel—as a foreign luxury—might account for its inclusion in the burial, like the silverware ewer and Sasanian glass bowl that were buried with Li Xian (see chapter 5). In his study on the trade of glass beads in Asia, Peter Francis has argued that "the farther from the manufacture one goes, the more a product is apt to be treated as a luxury item."[92] Most burials contained glass only in bead form—not whole vessels—

91. Munger and Frelinghuysen (2003).
92. Francis (2002: 57). Geographical distance is only part of the story. Distance from the

and this tells us something about the status of the buried man: the excavation team concluded he was a member of the elite.

The tomb was one of three excavated from the same small tumulus at Hengzhigang in the northeast of the city of Guangzhou. They were dated to the middle or late Former Han period by their structure, size, and burial goods.[93] The broken fragments of the three bowls were discovered in tomb no. 1. This had a burial chamber six meters below the original surface level of the earth and oriented south southeast. The surviving shaft was completely filled with fine sand. There were two gutters on the floor of the chamber used for the sleepers that supported the wooden burial chamber. Only a few blackened traces remained of the coffin.

Most of the goods had been placed in the north and west of the chamber. Among them were seventy-one ceramics, a bronze tripod, three glass bowls, and one glass *bi*. One of the bowls was placed in the north of the chamber; the other two, along with the *bi* and a bronze belt hook, were placed next to the coffin. The only other glass found was a green belt hook in tomb no. 2.[94]

The glass bowl had changed over the two thousand years of burial. It did not decay and disappear in the way of organic material, but its surface and composition were affected by the long period underground, making it look very different from when it was first produced. This so-called weathering is typically seen on buried pieces and is more common on potash glass than on soda-lime. The glass *bi* found in the same tomb did not survive excavation but disintegrated into dust, perhaps suggesting that the material was severely weathered potash glass. But the type of weathering seen on the bowl is consistent with other soda-lime pieces made in the Levant.

Moisture is the primary cause of deterioration, as it causes the alkali ions to be slowly leached out and replaced with hydrogen ions from the water. This usually occurs within a few years of the burial, and then a new cycle starts, so that the different layers can often be seen. They range in thickness from one to about twenty-five micrometers. Sometimes they protect the glass from further weathering by providing a sort of laminated layer that slows down access of moisture to the glass underneath.[95] The presence of moisture

potential owner in terms of cost is also a factor: a Gucci handbag is valued in China and Italy, even though manufactured in the former and branded to the latter.

93. For a description of Han tombs, see Erickson (2010: esp. 13–15).

94. Belt hooks are often also made of jade, so this one was probably emulating jade. As mentioned above, belt hooks were not part of traditional Chinese clothing.

95. See van Giffen (n.d.); Craddock (2009: 235).

is not surprising in a burial in this region and is supported by the fact that no surviving organic materials were found in the tomb and that both the corpse and the wood of the coffin and the tomb chamber had completely decayed. The excavators note the custom of this time of using sea sand to pack the wooden chamber—evidenced by the sand found in the shaft—and suggest that the moisture from the sand caused the wood to decay.

The glass bowl, which started life as a utilitarian object and became an exotic luxury, is now an aesthetic and historical artifact. It continues to be considered an item of value in the Chinese context. This is shown by the fact that, instead of remaining in a local or provincial collection or museum, it was sent to become part of the collections of the National Museum of China in Beijing (formerly the History Museum). As demonstrating one of the links across Eurasia in premodern times it has also acquired significance in a "Silk Road" context and has appeared in several exhibitions and publications—although erroneously labeled as Roman.[96] Its new life has just begun and it has many secrets yet to reveal.

As this piece was being made and transported, a new factor came into the equation that was to have an impact on the use and value of glass in China, namely the use of glass in Buddhism.[97] This is discussed further in chapter 4.

96. Exemplifying the dichotomous and therefore inevitably simplified interpretation of the Silk Road as linking China and Rome (see Whitfield 2008).

97. See Braghin (2002) for a discussion of this and Shen Hsueh-man (2002) for an inventory of glass in later Buddhist stupas in China.

THREE

A Hoard of Kushan Coins

IN THE SIXTH CENTURY a Christian church and monastery were built on the top of a steep-sided plateau in the highlands of what was then the kingdom of Axum (ca. 100–940), in present-day Ethiopia (plate 2). It is possible there was an existing shrine at the site, although no traces are recorded. Among the treasures found in the monastery grounds was a hoard of over a hundred gold coins, possibly contained within a wooden casket decorated with gold and green stone. The coins had been minted at the heart of the Silk Road when the Kushan Empire united Central Asia. They ranged in date from the early second century to the beginning of the third century.[1] The earliest showed signs of wear, but the newest—six gold staters of Vasudeva I (r. 190–230)—were in mint condition, suggesting they were probably taken to Axum during or shortly after his reign. Why, where, and how were the coins first minted, how did they travel to East Africa, and why did they end up in this Christian setting? And where are they now? To try to answer these questions, let us start their story in their homeland with the rise of the Kushan Empire in the first century AD and the Kushan use of coinage.

THE KUSHAN EMPIRE

The rise of the Kushan, like that of many Silk Road empires, is linked to the movement of peoples across the ecological rift that separates northern from

For places mentioned in this chapter see Map 4 in the color maps insert.

1. I owe a great debt to the work of numismatists for this chapter and would like to thank Joe Cribb and Robert Bracey in particular for their generous advice and suggestions. All mistakes, misunderstandings, and omissions are my own.

southern Eurasia (see chapter 1). Northern Eurasia, which David Christian has called "Inner Eurasia" but which is also called "Inner Asia," has an arid continental climate that cannot support large areas of sustained agriculture. Much of Inner Eurasia has long been home to peoples surviving by varying mixtures of agriculture and pastoralism, moving in search of pasture one or more times a year, and creating small settlements.[2] Christian calls the border with Outer Eurasia—a land of settled people living primarily from agriculture and with large cities—"the dynamo of Inner Eurasian history."[3] One such group of agricultural pastoralists living in Inner Eurasia were called the Yuezhi by Chinese historians.[4] They were a group of tribes living around the Tianshan (Heavenly Mountains), including in the Hexi corridor of what is now northwestern China. Attempts have been made to link the Yuezhi to the burials from an earlier period found in the Tarim basin to the west, but without further evidence such connections remain hypothetical. We can only speculate on the Yuezhi's language and ethnicity, if indeed they were one people.[5] When we do read about the Yuezhi in Chinese histories, it is after they have been pushed out of the Hexi corridor by invaders from the north. These were another confederation of steppe pastoralists, named the Xiongnu in Chinese (see chapter 1), who in the third century expanded their territory south across the Gobi Desert and into the Yuezhi homelands.[6]

For this early history we have to rely almost exclusively on the Chinese records.[7] But these were informed by firsthand accounts, primarily that of the imperial envoy Zhang Qian (d. 113 BC). He was sent in 138 BC by the Chinese emperor to seek an alliance with the Yuezhi against the Xiongnu, who were also pushing at the northwest borders of China. It is his intelli-

2. Agriculture is found here, but on a relatively small scale compared to Outer Eurasia. Cities are also found here.

3. Christian (1998: xxi).

4. See Chang et al. (2003) for a discussion of the Yuezhi as agropastoralists—farmers and herders.

5. Some have linked them to an Indo-European group known as the Tocharians, but this remains speculative.

6. The Yuezhi were renowned for their army of skilled archers, but the Xiongnu had mobile mounted warriors.

7. For a discussion of these, see Thierry (2005). For a detailed account of the Yuezhi migration, see Benjamin (2007). The historical record is always subject to support or otherwise from the archaeological record. They do not always tally, especially in the indiscriminate use of *Xiongnu* in the Chinese histories, where the archaeological record suggests different cultures.

gence on his return to China that informs *Shiji*, the great work of the so-called first historian of China, Sima Qian, and *Hanshu*, the subsequent history of the Former Han dynasty (206 BC–AD 9). The latter was compiled by Ban Biao and his son and daughter Ban Gu and Ban Zhao. Ban Biao had another son, Ban Chao, who also contributed his knowledge. Ban Chao rose high in the military, fought several decades of battles against the Xiongnu alliance, and became "protector general of the Western Regions." From the Han onwards the chapter on the "Western Regions" was to remain a mainstay of Chinese official histories.

We are told in the biography of Zhang Qian in these same histories that he was captured by tribes loyal to the Xiongnu alliance on his journey out and managed to escape only after a decade, having married a local woman and fathered a son. He reached the Yuezhi in 126 BC, and it is from his accounts given in the histories that we learn of their exodus:[8] "The Yuezhi originally lived in the area between the Qilian or Heavenly Mountains and Dunhuang, but after they were defeated by the Xiongnu they moved far away to the west, beyond Dayuan [Ferghana Valley], where they attacked and conquered the people of Daxia [Bactria] and set up the court of their king on the northern bank of the Gui [Oxus] River."[9]

Elsewhere in the histories the account is expanded. It is recorded that the Xiongnu killed a Yuezhi ruler and that the son of Modu, the Xiongnu leader, used his skull as a drinking cup. Some Yuezhi moved south, but most, it is recorded, first fled north across the Tianshan to settle in the Ili and Chu valleys—now on the borders of Kazakhstan and China.[10] When Zhang Qian embarked on his mission, he might have believed that they still lived in this region, close to the western borders of Xiongnu territory. However, probably around the middle of the second century BC, the Yuezhi were pushed out of this new homeland by other invaders from the steppe, called the Wusun in the Chinese accounts, and moved west again. They eventually settled in the land between the Sogdians—who lived north of the Amu Darya (Oxus)—and the Bactrians, who lived in the region just to the south of the river, in present-day northern Afghanistan. This was a long

8. Mainly in *juan* 123 of the *Shiji* and *juan* 96A of the *Hanshu*. Various translations are available for both, cited below.

9. *Shiji* 123, trans. Watson (Sima Qian 1993: 234).

10. Some probably stayed as well. A notable descendant of these was the Buddhist monk Dharmarakṣa (fl. mid-third century, Zhu Fahu). It is recorded that he came from a Yuezhi family that had lived for generations in Dunhuang.

way from their old enemies, and Zhang Qian's mission thus became longer than expected. But his journey further west in search of them was to result in intelligence that is traditionally seen as an impetus for the Chinese expansion into Central Asia.[11]

Zhang Qian spent a year with the Yuezhi and in Bactria to the south of the Amu Darya. He must have had many tales to tell on his return. Unfortunately, Chinese histories are terse, giving only brief descriptions of each foreign people.[12] That in the *Shiji* for the Yuezhi simply reads: "They are a nation of nomads, moving place to place with their herds and their customs are like those of the Xiongnu. They have some 100,000 or 200,000 archer warriors."[13]

The Chinese histories also suggest that the Yuezhi had conquered the lands immediately to the south of the Amu Darya, including the Hellenistic city of Balkh (see chapter 5), but that they remained a confederation with many leaders:

> Daxia is located over 2,000 *li* southwest of Dayuan, south of the Gui river. Its people cultivate the land and have cities and houses. Their customs are like those of Dayuan. It has no great ruler but only a number of petty chiefs ruling the various cities. The people are poor in the use of arms and afraid of battle, but they are clever at commerce. After the Great Yuezhi moved west and attacked the lands, the entire country came under their sway. The population of the country is large, numbering some 1,000,000 or more persons. The capital is called the city of Lanshi [Balkh] and has a market where all sorts of goods are bought and sold.[14]

Here we see a group of agro-pastoralists of Inner Eurasia, the Yuezhi, forced away from their home and eventually settling across the geographical rift, in the Outer Eurasia of agriculture and cities.[15] We might hope for archaeological sources and further written records from this time to supple-

---

11. And, by extension, as a major factor in the start of the Silk Road. See Whitfield (2018b) for further discussion of this.

12. As Holcombe has noted, "Three subjects that mainstream traditional Chinese historians seldom addressed were trade, Buddhism and foreigners" (1999: 285).

13. *Shiji*, trans. Watson (Sima Qian 1993: 234). The archaeological record suggests the Yuezhi were agro-pastoralists, but the nuances of the lives of different groups of the steppe were not necessarily acknowledged by the historians in China.

14. Ibid.

15. For a discussion of this interaction in relation to the Yuezhi, see Liu (2001).

ment the Chinese histories, but both remain frustratingly scarce.[16] Some of the main sources are coins.[17]

What has been pieced together is that a leader of one of the regional rulers of the Yuezhi took overall power in the mid-first century AD, marking the start of the Kushan Empire. This ruler, Kujula Kadphises, expanded his territory south into the Kapisa region (Bagram), Taxila, and Kashmir, and his successors moved into northern India. At the end of his reign he sent an army into the Tarim basin. This is reported in the *Hou Hanshu* (History of the Later Han; 25–220):

> More than a hundred years later, the *xihou* ("Allied Prince") of Guishuang (Badakhshān and the adjoining territories north of the Amu Darya), named Qiujiu Que (Kujula Kadphises), attacked and exterminated the four other *xihou* ("Allied Princes"). He set himself up as king of a kingdom called Guishuang. He invaded Anxi and took the Gaofu [Kabul] region. He also defeated the whole of the kingdoms of Puta and Jibin. Qiujiu Que (Kujula Kadphises) was more than eighty years old when he died.[18]
> His son, Yan Gaozhen (Wima Taktu), became king in his place. He returned and defeated Tianzhu (Northwestern India) and installed a General to supervise and lead it. The Yuezhi then became extremely rich. All the kingdoms call [their king] the Guishuang (Kushan) king, but the Han call them by their original name, Da Yuezhi [Great Yuezhi].[19]

The stability brought by the Yuezhi enabled a growth of trade north from Sogdiana, south into India, and from there to Barbarikon and the Indian Ocean routes, as well as east to the Tarim basin and thence to China, and west into Parthia and thence to Rome. As Millward notes in relation to the Tarim basin, this is "a phenomenon displayed over and over . . . a nomadic royal house and its followers forging a confederation and establishing imperial control over sedentary populations."[20] The rise of the Kushan confederation could be seen as the most important factor supporting the growth

16. As noted above, Chang et al. (2003) have studied contemporary settlements in southeastern Kazakhstan, supposedly the first stopping point of the Yuezhi, and have found evidence of an agro-pastoralist society.

17. See Michon (2015: 110–51) for a discussion of these.

18. There is considerable discussion about the equivalents of the place-names used by the Chinese. For example, Anxi is linked by some with Parthia and by others with the Parthian kingdom of Gondophares in Gandhāra.

19. *Hou Hanshu* 88, "Xiyu juan" [Chapter on the Western Regions], trans. Hill (2003).

20. Millward (2007: 15).

of sustained long-distance trade across Eurasia, the Silk Road: one striking example of how, again quoting Christian, "Inner Eurasia has played a pivotal role in Eurasian and world history."[21]

The paucity of written and archaeological sources continues to impede our understanding of this Central Asian empire.[22] The sources give little information, for example, about their religion. What there is points toward the Kushan kings practicing an eastern form of Zoroastrianism but patronizing other religions: in Raymond Lam's words, demonstrating a "profound cultural-religious eclecticism."[23] Buddhism was included in their patronage. Buddhist missionary activities had originally been given impetus in India by the Mauryan king Aśoka (r. ca. 268–232 BC). He made Buddhism his state religion and vowed to disseminate the faith throughout the world. According to tradition he sent his son and daughter to Sri Lanka and prominent monks to Central Asia, West Asia, East Asia, and Southeast Asia. Inscriptions above cave temples in Sri Lanka support the arrival of Buddhism at this time.[24] From the earliest period, therefore, Buddhism was a proselytizing faith with a penchant for long-distance travel.[25] The Maurya Empire (322–180 BC) included the city of Taxila, lying at the junction of trade routes leading between India and the Tarim, and this was to become one of the Kushan capitals. The region became a major center of Buddhism by the end of the Mauryan period, with famous stupas at Dharmarajika in Taxila and Butkara near Mingora in the Swat valley (see chapter 4). By the start of the second century BC the Maurya Empire had shrunk, and Menander, the Greek king of Kapisa/Gandhāra, had expanded his kingdom to the Kabul and Swat valleys.[26] The Pali text *Milinda Pañha* (The questions of Milinda) records that he became a Buddhist and recounts his debates with the Indian Buddhist sage Nāgasena.

By the start of the Kushan Empire under Kujula Kadphises in the first century AD there were Buddhist monasteries and stupas around the ancient city (near Jalalabad).[27] Buddhism spread northwest into the Kabul region

21. Christian (1994: 182).

22. "Writing Kusana history is like constructing a giant mosaic. Scholars have pieced together parts of the outer frame and a few internal configurations, but whole areas are still empty" (Rosenfield 2011: 10).

23. Lam (2013: 440).

24. Trainor (1997: 86).

25. By sea as well as land.

26. Holt (1988).

27. Dates for the Kushan and its early rulers are the subject of much debate, as discussed below, so no firm dates are given here.

during Wima Kadphises's reign and then moved further north into Bactria. The Kushan kings used imagery borrowed from Greek and Indian religions to represent their gods. For example, when Kujula Kadphises minted coins he chose the imagery of the Greek god Heracles to represent the Kushan god Wesho. Wesho was also shown in the imagery of the India god Śiva. Buddha appears on coins from the time of Kaniška, the only direct representation of an Indian "deity." As well as providing information about their beliefs, it is largely thanks to the Kushan coinage that it has been possible to construct a chronology of the kings of Kushan.[28]

KUSHAN COINS

Money has been needed from the earliest human cultures, with many objects taking the role of an object of value used for exchange—from livestock to obsidian, grain, and silk. Early societies also used objects with little value— such as cowrie shells and beads—to exchange for higher-value goods. But coins, manufactured solely for the purpose of exchange, appear in cities around the Aegean Sea, in India and in China between 700 and 500 BC, seemingly representing separate developments. By the time of the rise of the Kushan Empire, coins were in use by neighbors in regions they conquered and there were also coins in circulation from more distant cultures, such as Rome.

Coins had a use beyond simple objects of value for exchange. They also acted as symbols of power and authority, and some argue they were a means of asserting legitimacy and hegemony.[29] For the Yuezhi, who were invaders into the region, Daniel Michon argues that the minting of coins that were familiar to those they were seeking to rule presented an idea of continuity of power rather than change. He sees the Yuezhi making a conscious choice among the variety of coins that were in circulation, replicating ones that showed a horse rider on the obverse, for example, as they were themselves

28. For a recent discussion of the importance of coins for the historian, see Holt (2012), who calls them "the very backbone on which the frame of Central Asian history has been built" (31).

29. This is often asserted, but there is little evidence for these early-periods coins having a legitimizing purpose. Cribb, for example, is skeptical. For a discussion, starting from the coins of the early Yuezhi, see Michon (2015: 110–16). For a more general discussion, see Cribb (2009, esp. 500–503).

horsemen.[30] However, Joe Cribb sees the primary purpose of continuity in coin design as enabling coins to circulate and argues that existing designs were reused for this purpose: "The horseman design was the standard design for coinage before the Kushan arrived, so they were just copying it, not necessarily with any intention of alluding to their own horsemanship."[31]

We know the name of Kujula Kadphises only from the coins and one Bactrian inscription (he is assumed to be the Qiujiu Que mentioned in Chinese histories), yet as uniter of the Yuezhi clans under the Kushan he was of immense importance in Central Asian and indeed world history. During his reign both copper and silver coins were produced. They were diverse, both based on and reflecting the variety of existing coinage.[32]

His successor, Wima Taktu, reduced the variety of coins. But he still produced coins only in silver and copper. It was with the third ruler, Wima Kadphises (r. early second century AD), that the first gold coins were minted.[33] These were not an innovation: gold staters had been produced by the Hellenistic kings of Bactria and of Kapisa/Gandhāra and by Rome, the last imported into India. On current understanding, it appears that techniques of the first two of these were used by the Kushan, alongside newly developed techniques, but not Roman ones. However, in appearance they probably borrowed from existing Roman coins. Harry Falk makes the case that Wima Kadphises made a deliberate choice to follow the standard of Roman coins under Augustus (r. 27 BC–AD 14), although they are not struck to this standard.[34] In terms of the weight, Robert Bracey argues that they followed a Bactrian standard derived from the Greek stater.[35]

---

30. Michon (2015: 114).

31. Joe Cribb, pers. comm., May 2, 2016. Cribb also states that "the momentum of money is represented through the continuity of design. For money to continue to circulate it has to have some resemblance to pre-existing forms of money" (2009: 498) and that the debate on legitimacy has "obscured for many the primary function of the designs to enable the coin to be issued and used as money" (503).

32. "The copper coinage derived from silver and copper coinages of North India, Pakistan and Afghanistan current in the first century AD" (Bracey 2012: 188). Michon argues that the coins were part of a "process of 'imaginative remaking' of who he [Kujula Kadphises] was and who the Kuei-shang [Yuezhi] were" (2015: 130–31). Cribb argues that their diversity was to enable the coins to circulate rather than to assert legitimacy (see note 31).

33. Bracey (2009).

34. Falk (2015: 105–9). He further argues that the Kushan use of *devaputra* (son of god) to describe themselves was, at least in part, influenced by the use of *divi filius* on the coins of Augustus (107).

35. For a summary of discussions on this and alternative views, see Bracey (2009) and

Under Wima Kadphises gold staters appear in a variety of forms showing production by the same mint but in five different chronological phases.[36] The double staters, as found in the Axum hoard, date from phase 4, presumably well into his reign and the most productive of the phases.[37] They weigh about sixteen grams—double that of the standard, hence the name. Bracey notes that it is unusual to find coins of Wima Kadphises among coin hoards of later kings and suggests that this might be a result of a low level of production or a short circulation of such coins. In this respect, the Axum hoard is unusual if not exceptional. They were probably minted in Balkh.[38] New reverse and obverse dies were made for each phase, and Bracey suggests that each phase saw a period of days or weeks of intensive production with multiple workmen but that there might have been long periods when no coins were minted.[39] The Kharoṣṭhī inscription and images were prepared freehand onto the dies by different craftsmen, probably using a prototype or drawing. The Greek legend was created by drilling holes into the die to mark the end point of the letters and then joining these up with lines. The obverse die was then fixed into an anvil, and the reverse die joined others in a die box. To make each coin, the gold blank was placed between the observe die and the reverse die. The reverse die was struck twice to create the impression. The coin was then removed and the impression checked. If not clear enough, it was replaced and struck again. To create the impression would require strong blows, probably holding a hammer with two hands. Therefore either the coin and reserve die were fixed or a second workman held them in place. Other coin-making workshops used hinged dyes or sleeves to hold them in place, but the evidence suggests neither of these were used by the Kushan. The dies, however, were probably up to 50 percent larger than the finished coins.

The source of the gold for the coins has been subject to discussion. Gold is found in the Zerafshan and Ferghanan valleys, north and east of the Kushan in the lands of Sogdiana and Dayuan, and also in the steppes to the north. Trade is commonly found across the ecological border of Inner and Outer Eurasia, the steppe providing goods such as horses and gold in trade for grain, silk, and other commodities (see chapters 1, 6, and 8). There would be little remaining evidence of such trade—the grain consumed and the gold

Falk (2015: 105–9).

36. Bracey (2009).
37. Göbl (1970).
38. Bracey (2012).
39. Bracey (2009).

FIGURE 7. Coin of Wima Kadphises, found in the Debra Damo hoard.
After Göbl (1970).

reworked—and this source cannot be dismissed.[40] Southern Arabia has also
been suggested as a source, and for a long time it was argued that a large part
of the gold came from Rome in the form of coins. In an often quoted text,
the first-century Roman historian Pliny the Elder (AD 23–79) estimated that
the Roman Empire spent some 150 million sesterces a year for luxury products from India, including silks, gems, and spices.[41] Yet while coin hoards
have been found in Southern India, very few Roman coins have been found
in Kushan territory. Moreover, recent analysis has shown the gold used in
Roman coins to have a different source than that used in Kushan.[42] But perhaps we should consider a more local source. As Falk points out, there is plentiful evidence of gold in the Kushan area, in the mountains of what is now
eastern Afghanistan, and also brought down by the rivers.[43] And a large gold
hoard has been found in graves to the west of Balkh, at Tillya Tepe.[44] The
archaeologist in charge of the 1978 excavations of it, Victor Sarianidi, claimed
that these were graves of Yuezhi rulers, pre-Kushan.[45] However, the Yuezhi/
Kushan attribution has been questioned, as the grave goods have Parthian,
Saka-Samaritan, Xianbei, and Chinese affinities. Whether the people buried

40. As does Rosenfield, for example, when he writes, "It is difficult to imagine how the
Kushans paid for the raw metal" (2009: 21).

41. Pliny the Elder, *Natural History* 6.26, trans. Bostock (1855).

42. Rosenfield (1967: 21).

43. Falk (2015). Marshall (1951: vol. 2:620) suggested sources in Dardistan and Tibet.

44. For the treasure, see Sarianidi (1985). For the archaeologist's assertion that this was
an early dynastic necropolis of the Kushan, see Sarianidi (1990–92: 103).

45. See S. Peterson (2017: 47–58) for a review of the evidence, including recent studies
of the coins.

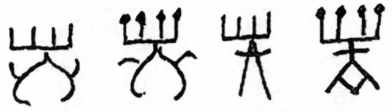

FIGURE 8. *Tamgha* of the Kushan kings used on the coins.

there had links with these cultures or whether they came from these cultures, both show the rich interconnections of Central Asia in the first century.[46] Sarianidi also claimed that the gold was local river gold, a view supported by more recent analysis of some pieces.[47]

The obverse of the five double gold staters found in the Axum hoard shows Wima Kadphises in profile facing right (figure 7).[48] He is bearded and wears a diadem and tall peaked cap. He is seated cross-legged on clouds with flames emanating from his shoulder. His dynastic symbol or *tamgha* is to the left (figure 8). *Tamgha* seem to have been developed by pastoralist people as a tribal symbol and used, for example, to brand their cattle, so this is another legacy of the Kushan's past.[49] The inscription on the coin—reading in translation "King Wima Kadphises"—is in Greek language and script. The reverse shows the Kushan god Wesho (sometimes associated with the Indian deity Śiva).[50] He is standing with a battle-ax trident in his right hand and an animal skin in his left in front of a bull—often identified as Nandi, the mount of Śiva. The symbol to the left is a *nandipada* symbol, sometimes associated with the Buddhism Triratna, but Bracey argues strongly against this, attributing its appearance to imitation: "It appears because it appeared on other

46. For discussions of different influences at Tillya Tepe, see Boardman (2012), Leidy (2012), and S. Peterson (2017).

47. Sarianidi (1990: 55); Hickman (2012: 80).

48. For images of the types of coins represented, see Göbl (1970). He identifies each coin by types based on his 1957 publication. This type is noted in the text here with the reference also to the type according to his 1984 publication, so this coin is "G16/G10/1" (Göbl 1957, type 16/Göbl 1984, type 10/1).

49. Rtveladze (1993: 84); Michon (2015: 126).

50. There is not space here to explain the complexities behind the origins (Hellenistic, Iranian, Indian, other) of the various deities shown on the coins of this region or their identifications with each other. In some cases we can only present hypotheses about how they were identified at the time. For a detailed discussion on Śiva, see Cribb (1997). Also see Rosenfield (1967).

FIGURE 9. Coin of Kaniška I, found in the Debra Damo hoard.
After Göbl (1970).

coins. Though some value was attached to it that is not why it was used."[51]
The inscription is in Prākrit, an Indian language, written using the Central
Asian Kharoṣṭhī script.[52] It reads: "Of the great King of Kings, lord of the
world, great lord, Wima Kadphises, the savior."

Here we see in one coin a microcosm of Central Asian complexity, of the
meeting and mixture of peoples, languages, gods, and symbols. This is not
an accidental or random mixture of cultures but the deliberate exploitation
and adaptation by a ruler of certain symbols, languages, and gods to send a
message both to the peoples under his reign and to neighboring and more
distant cultures.

Gold coins of the next king, Kaniška, also appear in a variety of forms,
and it is not clear whether the five gold staters in the hoard were of one or
more types.[53] Under Kaniška, for the first time some coins show images of
Buddha on the reverse: up until then the gods depicted were local, Iranian,
Indian, or Hellenistic. Robert Göbl indicates that the hoard did not include
the issue with Buddha but one showing a bearded Kaniška with his head
turned to the left (figure 9). Like all the kings depicted on these Buddha
coins, he is shown standing. He wears a tall conical hat and holds a spear in
his left hand and a goad in his right. With his right, he is tending an altar. The
legend is no longer in the Greek language but in the local Bactrian language,

51. Bracey (2009: 48).

52. A script seemingly invented by the Kushan and used only during the first to fourth
centuries in Kushan and in the Taklamakan oasis kingdom of Kroraina to the east.

53. Göbl (1970) shows only one type—as described here (G40/G68), but Mordini
(1967: 24) leaves it unclear ("Much more varied are the types of Kaniska, Huviskha and
Vasudeva I").

FIGURE 10. Coins of Huviška, found in the Debra Damo hoard. After Göbl (1970).

although still in modified Greek script. It reads, "Shah of Shahs, Kaniška the Kushan."[54] The Greek term found on his predecessor's coins, *basileus* (βασιλεύς), often translated as "king," has been replaced with the Iranian term for ruler, *shah*, and this continues to be used thereafter. On the obverse is the solar deity Mithra standing with head facing left, nimbate, holding the hilt of a sword in his left hand and with right hand outstretched in benediction. The Bactrian legend at right gives his name in Greek script as Miiro, while Kaniška's *tamgha* is to the left.

Coins from Huviška's reign form by far the greater part of the hoard—88 out of the 105 coins—and represent at least seven types (figure 10).[55] All show a bust of Huviška on the obverse. On these coins he is nimbate, faces left, and holds a filleted spear over his shoulder in his left hand and a mace scepter in his right.[56] The inscription—Bactrian in modified Greek script—reads, "Shah of Shahs, Huviška the Kushan." The reverse shows a variety of male and female gods. The ones in the hoard are all from the Iranian pantheon: Pharro, Nana, Ardoxsho, Miiro (Mithra), Teiro, and Ashaeixsho.[57]

The last coins found in the hoard are six gold staters from the reign of Vasudeva I showing a standing king facing left with a spear in his left hand and his right tending the altar (figure 11). The obverse shows Wesho with a bull. Although the history of this period remains obscure, this is generally

54. This is an Iranian phase. The modified Greek script has one additional glyph (Þ) to represent /š/ (*sh*), as in the words "Ku*sh*an" and "Kani*sh*ka."

55. Göbl (1970), G186–187/G280 (*pharro*, Khwarenah on obverse), G188/G281 (Nana), G192/G287 (Ardoxsho), G213/G228 (Mithra), G214/G234 (Teiro), G253/?G342 (Ashaeixsho).

56. In coins from earlier in this reign he holds the hilt of a sword in his left hand.

57. Although Huviška coins also contained Greco-Roman and India gods, see Bracey (2012: 198) for a table. Apart from Teiro, the other gods are the most commonly depicted among the known Huviška coins (Bracey 2012: 203).

FIGURE 11. Coin of Vasudeva I, found in the Debra Damo hoard. After Göbl (1970).

accepted to be a time of crisis and retrenchment for the Kushan Empire. Much of their territory in northern India was lost, and to the west their old neighbors, the Parthian kings (like the Yuezhi, originally settlers from the steppe), had been replaced by an Iranian dynasty, the Sasanians, commencing under Ardashir I (r. 224–42). He was threatening Kushan territory from the north and west. Some accounts tell that Vasudeva sought alliances at this time to counter these threats, joining with the Armenian king Khosroes I (r. 217–52) against Ardashir. The Chinese histories also report a diplomatic visit, probably sent by Vasudeva, to the Wei court of northern China in 230.[58] We do not know of any alliance resulting from this. However, given the composition of the hoard, with only six coins from Vasudeva's reign, it may be assumed that it left Kushan early in Vasudeva's reign before the start of the Sasanian campaign, perhaps on a more general diplomatic mission.

If we speculate that the hoard of coins of Vasudeva and his predecessors was a gift sent in a diplomatic embassy across the Indian Ocean, then they would have traveled from one of the Kushan capitals—possibly Peshawar or the summer capital Bagram. The mission would have undoubtedly had many other treasures to take as gifts for foreign rulers. From the city they would have followed well-traveled routes to the valley of the Indus River or one of its major tributaries.[59] From here it was possible to travel by river downstream. We have an early account of such a journey through Alexander the Great (r. 336–323 BC). He returned home this way in late 326 BC, marching first to the Jhelum River, where he had established the cites of Nicaea and

58. In the Chinese history *Sanguozhi* (Records of the Three Kingdoms; 220–80), discussed in Sinor (1990: 170).

59. See McIntosh (2008, esp. 15) for the geography of the Indus valley.

Bucephala on opposite banks earlier in the year. He assembled eight hundred river ships, many of them newly built, and set sail in November after the end of the monsoon when the river was navigable. The boats were rowed by Phoenicians, Cypriotes, Carians (from southwestern Turkey), and Egyptians, all seafaring peoples. Soldiers accompanied them on both banks. They traveled for ten days before reaching the confluence with the Ashkini, where several boats lost control and many people were drowned. Further downstream his army was attacked, and, in the ensuing battle Alexander was seriously wounded. He survived and his army eventually won. He had to fight other battles as they progressed, and the army did not reach the ocean until the monsoon in 325.[60]

At its greatest extent Kushan rule extended along the Indus River to the ocean, so there was less threat of such delays.[61] Vasudeva might not have had his own fleet and might instead have relied, as did many diplomatic missions of the time, on getting passage on a merchant ship, probably for the river voyage and, at Barbarikon, changing to a seafaring vessel for the crossing of the Indian Ocean.

 INDIAN OCEAN TRADE

Chapter 2 looked briefly at the maritime trade between India, the Red Sea, and the Gulf up to the first century BC. In the first centuries AD this trade continued and grew as new players came into the equation. In northern India and Central Asia the Kushan Empire provided a climate for trade by both land and sea. This was a major factor in the growth and success of the Silk Road. The stability provided by the Kushan enabled safe travel from the steppe to India through north-south routes, and from the Iranian Plateau to the Tarim, by east-west routes. Striking evidence for the trade is seen in the rock-cut graffiti at a way station called Shatial, high in the Indus River valley on the route from the north through Gilgit.[62] Most are in Sogdian, left by merchants from Samarkand, Penjikent, and other cities north of the Kushan. But there are also inscriptions in Bactrian, Middle Persian, and Parthian. The routes south

60. Alexander and a large part of his army chose to return by land across the Gedrosian Desert, which borders the coast.

61. Chakrabarti (1995); Seland (2013).

62. Known today as the Karakorum Highway.

led from the Kushan capitals—such as Bagram and Taxila—to the Indus valley and thence to the seaport of Barbarikon—near Karachi in present-day Pakistan. There is plentiful evidence, archaeological and textual, to show the existence of Kushan-Roman trade at this time, most notably the Roman bronzes and glass and the ivories uncovered during excavations at Bagram.[63]

One of the main textual sources is the *Periplus of the Erythraean Sea*, an anonymous handbook on Indian Ocean trade, written in Greek probably by a merchant based in Egypt in the mid-first century. Although at this time the Kushan Empire did not extend to the seaport of Babarikon, it is likely that items found in Bagram and elsewhere came in through this route and were traded at a site a little way inland. The *Periplus* lists glass as among the items traded there, along with gemstones, frankincense, textiles, silverware, wine, and coins.[64] It is supplemented by other texts, and although the imports from Asia have mainly long disappeared, scholars have made a strong argument for regular trade "undertaken for commercial profit, facilitated by the use of coinage and underwritten by accumulated capital."[65] By this time ships were making use of the monsoon winds. These are caused by the Asian land mass heating up during the summer months; the rising hot air creates a vacuum that is filled by air from the ocean, causing strong winds that blow from the southwest. The opposite happens in the winter months, with the winds changing direction to come from the northeast. This system is supplemented by other regular patterns, such as equatorial winds and southeast trade winds. It was possible for ships to take advantage to sail from the mouth of the Red Sea and the coasts of East Africa and southern Arabia in summer, helped by the southwest monsoon, and for ships to set sail in winter from the ports on the east coast of South Asia, from Barbarikon to Taprobane (Sri Lanka), to be helped across to the Gulf and Red Sea. There was also the alternative of coast hopping from port to port, used from earliest times.

From the western edges of the Indian Ocean, ships came from the ports of the Red Sea, southern Arabia, and the Gulf. Those from the Red Sea included Roman boats that sailed from the ports in the north but also ships made by the Axumites, a kingdom in East Africa in what is now Eritrea and Ethiopia.[66]

63. For Indian Ocean trade, see Tomber (2008, esp. 122–24). On Kushan trade, see Seland (2013). On Bagram treasures, see Whitehouse (1989).

64. Very few Roman coins have been found in Kushan.

65. Bellina and Glover (2004: 72–73). However, the importance of coinage in this trade is disputed by others, such as Bracey (pers. comm., April 12, 2017).

66. For more on Axum sea trade, see Whitfield (2015b: prol.).

In the third century the Axumites were a major political and trading power. Axum was listed as one of the four most important kingdoms in the world by the Persian religious teacher Mani (ca. 216–74)—alongside Persia, Rome, and China.[67] Two centuries earlier, the *Periplus* had noted Axum's importance as a market for ivory: "Here is brought all the ivory from the land beyond the Nile, across the region called Cyenum and thence to Adulis." This is sometimes given as the reason for the siting of the Axumites' capital, Axum, relatively far west from the coast, as it acted as a hub for ivory hunters working inland to bring their goods over the Sudanese steppes and through the Nile valley.[68] But the city also lay on fertile ground with ready access to water. Adulis, described by the *Periplus* as a "large village," had become the major port by the third century. From Axum, it was an eight- to ten-day journey over the highlands and down into the coastal plain and the port. Although the Axumites had a written language, Ge'ez, and also used Greek, there are no extant documents from this period. The name of the Axumite king contemporary with Vasudeva's reign is known from inscriptions found in southern Arabia. The script used for this gives consonants and no vowels, and in this unvocalized form he is named "GDRT."[69] This is tentatively vocalized as Gadarat. He was succeeded in about 230, the same time as the end of Vasudeva's reign, by "DBH" (possibly Azaba or Adhebah).[70] Although the Axumites started minting regular coinage only under King Endybis (r. ca. 270–ca. 300), they were familiar with the concept before this. The *Periplus* mentions that they were importing brass "for cutting as money" and also that they imported money for "use by the foreign community." When coins were minted by Endybis they were probably based on Roman coinage and produced in gold, silver, and bronze. They showed the head of the king and stalks of the indigenous wheat (*Eragrostis tef*) on the obverse, with a disc and crescent at the top. The inscription on the gold coins was in Greek, but the silver

---

67. Mani is the founder of Manicheanism. He traveled to northern India around 240—not long after the death of Vasudeva when the Kushan Empire was in decline. There is no record of his having visited Axum.

68. See Hatke's (2013: 34–35) discussion of this.

69. A bronze scepter found in northern Axum is inscribed with "GDR," and this could also be the name of the same king (Munro-Hay 1991: 75).

70. Also from inscriptions in southern Arabia; see Munro-Hay (1991: 73).

and bronze coins used the local language and script, Ge'ez, suggesting that the latter were for local use and the former for international trade.

Archaeology in Axum has revealed complex palace structures but also, most notably for this period, large stone built tombs (assumed to be royal burials) marked with carved stelae. The largest of these, which weighed 517 tonnes and would have been 32.6 meters tall if successfully erected, would have been the largest monolith to be raised by humans at that time.[71] It was made from granite quarried on a hill close by and possibly transported by elephants—although they are no longer found here. The stelae are carved with representations of the local architecture of multistoried monumental buildings. These were constructed of dressed granite with recessed facades, rebated walls, wooden tie beams, and monumental staircases. Archaeology of sites in Axum dating from the second century onward reinforces this, with remains of several substantial complexes tentatively identified as palaces but also large elite residences, indicating a society with considerable wealth.[72] Finds in the tombs and elsewhere show evidence for trade both north and south from Adulis, including Roman glass and Indo-Pacific beads.[73]

Even though the written and archaeological evidence is scarce, it suggests that the Axumites were probably used to foreign visitors—traders, religious figures, and diplomats. But we enter the area of speculation by proposing that the gift of coins was brought by a diplomatic mission sent by the Kushans directly to the Axumites. Possibly it was intended for some other recipient and was waylaid here, or it might not have been a single hoard at all.[74] We therefore have to make a leap of imagination to picture the Kushan mission disembarking at Adulis after their long sea journey. From here they would have taken the journey inland, perhaps accompanied by local officials and soldiers or simply joining a trading caravan. The gift was handed over and perhaps placed in the royal treasury. Here it possibly remained through a succession of kings.

A century later King Ezena (r. ca. 333–ca. 356) converted to Christianity, and a cross replaced the disc and crescent on the Axum coinage. Churches

71. See Phillipson (1998). It is unclear whether it was ever successfully raised; it is now lying on the ground. Also see chapter 4 for a comparison of height of monumental buildings: the Amluk Dara Stupa was over thirty-five meters tall.

72. For a review, see Finneran (2007: 159–65).

73. Tomber (2008: 91).

74. The latter is less likely given that there are no other Kushan coins in evidence to date and because of the lack of wear of many of the coins.

were built and monasteries endowed over the following centuries. In the late fifth century it is recorded that nine Christians came to Axum from various parts of the Roman Empire (27 BC–AD 1453) to avoid persecution after the Council of Chalcedon in 451. The council, convened by the Eastern Church, declared that Christ had two natures in one person, God and man. This was not a doctrine accepted by many parts of the Christian Church and resulted in a split in the Eastern Church. The churches not accepting this doctrine are often referred to as the Oriental Orthodox or Old Oriental Churches. The Axumite Church was among them—along with Coptic, Syrian, Armenian, and Malankara (Indian) Orthodox. The lives of the nine Christians are recorded in much later biographies, albeit with many contradictions. Among them was 'Aragawi Zä-Mika'el —the Elder Zä-Mika'el.

According to his later biography, Zä-Mika'el was the son of the Roman prince Yeshaq and of Edna (an Ethiopian name). The biography states that at age fourteen he received his name from and became a monk with Pachomius (ca. 292–348) in Egypt.[75] Other Christians joined them in what Pachomius established as a new form of monastic community, where monks and nuns formed one community with common property and were presided over by an abbot or abbess. This broke with the earlier tradition of ascetics living largely as hermits. Zä-Mika'el's mother Edna later became a nun here. Later Zä-Mika'el traveled to Rome and thence to Axum, which was by this time Christian. He invited his eight fellow believers to join him, and together with his parents they were welcomed by the king.[76] They lived at the court for twelve years before separating to evangelize in the countryside. Zä-Mika'el went with his mother and a disciple called Mattéwos to Eggala in the Tigray district. Here he decided to found a monastery—associated with Debra—on top of a steep-sided plateau. But he was unable to climb the cliffs until a serpent, living on top, let down his tail and pulled him up. The monastery was erected on the order of King Gabra Masqal, a large ramp being constructed

75. See Munro-Hay (2002: 336). The chronology given in the biography of the late fifteenth century is contradictory, as it says that he left the monastery seven years after Pachomius's death. This would have been in 355—a century before the Council of Chalcedon and before the traditional founding of Debra Damo. There are other contradictions in it as well concerning the order of the kings. See Irvine, Meinardus, and Metaferia (1975).

76. One of the other "Nine Saints" who came to Ethiopia at this time was Abba Garima. He also founded a monastery and is credited with having made manuscript copies of the Gospels. A recent carbon analysis of the two so-called Garima Gospels dates them to between 390 and 660 (mid-date 530), which would not challenge this.

to transport the building materials. On completion, the ramp was removed, making the perilous cliff climb the only route up. Zä-Mika'el's biography also reports that his mother Edna became part of the community, which suggests there might also have been nuns, as in Pachomius's original monastery.[77]

Tradition says that the king endowed the monastery with treasures. This is possibly another clue in the journey of our coins. Could the king have presented the coins to the monastery at this time? We have no evidence of this, but it is a possible hypothesis. It is, of course, also possible that the monastery was built on an existing shrine and that the coins were already there, or, indeed, that they did not make its journey to Axum until later. It is almost certain that we will never have the answers to such questions.

Treasuries are found in churches throughout the Christian world (see chapter 8) and present-day Ethiopia is no exception, laying claim to holding one of the greatest treasures of Christianity, the Ark of the Covenant. According to tradition, this gilded wooden chest contains the tablets giving the Ten Commandments received by Moses on Mount Sinai and was carried with the Israelites until the temple was built in Jerusalem to house them. Ethiopian tradition further records that the Ark left Jerusalem at the time of King Solomon, carried by his son with the Queen of Sheba, Menelik. It was kept safe until finally being enshrined in the Church of St. Mary of Zion in Axum, built by Emperor Haile Selassie in 1960 for this purpose. Today it is said to be in the treasury building adjacent to the church. Only the high priest is allowed to see it.

While most believe this story to be apocryphal, the treasury probably does contain some ancient treasure, just like many other churches in Ethiopia. Other treasures have been found at Debra Damo, including an Axumite coin of Armah (r. 614–31), gold and silver Arabic coins dating from about the eighth to the tenth centuries, and some textiles from the sixth to twelfth century, probably originating in Egypt.[78] Our coins probably remained safely there for centuries. However, oral and written histories tell of two major threats to Debra Damo and the Christian heritage of the Axumites in the intervening centuries.

The first, which appears mainly in oral tradition, was during the reign of Queen Gudit around the mid-tenth century. Some corroboration is provided

77. However, there is no record of this, and women are no longer allowed to enter the monastery or even to ascend the cliff.
78. Munro-Hay (2002: 337).

by a contemporary Arab traveler and geographer Ibn Ḥawqal in his work *Kitāb Ṣūrat al-ʿArḍ* (Picture of the earth), written in 977. "The country of the *habasha* [Abyssinians] has been ruled by a woman for many years now: she has killed the king of the *habasha* who was called *Haḍani* [from Ge'ez *haṣani*, modern *aṣe* or *atse*]. Until today she rules with complete independence in her own country and the frontier areas of the country of the *Haḍani*, in the southern part of [the country of] the *habasha*."[79]

Gudit (Judith) is said to have come from Axum's Jewish community, which had coexisted there for centuries alongside the Christians. Tradition tells that she killed the king to take the throne. It was usual at the time that royal princes were exiled on hilltop settlements such as Debra Damo—presumably to keep them from seeking power.[80] Queen Gudit duly went there, built a ramp to gain access, as Gabra Masqal had done, and killed the exiled princes to rid her of her rivals.[81]

The second event is better attested. It took place long after the end of the Axum Empire, starting in 1529 with the invasion of Ethiopia by Aḥmad ibn Ibrāhīm al-Ghāzī (r. ca. 1506–43), the ruler of the neighboring Muslim sultanate of Adal. He was named Gragn—"the Left-Handed" in Amharic. During this invasion many churches and monasteries were destroyed—including the Church of St. Mary of Zion, and, it is reported, many church treasuries were looted.[82] The Ethiopians asked for assistance from the Portuguese, who landed a force in 1541, and the invaders were eventually driven out. As Paul Henze noted, although these events took place centuries ago, they remain alive in Ethiopian culture: "In Ethiopia the damage which Ahmad Gragn did has never been forgotten. Every Christian highlander still hears tales of Gragn in his childhood. Haile Selassie referred to him in his memoirs, 'I have often had villagers in northern Ethiopia point out sites of towns, forts, churches and monasteries destroyed by Gragn as if these catastrophes had occurred only yesterday.'"[83]

During the invasion, the emperor, Dawit II (Lebna Dengel) (r. 1508–40), was forced to flee his capital and take refuge at the monastery at Debra

79. Taddesse Tamrat (1972: 39). See also Ibn Ḥawqal (2014).

80. Munro-Hay (2002: 337) points out that there is no other evidence of royal princes being exiled at this time.

81. Henze (2000: 48).

82. Tradition tells that the Ark had been removed to a safe hiding place before the invaders arrived and was returned only when the church was rebuilt a century later.

83. Henze (2000: 90).

Damo. He was wounded in a battle nearby in 1540 and died and was buried at Debra Damo. One of the Portuguese, Miguel de Castanhoso, records that Lebna Dengel's widow remained in Debra Damo, during which time Gragn laid siege to the mound for a year. But he was unsuccessful in gaining access. This makes sense when one reads Castanhoso's description of the place:

> The summit is a quarter of a long league in circumference, and on the area on the top there are two large cisterns, in which much water is collected in the winter: so much that it suffices and is more than enough for all those who live above, that is, about five hundred persons. On the summit itself they sow supplies of wheat, barley, millet and other vegetables. They take up goats and fowls, and there are many hives, for there is much space for them; thus the hill cannot be taken by hunger and thirst. Below the summit the hill is of this kind. It is squared and scarped for a height double that of the highest tower in Portugal, and it gets more precipitous near the top, until at the end it makes an umbrella all round, which looks artificial, and spreads out so far that it overhangs all the foot of the mountain, so that no one at the foot can hide himself from these above; for all around there is no fold or corner, and there is no way up save the one narrow path, like a badly-made winding stairs, by which with difficulty one person can ascend as far as a point whence he can get no further, for there the path ends. Above this is a gate where the guards are, and this gate is ten or twelve fathoms above the point where the path stops, and no-one can ascend or descend the hill save by the basket.[84]

When the Portuguese arrived, they met with Lebna Dengel's widow, and she accompanied them to the court of her son, Emperor Galawdewos. They joined forces and finally managed to defeat the invaders at a battle in 1543 with the help of Portuguese firearms that had been hidden at Debra Damo.[85]

It is possible that these events might have impinged on the life of our casket of coins. Perhaps it was not given to the monastery until this time, taken by the emperor when he took refuge. Or perhaps it was already there, stored in the treasury but removed to a niche on the cliff face during this period in case the site was ransacked. We do not even know for certain the date when it was found, said to be around 1940. The Italian archaeologist Antonio Mordini, who was carrying out excavations at the site, gives the following account:

84. Quoted in Munro-Hay (2002: 338).
85. Munro-Hay (2002: 337–38).

Toward the beginning of that year [1940], a young monk, entrusted with the repair works of the small wall sustaining the terrace where the church rises in the cemetery area of the convent, found in a small natural cave below the terrace, the relics of a wooden box along with eleven small gold plates, twelve [*sic*] small bands of same metal, and of various lengths, and a considerable number of gold coins. The coins along with the gold plates and bands (which presumably formed part of the ornamentation of the box), were brought to Asmara, and the prior of the convent, mamher Takla ab Tasfai sold the entire lot to an Italian jeweller; who, in turn, sold it to a person of culture, who felt interested in the hoard.[86]

This raises the question of the casket, for whose story we have even less evidence than for that of the coins, since at least we can be fairly certain of their origin. For a start, it is assumed that the pieces of wood, gold, and green stone found in the same place as the coins originally formed a casket. Mordini, one of the few people to see these, is confident on this point and describes them: "They consisted of ten small plates, partly rectangular and partly square; one large plate of hexagonal shape, slightly pyramidal and twelve bands of various sizes all decorated in light bas-relief with ornamental vines and stylish flowers of peculiar character."

In 1943 Mordini located the nook and sieved the earth in it to find more remains of the casket, including pieces of wood, about thirty gold nails, "which, it is clear, must have served to fix the plates and the bands to the casket," and some thin plates of green stone, which he could not immediately identify. He also found some potsherds that he judged to be from the Axumite period. In a later article, the Russian scholar S. I. Berzina suggests that the casket was Indian made and similar to a casket excavated by Neville Chittick.[87] However, since the casket was found in pieces and, as far as I have been able to ascertain, the pieces were not photographed or drawn, this conclusion must remain extremely tentative. David Phillipson gives information suggesting that the pieces of the casket were later discarded, so it is unlikely that we will ever know more.[88] The assumption that the coins were held in the casket is reasonable, given that we could expect such a rich hoard to be housed in some sort of receptacle. But whether this was the original recepta-

---

86. Mordini (1967: 23).
87. Berzina (1984); Chittick (1974: 199, fig. 23a).
88. Phillipson (2012: 18n4) notes that Göbl's files in Vienna include correspondence from Mordini to this effect. I have not seen the correspondence.

cle or one used later—perhaps when the coins were moved—and where the box originated remain too uncertain to call.

The sale of monastery treasures was not unusual—and continues to this day (see chapter 9). It is fortunate that Mordini had the opportunity to study the coins after they were sold on.[89] This was sometime prior to 1959, when Mordini published his original account. I have not been able to find the identity of the Italian jeweler or the "person of culture," although both might be noted in archives. The 1939 census of Asmara counted fifty-three thousand Italians among a total population of ninety-eight thousand in the city and a total of seventy-five thousand Italians in all of Eritrea. Among them there were presumably several jewelers. The nationality of the "person of culture" is unclear, but again details might be found in archives. As far as I know, this is the last record of the coins. While they might remain intact in a private collection, there is also the possibility that they were melted down to realize their value as gold.[90]

Whatever the story of these coins and how they traveled, they reflect many aspects of the Silk Road. Created in the "dynamo" of Inner Eurasian history by an exiled agro-pastoralist people who had perhaps largely adapted to a settled city life, they reflect the importance of the Kushan for trade by both land and sea. While the early pieces probably circulated as money, the newest issues were probably never used for this purpose, instead being kept unmarked and unworn as treasures. At some point they traveled from Central Asia to East Africa by land, river, and sea on routes used by Silk Road merchants, possibly in a wooden casket. They later became the property of a Christian church, surviving over centuries. We can only hope that they remain as a treasured collection. If so, although inaccessible to most, they continue their entanglement with their collector and to tell their story.

89. "Later I was able to examine the whole find" (Mordini 1967: 23). This is an English translation of Mordini's account in the *Proceedings of the International Congress of Ethiopic Studies, Rome, 1959* (published in 1960). In it, Mordini makes clear that he still expects to have access to the coins "through the courtesy of the present owner" (25). In a letter to the French numismatist, Côte, dated December 2, 1955, he explains that he has been very busy studying the Kushan coins (West 2009: 8). Also see Göbl (1970).

90. Thanks to Robert Bracey for this thoughts on this. He notes that he has not come across the collection, or parts of it, while preparing his study, which would be likely if the collection had been broken up and sold on (pers. comm., February 4, 2017).

FOUR

Amluk Dara Stupa

"WILD PERSIMMON HILL," the translation of the Pashto name of this stupa, Amluk Dara, reflects the fecundity of the Swat valley in which it was built. The stupa sits a terrace overlooking a mountain stream, a tributary of the Swat (plate 3). Its imposing dome rises from a square base, reached by a staircase from the upper slope of the mountain.[1] Behind the stupa rises Mount Ilam—a sacred site believed to have been the home of the Indian god Rāma during his forest exile and thus the focus today of annual Hindu pilgrimages.[2] It is also identified as Aornos, site of a famous battle of Alexander the Great (r. 336–323 BC).[3] But the stupa is a Buddhist structure, and to understand why it was built—and how it survived for a thousand years after Buddhism disappeared from here—we need first to trace the history of Buddhism in this region.

BUDDHISM IN THE SWAT VALLEY

The Swat rises in Kohistan in the heart of the Hindu Kush, the great mountain range that divides Central and South Asia. To the south the river flows

For places mentioned in this chapter see Map 5 in the color maps insert.

1. I am greatly indebted to Luca Olivieri for this chapter, both for the published reports of the Italians on their recent excavations of the stupa, led by Dr. Olivieri, and for his generous responses to my many queries and ready supply of excellent plans and photographs. All mistakes, misunderstandings, and omissions are my own.

2. Rāma is an avatar or incarnation on earth of the Hindu god Viṣṇu and the eponymous hero of the Indian epic the Rāmāyaṇa.

3. Mount Ilam has been a sacred site since ancient times. According to Hindu mythology, Rāma spent three years of his exile in the forest here. For Alexander, see notes 5 and 42 below.

through gorges until the valley widens. It joins the Kabul River near the ancient city of Pushkalāvatī (modern Charsadda) and the Peshawar plains. Less then one hundred miles after this the Kabul joins the Indus. The ancient city of Taxila (Takshaśilā) lies across the Indus. This flows southwest to join the Indian Ocean at the site of the ancient trading port of Barbarikon, from where ships sailed to Persia, Axum, and Egypt. Other routes from Swat followed the Kabul River west into Kapisa, the area around Bagram in what is now eastern Afghanistan, and the Indus River north deeper into Central Asia. Northwards from Swat travelers could cross to the Gilgit valleys and thence to the kingdoms of northern Central Asia and to the Tarim. Petroglyphs mark human activity on these mountain routes from ancient times. The Swat was known in the Sanskrit hymns of the *Rigveda* as the Suvastu—clear azure water, reflecting its source from the glacial melt of the Hindu Kush. Its lower valley was linked to Gandhāra, a kingdom recorded in ancient Indian sources, the Mahābhārata and the Rāmāyaṇa, as centered around Pushkalāvatī. The middle and upper reaches of the Swat valley and the lands across to the Indus were for part of history an independent kingdom, Udyāna.[4]

Owing to its position connecting North India through the mountainous Central Asia with the kingdoms and empires beyond, this was a strategic area. It often formed the borders of larger empires, with rulers based in India failing to expand north from here over the mountains and rulers from north of the mountains failing to expand further south from here into the Indian plains. However, one of the early invaders came from much further afield. Alexander fought famous battles here during his Central Asian campaigns. His army marched east from Alexander on the Caucasus (Bagram)—the city he had founded in the kingdom of Kapisa—and fought many battles to gain control of the region. Some of these were in the Swat valley and culminated with Alexander's successful siege of Aornos, a seemingly impregnable steep-sided mountain with a flat top watered by a spring where locals had taken refuge. Identifying the site of this ancient battle has occupied scholars for over 150 years, but two places stand out as the most probable candidates. Pir Sar, a mountain rising west of the Indus valley, was selected by Aurel Stein (1862–

---

4. *Udyāna* means "orchard" or "garden." The kingdom is also known as Oḍḍiyāna. But not all scholars agree with this, some arguing that Oḍḍiyāna refers to a place in eastern India. For further discussion, see Kuwayama (1991), and for a clear introduction to Buddhism in the region, see Behrendt (2004).

1943) after his survey of the region. However, although this is not rejected by all, the consensus now veers toward Mount Ilam, the summit of which is a day's walk from the Amluk Dara Stupa.[5]

When Alexander returned home, the Maurya Empire (322–180 BC), with its capital to the southeast at Paliputra on the Ganges (modern Patna), expanded northwest as far as Gandhāra. When a later Mauryan king, Aśoka (r. ca. 268–232 BC), started his patronage of Buddhism after a particularly bloody battle in about 260 BC, he ordered edicts to be carved on pillars and rocks throughout his kingdom. These included two rock inscriptions at Shabazgarhi between the Swat and the Indus (near present-day Mardan).[6] They are in the vernacular language of the region, Prākrit (also called Gāndhārī), written in a newly developed script, Kharoṣṭhī, which continued in use in Central Asia until the third or fourth century AD.[7] According to tradition, Aśoka also sent missionaries in all directions, including to the shores of the Mediterranean and the Tarim basin, while his son and daughter were sent to the island now known as Sri Lanka. Inscriptions above cave temples in Sri Lanka support the arrival of Buddhism during this period.[8] From its earliest days, therefore, Buddhism was a proselytizing faith with a proclivity for long-distance travel.[9]

A Buddhist text, the *Mahāparinirvāṇasūtra*, reports that after Buddha's *nirvāṇa* his cremated remains were divided into eight portions, which were distributed to the eight kingdoms in which Buddha had lived. Buildings called stupas were erected as giant reliquaries to house them.[10] None of these original stupa sites have been identified, but it is probable that they were simple mounds of earth—burial tumuli as seen in many cultures through-

5. Stein (1929); Rienjang (2012); Olivieri (2015a).

6. See Behrendt (2004: 39n1) for a list and references. See Errington (2000) and Falk (2006) for dating.

7. The inscriptions do not mention Buddhism as such. The Brahmi script was developed around the same time. Both seem to have been developed to transcribe the spoken rather than classical language—Prākrit rather than Sanskrit. See Falk (2014b).

8. No evidence exists of Buddhism reaching the Mediterranean or the Tarim at this time.

9. By sea as well as by land.

10. Fussman suggests that the relics were not so important in this early period as the memorializing aspect of the stupa, which would induce in worshippers "good thoughts" (1986: 44–45).

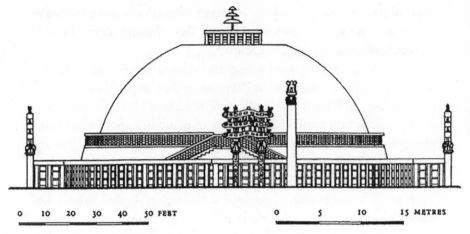

FIGURE 12. Plan of Sanchi Stupa. After Rowland (1977: 78).

out the world, including pre-Buddhist India.[11] At some point, possibly before Aśoka, the Buddhist stupa became more structural, built using wood and other materials.

Traditionally, Aśoka is said to have further divided these relics for eighty-four thousand stupas that he commissioned across his empire.[12] The earliest surviving stupas date from around this period, for example, that of Sanchi (figure 12). They were faced in stone but retained the basic form, resembling a mound built around a core or axis—the *yaṣṭi*—sometimes represented by a physical core, such as a tree trunk. From this a parasol (*chattra*) rose above the top of the dome.[13] The relic chamber was usually in the center of the base. There was space defined for circumambulating the dome.

The function of stupas widened over the following centuries: some were built to hold relics of famous monks; some covered objects used by the Buddha or his disciples; others commemorated actions or events in the life of the Buddha and his disciples; while others symbolized aspects of Buddhist theology or were built as shrines. The stupa was seen as an embodiment of the Buddha and was a focus for worship. Dharmarajika Stupa in Taxila has been identified by some scholars as a Mauryan-period structure, although

11. See Fussman (1986) for a discussion of the use and symbolism of the early stupa.

12. For a full discussion of relics in Buddhism, see Strong (2004).

13. Some stupas have a central core pillar, often made from a tree trunk, but many stupas lack this. See Fussman (1986: 42).

most place it no earlier than the second century BC. This was after the fall of the Maurya Empire, and the dating is largely based on coins found here from the succeeding Indo-Greek period.[14] The remains of a stupa, Butkara I, which is about ten miles north of Amluk Dara in present-day Mingora, are believed to date from the same period, probably as early as the third century BC.[15] Kurt Behrendt suggests that Butkara was the "hub of a provincial Buddhist centre, in contrast to the more important Dharmarajika complex, 130 miles south, which served the metropolis."[16] The role of Butkara as an urban sanctuary has recently been reassessed in light of the archaeological evidence from the urban site in the Mingora area.[17] Already we are seeing the spread of Buddhism northwards into the towns and villages of Central Asia. How did this happen?

Throughout the early Buddhist world we see a symbiotic link between Buddhists and merchants, enabling both the spread of Buddhism and the growth of trade. The Buddha was known as Great Caravan Leader (*mahasarthavaha*) for his role in protecting and leading followers from the world of *saṃsāra* to the world of enlightenment, *nirvāṇa*. Xinru Liu observes, "Abundant experience with long-distance trade provided the inspiration for these images of the Buddha as a guide for travellers and merchants."[18] Aśoka is credited with first sending monks to this region, but its position on important trade routes undoubtedly helped with the establishment and growth of Buddhism in this mountain valley over the following centuries. Buddhism continued here for over a millennium, despite numerous invasions and political changes throughout its history and rulers who did not always actively support the religion (although there is little evidence of persecution). Indeed, as one scholar notes, "It is possible that Buddhism flourished specifically because its religious institutions were not pillaged during times of war and thus provided stable way stations for the transient merchant communities."[19]

The following centuries saw many regime changes, archaeologically documented at Barikot. Toward the end of the first century BC, the Indo-Greeks

14. Behrendt (2004: 39–41). The Indo-Greek kings ruled various territories in this region during the last two centuries BC.

15. See Errington (2000: 191–92) for discussion of the dating of coins found in the remains. Also see D. Faccenna (2007) for an overview of the site in the pre-Kushan period.

16. Behrendt (2004: 48).

17. Iori (2016).

18. Liu (1994: 114–15).

19. Behrendt (2004: 23).

were replaced by a succession of rulers seeking control of these important passes, among them Indo-Scythians and Indo-Parthians (although it is not always certain that their rule extended into the Swat valley). Finds reflect the area's history, showing Hellenistic, Iranian, and South Asian motifs and coins with legends, often bilingual, in Greek and Prākrit.[20] In the first century AD Buddhism became more prominent, supported by the Indo-Scythian and Indo-Parthian rulers. Among the evidence for this is a schist reliquary with a Kharoṣṭhī inscription dating it to AD 5–6, saying that it contained relics of the historical Buddha and was donated by an Indo-Scythian prince, Indravarman, to earn merit for his extended family and to secure the happiness and welfare of his empire.[21] The earliest-known Buddhist texts, birchbark scrolls written in Gāndhārī using Kharoṣṭhī script, mention the Indo-Scythian rulers Aspavarma and Jihonika (Zeionises) and also date from the first century AD.[22]

In the mid-first century AD the region was seized by the Kushan Empire (see chapter 3), and their coins are found in stupas from here and westwards into present-day Afghanistan. Finds of coins in the structure of buildings help date the phases of work as stupas were expanded. For example, the second phase of work on Butkara I is dated by a coin of the Indo-Greek Menander I (end of the second century BC or later). The Pali text *Milinda Pañha* (The questions of Milinda) records that Menander became a Buddhist and recounts his debates with the Indian Buddhist sage Nāgasena. In this text Nāgasena explains that Buddha "is like a caravan owner to men in that he brings them beyond the sandy desert of rebirths."[23] "In a later phase, dated by coins of the Indo-Scythian ruler Azes II and then during further work dated by coins of the Kushan ruler Huviška (ca. 150–90), the stupa acquired a square terrace base with pilasters.[24] All these rebuildings strongly suggest

20. For example, see the stone dish in the Metropolitan Museum of Art showing Apollo and Daphne (Heilbrunn Timeline of Art History, "Dish with Apollo and Daphne," www.metmuseum.org/toah/works-of-art/1987.142.307/). Gāndhārī Prākrit was the language used in this region. See note 7 above.

21. Salomon and Schopen (1984). For an image, see Heilbrunn Timeline of Art History, "Inscribed Reliquary, Donated by King Indravarman," www.metmuseum.org/toah/works-of-art/1987.142.70a,b/. The reliquary contains an inscription saying it was brought from the Murykan Cave Stupa and secured in another place—presumably another stupa.

22. Lenz (2003: 100). See Salomon (1999) for an introduction to the manuscripts. Both rulers are known primarily through their coins.

23. Rhys-Davids (1890–94: 274), cited by Neelis (n.d.); also see Neelis (2013).

24. Errington (2000: 6). Errington identifies the coin as dating to Azes II, but the

that Buddhism was thriving in the region by the Kushan period and that there were wealthy patrons able to pay for the expansion of existing stupas and the establishment of new ones.

Stupas were usually at the center of monastic establishments, so their expansion also suggests a growing community of clergy. Much Buddhist activity took place during the reigns of the Kushan king Huviška and his successor, Vasudeva. As discussed in chapter 3, coins of Huviška and Vasudeva are among those found in an East Africa coin hoard. Amluk Dara was constructed around this time, the second or third century AD. It is not impossible—although purely speculative—that the casket of coins discussed in chapter 3 passed through the Swat on its way to the Indus valley and the ocean.

REACHING TO THE SKY—STUPA ARCHITECTURE

The need for an architectural infrastructure accompanies the growth of religious communities, and if the religious communities are patronized by the elite of the kingdom—the rulers and the rich—then the architecture is built on a monumental scale. This not only glorifies the relevant god or gods but also reflects the power and wealth of the local elite. Sacred buildings grow in size and scale depending on the level of wealth and patronage within the community. Whether they are village churches in Britain, mosques in Iran, or stupas in India, they are frequently rebuilt. Although buildings expand in floor space, the most notable increase is in height—the verticalization of buildings. So the original squat Norman church tower is knocked down and replaced by a taller, less earth-bound tower, which in turn is replaced by a spire, able to reach new heights because of developments in architectural and engineering technique.[25] The spire not only gives the building increasing prominence in its earthly setting—so it can be seen for miles around—but also, according to some scholars, serves as "a symbol of transcendental forces

existence of such a ruler and coinage has been questioned by Senior (2008), who concludes there was only one Azes of the Indo-Scythians and that he ruled around 58–12 BC. Joe Cribb argues that there were two different rulers, shown by a significant difference in the coinage (pers. comm., 2016).

25. A famous example is the Duomo in Florence, which was actually conceived without the engineering skills to complete it.

which are to fill the soul of worshipers with a deep longing for the celestial kingdom of God."[26]

The same process of verticalization is seen with stupa architecture. The original hemispherical or *classical stupa* form as found at Sanchi and elsewhere in northern India at the time of Aśoka, the dome on a circular base, persisted. It is seen in Gandhāra, for example at the early stupa at Butkara, but most especially in South India. Variations started to emerge from the original, with the hemispherical and relatively squat dome becoming a more elongated or verticalized parabolic shape. The height of this was increased with the addition of a *harmika*—a square enclosure at the top of the dome— and, rising above this, the *chattra* spire, often referred to as an umbrella or parasol (figure 12). The Italian archaeologists who have been excavating in the Swat since 1956 argue that the builders of stupas in the Swat valley paid attention to their siting to allow "as full a possible a side view" and to ensure that the stupa was "projected against an unencumbered sky . . . so as to make it appear larger."[27] A base might well have assisted in the stupa's elevation but also served to make a level platform in uneven mountain terrain. Further, "The lateral view of the monument was enhanced by the colours, the gilding and the pictorial and sculptural elements. . . . The sacred complex appeared already in the distance in such a way as to attract the worshipper with an immediate view of the principal monument, standing in the forefront and open to the faithful."[28]

Chronology is still uncertain, but there is evidence that an early development of a stupa form with one or more square bases or terraces (rather than the circular base) emerged in the Gandhāran region by the start of the first century AD just before the Kushan period (see chapter 2), for example the stupa Saidu Sharif I.[29] Like other Gandhāran stupas, it was built in stone and covered in plaster and stucco. This *terrace stupa* became dominant throughout Central Asia and, over the following centuries, developed in complexity and spread eastwards in the Tarim basin and thence to

26. These are the words of Ernst Gall, defining the Gothic. Von Simson quotes them in order to make the counterclaim that "verticalism is neither the exclusive property of Gothic nor even its most prominent feature. . . . I know of no historical evidence for the romantic assumption that the Gothic architect employed verticalism in order to fill the soul with longing for the kingdom of God" (1988: 156n).

27. D. Faccenna and Spagnesi (2014: 549).

28. D. Faccenna and Spagnesi (2014: 550). See also Behrendt (2004: 28n40).

29. Olivieri (2016).

China.[30] This is the architectural context in which Amluk Dara was conceived and built.

AMLUK DARA

Amluk Dara Stupa is on a site to the east of the Swat that runs from northwest to southwest along the bank of a stream known locally as Amluk Dara Khwar (*khwar* is the Pashto term for "torrent"), just half a mile southeast of the village of the same name. The stream is dammed at the southeastern part by large boulders to create a large pond used as a reservoir, probably there since antiquity. The whole area is filled with ruins of a Buddhist site. The main stupa sits on a roughly square base or terrace, 6.97 meters high and with sides between 32 and 35 meters long, as was typical of the terrace stupa dominant at that time. A stairway led up on its north side. The core was composed of a horizontal course of gneiss blocks and dark schist slabs interspersed with a thick course of mortar, made of a mixture of yellow clay and limestone fragments. It was faced with dressed blocks of granite of roughly equal sizes, and the spaces between them were filled with schist flakes. It was plastered and then painted. The floor of the base was made up of large slabs. The round base of the stupa was decorated in the same way, with another staircase leading up on the north side to the second story. Above this were two more stories, also round. These were plastered, and their tops were marked by projecting slabs supported by brackets, made of schist.

The hemispherical dome, almost eighteen meters in diameter, rose above this to a height of over ten meters (figure 13). At the floor of the dome were found fragments of six circular stone slabs that originally had formed part of the parasol or *chattra* rising above the dome on the central axis. The archaeologist working at the site since 2012, Luca Olivieri, has estimated that there were originally at least seven slabs, with the largest (which was placed at the bottom of the sequence) being over 7.5 meters in diameter and weighing around three tons when complete. The *harmika* and the *chattra* would have increased the height of the stupa by 8.8 meters, making the total height of the stupa around 35 meters.[31]

To the left (east) of the staircase was a small stupa. This bore the same dec-

30. Whitfield (2018a).
31. The Pantheon in Rome is 43.5 meters high.

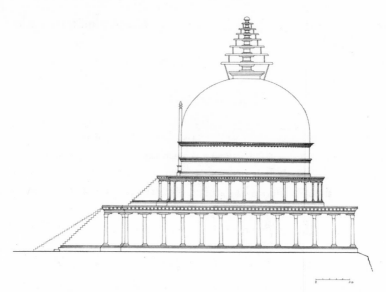

FIGURE 13. Plan of Amluk Dara. After Olivieri (2014, pl. 3). Drawings by F. Martore, ACT/Italian Archaeological Mission in Pakistan.

oration as the main one and was probably built at the same time. The pattern is seen elsewhere, such as at Baligram (Saidu Sharif) and Gumbatuna, both also in the Swat.[32] There were three other terraces, one to the northwest and two to the southeast, one of which probably was the site of the monastery buildings and all of which might have contained smaller stupas. The track to Mount Ilam is at the north of the site, while to the west are the pond and, a little further afield, remains of winepresses. Many smaller secondary buildings, probably built later by other, less wealthy or important patrons, are seen throughout the region, including at Dharmarajika Stupa at Taxila and at Butkara I. Evidence from the former site suggests they were built within a century of the main stupa and placed where there would have been numerous worshippers.[33] There were dwelling units further away, possibly for those seeking seclusion.[34] Rock shelters in the vicinity contain paintings from the same period.

This was a monumental building that, especially when plastered and painted, must have dominated the landscape in the way that medieval cathe-

32. Olivieri (2014: 352).
33. Schopen (1997: 118); Behrendt (2004: 90).
34. D. Faccenna and Spagnesi (2014: 549–51).

drals dominated the landscape of Europe. For comparison, it was almost the same height as the original twelfth-century tower of Ely Cathedral in Britain and only a few meters lower than the Pantheon in Rome. The archaeologist Aurel Stein noted that it was the largest of all the stupas he had surveyed in the Swat valley—and about four hundred Buddhist structures have been discovered here to date.[35] An obvious question that comes to mind is how it was constructed, most especially how the builders managed to erect the *harmika* and heavy stone *chattra* on top of a thirty-meter-tall building.

Luca Olivieri has considered this in his report of archaeological work at the site, also taking into account the work of Gregory Schopen, who has looked at the logistics of Buddhist architecture more generally, and Akira Shimada, who has researched Buddhist patronage during this early period in India.[36] First, we need to consider who was responsible for conceiving, planning, and then supervising the work. Was this the vision of a single patron, a group of local elite, or the monks themselves? We will probably never know. There are no known texts to give us any information on this, nor are there any inscriptions on the stupa itself. However, in other cases documents and inscriptions are found. For example, there are documents of King Aśoka and other rulers commissioning stupa building throughout their kingdoms— and presumably providing funds. In another case, when a seventh-century pilgrim monk, Xuanzang, returned to China to great acclaim, he asked the emperor to build a stupa in the capital, Chang'an. He also stipulated the style—to resemble the great stupa of King Kaniška I. In this case an eminent monk had the vision and the ruler was the patron. In other cases there are inscriptions on parts of the stupa, for example, the tree trunk *yaṣṭi* of the stupa at Pangoraria in Madhya Pradesh is inscribed as being donated by a nun and her disciples.[37] But, as Shimada has observed, there is little evidence of rulers acting as patrons at this period. Rather, inscriptions suggest that much Buddhist building, at least in this early period, was supported both by clergy and by "numerous collective donors from a wider section of society."[38] Shimada bylines stupas as "the architecture of collective patronage."[39] Monks and nuns also seem to have established and largely funded Stupa no. 2 at

35. Confirmed by D. Faccenna and Spagnesi (2014: 175).

36. Olivieri (2014); Schopen (1997); Shimada (2012: chap. 4).

37. Schopen (1997: 92). This is part of a larger discussion about the involvement of clergy in the stupa cult; see also 99–113 and 165–203.

38. Shimada (2012: 147), citing Dehejia (1992).

39. Shimada (2012: 163).

Sanchi and other stupas that contained the relics of the monastic dead. It is therefore possible that the monks would have been responsible for one or more of the smaller stupas at the site for such a purpose, though their involvement in the funding of the main stupa remains uncertain.

Why did a person or persons chose this location to build a major stupa? Its positioning depends not only on topography but also on proximity to people. A complex building such as this would have required not only patrons to enable its original construction but a local community and pilgrims to ensure its worship and maintenance. The close relationship between Buddhism and trade has been explored, and this stupa, like many others, is on a major trade route—an artery of the network of routes that connected distant regions by land and sea—the Silk Road.[40] It is not only on the main route up the Swat valley from the Peshawar plain but also on a route leading across the mountains both eastward to the Indus valley and southeast to the Kabul valley.[41] In terms of local settlements, it is only half a mile from a village, not much further away from Barikot, a larger urban site, while to the north are Udegram and Butkara.[42] It is also on a route to another sacred site—Mount Ilam. It would thus have been easily accessible to passing merchants and pilgrims and visible to other passing travelers.[43]

The orientation was also important, probably planned to be north and set by the sunrise. However, the stupa actually faces north northeast, with a difference of about thirty-five degrees to the astronomical north. This suggests that the stupa was planned after the autumn equinox when the sunrise was less than forty degrees to the east southeast.[44] Preferred orientations for stupas seem to have been east or north, but mountain topography often made this difficult.[45]

The location of the monastery and its central stupa was also dependent on the landscape. The fecundity of the Swat valley is well captured by the

40. D. Faccenna and Spagnesi (2014: 171).

41. Also to be considered is the vicinity of the Karakar road. Alexander the Great used this, and it remained in use from antiquity through to Mughal times. See Olivieri and Vidale (2006) and Olivieri (1996).

42. Barikot has been identified as the city of Bazira/Beira, described in Western sources as "opulent" and "carefully fortified" and conquered by Alexander in 327 BC (Callieri 2007: 135).

43. When W. W. McNair (1884: 5), a British engineer traveling in disguise, crossed into the Swat valley in 1883 he noted that he could see up to twenty stupas at any one time.

44. Olivieri (2014: 332); Snodgrass (1991: 15).

45. Olivieri (2014: 333); Fussman (1986).

description of the archaeologist Aurel Stein when he visited at the end of winter in 1926: "The deep-cut lane along which we travelled was lined with fine hedges showing primrose-like flowers in full bloom, and the trees hanging low with their branches, though still bare of leaves, helped somehow to recall Devon lanes. Bluebell-like flowers and other messengers of spring, spread brightness over the little terraced fields."[46] And the Italian archaeologists working there since 1956 have noted that "the entire complex blended in with the surrounding nature. From this it drew its charm, importance and beauty—all elements that are believed to have been taken into consideration both in the original plans and subsequent extension."[47]

Schopen makes the argument that monasteries were very closely linked to the Indian ideal of a garden containing an arbor or pleasure grove, evidenced by the shared lexicon in the first century AD. He writes that "Buddhist monks . . . attempted to assimilate their establishments to the garden, or actually saw them as belonging to that cultural category."[48] The framing of views from within the garden or monastery was an important element in its siting, a point noted by many travelers. So Stein writes of another site in the Lower Swat that it "proved a pleasing example of the care in which these old Buddhist monks knew how to select sacred spots and place their monastic establishments by them. A glorious view down the fertile valley to Thāna, picturesque rocky spurs around, clumps of firs and cedars higher up, and the rare boon of a spring close by—all combined to give charm to the spot. Even those who do not seek future bliss in Nirvāṇa could fully enjoy it."[49] Rock-cut or other seats were often placed at points giving a particular view.

To illustrate his argument for a "shared vocabulary," Schopen gives the example of a classical Sanskrit verse describing a garden as having trees in full bloom and resounding "with geese and cranes and peacocks, with parrots, mynas, cuckoos and pheasants." He compares this to a description of a Buddhist monastery "made lovely with various trees, filled with the sound of geese and cranes and peacocks, of parrots, mynas, cuckoos and pheasants, and made lovely with all kind of flowers and fruit."[50] The Sanskrit name for a Buddhist monastery, *vihara*, means "pleasure ground" or "garden," and, like gardens monasteries were situated outside but near settlements.

46. Stein (1929: 32–35). Devon is in southwestern England.
47. D. Faccenna and Spagnesi (2014: 550).
48. Schopen (2006a: 489).
49. Stein (1929: 17–18), quoted in Schopen (2006a: 499).
50. Schopen (2006a: 493).

In India both also were the focus of sightseeing excursions, especially for wealthy women.[51] Indeed, the same text makes clear that both resembled the "dwelling of a god," recalling the paradise scenes shown on the walls of Buddhist Central Asian cave temples. The stupas and monasteries were also decorated with paintings, which were used to attract pilgrims and potential donors.[52]

Most stupas are not, in themselves, complex architectural structures; in the words of Olivieri, "evoluted mounds." However, as he also points out, their size can make them complex to build.[53] Probably the core—the *yaṣṭi*—was erected first to act as a guide, even if it was not incorporated into the final structure. But, apart from this, there is little knowledge about the order of building or decoration.[54] Olivieri suggests that the nearby rocky slopes were possible starting points for ramps to transport materials as the building grew. Certainly his team's attempts to raise the massive dressed blocks of granite on the bamboo scaffolding used in the restoration were not successful, and Peter Rockwell, who has studied the stone-working techniques used in Swat, also concludes that "one of the mysteries of Gandhāran technology is how they lifted and placed the large disks."[55] Olivieri also questions the assumption that a "stupa was simply constructed from bottom to top" suggesting that the sequence was more complex.[56]

But before building the materials had to be obtained. Local sites show the evidence of stones being quarried, often cut out in the shape required, rather than worked into shape afterwards. One such is a quarry at Gogdara, north of Amluk Dara, which clearly shows the cutting of rock in the shape of the umbrella disks, and another is a schist quarry at Sakhakot, almost certainly used for sculptural work at this time.[57] Olivieri also suggests that some materials were possibly acquired locally by quarrying the cliffs adjacent to the site,

51. There is an interesting link to explore here with the role of women deities in Swat, reinforced by the Tibetan tradition in which Udyāna was the home of female spirits, *ḍākinī* (Tucci 1949: 212–13; Eck 2013: 292–93).

52. Schopen (2006a: 497).

53. Olivieri (2014: 337).

54. There is no sign of a *yaṣṭi* at Amluk Dara, but this does not mean that one was not used to measure out the axis of the building.

55. Rockwell (2006: 165). See also Olivieri and Vidale (2006), C. Faccenna et al. (1993), and Olivieri (2016).

56. Olivieri (2014: 339, also 337–38).

57. Rockwell (2006: fig. 4); Kempe (1986).

with the advantage that this could also increase the ground area available for building, as seen at Saidu Sharif I.[58]

Who organized this? Several textual sources record that monks, as well as collecting donations, were involved in other aspects of construction, such as purchasing materials and supervising the builders. One text, which tells an anecdote about the building of a monastery, gives a list of those involved: monk in charge of new construction (*navakarmika*); brickmakers; master builders; carpenters; plasterers; painters; day laborers.[59] From other texts we also know that monks sometimes did the work of day laborers, ending the day covered in mud and clay.[60] Buddha is said to have ordered this: "When a building project is not finished, the monks must help in the construction work."[61] The layout of a monastery was determined both by tradition and by the monks making decisions on the ground—essential in mountainous regions where the topography varied.

AMLUK DARA STUPA IN THE COMMUNITY

Apart from acting as patrons, builders, and skilled craftsmen, what was the role of the ordinary people of the surrounding community? It must be remembered that not all of them would have been Buddhist. There is no evidence that the Buddhists succeeded—or even sought—to convert all the local community. As Olivieri points out, citing the work of many others, "Buddhism . . . did not have universalist ambitions: at least in contexts such as these, its main target would have been to have on its side the political elites, the local landed aristocracy, merchants and craftsmen: in other words, the residents of the city."[62] The local pre-Buddhist religious practices—the "popular" religion—almost certainly survived in this region. It is also possible that the Buddhist monuments were incorporated into this belief system as something like beneficent spirits—suggested by the depiction of stupas in many of the local rock paintings. Just as possible is that they are indicators, in Olivieri's words, "of a cultural disparity"—that they might "represent a kind

58. Olivieri (2016).
59. Schopen (2006b: 231–33). He discusses each of these roles in turn; see 233–39. See also Silk (2008), esp. 75–100 on the role of *navakarmika,* and Shimada (2012: 158–60).
60. Schopen (2006b: 228–29).
61. Schopen (2006b: 240, 242–43).
62. Olivieri (2015b: 119).

of psychological response of the rural communities facing fast transformations affecting the most privileged areas of their territory."[63]

The Italian archaeological team has surveyed other contemporary archaeology in the area, and this includes remains of structures but also of many painted rock shelters and winepresses. They argue that during the heyday of Buddhism, when Amluk Dara was constructed, the land was under the control of local aristocrats who made parts of it over to Buddhist communities. But some of this was probably land already under agriculture and with existing irrigation infrastructures, as shown by a post-second-century AD inscription at Malakand, further up the valley. Some of the land might have continued to be worked by locals, not all of whom were necessarily converted. The account of the Buddhist traveler Hyecho (704–87) indicates the extent of community involvement here at this later date—though without the community having any choice in the matter: "Most of the king's villages and their inhabitants have been donated for the support of the monasteries. Only a few villages remain his own and even food and clothing from them are donated to the monastery."[64]

Even if this was not the situation in this earlier period, local people might have given labor for acquiring and producing goods necessary for the monastic community. As well as agricultural products, they may have supplied other foodstuffs such as fruits and honey and may have been involved in the production of oil for the lamps and perhaps even wine.[65] Whether the production of these was controlled by the monastery and the lay people acted as laborers—or indeed as slaves—or whether the lay people controlled production and sold on to the monastery is difficult to ascertain.[66] Elsewhere in the Buddhist world we see monasteries in control of the flour mills and oil presses needed by the local community and also acting as banks, making loans with considerable interest.[67]

Grapes grow wild in the valley, and grape juice production in the area is attested by the discovery of twenty tanks found at high altitude in local valleys. It is estimated these could have produced six to eight thousand liters of

63. Olivieri (2015b: 120n136).
64. Hyecho, ed. and trans. Yang (1984: 50). See below for more on Hyecho.
65. Olivieri (2015b: 20). He suggests that oil might have been made from mustard seeds, widely available in the valley. For mustard seed in Tibetan Buddhism, see Beer (2015).
66. See Schopen (1994) for forced labor; also see chapter 10 for a broader discussion of slavery in monasteries and elsewhere.
67. See Gernet (1995) for a discussion of the economies of monasteries in China, including their control of oil presses and flour mills.

juice per year. Tanks found near Buddhist complexes do not contain an exit hole, which suggests that they might have been used for fermentation rather than only for the original pressing of the grapes to extract the juice. This, in turn, might indicate that wine drinking was continued by local Buddhists.[68] One such press was found inside a shelter that also contains rock art, suggesting that the local community was involved in the production, perhaps selling some of the wine on to the monasteries.

The paintings in the rock shelters are contemporary with Buddhist life in the first millennium AD. Their motifs show a concern with local agricultural rites, production of wine, ibex sacrifice, and ritual hunting and shamanistic practices—the last attested until modern times in the middle and upper Swat and associated with groups speaking Kafir and Dardic languages.[69] But the painted shelters in this area cease around the end of the first millennium— around the time that we see a significant decline in Buddhist activity. Does this indicate a general decline in the area, including a decrease or move of the population? There is some evidence of later building—up to the thirteenth or fourteenth century—supported by at least one extant account, but nothing to indicate the level of Buddhist activity that continued during much of the first millennium.

WORSHIP AT THE STUPA

As discussed above, by the time Amluk Dara was built, the core—literally and metaphorically—of the stupa was the relic chamber. Although any relics from Amluk Dara are long looted and lost, other reliquaries have been discovered at nearby sites, such as at the stupas at Kaniška and at Jaulian. The reliquary from Kaniška Stupa, near Peshawar, dates from around AD 127 and is an inscribed and decorated gilded copper casket, seven inches high, which held in its base a hexagonal rock crystal reliquary containing three fragments of bone.[70]

Jaulian is on the east bank of the Indus, southeast of the Swat and near Taxila. The relic chamber of Jaulian Stupa A11 (fourth to fifth centuries) is ten and a half feet square and three feet eight and a half inches in height. It con-

68. Falk (2009).

69. Olivieri (2015b). The term "Shamanistic" is used advisedly.

70. The casket is in Peshawar Museum and the reliquary in Mandalay (Spooner 1908–9: 49).

tained a model stupa three feet eight inches tall just fitting inside. The stupa was made of stucco with a seven-*chattra* parasol. It was painted in blue and red and studded with garnet, carnelian, lapis, aquamarine, ruby, agate, amethyst, and crystal.[71] A hollow shaft ran down the inside, at the bottom of which was a decayed wooden casket, held by four iron nails. This contained lapis, ivory, gold-leaf, rock crystal, gold beads, some green vitreous paste, and coral—some of the seven treasures of Buddhism.[72] It also counted a smaller round casket of copper gilt, inside which was a smaller cylinder of the same material. This contained only dust, but we may presume it was the remains of the relic.

The stupa was the public part of the monastery. As we have seen, it was intended in its size and positioning to attract worshippers—and donors. Many stupas would have been gilded, making their domes even more prominent against the background of the sky, and they would have been "clothed" with silk flags and banners, much as statues of Buddha are clothed. Songyun, a Chinese pilgrim monk traveling around 520, noted this custom in the kingdom of Khotan in the Tarim basin: "Men of later times built several thousand Buddhist statues and stupas in the neighbourhood. Coloured canopies and banners hung over them in the tens of thousands."[73] He was able to date the offerings from the prayers written on them in ink. He mentions that one banner contained an inscription from the time of the pilgrim monk Faxian a century earlier, suggesting that the silks were left on the stupas and preserved by the dry desert air of Khotan. In the more humid Swat valley, such offerings would soon have disintegrated.

Worshippers might also have bought garlands of flowers for adornment, incense to burn in front of the stupa, or model stupas made from clay molds by the monastery. They might also have stuffed remnants of sacred manuscripts into the stupa's niches. Many ancient manuscripts have been preserved in this way—although not in the humid climate of Swat. A later Tibetan text enumerates the benefits from making offerings to stupas. Although apocryphal, it is ascribed to Padmasambhvara (Guru Rinpoche), a monk tra-

71. Marshall (1951: 373).

72. The seven treasures were traditionally gold, silver, crystal, lapis lazuli, carnelian, coral, and pearl, but other materials were used as substitutes. See Liu (1994, 1996) for a discussion of their role in trade.

73. Jenner (1981: 219–20). Also see Chavannes (1903b: 393). Songyun reports that he read the Chinese inscriptions on the banners and found most of them to date from 495, 501, and 513, with only one from the time of Faxian (ca. 400). See also Bhattacharya-Haesner (2003: 42).

ditionally believed to have been born in the Swat valley and to have taken Buddhism to Tibet.[74] It gives some idea of the many ways in which worshippers can show their devotion.[75] Below are just eleven of the over one hundred types of stupa offerings listed in the text:

> Whoever circumambulates the Great Stupa attains the seven qualities of divine happiness: noble birth, fine form, great pleasure, virtue and understanding, power and prosperity, freedom from disease and extreme longevity.

> . . . .

> Whoever offers flowers to the Great Stupa obtains ease and contentment, prosperity and health; whoever offers incense achieves pure action; whoever offers lamps has the darkness of unknowing illuminated; whoever offers perfume is freed from anxiety and suffering; whoever offers sacrificial food lives a life of concentration free from hunger.

> Whoever offers music to the Great Stupa spreads the Vibration of Dharma throughout the ten directions; whoever offers the sound of cymbals obtains deep and strong understanding and prosperity; whoever offers the sound of tinkling bells obtains a gentle and sweet voice—the sacred tones of Brahma.

> . . . .

> Whoever offers robes for the Image of Priest of the Great Stupa enjoys fine sensuous clothes; whoever gives a coat of whitewash to the Stupa acquires a fair and lustrous complexion, happiness, prosperity and health, attaining predominance over men, gods and demons. Whoever offers curd, milk and butter will possess the Ever Provident Cow and a herd of cattle; whoever offers molasses, honey and sugar receives celestial food.[76]

REBUILDING AND RENOVATIONS

As centers of worship, stupas, like most religious structures, are subject to frequent expansions and redecorations as new donors and communities of worshippers demand changes and extensions to show their piety. Amluk Dara

74. Padmasambhvara became central to the story of Buddhism's transmission to Tibet in the twelfth century. See van Schaik (2011: 96). For an early text on Tibetan pilgrims to the Swat valley, see Tucci (1940).

75. Although, of course, we have to be careful when making any assumptions about practice in earlier periods without other supporting evidence.

76. Dowman (1973: 33–34).

was no exception: Olivieri notes evidence for at least six subsequent rebuild-ings from the third to the ninth century. The stupa's redevelopment also tells us about the state of Buddhism in the Swat over this period.

The dates of all the renovations are not clear, but probably in the Kushan period the original blue schist decoration was replaced with the decorative elements made of *kanjur* stone, including pilasters, of a later variation of the type known as Gandhāran-Corinthian (figure 14). The carved pilasters and brackets were fitted into spaces left in the facade and were then plastered and painted. Also around this time the main staircase was rebuilt. Olivieri has suggested that it could have been damaged in an earthquake (earthquakes are not uncommon in this region).[77] The new staircase was built on top of the remains of the original and was thus higher and longer, throwing out the symmetry of the original building.

The Kushan Empire ended here by the fourth century, but Buddhism con-tinued to thrive in the valley, as shown in the architectural landscape. The political landscape is not so clear. Coin evidence suggests influence or rule by Kushano-Sasanians and Sasanians and then, from the fifth century, by the Kidarites, Hephthalites, Turki Shahi, and Hindu Shahi. In about 403 we have a report from Faxian, a Chinese pilgrim monk who stayed here on his way to India.[78]

Crossing the [Indus] river, we come to the country of Wu-chang [Udyāna]. The country of Wu-chang commences North India. The language of mid-India is used by all. . . . The dress of the people, their food and drink, are also the same as in the middle country [India]. The religion of Buddha is very flourishing. The places where the monks stop and lodge they call *saṅghārāmas*. In all there are five hundred *saṅghārāmas*; they belong to the Little Vehicle [Hinayana] without exception. If a strange Bhikshu arrives here, they give him full entertainment for three days; the three days being over, then they bid him seek for himself a place to rest permanently.

Tradition says: When Buddha came to North India, he then visited this country. Buddha left here as a bequest the impression of his foot. The foot-

77. Olivieri (2012: 109). Tucci in his 1958 preliminary survey, prior to excavations, also concludes: "I am certain that great disasters had ravaged Swat and been the chief causes of serious economic ruins which could not avoid influencing the religious situation. The preliminary study of the soil . . . has already convinced me that natural calamities such as earthquakes and terrific floods have been responsible for the destruction of the largest parts of the monuments" (212).

78. See Stein (1921: 5–9) for a retracing of Faxian's steps. Kuwayama (2006) raises issues about Faxian's and other pilgrims' accounts with translations (see note 91 below).

print is sometimes long and sometimes short, according to the thoughtfulness of a man's heart: it is still so, even now. Moreover, the drying-robe-stone in connection with the place where he converted the wicked dragon still remains.[79]

The Buddha footprint and the clothes-drying rock have both been identified with sites in the upper Swat valley that survive today.[80]

Faxian and some of his companions remained in Udyāna for the summer retreat—a practice developed in Indian Buddhism for monks to avoid the summer monsoon.[81] At the end of this they continued down the valley, to the lower Swat. Faxian reported that Buddhism was flourishing and identified a site where the Buddha had cut off a piece of his own flesh as a ransom to save the life of a dove: this is the subject of the Sivi Jātaka, one of the hundreds of tales of Buddha's former lives, collectively known as the Jātaka.[82] According to Faxian, the locals had erected a stupa on the site, adorned with gold and silver.[83] By his report it was another five days to the country of Gandhāra—presumably the Taxila area.

Faxian's account, describing a thriving Buddhist community, is supported by the archaeology, which shows that the patronage of Buddhism and its institutions continued despite changes in rule. Probably only a decade or two after Faxian's visit the region came under control of different rulers from the north, the Kidarites. These were the first in a series of invaders often referred to as "Iranian Huns." The paucity and confusion of the textual and archaeological evidence mean that the dates and extent of the rule of all these groups are not certain: coins produce some of the best evidence, and there are coins of the Kidarites in Swat, but this does not mean they ruled the area. During the Kidarite period, massive clay sculptures of Buddha and bodhisattvas were carved—some more than forty feet tall—although not in Swat.

In 467 the Kidarites were expelled from Bactria, possibly by an alliance of the Sasanians and Hephthalites, the latter another so-called confederation of

79. Beal (1884: xxx–xxxvi).

80. Noted by Deane (1896), who also took an impression of the carving. See also Tucci (1958). Later Chinese pilgrims, Songyun and Xuanzang, also mention these sites, summarized in Stein (1930: 56–58, 60, 65, 102). The footprints are currently conserved in the Swat Museum.

81. This practice, however, continued when monasteries were established in nonmonsoon lands, such as the Tarim basin.

82. For a translation of the Jātaka, see Cowell et al. (1895) Sivi Jātaka is no. 499 in vol. 4.

83. The archaeologist Aurel Stein suggested that this was Gumbutai Stupa.

"Iranian Huns" (see chapter 5). They probably held on to power around Swat for a decade or more. Then the Alkhan—part of the Hephthalite alliance—also crossed the mountains to take Gandhāra.[84]

We see more rebuilding to Amluk Dara during this period. A small temple was built in the center of the new staircase, and semicircular niches were cut in its side, probably to house votive stupas. Following further work on the staircase there is then some evidence of a period of abandonment or certainly neglect, perhaps when the monastic community and available patrons were too sparse to allow for its upkeep. It could be hypothesized that this was during the Hephthalite period, as the Hephthalites are not known to have been supporters of Buddhism. Songyun and Huisheng were envoys from the Tuoba court ruling North China, the Northern Wei (383–535), and they reported after their meeting with the Hephthalite ruler in 519 that the majority of the people "do not believe in Buddha. Most worship false gods."[85]

However, as Shoshin Kuwayama has pointed out, the monks do not mention any persecution of Buddhists or destruction of any Buddhist buildings or statues.[86] After meeting the Hephthalites to the north, Songyun's party traveled south across the mountains to Udyāna.[87] Here they met the local king who "pays adoration to the Buddha, both morning and evening." They visited some of the famous Buddhist sites mentioned by Faxian, such as the footprint of the Buddha, and even gave funds toward the construction of a stupa on the hill famous as the site of the Sivi Jātaka. Their reports indicate that Buddhism continued to thrive and to be patronized in this mountain kingdom.[88]

Frantz Grenet has proposed that the unification of Central Asia by the Hephthalites enabled a second fluorescence of Buddhism that was "more far-reaching than the first one in the Kushan period."[89] He points out that

84. Chinese sources record an embassy from the Kidarites in 477. Swat is identified as their base on numismatic evidence (Göbl 1967, vol. 2: 224). For the Hepthalites, see chapter 5 below. See also Kuwayama (1992).

85. Beal (1884: xcii). See also Chavannes (1903b: 405).

86. Kuwayama (1992).

87. Their route is described by Stein (1921: 9–11). See Chavannes (1903b: 406–15) for Songyun's time in Udyāna.

88. For much of the twentieth century, scholars linked this period with a decline of monasticism in Gandhāra. This was following Marshall's (1951) interpretation of his archaeology at Taxila. However, Errington (2000: 199–203) has summarized the weaknesses of this, and more recent archaeology has largely revised this opinion.

89. Grenet (2002: 213).

Buddhism influence in this period extended further than before, with a stupa founded at Merv (almost one thousand miles to the northwest of Taxila), a region also conquered by the Hephthalites.[90] Certainly there is evidence of ongoing trade during this period across Central Asia, with merchants from the north—especially Sogdians and Bactrians—leaving inscriptions at Shatial and other places in the upper Indus. And given the symbiotic link between trade and Buddhism, the thriving of Buddhism both here and also much deeper into Central Asia, including into the Tarim basin, might be expected.

The next surviving account, from the travels of another Chinese pilgrim, Xuanzang, paints a very different picture.[91] He arrived in about 630, having traveled to Gandhāra, like Alexander, from Kapisa to the west. He notes that "the towns and villages are deserted. . . . There are about 1000 *sanghārāmas*, which are deserted and in ruins. They are filled with wild shrubs, and solitary to the last degree. The stupas are mostly decayed. The heretical temples, to the number of about 100, are occupied pell-mell by heretics."[92] At this time Gandhāra east to the banks of the Indus was part of Kapisa, ruled from Bagram, while territory east of the Indus was ruled by Kashmir. It is not clear if Udyāna was under Kapisa.

The account of Xuanzang's travels says he then followed the Indus valley northwards from Udabhanda (Muzaffarabad), crossed the river—he does not say where—and traversed the mountains to reach the upper Swat valley, Udyāna. If he took this route, although this has been disputed, then it is possible he crossed by the Shangla Pass and thus passed Pir Sar on the western bank of the Indus. The account comments on the fertility of the Swat valley, where "fruits and flowers are abundant."[93] But it also notes that although

90. Callieri (1996: 399). The stupa inside the city walls at Merv, the westernmost confirmed evidence of Buddhism, was probably started in the third or fourth century (Herrmann 1997: 11). However, it has been suggested that it was halted because of the Sasanian state adoption of Zoroastrianism in 224, when other religions were not tolerated (Emmerick 1983: 957). The evidence of rebuilding during the Hephthalite period and the discovery of Hephthalite artifacts and a Buddhist manuscript add some support to the argument that there was a revival of Buddhism under their regime.

91. It is not, strictly speaking, a firsthand account, as it was written later, on the basis of Xuanzang's notes and other sources. Kuwayama (2006: 61) questions whether Xuanzang visited Udyāna or whether this is an account from someone else, possibly from a different period.

92. Beal (1884: 98).

93. Beal (1884: 120).

there were formerly 1,400 *saṅghārāmas* or monasteries on the banks of the Swat they "are now generally waste and desolate; formerly there were some 18,000 priests in them, but gradually they have become less, till now there are very few. They study the Great Vehicle [Mahāyāna], they practise the duty of quiet meditation and have pleasure in reciting texts relating to this subject, but have no great understanding as to them."[94] The account mentions the Buddha footprint rock and the place where he washed his robes. Among the other sites that Xuanzang notes in the southern reaches of the valley is Mount Hila, which the French archaeologist Alfred Foucher (1865–1952) identified as Mount Ilam.[95] Stein further identifies other sites described by Xuanzang, including Barikot and Gumbutai.[96] Amluk Dara does not figure among them.

Despite Xuanzang's bleak depiction, it is clear that Buddhism was still being practiced in Udyāna and the lower Swat, if not in Gandhāra to the south. The archaeology supports this, with evidence of sites being rebuilt in Swat during this period. As noted above, some of the damage to the structures noted by Xuanzang might have been earthquake-caused rather than manmade damage.[97] However, it certainly seems that the Buddhist community was much reduced from its heyday and that there was less patronage available than in former times, inevitably leading to the neglect of some of the many Buddhist structures here. Sometime around this period several square shrines were built in the middle of the steps of Amluk Dara.[98]

Extant records after Xuanzang include that of Hyecho, who traveled from Kashmir to Gandhāra on his way home from India in 727. He paints a very different picture, noting that the king "greatly reveres" Buddhism and has required most of the villages and their inhabitants to work for the monasteries, as cited above. He continues: "There are many monasteries and monks. There are slightly more monks than laymen." This account of a thriving Buddhist culture is reinforced by another Chinese traveler, Wukong, who visited in about 751.[99] He was part of a Chinese diplomatic mission to Kashmir but fell ill and remained behind when the mission returned to

94. Beal (1884: 120).
95. Foucher (1942–47: 48n3).
96. Stein (1921: 16–17).
97. See note 82 above.
98. Olivieri (2014: 356–60).
99. For translation, see Yang et al. (1984); for Wukong, see Chavannes and Lévi (1895).

China. It was over two decades before he returned home: he presumably joined a community of Buddhists in the region, which delayed his return.

That Buddhism was in some decline during Xuanzang's visit and then revived substantially by the mid-eighth century is possible, but it also should be observed that one scholar has cast doubt on whether Xuanzang actually visited Udyāna and has suggested that the account given is from other sources.[100] He suggests that the editors added Udyāna to the travels, as the site was well known to Buddhist China.

We have no accounts from the late eighth or ninth century, but sometime during this period, even if Amluk Dara was still in some use, its heyday passed. Its terrace became half buried by soil and rock. The once-clean plaster and painting were probably flaking and fading. A military watchtower was constructed next to the main stupa terrace by the Hindu Shahis who now ruled Swat.[101] While the stupa might have continued to be used by a small community for a century or so, it was probably finally abandoned in the ninth or tenth century and probably ceased its life as an active religious monument.

A MILLENNIUM OF NEGLECT:
TENTH TO TWENTIETH CENTURY

We have little idea of what happened to Amluk Dara over the next thousand years, but what is perhaps notable is its survival in a period when religions other than Buddhism became prevalent in the Swat. As discussed above, the local religion probably continued throughout the period alongside Buddhism, but from the time of the Hindu Shahis other religions supplanted Buddhism, primarily Islam. From the time when Peshawar was taken in 1005 by the Ghaznavid Empire (977–1186)—founded by Islamic Turks—the population of the Swat probably became more Islamized. Ghaznavid coins struck at the mint in Lahore have been discovered at a ruin near Udegram, just north of Amluk Dara and Barikot.[102] Excavations here have confirmed a period of Islamic occupation from the start of Ghaznavid rule through to the thir-

100. See note 91.
101. Olivieri (2003).
102. Guinta (2006).

teenth century, with buildings on top of preexisting Buddhist structures.[103] Remains of a mosque were discovered a little further down the mountainside from these and include an inscription from rebuilding carried out in 1048, making this the earliest dated mosque in this area. There is also a graveyard with about fifty Muslim tombs dating to the tenth and thirteenth centuries. Some of the paving stones in the Islamic settlement have been identified as the remains of the parasols from stupas. It is most likely that the umbrellas became unstable and fell off or were shaken off by earthquakes or floods, then were taken from the ground to be reused.

Regime changes followed fairly regularly, as in Swat's earlier history. Another empire ruled by Islamic Turks, the Khwarezmid (1077–1231), is evidenced by discovery of their Peshawar-minted coins in Udegram. They had been pushed south from their original base in Samarkand by the Mongols, but it was not long before the Mongol Empire (1206–1368) also reached here. By this time there was a cult in Tibet, mentioned above, of the monk Padmasambhava, who was believed to have been born in Udyāna and to have been a key figure in taking Buddhism to Tibet. A manuscript was discovered of the travels of a Tibetan monk who made this place the focus of his pilgrimage and reached here about 1260, around the time of the Mongol invasion.[104] He was named Orgyan Pa, meaning "From Udyāna." Like other travelers, he noted the lushness of both the valley and Mount Ilam: "covered by soft herbs and flowers of every kind of colour and smell. . . . To the east there is the mountain Ilo [i.e., Ilam]. . . . There is no medicinal herb growing on the earth, which does not grow here. . . . Sarabhas and antelope wander there quite freely. There are many gardens of grape and beautiful birds of every kind and of gracious colours make a deep chattering."[105]

From Ilam he went northwards up the valley, probably reaching Udegram, and noted that there were only one hundred houses in this and a neighboring settlement. This suggests that the Islamic settlement was almost abandoned at this time, a speculation supported by the archaeological evidence—or lack of it. However, Orgyan Pa also noted a sandalwood Buddhist statue still standing, at which he gave offerings, and he succeeded in collecting alms, suggesting that there were still some who respected if not followed Buddhism.

On Genghis Khan's death, this region became part of the Chagatai

103. Bagnera (2006).
104. See Tucci (1940) for a translation of this and another account.
105. Tucci (1940: 51).

Khanate, but how much control they exerted over the Swat—a mountain valley on the fringes of their empire—is unclear. The area was part of the Mughal Empire from the time of Babur (r. 1526–30). Although the Mughal Empire lasted until 1858, when the last emperor was deposed by imperial British forces, it is probable that Swat was more or less autonomous and ruled by local khans and nawabs for much of this period.

THE MODERN PERIOD:
ARCHAEOLOGY AND LOOTING

The fact that Amluk Dara was in such a complete state even after a thousand years of probable neglect strongly suggests that there was no concerted desecration of Buddhist monuments during this period by non-Buddhist inhabitants of the Swat. This is supported by the first person to visit and record an archaeological interest, the Hungarian-born scholar and archaeologist Aurel Stein.[106] Working for British India in Lahore, he made it to the Swat in 1926 (having attempted to visit since the 1890s). He writes of his first sighting of the stupa (figure 14):

> And just to delight the archaeologist, there arose against this grand background [of Mount Ilam] a big Stūpa . . . of carefully constructed masonry and in more perfect preservation than any I had ever seen. It had not been dug into of old for "treasure," like all the Stūpas I had so far examined. . . . The large monument still raises its fine hemispherical dome, about seventy feet in diameter, with its stone facing practically intact. . . . Nothing had fallen but the huge circular stone umbrellas that had once belonged to the "Tee" above the dome. Four of them now lay in a heap on the square base of the Stūpa. The largest of them measures fully fourteen feet in diameter: to raise it to that height must have been a task worthy of some Egyptian builder.[107]

Stein noted the damage on the northern part of the dome at the head of the staircase and took it for the attempts of looters, but Olivieri has suggested instead that this damage was caused by the falling of a large stone niche attached to the side of the dome—seen at other sites on the same position. And, as Stein notes, the hole found did not extend into the body of the dome. We can assume, therefore, that the reliquary might still have been

106. For a brief survey of archaeological and conservation activity, see Olivieri (2014).
107. Stein (1929: 34).

FIGURE 14. Amluk Dara in 1926, taken by Aurel Stein. British Library Photo 392/30(129). British Library Board.

intact at this period. When Stein returned here in 1933 he obtained a permit to excavate, but his plans were thwarted by an injury caused by a fall from his horse.[108] Stein visited again in 1941 but did not carry out further work at Amluk Dara.

The next account we have of the stupa is that left by the Italian scholar Guiseppe Tucci (1894–1984), who visited in 1955 to secure permission for archaeology and to undertake a preliminary survey. The surveyor accompa-

108. Olivieri (2014: 321).

nying him, V. Caroli, made two sketches, an elevation and a plan view, but they did not carry out any excavations at this time.[109]

The stupa was restored in 1958–59 under the direction of the Department of Archaeology and Museums, Pakistan.[110] Major restorations were made to the second story, using in-style intervention, where the same techniques and materials as the original build are used, making it very difficult to tell what is original and what is new.

In 1957 Caroli returned, but this time with Domenico Faccenna (1923–2008), whose archaeological work in the Swat, which he started in 1956, was to occupy much of his life. The next few decades were busy with many visits by the Italian team, more restoration by the Department of Archaeology and Museums in 1968, and a visit by Kuwayama in 1993.[111] Between 2012 to 2015 an Italian team led by Luca Olivieri carried out systematic excavation and published a full report.

The attention paid by archaeologists in the twentieth century has almost certainly been instrumental in causing greater damage to the stupa, as it has alerted looters to the site and the potential to market any finds. We do not know when the relic chamber was broken into, but there is a large hole and tunnel on the north side. This was probably only one of many such activities over the twentieth century culminating in large-scale looting in 2011 that was eventually stopped by police. In February 2012 the stupa was placed under protection. In 2016 the entire archaeological area was acquired by the provincial archaeological authorities. When excavations started in April 2012, the archaeologists were faced with excavating layers that were more than 90 percent disturbed by the illegal diggers and therefore mixed with other material, making stratigraphy almost impossible. Moreover, the illegal diggers had constructed retaining walls and ramps for their wheelbarrows to gain access and carry off finds. Only a few areas were found undisturbed.

But the third millennium has also seen the arrival of a much greater threat. In 2007 the Taliban gained control of the Swat valley. Although driven out by the Pakistan army in 2009, they remain active in this region—as can be seen in the shooting in Mingora of the schoolgirl Malala Yousafzai in 2012. Amluk Dara has survived a millennium of neglect, withstood floods and

109. Tucci (1958).
110. Khan (1968).
111. Khan (1968); D. Faccenna and Spagnesi (2014) reproduce many of Kuwayama's photographs.

earthquakes, and retained its majesty despite looters. However, the actions of the Taliban at the Buddhist site of Bamiyan leave little doubt as to the threat posed in the twenty-first century to this and other Buddhist remains in the Swat.

Despite this, there is a revival of Buddhist activity of the site after so many centuries of neglect. Since 2012 there have been thousands of visitors, many of them delegations of Buddhist monks from countries such as Bhutan, South Korea, Sri Lanka and Thailand who have circumambulated, prayed at, and performed other rituals at Amluk Dara.

FIVE

A Bactrian Ewer

THE GILT-SILVER EWER in plate 4 was discovered in the tomb of a sixth-century general in what is now northwestern China, but it was probably made in Bactria (present-day northern Afghanistan), possibly when the region was under Hephthalite rule.[1] It shows Sasanian Persian techniques and literary motifs from classical Greece with influences from India. The biography of this ewer therefore covers the geographical length of the Silk Road and raises many interesting questions, notably that of the use of objects in defining identity for cultures on the Silk Road. The ewer's antecedents are lengthy, dating back fifteen hundred years before its actual creation to classical Greece far west of its birthplace. Since its burial, it has spent fifteen centuries to the east of its birthplace in northwestern China. Understanding the ewer, its ancestry, production, and life, requires some understanding of the heart of the Silk Road in the ewer's presumed place of production in Bactria in Central Asia, around AD 500.[2] I shall refer to it throughout this chapter as the Bactrian ewer.

For places mentioned in this chapter see Map 1 in the color maps insert.

1. I would like to thank Judith Lerner for her detailed and extremely useful comments on this chapter, and many of the insights are hers. Also thanks to Jorrit Kelder for his thoughts over drinks during my Getty sojourn. All mistakes, misunderstandings, and omissions are my own.

2. This is an approximate production date, although the consensus is not earlier than the fifth century. If the date was in the first half of the fifth century, this would place its production when Bactria was under Sasanian rule.

Bactria, the area of present-day northern Afghanistan, lay between the Hindu Kush mountains to the south and the Amu Darya (Oxus River) to the north.[3] Rivers from the mountains had formed an alluvial plain where irrigation could support extensive agriculture, centered on oasis towns. The capital city, Balkh, was in the west of the kingdom on the Balkh or Band-e Amir River, and its citadel stood on a small rise in the landscape. To the east other cites were Tashkurghan (Stone Fort) on the Khulm River, Kunduz on the Kunduz River, and Ai Khanoum on the Kokcha River where it joins the Amu Darya. Bactria was a crossroads of routes, west to Merv, the Caspian, and Persia, north across the Amu Darya at Termez to Sogdiana and the steppe, east along the valley into the Tarim basin and China, and south to the Bamiyan basin, Kabul, and India. The route south was one of the easiest routes over the Hindu Kush mountains.

Bactria's position in the heart of Central Asia meant that it had many rulers over the years. In the first millennium BC the Achaemenids (ca. 550–330 BC) referred to the satrapy as Bactria and called its people Bactrians. But the name *Bactrians* is also now given to the peoples who ruled from around 250 BC, adopting many Greek practices (and who therefore are also referred to as Greco-Bactrian). A contemporary Roman historian wrote of "the extremely prosperous Bactrian empire of the thousand cities."[4] Examples of the Bactrian language and script—modified from the Greek script—survive from the succeeding Kushan period (first to third centuries AD; see chapter 3). By AD 500 Bactria was the center of the Hephthalite Empire (ca. 450– ca. 550). The Hephthalites, who are mentioned in many sources but whose exact origin is still uncertain, probably came from the north into Bactria,[5] taking

3. I use the name Bactria throughout for clarity, although the region was not always known as this. Leriche and Grenet ([1988] 2011) summarize: "It was in the Kushan period, however, that the name Bactria fell out of use. We do not know what name the region then bore. The geographer Ptolemy, writing in the second half of the second century A.D., states that it was then inhabited mainly by Tochari. In Middle Persian and Armenian, the name Balk denotes only the capital city. By the end of the Kushan period, Bactria had come to be known as Ṭokārestān. After the conquest of the region by the Sasanians, Ṭokārestān formed the core of their province of Kūšānšahr. In the Chinese sources Tu Kho Lo, undoubtedly a transcription of the new name, replaces the older Ta Hsia."

4. Marcus Junianus Justinus, *Epitoma historiarum Philippicarum*, bk. 4, Corpus Scriptorum Latinorum, www.forumromanum.org/literature/justin/texte41.html.

5. Kurbanov summarizes the many views on this subject in the opening chapter of his

it from the Sasanians. Here they made their capital, using the Bactrian script and issuing coins with Bactrian legends—Balkh had long been a mint city.[6] In the late fifth and early sixth centuries they expanded, taking the regions of Gandhāra to the south, Sogdiana to the north, and several of the Tarim states to the east.[7]

The Hephthalites were a significant new presence in Central Asia from the mid-fifth century, worthy of mention in Armenian, Arabic, Persian, Byzantine, Chinese, Indian, and other sources.[8] Why then, do we know so little about them? The textual evidence is fragmentary and sometimes inconsistent, while the archaeological record is currently extremely limited.[9] Their origins, ethnicity, and language are all uncertain.[10] They exemplify many of the issues of studying the Silk Road, when it is all too easy to give precedence to peoples and cultures for whom we have richer sources. What is certain about the Hephthalites is their military strength, as noted by their conquests and by contemporary observers from both ends of the Silk Road, including Chinese historians—who praised their archers—and the Armenian historian Lazar of P'arp (ca. 500), who noted that "even in times of peace the mere sight or mention of a Hephthalite terrified everybody and there was no question of going to war openly against one, for everybody remembers all too clearly the calamities and defeats inflicted by the Hephthalites on the kings of the Aryans and the Persians."[11] In absence of other knowledge of these peoples beyond the idea that they arrived from the north—the steppe—and threatened the settled empires, they were associated by Procopius of Caesurea (ca.

---

thesis and concludes that "most of these theories are based mainly on the often contradictory written sources. . . . The archaeological materials are hardly regarded and even when this is the case only a reduced selection is used to support one view or the other" (2010: 32).

6. Possibly the principal mint in the Kushan period, but certainly in the centuries after. See Bracey (2012: 121–24). See also chapter 2.

7. The taking of Sogdiana is supported by the fact that Sogdian embassies to China ceased and were replaced by Hephthalites (Litvinsky 1996: 140–42).

8. Although, as Judith Lerner and Nicholas Sims-Williams (2011: 18n6) point out, the term has been used somewhat promiscuously by historians, ancient and modern, to designate various groups, all classified as "Hunnic."

9. For a recent survey of the textual and archaeological sources, and the scholarship, see Kurbanov (2010). As he notes: "So far there are no monuments which can be directly connected with them" (37). Also see Sims-Williams (2007) for a discussion of recently discovered Bactrian documents from this period.

10. See La Vaissière (2007, 2009).

11. Cited by Litvinsky (1996: 139).

500–ca. 560), a Byzantine historian, with another steppe alliance, the Huns, who, by this time, were pushing at the borders of Europe.[12]

> Although the Hephthalites are a Hunnish people and are so called, they do not mix and associate with those Huns whom we know, for they do not share any frontier region with them and do not live close to them. . . . They are not nomadic like the other Hunnish peoples, but have long since settled on fertile land. . . . They alone of the Huns are white-skinned and are not ugly. They do not have the same way of life and do not live such bestial lives as the other Huns, but are ruled by one king and possess a legal state structure, observing justice among themselves and with their neighbours in no lesser measure than the Byzantines and Persians.[13]

The comment "white-skinned" has confused many historians, but in his study of the Huns across Eurasia, Hyun Jin Kim suggests that this arises because of their designation as "White Huns." This signified, not their complexion, but rather their position among the tribes: the four cardinal points were indicated with colors, so the White Huns were the Huns of the west.[14] Kim argues that the evidence is strong enough to associate them with the Xiongnu, although with the proviso that, like the Xiongnu, the Hephthalites were a political alliance and almost certainly encompassed many different peoples: "Given the heterogeneous nature of steppe political entities and dynasties, all of the above mentioned ethnicities and 'racial' groups [Turkic, Mongol, Iranian] were probably represented in some way in the White Hun Hephthalite state."[15] The rulers of northern China received Hephthalite embassies at their court from 456 to 559, but Chinese sources are equally uncertain about their origins—some saying they came from Turfan in the northern Tarim and others that they came from Kangju, in present-day southern Kazakhstan. Wei Jie, a seventh-century Chinese envoy to Central Asia, remarks on this confusion about their origins: "I talked per-

12. See Litvinsky (1996: 144) and for a fuller discussion La Vaissière (2007). Enoki originally proposed that they came from the western Himalayas, but this is now generally rejected; La Vaissière reviews this (119–20). See also chapter 1 for a discussion of the interactions between steppe alliances and cultures on their borders.

13. Procopius (1961), quoted in Litvinsky (1996: 136).

14. Kim (2016: 49), citing Pulleyblank (2000b). The other colors were black for north, red for south, and blue for east.

15. Kim (2016: 51 and chap. 3 for whole discussion). He goes on to argue, with La Vaissière and others, that the Xiongnu/Hephthalites were the same political grouping as the Huns who appear in later sources on the western steppe. Many scholars do not agree with this; see chapter 1 above.

sonally with some Hephthalites and discovered that they also called themselves Yituan. . . . This may mean they are descendants of Kangju. However, the information has come from remote countries, and foreign languages are subject to corruption and misunderstanding. Moreover, it concerns matters of very ancient times so we cannot know what is certain. Because of this it is impossible to decide."[16] The archaeological sources do not much help, mainly because there is very little, apart from coins, to identify sites as Hephthalite. One form of identification might lie in the practice of deformation of the skull, whereby babies' skulls are elongated by being bandaged or placed between boards. This is described as a tradition of the Huns in this period and is generally thought to have been transmitted westwards by their migrations.[17] It is found in graves from the Central Asian steppe to the Danube River valley in Europe. The Hephthalites have also been associated with this practice. However, the evidence is not conclusive. First there is the issue of the origins of this practice. Although usually associated with the Huns—on the basis of a Roman-period reference to the deformed Huns, images on coins, and corpses with such deformed skulls in areas and periods known to be Hunnish—an argument has been made that it originated in the Danube and traveled both east and west and might have little to do with the Huns.[18] Then there is the issue of whether deformation of the skull was indeed practiced by the Hephthalites. The evidence for this is again based largely on the portraits found on coins (figure 15). However, some scholars have identified such coins as belonging to Alkhan-Huns and have used these to make a distinction between the Hephthalites and Alkhan groups.[19] Archaeological evidence is problematic: if there is no other evidence to identify graves, we risk circularity if we conclude they are Hephthalite because of the presence of corpses showing skull deformities.[20]

16. From *Tongdian* (a Chinese history written at the beginning of the ninth century), quoted in Enoki (1959: 7) and La Vaissière (2007: 122).

17. Molnar et al. (2014).

18. See Holloway (2014).

19. Vondrovec (2014) and Alram (2016). The Alkhan-Huns are sometimes identified as the tribes of the south, the Red Huns—see note 14 above (Maas 2014: 185).

20. Kurbanov (2010: 41) supposes that the burial dating from the fifth century AD in Bezymyanny (Nameless) mound 4 near Pirmat-Baba-Tepe could relate to the Hephthalites. These two-row burials contained several individuals. On top of five people lay the burial of a man. Procopius of Caesarea notes the collective burials of the Hephthalites. Another indicator for the possibility that the burials belong to Hephthalites is that four of the seven skulls have artificial deformation. But see the discussion on coins below.

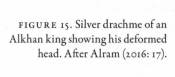

FIGURE 15. Silver drachme of an Alkhan king showing his deformed head. After Alram (2016: 17).

Coins are currently key to our understanding, almost the only firm ground we have among the many quicksands of uncertainties. Although not without issues, combined with the textual sources from neighboring and contemporary empires they can be used to construct a basic chronological narrative.[21] Having emerged as a major power in Central Asia in the mid-fifth century, the Hephthalites quickly expanded in the region.[22] An initial period of peace with their Sasanian neighbors—according to some sources they helped the Sasanian emperor Peroz I (r. 459–84) while he was still a prince[23]—soon came to an end, possibly because of the Hephthalite seizure of Balkh.[24] Peroz duly waged war against the Hephthalites. In the first campaign he was captured and was released only on a ransom paid in part by the Byzantine emperor.[25] He was defeated and captured again in the second campaign. There were insufficient funds in the Sasanian treasury for his ransom, and he left his son

21. See Bivar (2012) for a fuller version.

22. Coins found that date to the fourth century and that have reused the Sasanian dies of Shapur II (r. 309–79) and III (r. 383–88) contained the name Alkhan. These were probably minted in Kabul by the so-called Alkhan Huns. Some scholars have suggested the Alkhan Huns were Hephthalites, but most distinguish between them. Others have suggested that these coins were minted in Balkh, which was taken by Hephthalite/Alkhan peoples around 355. See Vondrovec (2014) and Alram (2016).

23. His younger brother had seized power on the death of their father, taking advantage of Peroz's absence.

24. Reported by the fifth-century Byzantine historian Priscus of Panium, cited in Litvinsky (1996: 138).

25. From a sixth-century Syriac chronicle attributed to Joshua the Stylite (1882: 8).

as a hostage in return for his freedom.[26] On his return home he imposed a poll tax, so raising sufficient funds to redeem his son.[27] Despite this, Peroz went to battle again. The Hephthalite response reveals their sense of themselves as a political power on a par with the Sasanians: "You concluded peace with me in writing, under seal, and you promised not to make war against me. We defined common boundaries not to be crossed with hostile intent by either party." Peroz was killed during this conflict, and in the following years there was peace in which the Hephthalites helped the new ruler, Kawad (r. 488–96) to regain Sasanian territory. The Hephthalites used as their currency the latest coins minted under Peroz—which were the third type of coin minted under Peroz's reign—and later started to replace these with imitations showing what appears to be a ruler with a deformed skull.[28] In the meantime they continued to expand, as far as Turfan in the Tarim basin by the end of the fifth century and north into Sogdiana around 509.[29] However, their rule was short. A subsequent Sasanian emperor, Khusrow I (r. 531–79), joined forces with armies of the Turks (their alliance was sealed by a marriage between Khusrow and the daughter of the Turkic *kaghan*), and they defeated the Hephthalites in a decisive battle near Bukhara around 560.[30] The description of the battle is found in Ferdowsī's poem—the Turks led by their *kahgan* (khan) and the Hephthalites (termed the Haitálians) led by Ghátkar:

Hear how the Khán and the Haitálians fought,

. . . .

Ghátkar heard of the doings of the Khán,
And chose an army from the Haitálians,
An army that obscured the sun, and called
For treasure, money, troops, and arms from Balkh,
Shaknán, Ámwí, the Zam, Khatlán, Tirmid,

26. This was not an uncommon practice.

27. Joshua the Stylite (1882): "He promised in his pride that he would give for the safety of his life thirty mules laden with silver coin; and he sent to his country over which he ruled, but he could hardly collect twenty loads, for by his former wars he had completely emptied the treasury of the king who preceded him. Instead therefore of the other ten loads, he placed with them as a pledge and a hostage his son Kawâd, until he should send them. . . . When he returned to his kingdom, he imposed a poll-tax on his whole country, and sent the ten loads of silver coin, and delivered his son."

28. Göbl (1967, vol. 2: 89–91).

29. Litvinsky (1996: 141).

30. Some sources suggest the marriage happened after the victory.

And Wísagird; he gathered troops from all sides;
From mount and waste, from sands and places bare,
They seethed like ants and locusts. When the Khán
Had passed the mighty river with his host,
With drums and lusty elephants, he massed
His powers round Mái and Margh; the sun became
As dusky as a falcon's plumes

.   .   .   .

As to the issue of that battlefield,
And whom the circling sun and moon would favour.
For one whole week those battle-loving hosts
Were opposites. On all sides lay the slain
In heaps, and dust and stones were cercis-like
With blood. So thick were spear, mace, sparth, and sword
That thou hadst said: "The clouds are raining stones!"
The sun vanished in the reek; dust filled
The eyes of eagles as they flew. It veered,
Upon the eighth day, 'gainst Ghátkar, the world
Was all bedarkened like night azure-dim,
The Haitálians were o'erthrown, irreparably
For years, the wounded scattered everywhere.[31]

The Sasanians and Turks divided the conquered territory between them,
using the Amu Darya as a border line. Menander Protector mentions
that when in AD 568 Turkic envoys arrived in Byzantine Constantinople,
Emperor Justin II (r. 565–74) asked them: "You have subjected all the power
of the Hephthalites?" "All," the envoys replied.[32]

Who were the Hephthalites, and how did they see themselves and choose
to place themselves within this Central Asian Hellenistic world? How did
their contemporaries see them? Did they adapt objects, such as this ewer
and the coins, to assert their own idea of themselves? Etienne de la Vaissière
downplays any strong sense of ethnic identity: "They were, as all the tribal
groupings of that period, an intricate mixture of political and clan relationships, not mainly an ethnic or linguistic entity."[33] But this does not mean

31. Firdausi (1915, vol. 7: 328–33).
32. Blockley (1985: 11).
33. La Vaissière (2007: 124). See also Bernshtam (1951: 119).

that others did not seek to identify them in terms of ethnicity or that at times they did not define themselves in these terms, especially to differentiate themselves from others.[34] As Sian Jones points out in her study of ethnicity: "Ethnic identify is based on shifting, situational, subjective identifications of self and others, which are rooted in on-going daily practice and historical experience, but also subject to transformation and discontinuity."[35]

La Vaissière suggests that the peoples who established the Kidarite regime in Bactria in the fourth century and those known as the Hephthalites might all have migrated into Central Asia from the steppe in the second half of the fourth century in one wave—and not in several, as has been suggested by others.[36] From the little we know from contemporary sources and sparse finds, it seems that one tribal alliance almost immediately allied themselves with the Sasanians, then under Shapur II (r. 309–79), helped them in battle, and minted coins with the word *kydr*—hence Kidarites. They probably established their capital at Balkh and expanded southwards into Gandhāra during the late fourth and early fifth centuries. There is then some evidence of their clash with the Indian Gupta Empire (ca. 320–550) to the south and with the Sasanians to the west and then the rise of the alliance known as the Hephthalites.

During the Kidarite period the Hephthalites did not seem immediately to have adopted a completely sedentary lifestyle, or to have taken over the systems and vocabulary of statehood used by the Kushan (see chapter 3), the previous rulers of this region, as did the Kidarites. They seem to have continued an at least partially nomadic lifestyle into the early sixth century, as reported by the Chinese Buddhist pilgrim, Songyun, who passed through their territories in 519 and noted that the people lived in felt tents, moving from place to place in pursuit of water and pasture. They moved to cooler areas in the summer and to warm regions in winter."[37]

Songyun's itinerary took him well south of Balkh, and it has been suggested that he met the Hephthalites at a summer camp.[38] If the peoples known as the Kidarites and the Hephthalites migrated into Central Asia

---

34. See discussion on the Xianbei below. I take here a processual approach to ethnic identity, as discussed in Jones (1996).

35. Jones (1996: 14).

36. La Vaissière (2007: 121–22) argues there was one wave of migration, from about 350 to 370, which included peoples who were formally part of the Xiongnu alliance.

37. Chavannes (1903b: 403–4).

38. Although he was traveling in the tenth month, well into winter. Given the itinerary

around the same time, it could be that the latter's retaining of elements of their former steppe lifestyle was a way of distinguishing themselves from their Kidarite fellow migrants—who were starting to assimilate into the local culture.[39] As Jones points out, assertion of ethnic identity is often a process to distinguish one's own group from another group. A parallel can be seen in the history of the Xianbei peoples, who had come into northern China from the steppe and established the Northern Wei (386–534). The deliberate push from their rulers to assimilate further into a Chinese world—moving their capital south and taking on Chinese dress and language, for example—caused a reaction from other Xianbei who set up an alternative regime, as discussed below. We know much more about the Xianbei than we do about the Kidarites/Hephthalites, but it is not an unreasonable assumption that the continuation of a nomadic lifestyle by the Hephthalites was as much a reaction to their fellow migrants' rejection of this shared past and a wish to remain distinct from them.

But at some point very soon after this, as La Vaissière puts it, "The Hephthalites went Bactrian."[40] Procopius, reporting in the second quarter of the sixth century, notes their settled lifestyle and distinctions from the still pastoralist Huns. And this was confirmed at the end of their rule by Menander, who reported an exchange between the Sogdian ambassador and the Byzantine emperor: "Do they live in cities or villages?" "My Lord, that people live in cities."[41] During their short reign from Balkh the Hephthalites appear to have adapted much of the existing administrative culture. Bactrian manuscripts suggest an orderly administration in which Bactrian was the official language and taxes were collected.[42] Some of the names of their early

---

in his account, he must have met them in southern Badakhshan, somewhere not far west of the Wakhan.

39. Although we need to be careful with assuming that the adoption of a certain lifestyle by the ruling elite was followed by all: the Chinese history *Beishi* notes that the Kidarites "move around following their herds, thus resembling the Xiongnu" (quoted in Zürcher 1968: 373–74).

40. La Vaissière (2007: 123).

41. This dating is from one of the Bactrian documents from Rob (present-day Ruy, near Bamiyan); see Sims-Williams (2000: 32–33). However, to date we have no structural remains that can be considered as Hephthalite (thanks to Judith Lerner for noting this).

42. The sixth-century historian Procopius of Caesarea says that they "live in a prosperous territory, are the only Huns with fair complexions, do not live as nomads, acknowledge a single king, observe a well-regulated constitution, and behave justly towards neighbouring states." He also describes the burial of their nobles in tumuli, accompanied by the boon companions who were their retainers in their lifetimes.

kings were Iranian, suggesting the influence of their Sasanian neighbors.[43] We also know that, on gaining control of the region, they used Sasanian mints to produce coins, using first the old dies and then new ones.

Apart from the coins, we have very little in terms of material culture that we can label as Hephthalite. Is this a lack of our knowledge, a reflection of the actual paucity of remains, or a result of Hephthalites' assimilation into the existing cultures? Probably all three factors play a role, but it limits our understanding and interpretation of objects created under their rule. Their contemporaries, as we have seen, also struggled to place them—Procopius striving to link them with the Huns, despite obvious differences, and the Chinese admitting confusion.

The attitude of the Hephthalites to religion is uncertain, and their tolerance or otherwise of existing religions—especially Buddhism—has been the subject of much discussion, but there is evidence for Zoroastrian, Buddhist, Manichaean, and Christian communities in Balkh, and also for the influence of Hinduism from India.[44] The religion of the Hephthalites themselves is not known, but Procopius mentions that they buried their dead in tumuli, often with companions. Although many sites have been excavated in this region, it is difficult to attribute any specifically to the Hephthalites, and finds are sparse. Among these are wall paintings and some statues and metal vessels.[45]

MINING AND METALWORKING IN CENTRAL ASIA

Central Asia has a particularly complex geological history leading to rich resources of metals and minerals. The major lapis mines of the Silk Road lie in present-day Badakhshan on the Kokcha River to the southeast of Balkh,[46] and there are many gold deposits along the Amu Darya valley. The Hephthalites inherited and continued the existing technologies of min-

43. La Vaissière (2007: 122–23).

44. See Nattier (1991: 110–17) for a discussion of the Hephthalite persecution of Buddhism.

45. See Kurbanov (2010: 73–86), although, as he notes, many of these identifications are tentative: for example, the Balalyk paintings are dated by some as post-Hephthalite (76).

46. Rubies and spinel are also found, the latter from mines in Badakhshan, although whether they were exploited as early as this is not known (Hughes 2013). Emerald is found in the Panshjr valley in Kapisa Province.

FIGURE 16. Design on the outside of the Chilek bowl, showing the bust on the base. After Dani, Litvinsky, and Zamir Safi (1996: fig. 18).

ing, minting of coins, and metalworking. Hephthalite coins originally were based on those of the Sasanian king Peroz I, whom the Hephthalites had defeated in 485. The silver drachmas showed his bust and the mint name *baxlo* (Balk) on the back: the additional legend in front of the bust, *eb*, has been interpreted as ēbodalo (Hephthal), supported by its appearance on other Hephthalite coins.[47] It is more difficult to ascribe specific metal ware to the Hephthalites, but pieces that have been tentatively identified, such as the Chilek bowl (figure 16) and a similar piece now in the British Museum, show a high level of skill.

The bowl was found at the village of Chilek near Samarkand in 1961.[48] It depicts six female figures. There is a bust on the base similar to that of the king's figure found on Alkhan coins. It is hammered with a repoussé design. The second, a silver-gilt piece, was given to the British Museum in 1912 with

47. Alram (1986). Although this does not prove the Hephthalites produced them.
48. It is held in the Samarkand Museum. See Litvinsky (1996: 160 and figs. 17 and 18).

the information that it had been found in the Swat valley.[49] It depicts four scenes with mounted hunters, with one of the stirrupless riders driving his spear down into his prey, similar in composition to the theme of the textile discussed in chapter 8 and common throughout West and Central Asia by this time. The museum identifies it as cast rather than hammered.

The minting of coins by the Hephthalites almost as soon as they took power and the fact that the coins were based on Sasanian models add credence to the idea that the Hephthalites inherited a metalworking tradition that they valued and used for their own political and cultural purposes. It is therefore also possible that they produced other wares, such as these bowls, adapting the designs to fit the demands or taste of their new patrons. There is no evidence of Hephthalite metalworking before, although the absence of evidence at this stage in our understanding means little. Metalworking is found from earliest times among both Eurasian steppe and settled communities, and the discovery and control of mines, especially those giving the metals required for stronger alloys such as bronze, are an important part of understanding the movement and meeting of peoples in ancient times.[50]

Among the metals known and used in the ancient world, silver and gold were the softest. Gold is often found in a pure form, in nuggets, and is workable as it is found. Other metals are found in ores and require heat to separate them from the rock, but these techniques were discovered early in human history. By the start of what we now call the Silk Road, all its peoples had metals, used for weapons, instruments, vessels, and ornaments. However, distinctions could be seen in the metals used and the forms they took. The gold working of the steppe peoples is discussed in chapter 1, while in West Asia through to Central Asia gold and silver wares were essential accouterments for the elite. In China, however, the elite associated themselves with objects in bronze and jade, materials valued more highly than gold and silver.

Silver at this time was primarily obtained by extraction from lead ores—although smaller amounts probably came from silver ores. The extraction process involved smelting the lead ore under reducing and/or oxidizing conditions to produce lead metal. Silver was then extracted by a process called cupelation—a cupel being a shallow and porous container. The lead metal was heated in the cupel under strongly oxidizing conditions, and the lead

49. British Museum, reg. no. 1963,1210.1.
50. For example, see the discussion on the sources of the copper and tin found in the Uluburun shipwreck, discussed in chapter 2.

oxide (litharge) that was duly formed was absorbed by porous material in the cupel. This material was usually made of bone or ground-up potsherds. The silver metal was left behind. This might be repeated several times. This process was probably carried out close to the mines. Adding copper to the silver improved its workability and this might also have been obtained from local mines.

Silverware, such as this ewer, used this alloy of silver and copper. Analysis has shown that, in the Sasanian tradition, objects such as ewers were made by hammering.[51] A sheet of silver was hammered into the correct shape, and the decoration was also hammered into the object—a method known as repoussé (from behind or over a mold). The handle was possibly cast by the lost-wax method. Sometimes the feet and lid were also made separately. The nonrelief sections were then painted with an amalgam of gold and mercury: gilding had originally been painted onto relief sections, but because of its tendency to run by the fifth and sixth centuries it was more commonly painted onto the background sections.

This is what we know of Sasanian silverware. Our subject here, the Bactrian ewer, was probably made in a region neighboring Sasania that had previously been under their rule. But Bactria also had a long tradition of metalworking: the Bactrian envoys depicted at Persepolis, capital of the Achaemenids (ca. 550–330 BC), are bearing gifts of cups and bowls, assumed to be their productions. Later, Bactria was influenced by Hellenistic wares, both metal and ceramics. And we must not forget the metalworking skills of the steppe peoples. The form and decorative elements of the ewer suggest a dialogue with other traditions, even if it contains elements that make it distinct.

The form, the ewer, is found in Sasanian metalwork from the fifth century, but several decorative elements set it apart from other Sasanian silverware as far as we know it. First, the handles of Sasanian pieces are usually square in section with terminals of onagers' heads and a ball-shaped thumb rest at the top. This piece has a hexagonal handle with terminals of camels' heads and a thumb rest shaped like a human head. Second, Sasanian pieces typically have a single register on the body, whereas this has two. Third, Sasanian pieces from this period often show no decoration on the neck and foot, whereas this has convex moldings and beaded decoration. A typical Sasanian piece that

---

51. P. Harper and Meyers (1981: 148).

shows these differences is a gilt-silver ewer dated stylistically to the sixth century, now at the Metropolitan Museum of Art.[52]

The beading and the double register on the Bactrian ewer are more typical of Roman wares of the fourth and fifth centuries AD. Several spectacular sets of silverware have been found from this period, and there are also depictions of silver tableware, such as on paintings at Pompeii. Ewers are typically part of these sets, including the fifth-century Sevso Treasure.[53] This group of silver objects contained the Dionysiac ewer, sixteen inches (forty-one centimeters) high, gilded with the revels of Bacchus. Such scenes from the stories and myths of ancient Greece decorate much of this silverware, the drunken revels of Bacchus being particularly appropriate for ewers for holding wine. Another piece, a Roman gilt-silver ewer from the first century, shows a scene from the Trojan War.[54] And we need to follow this tradition to understand the decoration of our Bactrian ewer. But to do so we must travel back over a thousand years before the start of the Silk Road and move west over three thousand miles onto its fringes, to ancient Greece.

THE TROJAN WAR

One of the enduring and oft-retold stories of ancient Greece was the Trojan War cycle. This story, possibly related to actual events from prehistorical times, tells of the ten-year siege of Troy by Greek armies after Paris of Troy took Helen from her husband, Menelaus of Sparta.[55] The story is found recounted in several surviving sources, including two epic poems ascribed to the eighth-century BC poet Homer, namely the *Iliad* and the *Odyssey*. These give only episodes, the former a period of weeks in the life of two of the protagonists, King Agamemnon and Achilles, and their dispute, and the latter

52. "Ewer with Dancing Females within Arcades," Heilbrunn Timeline, Metropolitan Museum of Art, www.metmuseum.org/toah/works-of-art/67.10a,b.

53. See Rosenthal-Heginbottom (2013).

54. From the Berthouville Treasure, a pitcher with scenes from the Trojan War. It depicts Achilles dragging the body of Hector around the walls of Troy. See Lapatain (2014: 53–56) and the images at *Ancient Luxury and the Roman Silver Treasure from Berthouville*, November 19, 2014–August 17, 2015, Getty Villa, J. Paul Getty Museum, www.getty.edu/art/exhibitions/ancient_luxury/.

55. There is continued debate over whether the accounts reflect an actual war, with belief that it might be a war of the twelfth-century BC. Troy is most commonly identified with Hisarlik in eastern Turkey. For a recent of the evidence, see Easton et al. (2002).

describing the return home of one of the war's heroes, Odysseus. Another cycle of poems recounts the whole course of the battle, but it is only partially extant and mainly survives in quotations in later sources. The poems are all believed to have existed alongside an oral tradition.

Illustrations from the Trojan War cycle are extant from the beginning of the seventh century BC, commonly found depicted on Greek vases from the sixth century BC but also on wall paintings.[56] Among the commonly depicted episodes are the judgment of Paris, the abduction of Helen, and the reunion of Helen and Menelaus. Paris is a Trojan prince and, as a young man, is charged by the gods with the task of selecting the most beautiful of the goddesses and presenting her with a golden apple engraved with "For the Fairest." He is herding animals on a mountainside when he is informed of this task by the messenger god, Hermes. Three goddesses come to him to be judged: Hera, Athena, and Aphrodite. Aphrodite wins by promising Paris that she will help him woo and win Helen, the most beautiful mortal woman, despite her already being married to Menelaus. He duly presents her with the apple.

The story continues. Paris visits Menelaus in Sparta, who is then called away to attend a funeral. In his absence, Paris successfully seduces Helen with Aphrodite's help and takes her back to Troy. This results in the ten-year Trojan War, at the end of which Troy falls and Helen is reunited with Menelaus.

Pots survive in comparative abundance from Greece in the first millennium BC. The black figure style—which appears in Corinth from about the end of the seventh century BC—is followed a century later by the red-figure style initiated in Athens, each in black and red showing the painted figures against a contrasting background. Both styles spread through the Greek world, and both carry depictions of the Trojan War.[57] They are found up to the fourth and third centuries BC. The extant scenes of the judgment of Paris are depicted in several ways, but often with Paris among his herds playing his lyre and the goddesses lining up for judgment with Hermes nearby. The apple is rarely seen. In these early examples, the goddesses are clothed in the traditional ankle-length Greek tunic, the chiton. The scene is also shown on other media such as the terracotta plaques on the wall of a mid-

56. Woodford (2003).

57. For examples, see the online British Museum resource, "Ancient Greece: Myths and Legends," https://www.britishmuseum.org/PDF/Visit_Greece_Myths_KS2.pdf.

sixth-century BC Etruscan tomb. Bronze, gold, and silver vessels were also being produced at this time, although few have survived—presumably they were melted down and their metal was reused. Both casting and hammering techniques were used: the remains of molds, matrices, and stamps have all been found at production sites across the region.[58] These sometimes show Greek deities, but there is too little evidence to confirm whether they were decorated with Trojan War scenes, like the Greek pottery. However, during this period it may be assumed that the story continued to be read and to be recounted by storytellers and was therefore widely recognized throughout the Greek world.

In the fourth century BC the Greek world expanded dramatically, thanks to the campaigns of the king of Macedon later known as Alexander the Great (r. 336–323 BC). For most of his adult life he sought to expand his territories eastwards and was largely successful. He reached Bactria in 329 BC and conquered it over the next two years. On his victory in 327 he took a bride, Roxane, who is usually described by historians as a Bactrian, daughter of Oxyartes.[59] Although Alexander's rule did not last long—he died in Babylon in 323 BC, possibly as a result of poisoning—the introduction of Greek language, administration, architecture, art, and culture eastwards into Central Asia was to have a significant influence, the so-called Hellenization of this region.[60] And this influence might have spread further east: some scholars have attributed to it the appearance of life-size realistic statuary in China—exemplified by the terracotta warriors guarding the tomb of Qin Shihuangdi (r. 221–206 BC)—suggesting its spread across the whole of Eurasia.[61]

After the death of Alexander, Bactria came under the rule of the Seleucids (312–63 BC), whose empire spread, at its height, from the shores of the Mediterranean. Greek elites dominated in the cities and were replenished by new migrants from the homeland. Hellenization was therefore an ongoing process, receiving new impetus and ideas from migrants, diplomats, traders, and soldiers and being adapted and assimilated by each new generation. But

58. Treister (2001: 382).

59. Some historians identify Oxyartes as a Sogdian.

60. Rotroff (2007: 140–41), however, makes the important point that Hellenization does not necessarily make itself immediately felt in the material culture, citing the case of classical pottery, which continued unchanged into the third century. "Clearly, it takes a long time for military and political events to have an effect on the way people make things" (141).

61. An idea long discussed in relation to Buddhism (see, e.g., Grousset 1948), but for this more controversial and more recent argument see Nickel (2013).

it did not necessarily overwhelm local traditions. For example, Greek Attic black gloss wares are seen in the early Seleucid Empire but then disappear by the third century, while in Mesopotamia the Greek pottery forms made in the local green-glazed ware and the fine eggshell ware, typical of the locality, continued to be produced alongside these.[62]

The Seleucids did not hold onto their Central Asian territory for long—they were driven out of Bactria and Persia by the Parthians in the mid-third century BC and thereafter ruled from bases in Syria. A local governor declared himself ruler of Sogdiana, Bactria, and Margiana in the mid-third century, and a marriage alliance in 210 BC between the Seleucid emperor's daughter and the local ruler consolidated the autonomy of what has been called the Greco-Bactrian kingdom (256–125 BC).[63] Seleucid and Bactrian coins show kings in the style of portraits of Alexander with Greek legends and Greek deities, such as Zeus, Apollo, and Heracles, on their obverse. Although it is uncertain about how united it remained over the following two centuries, Hellenistic influence certainly survived as aspects—such as the modified Greek script and the coinage—were adopted by the Kushans, who came to power by the first century AD (see Chapter 3).[64]

For a long time, historians and archaeologists sought to reconcile contemporary accounts of the richness of the Greco-Bactrian kingdom with the paucity of the archaeological remains. The Greek historian Strabo (63 BC–AD 24) described it as "Bactria of the thousand towns," but archaeologists throughout the twentieth century dug in vain at the presumed site of the ancient Bactrian city of Balkh, leading the French archaeologist Albert Foucher (1865–1952) to declare a "Bactrian mirage."[65] But in 1964 the remains of a large city were discovered at Ai Khanoum, east of Balkh on the junction of the Amu Darya and Kokcha Rivers. Over a decade of excavations followed, led by Paul Barnard, and the city was identified as the capital of eastern Bactria. Hellenistic influences are seen in the remains of typical Greek structures, such as a *heroon* (monument to the founder), a gymnasium, a theater, a fountain with sculptures, and peristyle courts.[66] But archaeologists have suggested that the large, centrally placed palace and the upper-class dwell-

---

62. Rotroff (2007: 147). See also Momigliano (1979).
63. Leriche and Grenet ([1988] 2011).
64. Mairs (2013) discusses the ethnic identity of this region.
65. "Bactrien mirage" (Foucher 1942–47: 73–75, 310).
66. Bernard (1981).

ings are clearly influenced by Iranian concepts, while the temples and the fortifications show signs of Mesopotamian inspiration.[67] As Rachel Mairs points out, looking from outside in time and place we risk viewing Bactria as "the somewhat schizophrenic sum of these influences, without sufficient attention being paid to the organic whole—the Bactrian polity and community—which these diverse influences combined to create."[68]

In addition to what we describe as Corinthian columns and sculptures of Greek gods uncovered in Ai Khanoum, silver and gold items have come to light from this period that show enduring Hellenistic themes. Most famous among these are the so-called Bactrian hoard, finds from a temple and tombs of the first century AD in Tillya Tepe dating from the end of the Greco-Bactrian period and the start of the Kushan.[69] These include an appliqué known as the "Aphrodite of Bactria" and rings showing Athena with her name inscribed in Greek.[70] Other finds tentatively dated to the Greco-Bactrian period (although their provenance is not certain) include three vessels with designs that have been interpreted as illustrations from the Greek playwright Euripides (480–406 BC). They are all hammered with repoussé designs.[71] Kurt Wietzmann suggests that they were modeled on earlier Greek and Hellenistic examples, where the story was often shown over several vessels.[72] But he also notes the changes from the assumed originals, particularly in the drapery: "The first changes in the process of copying even where the actions and the outlines of the figures are unchanged, occur usually in the treatment of the drapery. The shape of the woman's chiton on the New York bowl is no longer understood, and the manner in which it spreads in waves over the ground points to an intrusion of an oriental element."[73]

The chiton was a typical Greek form of clothing made of wool or linen and held at the shoulder. Women wore it ankle length, gathered below the

67. Bernard (1981); Barnard, Besenval, and Marquis (2006).
68. Mairs (2013: 370).
69. Excavated in 1978 and now in Kabul Museum (Sarianidi 1985). There have been worldwide exhibits, including Washington, D.C. (Hiebert and Cambon 2007). See chapter 3 for more on the Kushan.
70. The hoard also includes finds showing Indian, Chinese, and steppe influences.
71. Treister (2001).
72. Although, stylistically, these three pieces are dated over several centuries.
73. Wietzmann (1943: 319).

bust and sometimes with the extra material looping over the belt. On the vessel described by Wietzmann, the chiton falls below the feet and spreads over the ground. This is also clearly seen on the later Sasanian ewer from the Metropolitan Museum, where the women are bare-breasted. The motif seen on this latter vessel, of women dancing under arcades holding various attributes such as vessels and flowers, is also usually associated with imagery relating to Dionysius, the Greek god of wine and theater. Some scholars have suggested that, although this had its origins in ancient Greece, it had been assimilated into Sasanian culture as part of the cult of Anahita, the Iranian goddess of water and fertility.[74] Others propose that the motifs, although taken from Roman or Greco-Roman iconography, were associated by this time in Sasanian Persia with local seasonal festivals.[75]

While we can see aspects of the Greek legacy being adopted into Roman culture, and while it is plausible to believe that the designs of the Trojan war on, for example, the first-century Roman gilt-silver ewer mentioned above were readily understood by many, it is more difficult to grapple with how such images were viewed by the peoples on what was once the fringes of Alexander's empire. And if this was the case in the time of the Greco-Bactrian kingdom and the rise of the Kushan in the first century AD, then it would be even more so in Hephthalite Bactria several centuries later. But we should not totally dismiss the enduring power of stories: for example, the subjects of paintings and texts in seventh-eighth century Sogdiana have been plausibly identified as variations on *Aesop's Fables*.[76] Thus, when Boris Marshak and Anazawa Wakou suggested that the scenes on the Bactrian ewer were episodes from the Trojan War cycle, many scholars accepted this theory.[77] But we must remember that it is only a hypothesis and that even if the episodes can be traced back to a Greek mythology they might have been incorporated into some other narrative by this time and would have been described by their makers/owners in a way that we might not recognize. We simply do not know.

74. Shepherd (1964: 66–92); Ettinghausen (1967–68: 29–41); Trever (1967: 121–32).

75. P. Harper (1971: 503–15); Carter (1974: 171–202).

76. Possibly originating in India and moving westwards. For paintings at Penjikent, see Marshak (2002) and Compareti (2012). For texts, see the site Turfanforschung (http://turfan.bbaw.de/front-page-en?set_language=en). See also Zieme et al. (n.d.).

77. Marshak and Anazawa (1989). Reproduced several times since, including in Juliano and Lerner (2001), Watt et al. (2004), and Whitfield (2009: 89, cat. 55).

FIGURE 17. Design on the ewer.

THE BACTRIAN EWER

Let us return, then, to the Bactrian ewer and look at its design in more detail. The decorative frieze depicts three scenes, each showing a man and a woman (figure 17). Following Marshak and Anazawa's identifications, we see the judgment of Paris, the abduction of Helen, and the return of Helen. The first scene shows Paris and Aphrodite. In classical Greek art, Aphrodite's attributes include a magic girdle, a gold crown or stephane, and an apple, the last referring to this episode and hence to her beauty. She regularly appears seminaked or naked. Here the figure is clothed in a tunic somewhat like the Greek chiton, tied at the waist with the cloth falling over it. A belt below her bust possibly represents the magic girdle and the tiara-style headdress, the stephane. Unlike the other female figures, she is wearing earrings. The fingers of her left hand touch her chin. She is holding something between her thumb and forefinger of her right hand, but it does not seem to be an apple. Paris holds two objects that could be apples, although, of course, in the original story he has only one apple to give away. He is also wearing a Greek-style tunic, this one at knee length, and calf-high boots.

In the scene to the left—going clockwise—that has been identified as the abduction of Helen, the female figure is similarly clothed but without the girdle or earrings. The man is naked except for a cloak over his shoulders, a helmet, and the same boots. The gesture, with his fingers touching her chin, is recognizable as the typical love gesture in Greek art. His other hand holds her wrist. Although there is no ship depicted, she is shown stepping upwards, plausibly as if onto a ship.

In the third scene Helen wears a different headdress. She is shown face on in a pose—often called the *tribhaṅga* or tri-bent pose—typical of Indian art. It is found on contemporary statues of bodhisattvas, for example, from India and Central Asia through the Tarim and into China. The folds of the fabric over her hips—rather than below the bust as is common on many Greek representations—are also reminiscent of Indian art, as is the way the fabric folds and clings to the legs. She too is touching her chin with the fingers of one hand, her right. Her left arm is bent to hold a small container. Boris Marshak suggested this represents the box of treasures previously stolen by Helen and Paris from her husband. The male figure, assumed to be her husband, Menelaus, has a spear and a shield, showing his warrior status, although he seems to be leaning on the shield without it having any visible means of support. He is also dressed in the short Greek tunic but, like the women, wears sandals. How much of this iconography was chosen deliberately to identify the figures and their feelings or actions, and how much was copied without an understanding of the significance, is an open question.

THE JOURNEY TO CHINA

We do not know how the Bactrian ewer piece traveled east from its presumed Central Asian production site into northern China or how, where, or when it came into the hands of the general Li Xian (502–69), but we do know something about Li Xian, as he was important enough to receive biographies in two Chinese histories: *Zhoushu* (History of the Northern Zhou; 557–81) and *Beishi* (History of the Northern Dynasties). His tomb, in which the ewer was discovered, also contains epitaph tablets for him and his wife. All these tell us that Li Xian was born in 502 to a prominent family in the Guyuan area—in present-day Ningxia Province, China, where the tomb is located, then under the rule of the Northern Wei. His family were migrants to this area. The biographies record that his tenth-generation ancestor Yidigui had come southwest from the steppe across the Yin Mountains.[78] These mountains mark the southeastern border of the Gobi Desert in Mongolia, start-

78. Assuming twenty to twenty-five years for a generation, this would have put the migration south to the third century.

ing at the northernmost part of the Yellow River where it loops around the Ordos. They extend northwest, passing by present-day Beijing—a provincial city under the Northern Wei—and into the Manchurian region north of the Korean peninsula. Guyuan is within the Yellow River loop to the south of the Ordos Desert. The biographies record that before settling in Guyuan, Li Xian's great-grandfather, who had already taken the Chinese surname Li, was General of Pacifying the West and was the prefectural governor in the Tianshui area in present-day Gansu Province. This was further south on the main route leading from the previous Chinese capital of Chang'an (present-day Xian) to the Tarim, an important section of the Silk Road. Li Xian's father probably moved the family to the Guyuan area. We do not know whether they had retained their own language—or indeed what this was, but probably an Altaic language—or whether they spoke Chinese at home. But, as we see from the biographies, they had not lost the knowledge of their northern steppe ancestry.

China was culturally complex, with waves of invaders and migrants especially from the porous and oft-challenged borders to the north and north-west.[79] We should not assume that it was accustomed to being unified or that everyone in the region we now know as China saw this as the norm or ideal. At this time northern China and west into the Hexi corridor was under the Northern Wei dynasty. They were a clan of the Xianbei who came from the northern steppe. China had not been united since the fall of the Han in 206 AD. The Northern Wei are immensely important in our understanding of China's role in the Silk Road, as it was during their reign that Buddhism became embedded in northern China. Their patronage of Buddhism is exemplified by the two large Buddhist cave temple complexes, Yungang and Longmen, near the Northern Wei's successive capitals of Datong and Luoyang. With their rule extending along the routes west from the Yellow River valley into the Tarim, security for pilgrims and traders was ensured.

At the birth of Li Xian the Northern Wei were ruling from Luoyang on the Yellow River, but the empire was in trouble. Rebellions in the north and battles between competing factions led to its division in 534. One of the reasons given for this unrest was the growing divide between the regional rulers in the north, still retaining their contacts with the steppe, and what they saw as the increasingly distant and sinified elite in the capital. The capital had

79. Like all the settled empires on the borders of the steppe; for a broader discussion of this interaction, see Christian (1998) and chapter 1.

been moved south to near Luoyang on the Yellow River in 494, and a series of reforms were passed that included the banning of Xianbei clothing at court, the necessity to learn Chinese, and the need to adopt Chinese one-syllable surnames. People were moved from the steppe to populate the new capital. The emperor who introduced these measures had a Chinese mother, and his move to Luoyang and his reforms were a signal of a process of sinicization: a move away from the existing ethnic identity as military and steppe peoples, separate from the Chinese.

This unrest led to the fall of the Northern Wei. Guyuan fell within the territory of the succeeding Western Wei (535–57) controlled by Yuwen Tai (506–56), a powerful Xianbei military commander who established his capital in Chang'an. The Eastern Wei (534–50) controlled most of the territory of northern China to the east of the Yellow River, including the former capital of Luoyang. Li Xian rose through the military ranks under the Western Wei and was trusted with the command of strategic points on the western borders, including that of Dunhuang, which had first been established as a military garrison by the Chinese Han dynasty at the end of the second century BC. He lived to see Yuwen Tai's son seize the throne from the final emperor of their rivals, the Eastern Wei, and establish a new empire—that of the Northern Zhou (557–81). However, the territory east of the Yellow River bend, formerly under the Eastern Wei, remained under separate control. The Northern Zhou expanded, but south rather than east to the borders of what is now Vietnam. The next two emperors were also Yuwen Tai's sons, and it was during the reign of the first, Yuwen Yong (r. 561–78), that Li Xian died (569).

As a military commander posted to frontier stations, Li Xian would have traveled considerably, and many of his travels would have taken him along the trade routes of the Silk Road as well as to the capital to give reports and receive orders. We do not know how the Bactrian ewer came into his possession: there are several possibilities. It could, for example, have been taken to the Northern Wei or Northern Zhou court as a gift by one of the Hephthalite embassies that visited between 456 and 559. We know also the Li Xian was governor of Dunhuang, which had by this time become a thriving Silk Road town with wealth and patrons to start excavating Buddhist cave temples of their own in sites around the town. He would have had access to the markets and the merchants passing through. As prefectural governor, he would presumably have been presented with gifts by prominent local families keen to secure his favor. And he might have taken booty or simply seized objects he coveted from areas under his control. So we do not know when or where or from whom he acquired the ewer. We can assume that it was only one among many valuable objects acquired by the family.[80] When his granddaughter died, at the age of nine, her tomb was also furnished with silver and gold vessels.[81]

There is one possible direct connection between Li Xian and the Hephthalites, discussed by Wu Zhuo. A Hephthalite envoy passed through Guyuan en route to Luoyang around 525.[82] He was reported to have been taking a lion as a diplomatic gift and was delayed at Guyuan owing to a rebellion. He reached the capital after this: the fate of the lion is not recorded, but it was not a unique gift. There are records of lions being presented to the Chinese by the Tocharians in the seventh and eighth centuries, and another sent from Samarkand in 635 received an imperially commissioned rhapsody in its honor.[83] Li Xian would have been only a young man, but given the status of his family it would be expected that they would have met and entertained the envoy during his enforced stay.[84] It is possible that his family entertained later envoys en route to the capital or that Li Xian met then during his border postings or in the imperial court. By 508 the Hephthalites had taken Karashahr and Turfan in the Tarim, and Li Xian would have been well aware of them as both a political ally and a potential threat to the Northern Wei borders.

How did Li Xian see and use the ewer? Was it an exotic piece brought out for formal banquets, filled with the local grape wine for his guests and intended to reflect his status and cosmopolitanism? Or was it used at less formal occasions—or not used at all?[85] For all we know, he might have acquired it only shortly before his death and never put it to use. These are tantalizing

---

80. Others are known from his tomb, although most contents were probably robbed. See below.

81. Princess Li Jingxun (d. 608). Her ancestry shows how the Li clan continued to thrive: her maternal grandparents were an emperor of the Northern Zhou and the daughter of the first emperor of the Sui dynasty and sister of the second emperor. She was buried near Xian and her tomb was excavated in 1957. For examples of the objects, see Watt et al. (2004: cats. 186–88).

82. Wu (1989: 66, 68).

83. For translation, see Schafer (1963: 85).

84. He also spent time as a young man in the imperial court as a companion to the young emperor.

85. Although we know a fair amount about the eating and drinking culture of the Greeks and Romans, and the use of similar ewers, little is known of the Xianbei. For their tombs, see Dien (1991).

questions but ones on which we can only speculate. The same goes for what Li Xian made of the design on the ewer. Did he know anything of the Trojan War story, even if it had become assimilated into local myths? Or was the piece interpreted as depicting another local story? Or not interpreted at all, just seen as an attractive or an exotic design? Not all people ask questions about the world around them and the objects they encounter. Indeed, perhaps this ewer was of more interest and value to his wife: theirs was a joint tomb. Then there is the question of why it was buried with them. This is also a question on which we can only speculate, especially as we do not know the original tomb inventory.[86]

Li Xian was presumably buried in 569 shortly after his death in Chang'an. His wife, Wu Hui, had died in 547, and she was removed from her original resting place in her family cemetery and reentombed with him.[87] The ewer lay in the tomb from Li Xian's death until the site was excavated by Chinese archaeologists in 1983.[88] Robbers had broken into the tomb before then, but the roof had collapsed on top of the ewer and so they probably did not see it. Again, we can do no more than speculate about what they might have taken and whether this included other silverwares. Along with his wife's seal ring, a Sasanian glass bowl and a Sasanian sword survived the robbery. The Bactrian ewer is now in the collection of the Guyuan Museum, where Li Xian's tomb is reproduced. It has traveled to many exhibitions both in China and abroad.[89]

86. Because of robbery.
87. She was found with a gold ring with a Sasanian seal.
88. Shaanxi sheng kaogu yanjiusuo (2005).
89. Including Zagreb (Lukšić 1996), New York (the Asia Society [Juliano and Lerner 2001] and the Metropolitan Museum of Art [Watt et al. 2004]), and Brussels (Whitfield 2009).

SIX

A Khotanese Plaque

THE WOODEN PLAQUE in plate 5 with a triangular top is painted with images of a dappled horse and a camel. The rider of each animal is haloed, wears a sword hanging from his left side, and holds a bowl in his right hand. The back of the plaque has five holes that were probably used for dowels to fix it to a wall. It was discovered during excavation of Buddhist ruins in the eastern Silk Road kingdom of Khotan at a site, now deep in the Taklamakan Desert, called Dandan-Uliq, or the "Place of Ivories." Scholars have variously dated this object to the sixth to eighth centuries and have assumed, on the basis of its find context and other objects found nearby, that it was created as a Buddhist religious object. This assumption is reinforced by the halo, common to saints, divinities, and sometimes rulers in both Judeo-Christian and Buddhist contexts. However, a century later, elements of the iconography remain puzzling.[1]

The plaque was discovered in 1900 by the archaeologist Marc Aurel Stein (1862–1943) on the first of his four expeditions to Chinese Central Asia.[2] Dandan-Uliq had previously been visited by the Swedish explorer Sven Hedin (1865–1953), who carried out preliminary excavations there. But Stein's

---

For places mentioned in this chapter see Map 6 in the color maps insert.

1. I must thank Joanna Williams for her interest in—and thesis on—Khotanese art, which discussed this piece, for drawing my attention to it, and for reading this chapter; to Yidriss Abdurusal and his colleagues at the Xinjiang Institute of Archaeology for enabling my travels to see many of the sites of ancient Khotan; and to Zsuzsanna Gulácsi for reading this chapter. All mistakes, misunderstandings, and omissions are my own.

2. On Stein, see Mirsky (1998) and Walker (1998). For Stein's popular and scholarly accounts of his first expedition, see Stein (1904, 1907).

was the first systematic excavation of the Silk Road towns and temples long covered by the desert sands of the Taklamakan.[3] He had come to Khotan, described in Chinese sources in the first millennium AD as a prosperous Buddhist kingdom, as he believed it would be a place where Indian, Iranian, and Chinese influences met and mingled. He was not to be disappointed, naming it "a kingdom of remarkable diversity" after this first expedition.[4] The plaque exemplifies that diversity. But first we should consider why it was made and for whom, and to address that we must understand more about its context, starting with Khotan and Khotanese Buddhism.

THE KINGDOM OF KHOTAN

Khotan was an oasis kingdom thriving throughout the first millennium AD until it was conquered around 1006 by the Karakhanids (840–1212)—an Islamic Turkic people who invaded from west of the Pamir mountains.[5] Until excavations of the early twentieth century we knew of Khotan primarily through the Chinese histories and records of the monks who had passed through here on their way between China and India. For example, the *Hanshu*, the history of the Former Han dynasty of China (206 BC–AD 9), written after the fall of the Han, notes that the Khotan had 3,300 households, 19,300 individuals, and 2,400 people able to bear arms.[6] The capital was situated between two rivers flowing north from the Kunlun Mountains. The rivers, called the White Jade and Black Jade (Yurung kash and Kara kash), were sources not only of water for irrigation but also of jade. The stone was also mined in the mountains and exported—certainly from the first millennium BC, when we see Khotanese jade in central China.[7] The jade—and the rivers—ensured Khotan's prosperity.

3. Hedin visited in 1896. For a lively account of these early explorers, see Hopkirk (2006).
4. Stein (1907: 429).
5. Biran ([2004] 2012) gives a good summary of this period, with more detailed references.
6. Abel-Rémusat (1820) provided a compendium of translations (into French) of the notices of Khotan from Chinese sources. More recent translations are available in print and online; see, for example, Hill (2015).
7. Notably some of the 755 carved jades found in the tomb of the Shang queen and general Fu Hao, dated ca. 1250 BC. Online images of some jades can be seen at "Jades from Fu Hao's Tomb," http://depts.washington.edu/chinaciv/archae/2fuhjade.htm. Early Chinese sources note that the Yuezhi were suppliers of Khotanese jade at this time (see chapter 1). But

The rivers joined beyond the town and flowed north across the Taklamakan Desert as the Khotan River, although probably disappearing below the sands for some of the year. The river provided a viable route to the northern kingdoms of Aksu and Kucha: a fort was built on a bluff overlooking it about halfway into the desert to guard against invasions from the north. To the west, routes led to the small kingdom of Suoju (present-day Yarkhand). The traveler then went either northwest to the Shule kingdom (present-day Kashgar), south to the Tibetan Plateau, or southwest to the mountain passes of the Pamir, Hindu Kush, and Karakoram, leading to Central Asia kingdoms such as Bactria and Gandhāra, and thence to northern India. To the east was the neighboring kingdom of Kroraina. The small kingdom of Caḍota (now known as Niya) snaking up the river about 150 miles east of Khotan's capital marked the border, falling under Khotanese or Krorainic control at various times.

The early history of Khotan is uncertain. A story that claims the kingdom was founded by exiles banished from Taxila in Gandhāra by King Aśoka (r. ca. 268–ca. 232 BC) is told in seventh-century texts but has no supporting evidence.[8] By the seventh century, documents were being produced in the local language, Khotanese, which is of the Middle Iranian group. Some scholars have argued that Khotanese replaced an earlier Tibeto-Burmese vernacular, but the existence of either of these languages would not offer any support for the story of Gandhāran exiles.[9] There are, however, finds of bronze Sino-Kharoṣṭhī coins from the first few centuries AD that name Khotanese kings; the kings have Iranian names.[10] The coins combine two coin systems, that of the Kushan (see chapter 3) and that of the Chinese.[11] The neighbor-

---

also see discussion in chapter 1 on recent doubts as to whether Khotan is really the source of early jade found in Fu Hao's tomb and elsewhere in central China.

8. The story of the exiles is found in a Tibetan text, "The Prophecy of Li County," and is told by the seventh-century Chinese pilgrim monk Xuanzang (Emmerick 1967: 15–21; Beal 1884, bk. 12: 309–11).

9. Schafer (1961: 47 ff.).

10. Cribb (1984, 1985). There is also a document found in Endere, east of Caḍota—a contract for the purchase of a camel written in Prākrit, dated to the third year of the reign of the Khotanese king Vijita-siṃha (Burrow 1940: 137)—that gives "the earliest local form of the king's name," along with "an Iranian epithet *hināza* (army leader) as well as a few other, clearly Iranian, personal names. Thus it shows that the royal family, as well as a substantial part of the population, was Iranian at that time" (Kumamoto 2009).

11. See H. Wang (2004: 37–39) for a review both of the Sino-Kharoṣṭhī coins and of Chinese coins found in the region.

ing kingdom to the east, Kroraina, which thrived from the first to fourth centuries AD, produced documents in Prākrit in Kharoṣṭhī script. These documents and the coin evidence suggest that migrants might have moved from Gandhāra to southern Taklamakan, but possibly not until the Kushan period (first to third centuries). From his study of the coins Cribb concludes that "the issuers of the coins were in close contact, whether political, cultural or economic, with the kingdoms of Bactria and NW India during the period of transition from Indo-Scythian and Indo-Parthian to Kushan control and particularly to the period immediately after that transition."[12] The coins are also interesting in the context of the Khotanese plaque, in that a riderless horse or camel is depicted on the side bearing the Kharoṣṭhī inscription. Horses and camels are found previously on a variety of coins, including Indo-Scythian, Indo-Parthian, and Kushan. One type of Sino-Kharoṣṭhī coin is probably a copy of a Kushan coin, some coins are overstrikes on Kushan copper drachmas, and all types show a *tamgha*, or tribal symbol—used among the Kushan (see chapter 3).[13] But the weight of the coinage, three, six, or twenty-four grains, copied weights of Chinese coins.[14] So while the Kushan across the Pamir to the west clearly had a strong influence on Khotan, at the same time they were linked into the Chinese economic system to their east. Given Khotan's trade with China in jade and other stones, this would have been important.

The Chinese histories report that in the first century AD Khotan probably expanded its control both eastward to include Caḍota and westward to include Suoju.[15] When the Chinese armies came from the east, the Chinese governor-general was stationed at Khotan for a brief period (77–91). In the second century Khotan sought to expand its kingdom beyond Caḍota further into Kroraina. Although not successful, Khotan remained secure during

12. Cribb (1984: 141).

13. Cribb (1984: 142–43).

14. H. Wang (2004: 37–38). Also see chapters 2 and 5 for Kushan coins, Bactrian minting, and Hephthalite overstriking of Sasanian issues.

15. "During the Yongping period (AD 58–76), in the reign of Emperor Ming, Xiumo Ba, a Khotanese general, rebelled against Suoju (Yarkand), and made himself king of Yutian (in 60 CE). On the death of Xiumo Ba, Guangde, son of his elder brother, assumed power and then (in 61 CE) defeated Suoju. His kingdom became very prosperous after this. From Jingjue (Niya) northwest, as far as Shule (Kashgar), thirteen kingdoms submitted to him. Meanwhile, the king of Shanshan (Kroraina) had also begun to prosper. From then on, these two kingdoms were the only major ones on the Southern Route in the whole region to the east of the Congling" (Hill 2015: sec. 4). See also Zürcher (1959: 62n187).

the third and fourth centuries. In 260 a Buddhist monk from central China, Zhu Shixing, traveled to Khotan in search of scriptures and, on discovering a copy of the *Prajñāpāramitāsūtra* in Sanskrit, he wanted to send it to China. This was initially blocked, his biography records, by local Buddhists who thought its teachings heterodox: the surmise is that they followed Śrāvakayāna (Hinayana) teaching. However, Zhu Shixing managed to send the text to Luoyang, where it was translated. He remained in Khotan, and in 282 a Khotanese monk went to China with another copy of the same text.

Mahāyāna seems to have become dominant after this. The Chinese monk Faxian and his companions arrived in Khotan in 400 on their way to India, describing it as

> prosperous and rich.... The people are very wealthy, and all without exception honour the law (*of Buddha*). They use religious music for mutual entertainment. The body of priests number number even several myriads, principally belonging the the Great Vehicle [Mahāyāna]. They all have food provided for them. . . . Before their house doors they raise little towers [stupa], the least about twenty feet high. There are priests' houses for the entertainment of foreign priests and for providing them with what they need.[16]

The king of Khotan housed Faxian and his companions in a large Mahāyāna monastery that, Faxian records, had three thousand monks. Faxian also mentions four other large monasteries, including one outside the city called the "King's New Monastery," which "was eighty years in finishing, and over after three kings (*reigns*) was it completed. It is perhaps twenty *chang* in height (290 *feet*). It is adorned with carving and inlaid work, and covered with gold and silver. Above the roof all kinds of jewels combine to perfect it. Behind the tower there is a hall of Buddha, magnificent and very beautiful. The beams, pillars, doors, and window-frames are all gold-plated."[17]

Jade alone did not account for this prosperity. Reports suggest that Khotan was a center of trade, especially in semiprecious stones. As well as the local jade, these included lapis lazuli, emeralds, and rubies from Badakshan across the Pamir Mountains to the west. Within the first few centuries AD, Khotan also developed silk and papermaking industries (see chapters 8 and 9). The wealth from trade enabled the building of gold-covered Buddhist stupas, their relic chambers probably filled with some of the semiprecious

16. Beal (1884: xxv). For a compendium of translations (into French) of Chinese accounts of Khotan, see Abel-Rémusat (1820).

17. Beal (1884: xxvii), Jenner (1981: 219–20).

stones that passed through its markets and, as the monk Songyun describes, adorned with votive silk: "Men in after ages built towers [stupas] around this [Buddha] image of 18 feet, and the other image-towers, all of which were ornamented with many thousand flags and streamers of variegated silk. There are perhaps as many as 10,000 of these and more than half of them belong to the Wei country."[18]

Traveling in 518–22, Songyun, a pilgrim monk born in Dunhuang to the east, records a local story about the founding of Buddhism in Khotan when a merchant introduced a monk to the king. The monk subsequently built a stupa with the king's patronage.[19] The patronage of Buddhism by the elite and the close link with merchants and trade are well evidenced and were major factors in the success of Buddhism's spread across central, South, and East Asia.[20] Songyun also mentions that the women dressed like the men in trousers and short tunics "girded with belts" and that they "gallop on horseback just like the men."[21]

During this period the Hephthalites were extending their power from their base in Bactria—present-day northern Afghanistan—across the Pamir mountains to the Tarim, taking Shule and the northern kingdom of Kucha (see chapter 5). Songyun passed through their territory after leaving Khotan, although he did not visit their capital, and he noted that the Khotanese sent envoys to the Hephthalites. The extent of Hephthalite influence in Khotan is uncertain, but they would have been important to keep as allies, as they controlled many of the mines producing the stones traded in Khotan. Songyun's account suggests that Buddhism was thriving in Khotan during this period.[22]

Khotan continued to prosper, although subject to the rise and fall of empires on its borders. From the seventh century it was variously under the control of the Chinese, Tibetan, and Western Turkic empires, and their cultures reveal two-way influences such as paper and silk technologies coming from China and Khotanese Buddhist texts transmitted to China and Tibet. There continued to be residents of Indian origin, as seen in the dedications

18. Beal (1884: lxxxvi). This description was of a town en route to Khotan's capital. Also see Jenner (1981: 219–20).
19. Beal (1884: lxxxviii).
20. For a discussion, see Liu (1994) and Whitfield (2016). Songyun also mentions the riding camel in Khotan; the Bactrian camel was generally used as a pack animal.
21. Chavannes (1903b: 394).
22. Mariko Walter (2014) suggests otherwise. For other references, see King (2015).

to some manuscripts.[23] And Khotanese, an eastern Iranian language, is written using Brahmi, an Indian script, on a form of manuscript based on Indian palm leaf manuscripts—the *pothi*.

In the early seventh century Khotan was probably subject to the Western Turkic Empire, whose center of power was based in the steppe to the north of the Tianshan. Xuanzang, the seventh-century Chinese pilgrim monk, stayed in their lands for several months and was given a letter of safe passage by the resident Turkic ruler or *tundun*.[24] He visited Khotan on his return, noting it was "renowned for its music; the men love the song and dance. Few of them wear garments of skin *(felt)* and wool; most wear taffetas and white linen. Their external behaviour is full of urbanity; their customs are properly regulated. Their written characters and their mode of forming their sentences resemble the Indian model; the forms of the letters differ somewhat; the differences, however, are slight. The spoken language also differs from that of other countries. They greatly esteem the law of the Buddha. There are about a hundred *saṅghārāmas* with some 5000 followers, who all study the doctrine of the Great Vehicle [Mahāyāna]."[25]

The Khotanese king sent an envoy to the Chinese court in 632, and Khotan became a pawn in the diplomatic negotiations between the Chinese and the Western Turks, resulting in the Khotanese king leaving sons in the Chinese capital as surety and offering allegiance to the Chinese emperor. But to the south of Khotan a new Tibetan empire had formed, and they pushed north and took Khotan in 670. Thereafter Khotan was subject to the power struggles between the Chinese and Tibetan Empires in the region, with the Chinese having dominance during the late seventh and early eighth centuries but then, following the outbreak of civil war in central China, being forced to withdraw their armies. This enabled the Tibetans to move in again, and they controlled Khotan from the end of the eighth century. By this time the Western Turks had been replaced in the Mongolian steppe by another confederation of Turkic tribes, the Uygur. But throughout this period, Khotanese kings continued to reign in this Taklamakan kingdom.[26]

The Tibetan and Uygur Empires both fell in the mid-ninth century. Many Uygurs moved south into the Taklamakan, establishing kingdoms to the

---

23. Burrow (1940).

24. The *tundun* was assassinated shortly after Xuanzang had left (Chavannes 1903a: 194–95).

25. Beal (1884: 309).

26. See Hill (1988) for discussion of dating of this period.

north and east of Khotan. In the tenth century Khotan had resumed relations with China but was also very close to its neighbors in Dunhuang. Their ruling families intermarried, and Khotanese patrons are depicted on the walls of the Dunhuang Mogao Buddhist cave temples from this period. The Dunhuang Library Cave is also a major source of Khotanese manuscripts, some of them Buddhist but including several more mundane documents such as a receipt for goods from Dunhuang for a Khotanese monastery.[27] Khotan again expanded westward to Kashgar, sending an envoy to the Chinese court in 971 with an elephant captured during this campaign. But this was part of a larger battle with the Turkic confederation then ruling much of northern Central Asia west of the Pamir, the Karakhanids (Ilkekhanids). Islamic sources record that the Karakhanids took Khotan in 1006, sending an envoy to the Chinese court in 1009 under the name Kara Kaghan (the Black Khan).

BUDDHISM IN KHOTAN

Khotan was Buddhist throughout this period.[28] The earliest Buddhist remains are from around the third century.[29] Certainly by the time of Faxian's visit there were large monasteries, although Dandan-Uliq might well not yet have existed—archaeologists have usually dated its origins to the sixth century.[30]

That Buddhism in Khotan during the early period was Śrāvakayāna is supported by the account of the third-century monk Zhu Shixing. But the surviving Khotanese Buddhist literature dates from a later period, probably from around 700 onwards. These manuscripts, written in the Brahmi script

27. The British Library, IOL Khot 140, is a list of goods for a Khotanese monastery in the tenth century. On the list are coats of silk and wool, trousers, undergarments, shoes, blankets, a camel-skin pouch, a silver cup, incense, and more.

28. For a review of Buddhism in Khotan with useful bibliography, see Emmerick and Skjaervo (1990). For images of Vaiśravaṇa sponsored by Khotanese "for a long life," see Maggi and Filigenzi (2009).

29. See Whitfield (2016) for a discussion of Buddhism in the Tarim, addressing Zürcher's assertion that monastic Buddhism was not established until the third century. There is a record of persecution of Buddhism under an eighth-century Khotanese king, but this seems to have been short-lived (Hill 1988). Yamazaki (1990: 68–70) suggests that Zoroastrianism was also present in Khotan, perhaps even dominant in the early period. We have evidence of a Zoroastrian community in Dunhuang from the fourth to the tenth centuries (see Grenet and Zhang 1996).

30. Whitfield and Sims-Williams (2004: 158).

FIGURE 18. A folio from the Khotanese Buddhist text, the *Book of Zambasta*. British Library Or.9614.

(as Xuanzang observed), contain both Sanskrit texts and translations into the local language of Khotan. This body of literature is Mahāyāna and probably reached Khotan through Gilgit in northern India. But Khotan was on the route between northwestern India and China, also a major route for the Tibetans when they made their incursions into Central Asia. This position ensured Khotan's importance in the transmission of Mahāyāna Buddhism from India to China and Tibet. Khotanese texts also were found in the library cave in Dunhuang, indicating links between Khotanese Buddhists and the Chinese and Tibetan Buddhist communities further east.

The Khotanese Buddhist texts are almost all translated directly from Sanskrit texts, and there are a few texts known only in Khotanese, such as the *Book of Zambasta* (figure 18).[31] This is based on Indian texts but is not a direct translation. Other texts, such as a Khotanese poem, also show an Indian connection. This poem is in essence the Hindu Indian story of the Rāmāyaṇa, but given a Buddhist interpretation: the heroes Rāma and Lakṣmaṇa are identified with the Buddha Śākyamuni and the future Buddha Maitreya.

Vaiśravaṇa, the Guardian of the North, played a central role in Khotanese art and Buddhism and also features in understanding our plaque.[32] Seventh-century texts recount a legend of the founding of the kingdom. The founding king prayed at the Vaiśravaṇa Temple for a son and heir. A baby boy duly emerged from the statue's head. The king took him home, but the baby would not eat. The king returned to prayer again at the temple, whereupon a breast emerged from the earth at which the baby suckled and grew strong. The king established a new Vaiśravaṇa temple that Xuanzang identified as one he vis-

31. Emmerick (1968).
32. For images of Vaiśravaṇa produced by Khotanese, see Maggi and Filigenzi (2009).

ited, full of rare and precious objects. Texts also tell of Vaiśravaṇa being delegated by Buddha to protect Khotan.

Archaeologically, little is left of the ancient capital of Khotan—Yotkan—which lies about five miles west of the modern city and is buried under meters of silt. The main finds from here, apart from flakes of gilt, were hundreds of small terracotta models, many of them monkeys, some in sexual poses, their significance and use still debated.[33] But a magnificent stupa remains some twenty miles to the northeast, called Rawak Stupa (not to be confused with Rawak, a settlement north of Dandan-Uliq). With its tiered stupa bases and staircases on each side, it follows a style probably developed to the west and seen in Gandhāra in Kaniṣka's stupa at Shah-ji-ki-dheri in the Peshawar Valley; at Top-i-Rustam in Balkh, Afghanistan; and at Bhamala Stupa in Taxila (see chapter 4). These appear to follow a textual description in the third-century *Divyāvadāna*, which describes a stupa as having four staircases, three platforms, and an egg-like dome as well as the other usual elements. The development of this form at Rawak suggests strong and continued links with its Buddhist neighbors across the Pamir Mountains to the west.[34]

Statues, both monumental and life-size, stood along both the inside and the outside of the two perimeter walls, which were also painted. The walls of one gate are flanked by guardian statues, with the bare torso of a small woman shown between their feet. Scholars have suggested that this depicts the founding myth of the baby being suckled by a breast from the earth, with Vaiśravaṇa as the guardian.[35] A statue of Vaiśravaṇa also appears at Dandan-Uliq, a site that lies about sixty miles northeast of the present-day city between the Keriya and Khotan Rivers.[36] The name means "the houses with ivory." This was the find-site of the plaque and it is worth looking in detail at its excavation by Stein to understand more about the context of the plaque.

33. For examples, see Whitfield and Sims-Williams (2004: 139–41, cat. 29–33).
34. For further discussion, see Whitfield (2016, 2018a).
35. Hansen (1993: 81). She quotes Alexander Soper to explain why the breast is shown in the form of the woman. However, this divergence from the story and the dating—Rawak dates to the third/fourth centuries, while the founding myth is only recorded in the seventh century (but then again, we have no textual sources from earlier anyway)—makes this identification uncertain.
36. Stein (1907: 252–53).

Stein arrived at the ruins of Dandan-Uliq on December 18, 1900, with a terrible toothache: "The neuralgic pains it gave me were never more exquisite than at night."[37] With the nighttime temperature falling to zero to minus ten degrees Fahrenheit, he slept fully clothed in his tent with his head inside the end of his fur coat, making the sleeve a breathing tube. It had taken his party five days' march from the Khotan River to reach here. The Keriya River was another three days' march eastwards. Yet despite this inaccessibility, he found many of the ruins already "'explored' by treasure-seekers," certainly among them his guide, "Old Turdi," who "felt quite at home among these desolate surroundings which he had visited so frequently since his boyhood. It was the fascinating vision of hidden treasures which had drawn him and his kinsfolk there again and again, however scanty the tangible reward had been of their trying wanderings."[38]

Dandan-Uliq must once have had a plentiful supply of water to support the considerable settlement. The American geographer Ellsworth Huntington (1876–1947) surveyed the old route of the Chira River here in 1905 (and subsequently formulated a theory about climate change in Asia).[39] The river, like all those in the southern Taklamakan, flowed northwards from the Kunlun Mountains west of the Keriya and disappeared somewhere in the desert northwest of Dandan-Uliq. It must have flowed for several centuries to ensure the development of this settlement—which covers an area of over 8.5 square miles, the core area being about 1.7 square miles. At some point the site was abandoned: Stein suggested this was around AD 800, on the basis of the discovery of documents dated between 781 and 790 and some eighth-century Chinese copper coins.[40] Nothing has been found since to challenge

37. Stein (1907: 276–77).

38. Stein (1907: 279). This shows that, while the arrival of foreign explorers might have increased the possibility and size of the "rewards," they did not precipitate this treasure seeking. Indeed, Khotanese had been doing it for centuries, digging for jade along the ancient riverbed, much like more recent gold prospectors.

39. See Huntingdon (1906: 363; 1907: 170ff.) and Wagner et al. (2011: 15737) for a summary of more recent research. See Foret (2013) for an interesting discussion of the theory of climate change at that time.

40. Stein (1907: 236–88). His view was that there had been an irrigation canal supplying water but that increasing dessication had made this site unviable in the eighth or ninth century. After Stein the site was visited by the Ellsworth Huntington and, in 1928, by Emil

this hypothesis. The suggestion has been made that the abandonment of the site was a result of the end of Chinese rule in the area, prompted by civil war in central China and the withdrawal of their troops from outlying garrisons. However, as in other sites, there could have been other reasons for the abandonment, such as a change in the water's course, a reduction in the water's supply, or a drop in population that made maintenance of the irrigation unviable.

The date of the founding of Dandan-Uliq is less certain. Even with a water supply, it is not on a major route. But it was more than a small farming settlement, as shown by the number of Buddhist shrines uncovered to date. It was not the most outlying settlement along the Chira River: about eight miles to the north, Stein also excavated two small mounds (possibly once stupas) named Rawak (not to be confused with Rawak Stupa, which is much closer to the capital).[41]

Stein started work immediately on his arrival, uncovering a small shrine with many stucco ornaments used to decorate the walls (D.I, the "D" being short for Dandan-Uliq), and then two adjoining shrines containing sculptures and wall paintings (D.II). Three wooden panels were found against the lotus pedestal of the remains of the main Buddha image, all painted (although much faded) and assumed by Stein to have been placed there as votive offerings.[42] Interestingly, however, Stein found evidence that the remains of manuscripts had been pasted over the paintings, and it is not clear if the original plaque, the manuscript, or both were intended to carry most of the votive force.[43] The remains of the wall paintings were mainly of multiple Buddha images, but on the inside of the north passage wall Stein discovered

Trinkler (1896–1931) and Walter Bosshard (1892–1975). In 1996 the Xinjiang Institute of Archaeology surveyed the site, preparatory to a joint excavation with the Niya Research Institute of Bukkyo University, Japan, which took place in 2002. They discovered another temple and removed its murals to Urumqi. In between, an unofficial group led by two Europeans visited the site in 1998, carrying out excavations and removing more wall paintings. Fortunately these were later recovered and are now also held at the Xinjiang Institute of Archaeology in Urumqi.

41. Stein (1907: 304–5). It is conceivable that other ruins may yet be found. The Sino-French team of archaeologists at Karadong, to the east, have discovered sites deeper into the desert than those identified by Stein, suggested to be on a cross-desert route (Debaine-Francfort and Idriss 2001).

42. D.II.2, 4, 03; see Stein (1907: 247). Now in British Museum, reg. no. 1907,IIII.63.

43. Or perhaps the wooden plaques had been used as one of the boards enclosing a *pothi*-style manuscript?

MAPS

MAP 1. Silk Roads by land and sea across Afro-Eurasia. For detail of area marked, see maps 5 and 6.

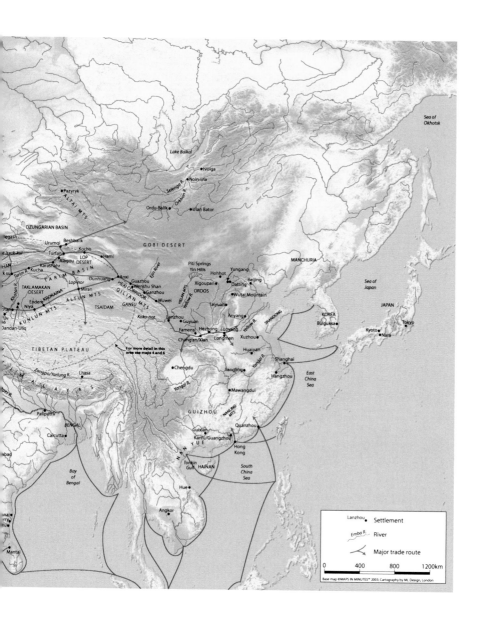

Sea of
Okhotsk

Lake Baikal

Ivolga
Noin-Ula
Selenge R.   Orkhon R.
Ordu-Balik   Ulan Bator

DZUNGARIAN BASIN

GOBI DESERT   MANCHURIA

Beshbalik
Urumqi
Kucho
Turfan   Hami   Piti Springs
Alagou LOP   Yin Hills   Yungang
Karashahr DESERT   Hohhot   Datong   Beijing
Dunhuang Anxi   Xigoupan   Sea of
TARIM BASIN   Guazhou   ORDOS Wutai Mountain   Japan
Lopnor Wenshu Shan   JAPAN
TAKLAMAKAN Ganzhou   Taiyuan
DESERT Miran Wuwei
Niya ALTUN MTS QILIAN MTS   KOREA   Kyoto
Endere   Anyang   SHANDONG Bulguksa   Nara   Tokyo
Khotan KUNLUN MTS GANSU MTS Lanzhou   Yellow R.
Dandan-Uiliq   Koko-nor Guyuan Hezhong Luoyang
TSAIDAM   Famensi Longmen Xuzhou Sea of
For more detail in this Chang'an/Xian   Japan
area see maps 4 and 6   Huaian

TIBETAN PLATEAU   Chengdu Jiangling Yangzi R. Shanghai
Zangpo/Yarlung R. Lhasa   Hangzhou East
HIMALAYAS   Mawangdui   China
                                              Sea
Pataliputra
BENGAL   GUIZHOU
Calcutta   Guixian Quanzhou
                           Kanfu/Guangzhou
                           Hong NANYUE
Bay   Kong
of   Tonkin HAINAN South
Bengal   Gulf   China
                           Hue   Sea
                           Angkor

Mantai

Lanzhou • Settlement

Emba R. River

  Major trade route

0   400   800   1200km

Base map ©MAPS IN MINUTES™ 2003. Cartography by ML Design, London

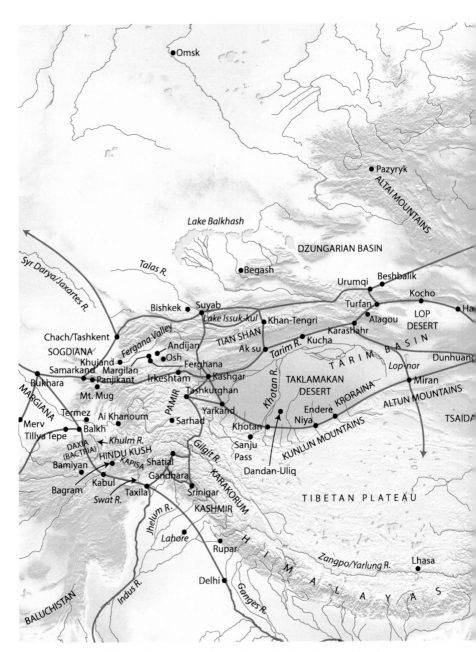

MAP 2. Silk Roads by land in central and East Asia with places discussed in Chapter 1.

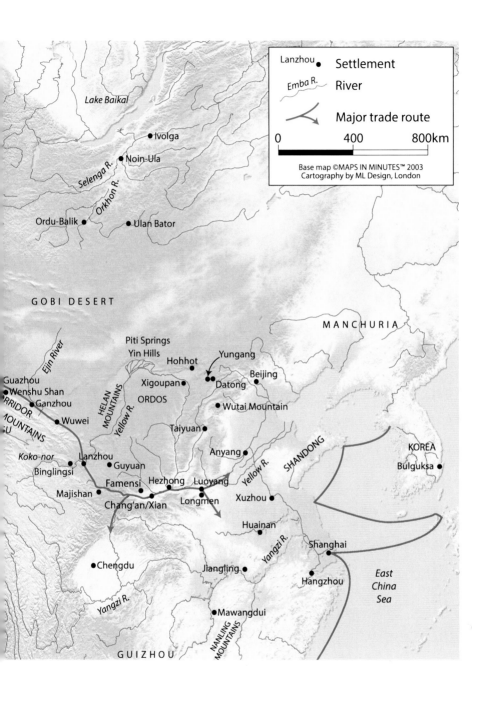

Lanzhou ● Settlement

Emba R. River

Major trade route

0   400   800km

Base map ©MAPS IN MINUTES™ 2003
Cartography by ML Design, London

Lake Baikal

●Ivolga

Noin-Ula●

Selenga R.

Orkhon R.

Ordu-Balik ●   ●Ulan Bator

GOBI DESERT

MANCHURIA

Ejin River

Piti Springs
Yin Hills   Hohhot●   ●Yungang
Guazhou   ●Beijing
Wenshu Shan   Xigoupan●   ●Datong
Ganzhou   ORDOS
CORRIDOR   HELAN   Yellow R.
●Wuwei   MOUNTAINS   ●Wutai Mountain
MOUNTAINS

Taiyuan●

Koko-nor   Lanzhou●   Anyang●   KOREA
Binglingsi●   ●Guyuan   Bulguksa●
Majishan●   Famensi Hezhong Luoyang   SHANDONG
                Chang'an/Xian Longmen ●Xuzhou
                                Yellow R.
                        Huainan●
                                    Shanghai●
●Chengdu   East
        Jiangling●   Yangzi R.   China
                                Hangzhou●   Sea
Yangzi R.
                ●Mawangdui
GUIZHOU   NANLING
               MOUNTAINS

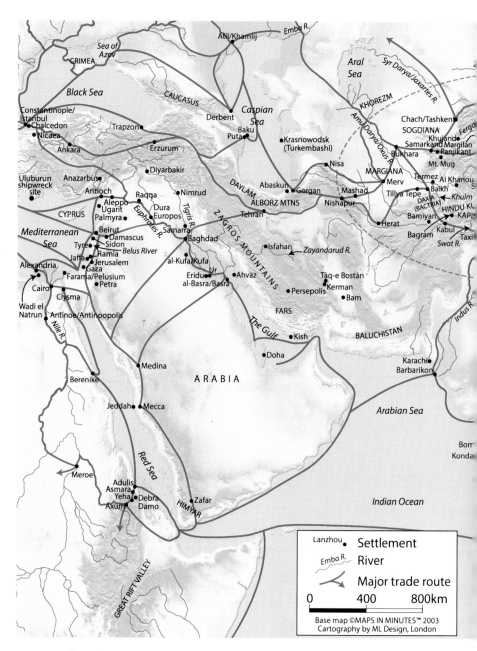

MAP 3. Silk Roads across Asia with places discussed in Chapter 2.

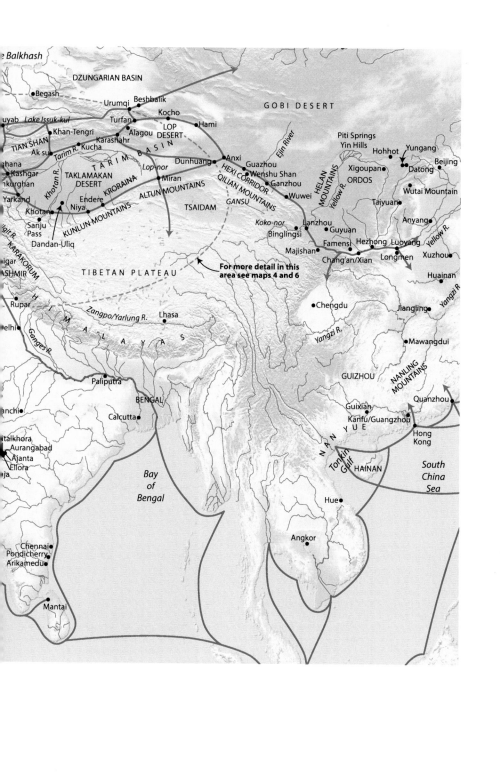

Balkhash

DZUNGARIAN BASIN

GOBI DESERT

Begash

Urumqi · Beshbalik

Kocho

uyab · Lake Issuk-kul

Turfan · Hami

Piti Springs
Yin Hills

Khan-Tengri · Alagou

Hohhot · Yungang

Beijing

TIAN SHAN

Karashahr

LOP
DESERT

Xigoupan · Datong

Ak su · Kucha

Tarim R.

BASIN

Anxi

ORDOS

Wutai Mountain

hana

Lop-nor

Dunhuang · Guazhou

Wenshu Shan

Taiyuan

Kashgar

TAKLAMAKAN
DESERT

Miran

Ganzhou

Anyang

kurghan

Khotan R.

TARIM

Wuwei

HELAN
MOUNTAINS

Yellow R.

Yarkand

Endere

KRORAINA

ALTUN MOUNTAINS

QILIAN MOUNTAINS

Khotan · Niya

TSAIDAM

GANSU

Koko-nor

Lanzhou · Guyuan

Hezhong · Luoyang

Yellow R.

Sanju
Pass

KUNLUN MOUNTAINS

Binglingsi

Famensi

Xuzhou

Dandan-Uliq

Majishan

Chang'an/Xian · Longmen

Huainan

KARAKORUM

TIBETAN PLATEAU

For more detail in this
area see maps 4 and 6

Rupar

Chengdu

Jiangling

Yangzi R.

elhi

Zangpo/Yarlung R. · Lhasa

H
I
M
A
L
A
Y
A
S

Yangzi R.

Mawangdui

Ganges R.

Paliputra

GUIZHOU

NANLING
MOUNTAINS

anchi

BENGAL

Quanzhou

Calcutta

Guixian

Kanfu/Guangzhou

talkhora
Aurangabad

N
A
N

Y
U
E

Hong
Kong

Ajanta
Ellora

Bay
of
Bengal

Tonkin
Gulf

HAINAN

South
China
Sea

Hue

Chennai
Pondicherry
Arikamedu

Angkor

Mantai

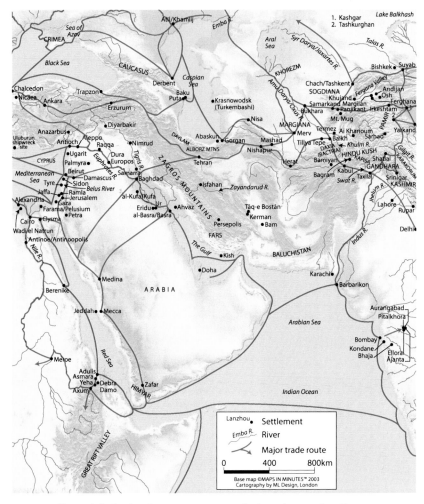

MAP 4. Silk Roads by land and sea in West Asia with places discussed in Chapter 3.

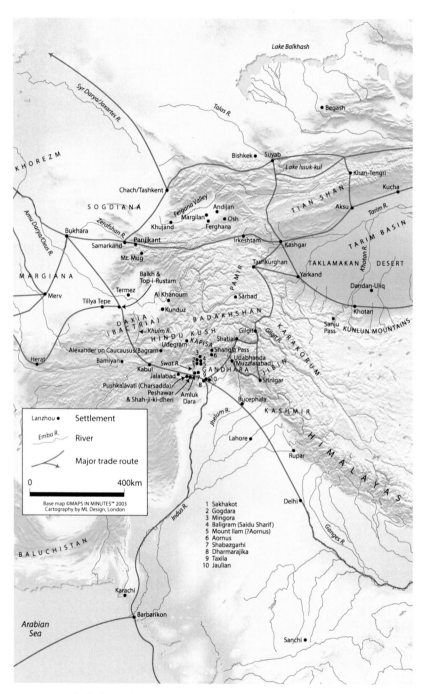

Lake Balkhash

Syr Darya/Jaxartes R.

Talas R.

Begash

KHOREZM

Bishkek • Suyab

Lake Issuk-kul

Khan-Tengri

Chach/Tashkent •

Kucha

SOGDIANA

Fergana Valley

Andijan

TIAN SHAN

Aksu

Tarim R.

Zerafshan R.

Margilan •

• Osh

Amu Darya/Oxus R.

Bukhara •

Khujand •

Ferghana

TARIM BASIN

Samarkand •

Panjikant •

Irkeshtam

Kashgar •

Mt. Mug •

Tashkurghan •

TAKLAMAKAN DESERT

MARGIANA

Balkh &
Top-i-Rustam •

PAMIR

Yarkand •

Khotan R.

Dandan-Uliq •

• Merv

Termez •

Ai Khanoum •

• Sarhad

• Khotan

Tillya Tepe •

• Kunduz

BADAKHSHAN

Sanju
Pass •

KUNLUN MOUNTAINS

DAXIA
(BACTRIA)

Khulm R.

KUSH

Gilgit •

KARAKORUM

HINDU

KAPISA

Shatial •

• Herat

Alexander on Caucausus/Bagram •

Udegram •

Shangla Pass

• Bamiyan

Swat R.

3

6

Udabhanda
(Muzzfarabad)

TIBIN

Kabul •

GANDHARA

5

Jalalabad •

9

10

• Srinigar

Pushkalavati (Charsadda) •

8

Peshawar
& Shah-ji-ki-dheri •

Amluk
Dara

Bucephala •

KASHMIR

Jhelum R.

Lanzhou •   Settlement

Lahore •

HIMALAYAS

Emba R.   River

Rupar •

Major trade route

0   400km

1 Sakhakot
2 Gogdara
3 Mingora
4 Baligram (Saidu Sharif)
5 Mount Ilam (?Aornus)
6 Aornus
7 Shabazgarhi
8 Dharmarajika
9 Taxila
10 Jaulian

Delhi •

Ganges R.

Base map ©MAPS IN MINUTES™ 2003
Cartography by ML Design, London

BALUCHISTAN

Indus R.

Karachi •

• Barbarikon

Arabian
Sea

Sanchi •

MAP 5. Detail of Silk Road in Central Asia with places discussed in Chapter 4.

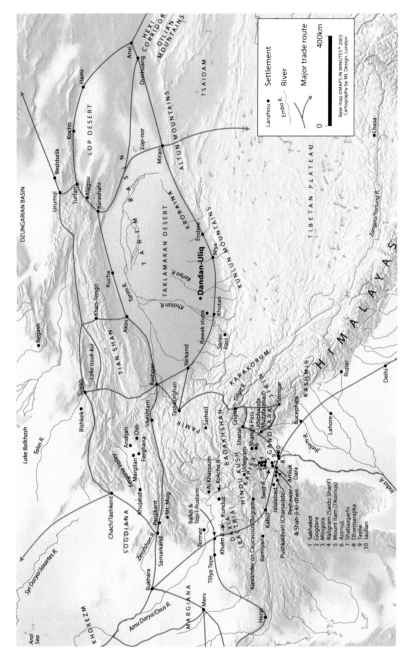

MAP 6. Silk Roads by land in Central Asia with places discussed in Chapter 6.

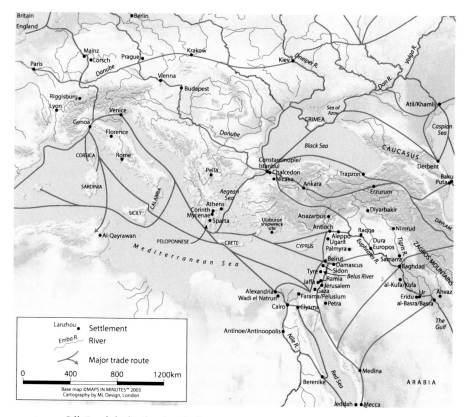

MAP 7. Silk Roads by land and sea linking Europe, North African and West Asia, with places discussed in Chapter 7.

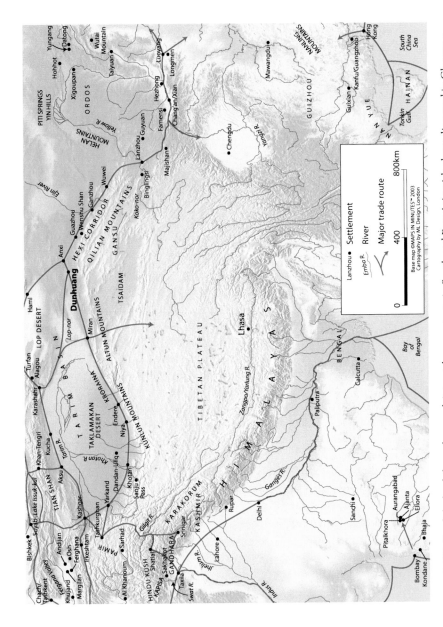

MAP 8. Silk Roads by land through central Asia with sea routes to in South and East Asia with places discussed in Chapter 9.

the remains of the depiction of "three rows of youths riding Bactrian camels or else dappled horses, four or five in each row, each holding a cup in his outstretched right hand, while above one of the riders a bird is swooping down on this offering."[44] This is the same image as depicted on the plaque.

Another four painted wooden panels were discovered in the adjoining shrine (D.II.010, 79, 16, 21), also Buddhist but much faded, one showing Ganesha; again, Stein surmises, these were placed there as votive offerings. A small cotton bag was also found in the same shrine containing human teeth and small fragments of bones: Stein asks, "Were they ex-votos deposited with some superstitious object, or had they been brought here by visitors as reputed relics?"[45] The room also contained the remains of a statue of an armor-clad guardian standing on the body of a demon. It held in its left hand an object that Stein identified as a money bag; Stein suggested, therefore, that this was a figure of Vaiśravaṇa.[46]

The next ruin to be excavated, named by Stein as D.III, was that of a small dwelling and yielded the first significant manuscript finds. These included several almost complete *pothi*—paper folios of texts in a rectangular form emulating the shape of the Indian style of books made from palm leaves and fastened together with string. They were mainly in Sanskrit and contained Mahāyāna Buddhist texts. Stein suggested that the building was a monastery and that the *pothi* were the remnants of its library.[47]

The plaque was discovered in the seventh building Stein excavated—D.VII. The building was typical of contemporary wood frame structures that continue to be built in the local villages. Their poplar wood frames made using mortise and tenon joints were filled in with reed or tamarisk mats, which were then covered in clay and plastered. D.VII was set slightly apart from D.I–V, with a Buddhist shrine (D.VI) nearby (figure 19). It consisted of two square rooms, one with a fireplace on the wall showing signs of a molded plaster surround. On the basis of the remains and the debris on the floor Stein surmised that this had been a two-story building but that the top floor had caved in. He suggested that this might have been the reason that the plaque, which he believed had originally been fixed high on the wall of the ground-floor room, had fallen off and was therefore discovered on the floor

44. Stein (1907: 248).
45. Stein (1907: 251, D.II.013).
46. Stein (1907: 251–53).
47. Stein (1907: 258).

PLAN
OF
RUINED STRUCTURES D.VI, D.VII
DANDĀN-UILIQ.

SCALE

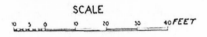

10   5   0   10   20   30   40 FEET

D.VII

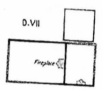

Fireplace

D.VI

Inscribed
fresco

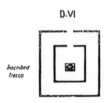

Wall of timber and plaster.......... ▬▬
          Ditto   ruined.. ▬▬
Rush wall..................................... ▬
Fireplace.......................................
Statue base of plaster.............. ▬▬

M A STEIN & RAM SINGH Del.

FIGURE 19. Plan of Dandan-Uliq, house no. 7. After Stein (1907).

covered by debris. Two other plaques of different shapes, one with paintings on both sides, were found nearby along with several paper fragments containing Chinese text.[48]

The texts give us names of Chinese Buddhist monks living here in the late eighth century and suggest that this was an outlying property under the jurisdiction of a larger monastery called Huguo ("protect the country"). One document is an order from the head monks of Huguo to other monks to supervise the maintenance of the outlying property, including its land.[49] On its receipt at Yangling, all the servants of the temple were supposed to be employed for three days in cutting the grass, while one man only would be left to see to the irrigation of the fields. Stein concludes that it is therefore likely that this outlying place was called Yangling and that the order was sent from the more centrally situated monastery of Huguo. Despite the seeming remoteness of this site, Yangling residents were not poor. Among the documents is a loan document made by the monk Qianying of Huguo Monastery in 782 to a solder, Ma Lingzhi, for a thousand copper coins—a string of cash. The soldier had pledged all his movable property against the loan and was paying a rate of 10 percent interest to the monk.[50]

Stein continued to find more manuscripts and plaques in other ruins, including D.X. One bore the image of three figures, the middle one identified by scholars as "the silk-bearing princess" (D.X.4).[51] Another showed again the motif of the dappled horse and rider. A plaque from D.IV depicts a local legend of a rat king.[52] Stein left on January 4, 1901, but while he was excavating at Rawak to the north the locals continued digging on their own and discovered a crumpled-up ball of paper from D.XIII. Once conserved, this proved to be a letter in Persian transcribed in Hebrew script.[53]

The plaques and other finds were first sent to the British residency at Kashgar, Chini Bagh, to await Stein. He returned there at the end of his expedition on May 12, 1901.[54] Stein had received permission from the Russian

48. Stein (1907: 275–77). For a translation, see Chavannes (1907).
49. British Library Or.8210/S.5868 (D.VII.7); Stein (1907: 276).
50. British Library Or.8210/S.5867 (D.VII.2); Stein (1907: 275–76). For comparison, a contemporary document notes the sale of a donkey for six thousand cash (H. Wang 2004: 103).
51. Stein (1907: 259–61, D.X.3, 4, 5, 8).
52. Stein (1907: 264–65). Whitfield and Sims-Williams (2004: 1367).
53. Stein (1907: 306–8 and Appendix C): the document is now in the British Library, Or.8212/166.
54. Stein (1904: 491–93).

authorities to travel to Europe using the Russian-Turkestan Railway and for the finds to accompany him to Britain for preliminary sorting. In Kasghar, he repacked them into twelve large boxes for their long journey. These were presented at the Russian Consulate in Kashgar for a customs examination and were duly sealed, stamped with the Russian imperial eagle. On May 29 Stein set out across the mountains for Osh via the Chinese-Russian border at Irkeshtam, with "six sturdy ponies carrying my antiquities."[55] The ponies had to negotiate many rivers swollen by exceptional rain, a daily anxiety" to Stein, but they forded them all safely. He arrived after ten days. After a short rest, it was only a four hours' drive to Andijan and the terminus of the railway. He left by train on June 11, making brief stops at Margilan, Samarkand, and Merv. At Krasnowodsk (present-day Turkembashi) on the eastern coast of the Caspian Sea, Stein and the boxes crossed by boat to Baku and took another train. He had to take another sea crossing of the Channel before arriving in London on July 2. The twelve boxes of finds were placed in temporary deposit in the British Museum, their Russian seals intact.

Who made these plaques, why, when and where? The depiction of the same themes found on wall paintings in Buddhist temples elsewhere in Khotan, which must have been done in situ, points to these having been made locally, and probably by the same painters. The lack of plaques found outside Khotan reinforces this. The craftsmen would have had a ready supply of wood from the local poplars and orchards, and possibly these plaques were made from leftover pieces used in buildings or furniture. The painters must have also had a supply of pigments for the wall paintings: again, it would have been a relatively simple matter to produce plaques, perhaps from the paint remaining at the end of a commission.[56]

We know next to nothing of painters' practices at Khotan, although by this time in Dunhuang, as Sarah Fraser has shown, painting was a profession supported by the rich and pious. Many of the Buddhist murals and paintings on textiles have inscriptions giving the name of the patrons. We cannot know whether this piece was made to order or prepared for sale to any buyer. Its making would have been quite straightforward, but it shows a confident and practiced hand. Once the wood had been fashioned into shape it had to be treated with size—some sort of glue mixture—to provide a ground for the

55. Stein (1904: 495).

56. Analysis of the paints used in the wall paintings and on the plaques would help confirm this but has not yet been done.

paint. The plaque was then painted white, possibly with a mixture of kaolin used as a ground for the wall paintings or with lead white, frequently used at the time. The animals and riders have been drawn in confident ink lines and colored with red and green wash.[57] The colors have not been analyzed, but the ink is almost certainly carbon ink—what we would now call India ink. The pigments to make the red and green paints used on Buddhist cave murals, portable paintings, and illustrations on manuscripts from the region and period are often from cinnabar (vermilion) and malachite, but organic colorants are also found, such as lac, safflower, and madder for reds.

The shape gives a clue as to its purpose. The triangular top is common on Buddhist votive plaques, both painted and sculpted, possibly reflecting the shape of a stupa. Model stupas were also produced as votive offerings (see chapter 4). The shape is not restricted to Buddhism. Wooden plaques with triangular tops and depicting a horse are called *ema* in Japan and are given as messages to the gods in both the Shinto and Buddhist traditions.[58] *Ema* means "horse picture," and Ian Reader argues that the plaques originated in Shintoism, dating from the eighth century, and originally held an image of a horse. The horse was a messenger of the gods, and important Shinto shrines probably used real horses, but as Reader points out, "This replica or substitute horse was simultaneously an offering and a means of conveying petitions that allowed people from all walks of life to transmit their wishes and needs to the kami."[59] While Reader sees the practice only as being adopted by Buddhists in Japan in the twelfth century, the prior existence of votive stupas and triangular-headed plaques in Central Asia—and presumably China—suggests a possible earlier influence.

This piece was not left at a shrine, but, judging from its find-site and the holes in its back, it was fixed to the wall of a residence. Possibly it was used as a shrine for the resident monks. If so, it is curious that these plaques were discarded when the residents left. It would have been a simple matter to remove them from the wall and take them to the monks' next home. It would perhaps make more sense if they had been found in the Buddhist temple, left as a votive offering. The number of similar plaques found at Dandan-Uliq sug-

57. The green is quite faded and could have originally been blue.
58. Reader (1991).
59. Reader (1991). The horse is also a messenger to the underworld in Buddhism; see, for example, the illustrated copies of the *Sutra of the Ten Kings*.

gests that they were not uncommon, and indeed perhaps other plaques were removed by the monks when they left.

If the plaque was fixed to the wall as a house shrine, then the motif clearly had significance to the residents. It is distinctive, with the bird flying into the bowl and, as mentioned above, was found by Stein depicted elsewhere in Khotan.[60] More recently, the same motif has been discovered on another mural at Dandan-Uliq and at a small shrine on the route east of the capital near the present-day town of Domoko.[61] In the latter it makes up the frieze around the bottom of wall, as at Dandan-Uliq, with multiple Buddhas above. It has not been discovered in other oasis kingdoms of the Taklamakan and Gobi deserts, despite the extensive mural decoration extant at the Mogao and other cave temple sites at Dunhuang and, to a lesser extent, at sites near Kucha and Turfan.

Joanna Williams, in the only comprehensive treatment of Khotanese art written to date, provides one possible hypothesis to explain the iconography.[62] In brief, she links it to a story, told in the works of the Fifth Dalai Lama (1617–82), about Vaiśravaṇa and Pekar, the tutelary hero of the "Bhaṭa Hor" Turks.[63] Pekar took the form of a bird of prey but was shot down by an arrow from one of Vaiśravaṇa's *vajra* attendants.[64] This episode seems to be illustrated in a painting from Dunhuang.[65] There is one known example from outside Khotan linking a rider with a bowl and bird—although in this case the rider is armored and the shallow bowl holds a vase. It is a drawing on paper found at Yarkhoto near Turfan.[66] In Pekar's biography there is also an episode where a great bird settles on a tree at the consecration of a stupa on the border between Tibet and Mongolia.

Tucci identifies the "Bhaṭa Hor" Turks of the Tibetan account as the people who originally lived around Lake Baikal, probably Uygur Turks.[67] They

60. Stein (1907: 278) identifies the bird as a wild duck, on the basis of its depiction in D.X.5.

61. See Whitfield (2009: 184–85, cat. 157) for the former. The latter is preserved at the Tuopuklun temple museum near Domoko.

62. J. Williams (1973: 150–51).

63. The story is recounted in Tucci (1949: 734–35). Pekar or Pe-dkar became a major figure in Tibetan Buddhism, legends recounting that he moved from the land of Hor to take residence at Samye in Tibet.

64. Also see Lin Shen-Yu (2010: 18) for a discussion of this passage.

65. British Museum, reg. no. 1919,0101,0.45.

66. Von le Coq (1913: pl. 48).

67. Tucci (1949): 736.

emerged into history in 744 when they formed a confederation that took control of the lands to their south, much of present-day Mongolia, up to the borders of China, north of the Tianshan and west to the Caspian.[68] They ruled for almost a century until they were driven out by another group from the north, the Kyrghyz. This was in 840, and some then moved south into the Tarim. But the move of the Uygurs south was almost certainly after the abandonment of Dandan-Uliq and, if the plaque dated from the seventh or early eighth century, this was when the Uygurs were still living to the far north around Lake Baikal.

A Turkic presence in Khotan is known from earlier, as seen in the seventh-century account of Xuanzang, mentioned above, and in the Chinese historical records, which record that the Khotanese king was beheaded in 725 on the orders of China for having conspired with the Turks. Whether the scene represented has a Turkic origin is impossible to know for certain: the Tibetan source is much later and clearly identifies Pekar as a large bird of prey, not consistent with the image here. But it could be a Khotanese retelling of a Turkic legend in which some elements have been distorted.

Emil Esin also identifies several Turkic and Uygur themes in the painting, such as the dress of the rider—"the nomad's breeches and boots and the short Scythian tunic worn in later times by Turkic Balbals"—the flowing hair bound with a scarf, and the spiked wheel ornament on his forehead.[69] He also suggests that the motif of a cup in hand is common to other Turkic paintings representing "supernatural personages of royal rank." The dappled horse is a royal mount, its importance reinforced by the sun and moon (disc and crescent) emblem on its head ornament. However, the dress, the flowing scarf, and the sun and moon are not restricted to art of the Turks—if we can indeed identify such a corpus. For example, the clothes of the riders are found across the region, even being adopted by Chinese elite in the Tang. It is not hard to imagine that they were worn by the Khotanese. The sun and moon emblem is also more widely found: for example, it often appears in Buddhist and Manichaean art.

Perhaps there is also a Sogdian connection. Yu Hong (d. 592) was probably a Sogdian immigrant who had served on an embassy to Sasanian Iran and settled in China in the mid-sixth century. His funerary couch or sar-

68. J. Williams (1973: 151–52); Reynolds (2007: 356).
69. Esin (1965). Although most have interpreted the scarf as tied around his neck and then curled round his upper arms, in the form of Buddhist *ullarīya*.

FIGURE 20. Details of a scene from the sarcophagus of Yu Hong (d. 592).

cophagus, discovered at Taiyuan in northern China, is decorated with scenes reflecting his life and beliefs.[70] One scene shows a horseman holding a bowl in his right hand (figure 20). A bird flies overhead. The similarities with the scene on the horse plaque are clear, although as far as I know they have not previously been connected.

It is, of course, also possible that this plaque represents what was originally a Khotanese legend that became associated with the Uygurs after they moved into the Tarim, to be recorded, centuries later, by Tibetan historians. Given that archaeology in Khotan continues to reveal new sites and finds, it is conceivable that we may yet learn more about this plaque and its story.

Whatever its origin, this was clearly a scene of significance to Khotanese Buddhism that would not have needed explanation to the local people of the

70. Zhang et al. (2002); Wu Hung (2002).

time.[71] Leaving aside for now the overall meaning, the individual elements of the design reflect the multicultural influences on Khotan and its place on the Silk Road. These include the nimbate figures, the flying scarfs, the crescent and disk decoration, the pom-poms, and the Bactrian or two-humped camel.[72] Discussion of each of these could occupy a chapter in itself. Here I will discuss briefly one element only, the dappled horse.

THE DAPPLED HORSE

While the camel is often used as the animal representation of the Silk Road, the horse played an equally if not more important role. The horse was integral to the settlement of the steppe, and its domestication probably goes back to at least 3500 BC. It enabled the great Bronze Age migrations that brought peoples from the borders of Europe to Mongolia, Tarim, and India. DNA sampling shows that all horses derived from a common stallion line but that the mare genes are diverse, suggesting that mares from wild stock were introduced into herds for breeding throughout the horse's early history. The horse was used for a portable two-wheeled chariot that transformed warfare and gave these peoples control of the ores mined from Mesopotamia to the Altai. These ores were used to make and decorate the horses' tack, and the horse became part of myth and art. We have remains of tack—including bits and saddles—from burials in the Taklamakan dating to the first millennium BC.[73] Scholars have also found evidence of mounted pastoralists in the Kunlun Mountains to the south of Khotan in this period.[74] By the time of

71. Although the monks living in Dandan-Uliq included Chinese, their use of a local motif suggests their adoption of Khotanese culture: it is possible they were second- or more generation Chinese, born in Khotan.

72. In some places it is described as a dromedary, but a hairy hump behind the rider is clearly depicted. Although the Bactrian camel was most often used as a pack animal rather than as a riding animal, the Chinese monk Songyun notes "riding camels" (Abel-Rémusat 1820: 22; Stein 1907: 278). The camel also has a mane and beard of long hair on its neck and throat. Both horses and camels are found on the Sino-Kharoṣṭhī coins (see chapter 5). For the tassels on the horse's tack see Ilyasov (2003), and on the horse's crenellated mane see Trousdale (1968).

73. Whitfield (2009: cat. 69) from tombs at Subeixi. See also Timperman (2017) for more examples of tombs containing horse tack.

74. Wagner et al. (2011).

the start of the Silk Road, the horse had been adopted for military cavalry by the lands adjacent to the steppe, including China.

The horse played an important part throughout Silk Road history in economics, diplomacy, warfare, art, and culture. For example, as Thomas Allsen has shown, the hunt on horseback became a mainstay of royal life across the empires and kingdoms of settled or Outer Eurasia. With a common lexicon, it was an ideal pursuit to entertain and honor high-level diplomatic visitors.[75] Polo played a similar role, with strings of polo ponies kept in the imperial stables from Sasanian Persia to Tang China.

However, while successful horse breeding and equestrian skills are celebrated by many of the early Eurasian empires, including the Achaemenids of Iran and the ancient Greeks, they are less visible in ancient China.[76] While the Persian prince would always be on horseback, his Chinese counterpart—the Confucian gentleman—did not figure horsemanship among his skills.[77] The traditional Chinese clothing—ankle-length gowns with very wide sleeves—would have made riding very difficult. It is not that his skills were not military; he was expected to be able to draw a bow and drive a chariot.[78] The histories of the kingdoms that ruled China in the second half of the first millennium BC record that the king of Zhao was the first to order his military to incorporate cavalry divisions in about 300 BC.[79] Cavalry then became part of the armies of the other kingdoms, including that of the Qin, who in 221 BC finally defeated the last of their neighbors to unite the Chinese plains under single rule—the period of the "First Emperor of China," Qin Shihuangdi (r. 220–210 BC). The massed ranks of terracotta soldiers guarding his tomb include cavalry divisions and chariots. His success would almost certainly not have been possible without these.

The Qin fell soon after the First Emperor's death, and the family who took power after defeating their main rebel rivals named their dynasty the Han. The story of the Han's eventual defeat of the steppe confederation to their

75. Allsen (2006).

76. For a summary of horse breeding in ancient Iran, see Shahbazi ([1987] 2011). For Greece, see Carlà (2012). The Achaemenids were probably responsible for introducing the fodder alfalfa (lucerne) into Greece, as it is called Median grass.

77. According to the sayings attributed to Confucius, the Six Arts were rites, music, archery, charioteering, calligraphy, and mathematics.

78. We see evidence of horse-drawn chariots in China around 1200 BC, probably adopted from the steppe cultures to the northwest.

79. See chapter 1 for further discussion.

north and west, the Xiongnu, is told in chapter 1. Part of this story is the mission of the Chinese imperial envoy, Zhang Qian, to the lands of the Yuezhi in the mid-second century BC (see chapter 3). Zhang Qian traveled through the lands of the Ferghanan valley, an oasis of plenty in the midst of Central Asian mountains and steppe.[80] Here he encountered a breed of horse that bore little resemblance to those in China. After the Chinese Empire spread westwards and established military garrisons to secure the route, diplomatic and trade missions followed in both directions to secure allies and goods. Prime among the latter for the Chinese, as recorded by their histories, were the Heavenly Horses of Ferghana. The horse continued to be a major part of trade throughout Chinese history and, for much of this period, was purchased with silk.

Archaeology shows the existence of the domesticated horse in the area of what is now China from Neolithic times. And horse-breeding programs are recorded from the first millennium BC. Despite this, the land of China does not ever seem to have been successful either in producing new sustainable breeds or in producing sufficient stock of existing breeds to supply the military.[81] A second-century BC Chinese author notes that Chinese-bred horses cannot rival those of the Xiongnu "in climbing up and down mountains, and crossing ravines and mountains torrents."[82] A large part of the reason for this must have been the lack of suitable pasture—the plains of northern China were devoted to agriculture.[83] Over a millennium later another Chinese official wrote: "The reason why our enemies in the north and west are able to withstand China is precisely because they have many horses and their men are adept at riding; this is their strength. China has few horses and its men are not accustomed to riding; this is China's weakness."[84]

Yet during this period, as Creel points out, "China's foreign relations, military policy, economic well-being, and indeed its very existence as an inde-

80. Today (as of 2013–14), the population of Uzbekistan, Kazakhstan, and Tajikistan combined consists of approximately fifty-five million people, of whom fourteen million live in the Ferghanan valley, even though it is a small part of the total territory.

81. Erkes (1940); Sinor (1972). India, where the horse was introduced much earlier, had similar problems with maintaining breeding programs and also imported horses, by land and sea (Gommans 1995: 15–16; Karttunen 1989, 2014).

82. Quoted in Creel (1965: 657). This passage is interesting in showing that the author was considering the landscape of northern China rather than that of the south, which was full of mountains, ravines, and torrents.

83. Alfalfa (lucerne), a principal horse fodder, was introduced into China by the second century BC.

84. Song Qi (998–1061), quoted in Creel (1965: 667).

pendent state were importantly conditioned by the horse."[85] And the horse was certainly valued: it appears in literature, art, and religion. Moreover, several of the rulers of northern China from the end of the Han period had ancestry from the steppes. This was true of the Tang emperors, believed to be of partly Turkic ethnicity. And during the Tang we see paintings of polo and royal hunts depicted on the walls of the princes' tombs, and the emperors' favorite steeds celebrated in art. Yet there were dissenting voices about participation in the royal hunt.[86] And still the Tang was forced to buys tens of thousands of heads of horses from its Uygur and other neighbors.

It seems, as Creel suggests, that the horse never became entirely adopted into Chinese culture and remained "exotic," even through the Chinese had a desperate need of it.[87] "It is hard to avoid the impression that to Chinese in general the riding horse remained something strange, almost foreign in nature. Horses, and horsemen, were in general associated with the border areas of the north and west. It is a striking fact that the grooms and handlers of horses appearing in Chinese art seem almost always to be depicted as non-Chinese."[88]

And perhaps it was this very lack of confidence in equestrian skills that led Chinese to the invention of the rigid stirrup.[89] Even after its invention many of their equestrian neighbors continued to ride without it, and some sources suggested that the skilled rider felt no need of it.[90] Silks and silverware contemporary with our plaque but produced in Persia and Byzantium almost always depict the royal hunter without stirrups (see chapter 8).

But Khotan, although it had a Chinese population and Chinese garrisons at times, was far removed from the agricultural plains of China and as much

85. Creel (1965: 648).

86. The Chinese emperor Taizong (r. 627–40) was criticized by his advisers for his participation in the royal hunt, but he justified it in terms of the hunt's importance for his Iranian and Turkic neighbors (Marshak (2004: 47). See also Allsen (2006) for Taizong and the royal hunt (109).

87. See chapter 2 for a discussion about the "exoticism" of glass and the lack of its assimilation into Chinese arts.

88. Creel (1965: 670).

89. The earliest known depiction of the rigid stirrup is on a statue from around AD 300 from a tomb in China. However, other finds might revise the conclusion that the stirrup was invented by the Chinese, so this argument is entirely speculative. See Dien (2000) for a discussion on the stirrup in China.

90. See chapter 8 and Shahid (1995: 577).

part of Iranian, Indian, and Central Asian culture. The horse was probably therefore an accepted part of life.[91] Khotan was on routes to the north and northwest, where there were fertile equine breeding grounds.[92] But the horse might also have been bred closer to home. Stein noted the similarity of the horse on the plaque to a modern local breed: "The horse, which is well drawn even to its legs and hoofs, by its colour—white with large spots of black— curiously recalls the appearance of the piebald 'Yarkandi' horse which until recent times was much fancied by natives of Northern India."[93]

The color of the horse is almost certainly significant. In Indo-European cultures the white horse is highly valued, being associated with the sun god.[94] It appears in numerous contexts such as Buddhism, where Buddha departs his father's palace on a white horse, befitting his princely status. The white horse continues to be a theme in Buddhism: for example, legends of the introduction of Buddhism into China tell of two monks coming from the Yuezhi territories on the Amu Darya on white horses, and the seventh-century Chinese pilgrim monk Xuanzang famously selected a white horse to take him on his journey to India.

But the dappled horse is also prominent: Greek legend tells of Poseidon giving two immortal horses, Xanthos and Balios, to Peleus, whose son Achilles later used them to draw his chariot in the Trojan War.[95] They were "blond" (white) and dappled.[96] The dappled horse also has importance in

91. Sino-Kharoṣṭhī coins produced in early Khotan show horses and camels. See Cribb (1984, 1985) and H. Wang (2004: 37–38).

92. "The pastures of western Iran and Armenia had long been renowned for their horses, the Armenians being expected to contribute twenty thousand foals to the king on Mithra's holiday." Creel (1965: 652) quoting Tretiakov and Mongait (1961: 62).

93. Stein (1907: 278). The Yarkandi, a now extinct breed, was probably bred on the Pamir plateau and brought to the oasis of Yarkhand in Khotan for sale. Although India is not discussed here, it also had a demand for horses met in large part by Central Asia to its north (see note 81 above). Gommans (1995: 16) discusses the later trade through Balkh and Bukhara. Also see Moorcroft (1886), who concludes, "It seems proved that the more sandy and dry the soil, every thing else alike, the more healthy are the horses" (27). Horses were also transported by river and sea.

94. Mallory and Adams (1997: 277–78).

95. *Iliad* 16.148.

96. The white (gray) and the dappled horse also appear together in a Chinese poem by Du Fu (712–70) praising a painting: *(continued on next page)*

Central Asian culture.[97] Rustam, the hero of the Persian epic the *Shahnameh* (The books of kings), by Ferdowsī, rode a dappled horse, Rakush, who came from the land of the Kushan (see chapter 3). The story tells that Rakush was chosen from among thousands of horses and that he sired many beautiful spotted foals. In Turkic cultures the "Northern Alayondlu, the Alakcin Tatars, the North and East Asian Basmils, the Turkhsi, the Chaghanina Oguz, and Multan area's Qaiqaniah Turks, all specialised in dappled *alaca* horses."[98] The Basmil lived to the north of the Kok-Turks but later settled in the Turfan area before the Uygurs arrived there.[99] In Seljuk culture the black and white dappled horse of the wheel was a motif signifying the march of time, with the black and white patches representing night and day, as in the lines from the ninth-century *Irk Bitig* (The book of omens) "I am the deity with black and white dappled horse, / who drives day and night."[100]

The eleventh-century Turkic lexicographer Mahmud al-Kashgari would also note many Turkic words across different dialects to describe dappled horses of various colors and patterns.[101]

(continued from footnote on previous page)

> Since the birth of the dynasty, of those who painted saddle-horses
> Only the Prince of Jiangdu was reckoned a wonder,
> Till General Cao won a name, in the last thirty years,
> And men saw again the true yellow thoroughbreds.
> When he drew the late emperor's gray, "Night-shiner."
> Thunder-claps rolled for ten days over over Dragon Lake.
> In the Inner Treasury was a red cornelian bowl:
> Court ladies passed an order to the maids of honor to fetch it,
> The bowl presented, the general made obeisance and danced home elated.
>
> . . . .
>
> In past years, the emperor Taizong had a curly-maned dun;
> In our days, General Guo has a piebald called "Lion";
> Here in this freshly painted picture are the two horses together.

"A Drawing of a Horse by General Cao at Secretary Wei Feng's House," translation after Herdan (1973: 108).

97. Interestingly, the eleventh-century Turkic lexicographer Mahmud al-Kashgari noted that *ak* meant "dappled" in every Turkic dialect except that of the Oguz Turks, where it meant "white" (Esin 1965: 176). Some trace the origins of the Appaloosan horse to these Central Asian forebears.

98. Esin (1965: 168).

99. The Basmil Turks were one of the tribes who formed the Karakhanid confederation, who were to take Khotan in 1006.

100. Esin (1965: 179). During his investiture rights the Seljuk monarch was mounted on such a horse. The wheel as a symbol of time is found more widely—for example in Vedic culture in India—and might show a Buddhist rather than a Turkic influence.

101. Esin (1965: 177n6) cites a list of modern terms, such as *ciren* (brown and reddish spots), *kok* (bluish gray dapples), and *bogrul* (spots on flanks only).

• • •

Over a thousand years ago a group of monks in the oasis kingdom of Khotan traveled from the capital northeast into the desert. They passed through small farming settlements at the edge of the oasis and along an irrigation canal for a week deep into the desert. Here they came to a settlement, with orchards of apples and apricots and oleaster trees. This was a place dotted with the stupa domes of small temples. The monks lived in a small two-story house on the edge of the settlement. Their days were spent looking after one of the temples and its grounds—which included a smallholding. They swept the grounds, cut the grass, irrigated the fields, and tended the crops. They probably also officiated at local ceremonies and carried out their own private worship. They were able to circumambulate the stupas along corridors adorned with murals.

Votive offerings were part of the everyday life of a Buddhist shrine. Miniature clay stupas and wooden and terracotta plaques were made by the local temple and sold to visiting pilgrims and worshippers to offer to the temple, so individualizing the act of workshop. Although the plaques were decorated with Buddhist scenes, these reflected the Buddhism of Khotan. Over time the monks decorated their small dwelling, making holes in the wall above the fireplace to hang some of the plaques to act as a shrine. When they left, the plaques remained, and over time, as the building collapsed in on itself, they were displaced from the wall and buried under rubble. So protected they lay undisturbed until uncovered by archaeologists from afar. Today they rest in the storage vaults of a museum, far removed from their original context and purpose. They are valued now not for their votive power, but in their capacity as a historical and artistic record of a long-extinct and still little-understood culture.

SEVEN

The Blue Qur'an

WE JOIN THE OBJECT discussed in this chapter at a time in its life when it has already been fragmented and its parts have been dispersed worldwide. It is highly improbable that it will ever be complete again, even digitally. It is—was—a bound book, in the codex form, of possibly as many as six hundred folios. The Arabic text is the Qur'an written in gold in Kufic script with decorations in silver on indigo-colored parchment (plate 6).[1] The object offers us an insight into the modern art and book market and raises the conundrums faced by public museums when working in the same arena as the private market. But before considering the relatively modern plight of this object, we will look at why, when, and where it was first created over a millennium ago, starting with a discussion of book production in the medieval world.

A WORLD OF BOOKS

When discussing the history of books (in the broadest sense) we can make a basic distinction between, put simply, those produced to last and those

For places mentioned in this chapter see Map 7 in the color maps insert.

1 Jonathan Bloom's and Alain George's work and ongoing debate on the Blue Qur'an have been invaluable sources for this chapter and I recommend reading George (2009) and Bloom (2015) for its current status. Emily Neumeier (2006) has produced a clear summary. I must thank Alison Ohta and Cheryl Porter for their most useful comments and for their generous sharing of their knowledge. Jiří Vnouček and Peter Sellars both offered insightful comments and infectious enthusiasm, Jiří on parchment, and Peter on aspects of the Qur'anic tradition. Conversations with them have been an unexpected highlight of choosing this object. All mistakes, misunderstandings, and omissions are my own.

intended as ephemeral objects: the difference, for example, between a published book and a shopping list today. While there is a large gray area in between these two extremes, religious texts, especially expensively produced canonical works of the major religions, such as this copy of the Qur'an, are usually produced for permanence.[2] This chapter relates to religious material; discussion of a more ephemeral text—an almanac—is found in chapter 9.[3]

As Islamic rule and culture developed and spread from the late seventh century, it would have encountered several established manuscript cultures that showed varieties in the format and medium of books in different parts of Afro-Eurasia.[4] How and to what extent Islamic book culture was influenced by the surrounding cultures is very difficult to ascertain, but by this time in Europe, West Asia, and North and East Africa the codex was the dominant form in the Christian tradition.[5] The codex is the form used for modern printed books where sheets or folios—usually folded—are bound at one side, creating pages that can be leafed through.[6] It is the original form of this copy of the Qur'an and probably used for the earliest copies of the Qur'an.[7] In the form seen in Christian and then in Islamic codices, several folios are folded together to form quires before the quires are bound in groups at their folded edges to form the book. The pages are protected by the binding.[8] In the Christian world at this time, book production was largely controlled by the clergy, the literate elite, from their monastic centers, and we see the codex form standardly used for Bibles in both the Eastern and Western

2. *Qur'an* refers to the revelation given to the prophet Muhammed. Copies of the Qur'an, whether in oral or written forms, are *mushaf*. However, I use the term *Qur'an* here as in common English usage, to refer to the copies as well.

3. This chapter concentrates on a few formats, such as the codex, scroll, and *pothi*, which were commonly used for important texts. There were a wide range of other formats and materials. For examples in Central Asia, see Whitfield (2015a).

4. Arabic inscriptions on stone exist from before this, and there are references to texts on palm bark and parchment, but none are extant (Roper 2010: 321).

5. Pedersen (1984: 101) suggests that the codex format was transmitted to Muslims by Axumite (Ethiopian) Christians, as the work *mushaf* came from their language.

6. The seminal work *The Birth of the Codex* describes the form as "a collection of sheets of any material, folded double and fastened together at the back or spine, usually protected by covers" (Roberts and Skeat 1983: 1).

7. Although Déroche (2006: 174) suggests that there is some evidence that early Qur'an were scrolls. Ohta (2012: 40n1) notes a Qur'an in scroll format (arabe 6088) dating to 1400 in the Bibiothèque nationale de France. Note also that this Qur'an is in horizontal format, a feature discussed below.

8. The bindings vary over time. Discussed briefly below.

Christian traditions.[9] Famous examples are now commonly referred to after their place and format, such as "Codex Sinaiticus"—a mid-fourth-century codex from Sinai.[10]

But the codex form of the book only emerged as dominant in the classical and Christian traditions around AD 300.[11] Before this such texts were mainly in scroll format.[12] Originally scrolls were commonly made of sheets made from the papyrus plant, *Cyperus papyrus L.* Such books are extant from the mid-third millennium BC in Egypt.[13] The papyrus plant was common across the Egyptian Empire and was widely exploited, not only for books, but also for everyday items, such as baskets, ropes, and sandals. But it formed sheets that were brittle and difficult to fold. At the end of the first millennium, parchment also started to be used and came to largely replace papyrus over the following centuries in West Asia and Europe.[14] *Parchment* refers to prepared animal skins—mainly sheep, goat, and calf.[15] The finer skins are also called vellum.[16] The terms are not always used precisely: sometimes *vellum* refers to finer parchment, whether sheep, goat, or calf, and sometimes it

9. Production later moved into cathedral schools, universities, and commercial outlets (Beit-Aíré 2009: 22). The name *Bible* derives from the Greek *biblia,* a collection of books. Codices contained parts of the Bible we know today as the Old and New Testaments.

10. These are recent names given by collectors and holders and do not indicate the origins of the book. In this case, the codex was held at the Monastery of Saint Catherine, Mount Sinai, until the nineteenth century, when it was broken up and dispersed (although between only four institutions, making it feasible to reunite the fragments digitally online (see "History of Codex Sinaiticus," n.d., Codex Sinaiticus, accessed September 23, 2017, www.codex-sinaiticus.net/en/codex/history.aspx).

11. Various theories have been put forward to explain the change from scroll or codex; see Roberts and Skeat (1983) and Skeat's update (1994). However, none are totally satisfactory. See further discussion below.

12. See Skeat (1994). Other formats and materials continued in use; as noted above, we are concentrating here on the form used for books intended to last.

13. Discovered by a joint Egyptian-French team in 2013 at Wadi al-Jafr, an Egyptian harbor on the Red Sea (Tallet 2012).

14. Although papyrus continued to be used in certain contexts, including codices. Ohta (2012: 40n1) notes a ninth-century papyrus scroll in the Heidelberg papyrus collection. Papal bulls, for example, continued to be written on papyrus until 1022 (Diringer 1982: 166). Hebrew texts were also written on leather.

15. Although skins from other animals are also used.

16. I owe most of my meager knowledge on parchment to Jiri Vnouček, a conservator at the Royal Library, Copenhagen, who did a PhD on the subject for York University (Vnouček 2018). I thank him for many fascinating conversations and practical demonstrations at the Getty Research Institute in 2016 and since. All mistakes or misunderstandings are my own.

is used to refer only to calf skin.[17] The skins are not tanned, distinguishing them from leather.[18]

Malachi Beit-Arié argues that relatively high literacy among Jewish communities combined with their lack of a centralized political or intellectual establishment "shaped the individual and personal nature of Hebrew book production and precluded the standardization of the reproduced texts."[19] In other words, he argues that Hebrew books were produced in a variety of forms, which were influenced by the local culture. But we see from finds that the scroll remains for several centuries after Christian codices become common: in the Jewish world the codex does not seem to have started replacing scrolls until the ninth century. The earliest extant Hebrew codices that can be dated are from the tenth century. This was not a case of the codex being unknown: the Islamic, Christian, and Hebrew communities lived side by side, and there is evidence of mutual influence and sharing of book production.[20] All extant early copies of the Qur'an are in codex form.

As Islam expanded eastward, it came into contact with communities who had other religions, such as the Zoroastrians of Sasanian Iran. This religion had developed in Central Asia and spread to Iran in the first millennium BC, becoming the religion of the Achaemenid kings. Like Judaism and Christianity, it looked to the sacred word, in its case the Avestan texts. But written documents are conspicuously rare, which has led many scholars to conclude that Zoroastrianism perpetuated an oral tradition whereby the Avestan texts were not transcribed.[21] Although there is some evidence that texts, including the Avesta, were written under imperial patronage in the third century AD, the earliest extant Avestan manuscript is ninth or tenth

17. As noted in the Introduction, the lack of identification of the animal skin used in most catalogs of medieval manuscripts shows the comparative lack of interest among most scholars—and curators (with honorable exceptions)—in the materiality of these objects. This lack of precision is not restricted to European medieval manuscripts. Just as the term *vellum* is ambiguous, so the terms used for Chinese and Japanese manuscripts—*hemp* and *mulberry* paper—can be equally misleading, referring to a type of paper rather than the fibers used. Of course, there is the issue of funding for analysis on the materiality, but if there were sufficient interest among curators and scholars in these questions, then funding would surely be found.

18. Leather, wood, and a variety of other materials were also used for writing—for example, some of the Dead Sea scrolls are on leather—but I am concentrating here on the main materials used for religious texts.

19. Beit-Arié (2009: 23).

20. Beit-Arié (1993; 2009: 27–29).

21. Kellens ([1987] 2011), Skjærvø (2012).

century and was unearthed at a site in Central Asia.[22] Although only one sheet of paper remains, it was probably originally in vertical scroll format, evident from the glue marks on the bottom of the sheet.

This reliance on oral transmission is common in many religions, including Buddhism, which developed in North India and in which, tradition tells us, the lectures of the historical Buddha were not written down until some centuries after his death. It would be a mistake, however, to think that the oral and written traditions were exclusive: more often they were complementary.[23] The Qur'an, as well as Hebrew and Buddhist scriptures—and other religious texts—are still learned by heart in religious teaching.

The earliest extant Buddhist manuscripts are found in Central Asia written on scrolls made of birch bark.[24] But in India Buddhists used the traditional writing material of palm leaves for their books, inscribing the letters and rubbing ink over them. The palm leaves were strung together with one or two strings through the center of the leaf and bound between wooden boards: this form is often referred to as *pothi* or *pustaka*. This tradition spread into Southeast Asia. Elsewhere, Buddhism seems to have adapted to the local materials, sometimes retaining the Indian format—seen in the large paper *pothi* of the Tibetans—and sometimes adopting the local format—as in the paper scrolls of East Asia.[25]

Buddhism almost certainly spread westwards into Sasanian Iran, perhaps even as far as modern-day Turkey, but there is sparse remaining evi-

22. British Library, Or.8212/84. See Whitfield and Sims-Williams (2004: 118, cat. 2).
23. "In medieval Islamic society the written text, therefore, was not an end in itself but served primarily as an adjunct to memory" (Bloom 2001: 95; for general discussion of this topic, see 94–99).
24. Salomon (1999).
25. In East Asia the scroll—formed of silk or wooden strips tied together—was used in the first millennium BC for canonical texts and continued through much of the second millennium. But by the first few centuries AD scrolls were commonly made of paper: cheaper than silk and more convenient and lighter than wood. It was only in the ninth to tenth centuries that codices start to be seen, becoming prevalent over the following centuries (Whitfield 2015a). I will not enter a debate about the move from the scroll to the codex except to express some caution when considering the argument often given, especially by medievalists of the Western world, that it was a superior form. This is far from clear, as the nature of the script and the purpose of the text are both factors. See Gamble (2006: 25) for a clear summary of the issues for Christian texts. It is also possible that, in both the medieval West and China, part of the impetus for the move was for economic reasons. According to Xin Wen's research, early codices in China show a very economical use of paper (forthcoming; pers. comm., September 2016).

dence.[26] However, Islamic communities would have encountered this religion—and its texts—as they moved eastwards. But Sasanian Iran was the birthplace of another religion that placed great emphasis on the book, that of Manichaeism. Its third-century founder, Mani, probably grew up in South Mesopotamia among a Jewish-Christian Baptist community—the Elkhasaites. The religion spread both west, into the Roman-Byzantium world, and east, into Central Asia and thence to China. As in Buddhism, Manichaean texts, originally written in Syriac (Eastern Aramaic), were translated into numerous languages—from Coptic translations of the fourth century to Parthian, Middle Persian, Sogdian, and Turkic translations—and they appear in both scroll and codex format.[27] Many of these were illuminated, supporting the mention in early sources of "Mani's Picture Book," which was used for teaching.[28]

We therefore see a medieval world of books far more diverse than often suggested by the emphasis on the Western medieval codex, and it is this world that Islamic scribes, scholars, teachers, and patrons encountered when they variously considered their committal to text of the teachings of Islam.[29]

ISLAMIC BOOKS AND THE QUR'AN

According to Sunni tradition, the teachings of Islam received by the Prophet Mohammed in the early seventh century were first preserved by oral transmission—as in other religions, such as Zoroastrianism and Buddhism. But Sunni tradition also tells that only two decades after his death, during the leadership of the third caliph, Uthmān ibn 'Affān (r. 644–56), an authoritative edition was preserved in writing, forming the Qur'an.[30] In 2015, radiocarbon dating was carried out on two parchment folios remaining from a Qur'an in codex form preserved in the University of Birmingham. The tests gave a date between 568 and 645.[31] The dates for the text have not been unequivocally accepted—some scholars suggest that the parchment had been

26. For an interesting discussion, see Vaziri (2012).

27. Gulácsi (2005).

28. Gulácsi (2011, 2015).

29. There is no suggestion that there was a consensus or any formal discussion on this.

30. Schoeler (2006). For an overview of the written transmission of the Qur'an, see Déroche (2006).

31. "The Birmingham Qur'an Manuscript" [frequently asked questions], n.d., Cadbury

reused so that the text is later—but several other extant Qur'an manuscripts are accepted as dating from the seventh century.[32]

The Qur'an is written in Arabic using a script probably developed by the Nabataeans, a people who ruled a kingdom around Petra in Jordan from the middle of the first millennium BC. Inscriptions in this script in the Aramaic language are found from the second century AD. Later texts written in papyrus show its development into a cursive form, which over the centuries evolved into the Arabic script. The earliest example using the Arabic script is a trilingual inscription—in Greek, Syriac, and Arabic—written in 512.

Although some texts, mainly poetry, survive from before the Qur'an, Arabic developed and flourished as a written language with the rise of Islam.[33] The original script allowed many ambiguities in reading, as it did not, for example, transcribe short vowels, leaving the reader to use context to identify them. But over the following centuries, almost certainly at least in part as a result of the desire to provide a canonical written version of the Qur'an, the script was refined. The script used for manuscripts of the Qur'an up until the eleventh century is called Kufic, named after Kufa in Iraq.[34]

It was in this context that the Blue Qur'an was produced. Before discussing the when and where—over which there is continuing debate—we will look at the how, which is less contentious, although not without some uncertainties.

MAKING THE BLUE QUR'AN

The Blue Qur'an is made from parchment, the material of choice for books in the western Eurasian world by the third century, although it had been

---

Research Library, University of Birmingham, www.birmingham.ac.uk/facilities/cadbury/TheBirminghamQuranManuscript.aspx.

32. For a discussion of carbon dating of these early manuscripts, see "Radiocarbon (Carbon-14) Dating of Manuscripts of the Qur'ān," Islamic Awareness, updated August 14, 2016, www.islamic-awareness.org/Quran/Text/Mss/radio.html.

33. "Because the overwhelmingly powerful revelation had come in the form of a book, textuality became the preeminent characteristic of Arab and Muslim cognitive processes, and came to permeate Muslim society" (Roper 2010: 322). A tenth-century bibliography gives forty-three thousand Arabic authors (323).

34. See George (2010). There is another interesting avenue of discussion here, namely the importance of calligraphy and why it became so highly valued in some traditions—such as Islamic and Chinese —but not so much in others, such as Roman.

used since the second century BC if not before.[35] Parchment is formed from animal skins—mainly calf, sheep, or goat. While calf skins had to be taken from calves that were either stillborn or less than a week old—otherwise the skins became too thick to use—skins from full-grown sheep and goats were suitable, as they were much thinner.[36] The parchment of the Blue Qur'an is sheepskin.[37] Preparation of the skins was a skilled but slow and messy business.[38] They were soaked in a solution of lime for several days before the hair was scraped off and the skin stretched taut on a frame (figure 21). If stretched too much then it might break. Small holes could be repaired and can be seen on the finished books. The skin was scraped again while wet and stretched further. It might be rubbed with pumice in order to enable the surface to take the ink before being left to dry. If the surface still contained grease after drying, making it difficult for the ink to adhere, then it was treated with a calcium compound such as lime, chalk, or wood ash, which was applied as either dry powders or wet pastes.[39] A single skin might typically produce one to four folios, depending on its size and that of the folios required. The parchment of the Blue Qur'an is made from sheepskin, and the size of its folios —thirty-one by forty-one centimeters—suggests a large skin that might have been able to produce as many as two bifolia—each folded in half, so forming four folios or eight pages (figure 22).[40] A book like this with an estimated six hundred folios would therefore have required at least 150 animals.[41]

The Qur'an has been colored blue by a dye extracted from an indigotin-bearing plant. Indigo had been used as a dye for textiles since ancient times, independently developed wherever the plants grew.[42] Examples are found in

35. Parchment, *pergamaneum* in Latin, takes its name from the town of Pergamum. Pliny recorded that a king of the second century BC invented it during a trade blockade on papyrus. For clear summaries of this and of parchment preparation, see Curci (2003) and Baranov (n.d.).

36. My comments on parchment are based on Jirí Vnouček's extensive research on medieval manuscripts and hands-on experience with making and using parchment (Vnouček 2018). His conclusion about the use of skins of stillborn or very young calves and the unsuitability of the skins of older calves is not accepted by all. For recent analysis, see Fiddyment et al. (2015).

37. After tests done by Sarah Fiddyment at York University, UK.

38. See the short video *Making Parchment* (British Pathé, 1939), www.britishpathe.com/video/making-parchment-issue-title-is-the-very-idea.

39. R. Reed (1975: 90).

40. Porter (2018).

41. The original size of the book is an estimate based on the length of the Qur'an.

42. Sandberg (1989); Balfour-Paul (1998); Cardon (2007).

FIGURE 21. Woodblock print showing a parchment maker. After Josef Amman, *Das Ständebuch* (1568).

South America from around 4000 BC, in the Middle East around 3000 BC, and, on linen mummy cloths in Egypt around 2400 BC.[43] After this we have more examples both on linen and on wool through the second millennium BC. Indigo as a dye is derived from two main plant species, although found in many others: true indigo or *Indigofera tinctora*, and the woad plant, *Isatis tinctoria*. The former is a much more efficient source of the dye, but as a subtropical and tropical plant it is not indigenous to much of northern Eurasia or North Africa. Woad is found across the Eurasian steppe and desert, from the Caucasus, West Asia, to eastern Siberia as well as in parts of North Africa. It was cultivated throughout Europe, and seeds have been found in

43. At the Huaca Prieta Temple in Peru (Splitstoser et al. 2016).

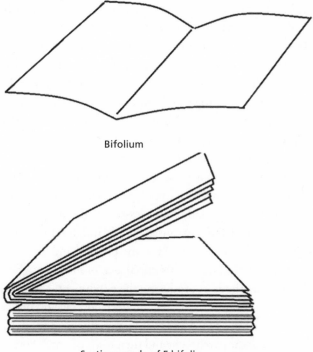

Bifolium

Sections made of 5 bifolia

FIGURE 22. The formation of quires or sections using five bifolia. After Marzo (n.d.).

Neolithic contexts. It continued in use into the first millennium, but for textiles. Because the main detectable components of indigo dye are common to all sources—whether woad grown in Turkey or true indigo from India—little provenance information can be gained from any analytical tests.[44] It is therefore not possible to know which plant was used to create the indigo for the Blue Qur'an.[45]

From the sixth century we see Bibles made from parchment colored reddish-purple.[46] Purple dye was highly valued in several ancient societies. Much was produced from boiling the *murex* sea snail, its discovery credited to the citizens of the Phoenician city of Tyre by the fourteenth century BC, hence

44. Ferreira et al. (2004: 330).
45. Bloom (2015: 208) expresses some doubts about whether dyeing of parchment is possible, while George (2009:76) cites unpublished microscopic analysis in support of dyeing.
46. For examples, see Evans and Ratliff (2012: 40–41).

Tyrian purple.[47] It was very expensive, as a large number of shellfish were required to produce a small amount of dye.[48] In AD 301 in the Roman world one pound cost 150,000 denarii or around three pounds of gold.[49] But purple dye made from lichen (orchil) was also used from this time, and some texts give recipes where they were used in combination.[50] In Rome purple was used for status: the senators wore togas and tunics with a stripe of purple. This link continued into Byzantium, where it became the imperial color and its use was highly restricted. It was at this time that purple started to be used for books. While it was long assumed that these were dyed with *murex*, almost all tests on such work to date have shown the dye to be from lichens.[51]

Early modern experiments with dyeing parchment using similar methods to dyeing textiles were originally unsuccessful, as the purple color did not adhere to the parchment and also caused it to shrink. But many technologies of the past have not been bequeathed to the present, and we often struggle to replicate them today. Much of this initial lack of success might have been owing to different methods in producing the parchment. More recent work has produced successful results, with good deep coverage on both sides and with the parchment restretched afterwards. Equally good results have been obtained by painting the parchment and then restretching.[52] Some medieval manuscripts show brush marks, suggesting that the second method was used in these cases, but Cheryl Porter, who has examined several folios of the Blue Qur'an, notes the lack of any brush marks, although she argues, on the basis of experimentation, that brush marks disappear on a second application of

47. *Murex trunculus, Purpura lapillus, Helix ianthina*, and especially *Murex brandaris* (Ferreira et al. 2004: 331; Cardon 2007).

48. Beatrice Caseau, quoted in Bagnall et al. (2012: 5673), gives a figure of ten thousand shellfish to produce one gram of dye.

49. Price edict under the Emperor Diocletian.

50. See Casselman and Terada (2012) for an interesting discussion on the economics and politics of the dyes and the use of combinations of the dyes.

51. Porter (2008). Also see Muthesius (2002: 159–60), which discusses the uses of combinations of murex and lichen and of madder and indigo to emulate the more expensive purple on silk produced for diplomatic gifts.

52. See Vnouček's PhD dissertation (2018) for successful use of dying and painting parchment with purple dye and Cheryl Porter's (2018) article reporting Isabelle Whitworth's successful dying of sheepskin with indigo. The artist Inge Boesken Kanold (2005) has also achieved successful results by using a cold vat of dye and adding detergent; see her website, www.artemision.free.fr/boesken/index-en.php) for other references to her work. But Vnouček has achieved excellent results without the addition of detergent. See also Biggam (2002: 32).

the dye.[53] She also notes, from her own observations of several folios that contain surface abrasions, that brush-applied color sits on the surface.

The bifolia for the Blue Qur'an then had to be prepared from the colored parchments.[54] Their size, as noted above, is unusual. Also of note is the orientation. This codex is in horizontal rather than vertical format—landscape rather than portrait. Early codices, whether in the Christian or Islamic tradition, are usually vertically oriented. Later Islamic codices also revert to the vertical format. One explanation for the move to horizontal format is the adoption of the Kufic script, but given the relative lack of extant early Islamic codices it would be rash to jump to any conclusions.[55] However, by the sixth century we see Greek manuscripts in vertical format but of similar proportions, some colored in purple, such as the *Codex Purpureus Petropolitanus*, which has 231 folios sized thirty-two by twenty-seven centimeters. However, unlike this and most other Greek counterparts, the text in the copies of the Qur'an is written in a single column. The sheets were prepared for writing by incising in dry point a fifteen-line text box grid, possibly using a frame with cords.[56] The text was then added.

It was originally assumed that the text was written in gold ink, a technique called chrysography.[57] This is seen used on Christian manuscripts and is described in Islamic texts, such as a tenth-century manual on calligraphy.[58] At this time, reed pens were commonly used: the reed was soaked in water and then sharpened to form a nib. The shape of the nib shows not only regional variations—especially between Spain/North Africa and central and eastern lands—but also variations between calligraphy masters.[59] Cases have been found that incorporated an inkwell.

There are many extant copies of the Qur'an written using gold. However, microscopic examination by Cheryl Porter of a folio in the Museum of Fine Arts, Boston, showed that gold leaf was used instead.[60] The scribe wrote the letters using some form of adhesive—possibly gum arabic—and then the

53. Porter (2018).

54. It is assumed that this was done after coloring, but of course it is also possible that the folios were prepared before coloring.

55. Ohta (2012: 41–43).

56. George (2009: 77); shown in Bloom (2015: figs. 2 and 5).

57. George (2009: 75).

58. By 'al-Mu'izz ibn Baid (d. 1062), as noted by George (2009: 75).

59. Roper (2010: 324; Schimmel 1984: 39–40).

60. Porter (2018). Cited in Bloom (2015: 210–11).

gold leaf was applied, brushed to remove loose fragments, and possibly burnished.[61] The letters were outlined using an iron-tannate ink that was brownish in color.[62] Such ink had been used since antiquity. As Jonathan Bloom notes, Arabic recipes for ink give gallnuts as the source of tannin, but elsewhere walnut shells and pomegranate bark were also used.[63] The tannic acid was mixed with ferrous sulfate. Bloom argues that the outlining of the characters in brown ink, as noted by Alain George, was to "tidy up" the feathery edges of the gold leaf.[64] The text would have almost certainly been written by a professional scribe, but we know little of such groups—although we do know that they were not only male. One reference mentions 170 female scribes writing the Qur'an in Kufic script in tenth-century Cordoba in southern Spain.[65]

Headings and markers were added in silver. Again, we see a difference in interpretation between George and Bloom. The former argues that these were added later—along with a silver-illuminated folio that was applied over existing text.[66] The latter argues that they were contemporaneous with the rest of the manuscript.[67]

Finally, and there is consensus on this, the folded leaves—or bifolia—were grouped together in the appropriate order into quires, which were then secured inside a binding (figure 23). The binding is not known and probably long lost: as Alison Ohta has noted, a substantial number of bindings are found only by the Mamluk Sultanate (1260–1516), long after the probable production of this Qur'an.[68] However, as she notes, several scholars have suggested that bindings and decoration during the early period were influenced by Coptic bindings. The earliest extant Islamic bindings

61. Porter (2018). The examination was carried out with Joan Wright. She lists as possible adhesives "gum, glair (egg white) or plant or animal adhesive such as fig sap, parchment shavings or fish collagen."

62. "This result was obtained by Joan Wright at the Museum of Fine Arts, Boston, and confirmed—using Laser Raman Spectroscopic analysis—at the New York Metropolitan Museum" (Porter 2018: n15).

63. Bloom (2015).

64. Bloom (2015: 2011–12). Such ink has a corrosive effect on paper, and after it started to be used black ink started to be made from soot and gum, already in use for papyrus and closer to inks used since early times in India and Central and East Asia (Roper 2010: 324).

65. Roper (2010: 329).

66. George (2009: 89-92).

67. Bloom (2015: 212).

68. Ohta (2012: 40).

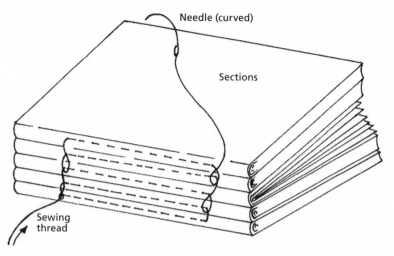

Needle (curved)

Sections

Sewing
thread

FIGURE 23. The sewing together of quires to form a codex. After Marzo (n.d.).

date to the ninth century and are box bindings made of wood covered with leather.[69]

When and where the book was made are uncertain. Scholars have argued for dates of production ranging from the late eighth to tenth centuries and places of production from Iran, Tunisia, and Iraq to Spain and Sicily.[70] In a 2015 article that reviews all previous discussions, Bloom argues on the principle of Ockham's razor—the simplest explanation should be given most weight—for a Tunisian production. He cites three potential pieces of evidence to support this. First, there is one known surviving folio of another copy of the Qur'an in gold ink on blue-dyed paper dating from the fourteenth century. It is written in a script developed in North Africa—the Maghribi script.[71] Second, the library of the Great Mosque of Kairouan was invento-

69. See Ohta (2012: 41–42 and rest of chapter) for a full discussion of this. See also Hobbs (n.d.) for a discussion with illustrations. For further discussion of box bindings, see Dreibholz (1997). Some of these have been found at Kairouan, Tunisia, one of the possible production sites of the book.

70. The history of this discussion is most recently summarized by Bloom, who himself argues for Kairouan in Tunisia in the tenth century (2015: 204–6). For the Spanish attribution see Stanley (1995), and for the Sicilian connection see Fraser and Kwiatkowski (2006).

71. Bloom (2015: 205) notes other manuscripts with some similarities, such as a page in Kufic script in the Freer Gallery that has blue decorations and a fifteenth-century Qur'an written in silver and gold on purple and brown-dyed paper. The latter was produced in North Africa (Blair and Bloom 1994: 116–17).

ried in 1293, and the inventory listed several copies of the Qur'an, including one "in large format, written in gold, in Kufic script, on dark-blue (*akhal*) parchment . . . the *sūras* and number of verses and *aḥzāb* in silver, covered in tooled leather over boards, lined with silk."[72] Third, the sixty-seven folios of the Blue Qur'an now held in the Raqqada National Museum of Islamic Art (about seven miles southwest of Kairouan) almost certainly came from the library of the Great Mosque of Kairouan.[73]

Without further evidence to the contrary, the argument for this manuscript's Tunisian origins is therefore strong, if not decisive. The mosque, established in 670, became an important center of learning in the Islamic world, especially from the ninth to eleventh centuries.[74] Situated on Mediterranean trade routes and within easy access to Egypt, Sicily, and the Levant, this region was well connected to the rest of the Islamic world. The House of Wisdom (Bayt al-Ḥikma) established there was said to rival the one in Baghdad in the study of medicine, astronomy, engineering, and translation.[75] The 1293 library catalog, noted above, stated that the mosque library had developed from the endowment of books, including copies of the Qur'an, and was supplemented over time with more bequeathed by local scholars and famous families.[76]

The evidence for the dating—the when—is also uncertain, with strong arguments being given by both George and Bloom for late eighth-/early ninth- and early tenth-century dates respectively. I do not intend to discuss these, as the topic is far outside my expertise, but it is possible that further evidence will come to light or that analytic techniques will provide more information in the future.

This leaves the question of why. This question comes in at least two parts. Without knowing more about the when and where, we cannot be specific about the impetus for the production of this copy of the Qur'an and can do little more than assume that it was commissioned by a very wealthy and elite

72. Shabbūḥ (1956) quoted in George (2009: 79). As several scholars have pointed out, this description does not accord strictly with the Blue Qur'an. Stanley (1995) has discussed this and provided a potential explanation.

73. George (2009: 75) cites the figure of sixty-seven folios from a personal communication he received from the keeper of manuscripts. Others have treated it with some skepticism, since the folios have not been published or studied by scholars (Bloom 2015: 205).

74. Laugu (2007: 103, 105). See also Othwa ([2002] 2010).

75. al-Rammah (1995: 29).

76. Ibn al-Nadim (1872: 8, 29); Othwa ([2002] 2010).

person. Its large size and sumptuousness—its "conspicuous virtuosity"—suggests a public and ritual function: it was not produced to be hidden away.[77] The very richness of the materials used showed not only the patron's largesse but also God's providence.[78]

But we have to hope for more evidence before we can learn anything more. The second part concerns why this color scheme was chosen. We know of no precedents and only one later copy of the Qur'an using the same color scheme. This therefore brings us to the issues of color symbolism and aesthetics and raises several intriguing questions.

WHY BLUE AND GOLD? THE PERCEPTION, AESTHETICS, AND SYMBOLISM OF COLOR

When folios of this manuscript first appeared in the world of the Western book collector, the assertion was made that the manuscript had come from Mashad in eastern Iran and had been commissioned on the death of the Abbasid caliph Hārūn Ar-Rašīd (r. 786–809), by his son, as blue was the color of mourning.[79] There seems to be little evidence given to support either the provenance or the symbolism of blue, but it was nevertheless accepted and even embellished by other scholars.[80] Most importantly, however, it gave a provenance for a manuscript on the market. While the provenance, as mentioned above, remains uncertain, since then there have been more informed discussions about the choice of and potential influences on the color scheme, although without consensus.

As noted above, Byzantium culture linked purple dye with the imperial family and used purple for clothing but also for imperial edicts.[81] By the sixth century, purple-dyed parchment starts to be used for Christian

---

77. Touati (2010).

78. In both the Islamic and Christian traditions, "Precious materials—particularly gold, silver, ivory and silk—and conspicuous virtuosity came to carry auspicious connotations of God's providence as the gifts and wonders of creation" (Schoeler 2006: 124).

79. F. Martin (1912, vol. 1: 106, 141).

80. Arnold and Grohman (1929: 20), cited in Bloom (2015: 197). The only evidence for a Persian origin is a Persian custom stamp, which Bloom notes on the folio later sold to Harvard (Bloom 2015: 199).

81. Images of "Christ the king" also showed him dressed in purple. It is worth noting that Chinese Buddhists also adopted the imperial color—in their case, yellow—as the color of their sacred texts. Paper used for sutras was usually dyed with *huangbo*—derived from the

Bibles that were written in gold or silver.[82] In a poem written by the scribe Godescalc at the end of a Christian text produced for the then king of the Lombards, Charlemagne, in 781–83, is the following verse:

Golden words are painted here on purple pages,
The Thunderer's shining kingdoms of the starry heavens,
Revealed in rose-red blood, disclose the joys of heaven,
And the eloquence of God glittering with fitting brilliance
Promises the splendid reward of martyrdom to be gained.[83]

This symbolism of the juxtaposition of the stars, representing the golden words of God, against a night sky—the light in the dark—is a trope in many, if not most, religions. George has rejected the suggestion that these purple/gold books could have been a possible influence on the color scheme of the Blue Qur'an. His argument, based on the difference between the reddish-purple hues of the Bibles and the dark-blue hue of the Qur'an, and suggesting that such a difference would have been perceived acutely "at a time when . . . brightness and darkness were fundamental aspects of colour perception," is not, I believe, enough to reject totally a potential influence.[84] As the above verse shows, while there was a different aesthetic, the same idea of light and darkness was being explored in the Christian manuscripts.[85] We also have to bear in mind the possible change in color of the purple Bibles over time. Although Tyrian purple was notably resistant to fading, the same is not true of dye made from lichens.[86] However, the symbolic association of purple with the blood of Christ, also noted by George, would not have resonated in an Islamic context.[87]

An obvious example of the juxtaposition of deep blue and gold is found naturally in lapis lazuli, a stone mined in what is now eastern Afghanistan

---

bark of the Amur cork tree—which had berberine as its main constituent. The dye had other benefits, giving the paper water- and insect-repellent properties.

82. Examples from the sixth century include the Rossano and Sinope Gospels and the *Codex Purpureus Petropolitanus*. See Evans and Ratliff (2012: 40–41).

83. From a manuscript in Paris, BnF MS, nouv. acq. lat. 1203, 26v–127r, quoted in H. Kessler (2006: 77). For further discussion, see 102–3.

84. George (2009: 95).

85. And in other contexts: as Thomas notes in relation to silk, "Byzantine aesthetics appreciated colour allied with brightness" (2012: 128).

86. Casselman and Terada (2012) explore the color fastness of the two dyes used alone and in combination. There is also the change of the ink.

87. George (2009: 97).

and imported to North Africa and West Asia from at least the second millennium BC. Lapis was a valued gemstone and pigment in the Islamic world and was exported to the Christian world.[88] Gold-colored pyrite flecks are often found in the mined stone.[89] This combination of blue and gold was also used in Byzantine mosaics and in Islamic and other monumental inscriptions, such as the inscription on the Dome of the Rock.[90] On a more domestic note, the ninth-century poet Ibn al-Rūmī celebrates an inkwell made of ebony inlaid with gold, comparing it to a black African woman "who likes to wear yellow dresses."[91] Lawrence Nees has argued for a possible connection "with peacocks and with Solomon, and a conception of rulership not founded primarily upon Roman inspiration."[92]

The Dome of the Rock early mosaic inscriptions are in gold on a ground of what has been described as dark green rather than blue. But the green-blue distinction is one that has been subject to much scientific scrutiny. Some anthropologists and neuroscientists have argued that there is a relation between a culture having a name for a color and members of that culture learning to distinguish it from other colors.[93] Many of the cited experiments in these cases have involved the distinction—or lack of—between perceptions of green and blue in cultures without a word for what we would recognize as blue. Bloom argues that there is no world in classical Arabic for "blue" as such. In the Qur'an, he notes, the word azraq is used only once, to refer to the evil blue-eyed people, whereas other colors receive repeated mentions. Bloom suggests that the color of the sea, for example, would have been described by the word we translate as green or dark/black (khadra), which is supported by the fact that in some Arabic texts the sky is also described as khadra.[94] As mentioned above, George sees the use of gold on dark blue as producing a "resonance of light over darkness," which is key to understanding the aesthetic and symbolism of this color scheme. He cites a ninth-

88. Hoffman (2007: 324).

89. This precedent is noted by Bloom (2015: 214–15).

90. Dating to the late seventh century. For a recent discussion, see Nees (2011).

91. Quoted in Schimmel (1984: 40).

92. Nees (2011), quotation from abstract at "Islamic Art Symposium Podcasts," 2014, http://podcast.islamicartdoha.org/2009/laurence-nees/.

93. There is an extensive literature on this, but see, for example, Kowalski and Zimiles (2006).

94. This recalls Homer's much-discussed description of the sea as "wine-dark." There are also parallels with classical Chinese, where the color term qing is used to describe grass, sky, and sea. It is also used for dark shades—gray and black.

century Syriac encyclopedia that describes the color spectrum as based on "whiteness and blackness, which are the universal."[95]

Taking this further, it could be argued that the production of the Blue Qur'an, with its light-dark aesthetic of the light gold word on the dark indigo background, represents in a physical form the power of the word to bring unbelievers from the dark into the light, from night to day—a concept oft repeated in the text itself.[96]

> Allah is the protector
> Of those who have faith:
> From the depths of darkness
> He leads them forth
> Into Light. Of those
> Who reject faith the patrons
> Are the Tagut; from light
> They will lead them forth
> Into the depths of darkness.
> —Sura 2:257

But the difficulties with all these proposals, however plausible, is that if this combination had a recognized symbolism and aesthetic in the Islamic world, then we might expect to see more copies of the Qur'an using it throughout the Islamic world. However, as mentioned above, there is only one other later folio extant.[97] We could put forward various reasons for this: first, there were other Blue Qur'an, but they have all been lost—apart from the one; second, it was very expensive and difficult to produce; and third, the aesthetic and symbolism was local, or the books were produced in a fairly isolated community. The third hypothesis would be reinforced if we accept the argument that many Qur'an were hidden away, seen by very few.

To address these points briefly, first, we have a significant number of extant Qur'an from this period, from different places. Although not impossible, it is implausible that no copies of a fine production would have survived from throughout the Islamic world. To follow through on this, if there were

95. Job of Edessa (1935), cited in George (2009: 105). See also the discussion in Bloom and Blair (2011).
96. See, for example, Berrada (2006).
97. Although blue and gold were extensively used in other copies for illumination. For several examples, see Canby (2012).

other copies we might also expect to see an influence on other book cultures (but see comments below).

Second, expenses and difficulty in themselves would not have been a barrier to production. Indeed to a rich and pious patron they might have been an incentive. And there is no shortage of very finely and richly produced copies of the Qur'an. Also, as shown above, the use of gold ink was well known, and dyeing or brushing was not a difficult technique to master. Both gold and indigo were available: we see many copies using both.

Third, the aesthetic of blue/green and gold was certainly not restricted to a local use, as it is used on Islamic architecture and in other copies of the Qur'an with blue decoration. Nor was the Islamic community in North Africa isolated from the rest of the Islamic world at this time.

However, while blue/gold might have been a recognized symbolism and aesthetic, possibly the use of solid blue background fell quickly out of aesthetic appeal, with patrons preferring a more delicate and decorative effect.[98] The early inscription on the Dome of the Rock shows an aesthetic similar to the Blue Qur'an, with the square Kufic script only partly breaking up the green background. But this is markedly different from inscriptions seen from a later period as the Kufic script itself becomes more decorative. By the eleventh century a cursive script, Naskh, had largely replaced Kufic for manuscript copies of the Qur'an, consolidating a very different aesthetic.[99]

There is one more point to note. Rare and valued Buddhist scriptures appear in East Asia around the same time dyed with indigo and written in gold or silver ink—although in the form of paper scrolls, the ubiquitous medium and form for books in this region.[100] The links between the Islamic world of Central and West Asia and the Buddhist world of East Asia at this time are not well explored, but there were certainly contacts and commonalities, with both cultures sharing a great respect for calligraphy.[101] However, in Buddhism—and then in Daoism—manuscripts using this color scheme were unusual but probably not extremely rare.[102] It became one of the choices avail-

98. Analogous in some ways to the Japanese preference not to use too many *kanji*—Chinese characters—in a page of text as it makes the writing too dense.

99. See Schimmel (1990: 1–33) for a discussion of the scripts.

100. Tucci (1949: 212–13) notes an interesting early Tibetan textual source to Tibetan Buddhist texts written with lapis on gold leaves, that is, with the paper dyed gold.

101. George (2009) notes this possible link.

102. Pre-tenth-century fragmentary examples are found in the library cave at Dunhuang;

able for patrons who commissioned the production of the manuscripts and spread to Japan, Tibet, and Nepal. It was an aesthetic that persisted.

BREAKING THE CODEX

In 2015 a single folio of the Blue Qur'an offered at auction fetched £365,000.[103] How did this manuscript come to be broken up and dispersed? And what effect has the market had on its survival, its dispersal, and its scholarship?

If the manuscript was held in the library of the Great Mosque of Kairouan in 1293, why and when was it first broken up, and why and when were parts removed from the mosque? Without further evidence we cannot know, but Bloom hypothesizes that this started in the sixteenth century after the Ottomans captured Tunisia. They could have removed a section of this astonishing and almost unique find to Istanbul. Given the book's splendor and rarity, the Ottoman conquerors' desire to obtain part of it is understandable. Almost all the known folios held in collections outside Tunisia come from the first part of the Qur'an, chapters 2, 3, and 4, so it is possible they removed part of the whole. This, of course, would have entailed breaking the binding.[104]

The main basis for this argument is the fact that the Blue Qur'an first came to the attention of the market when a Swedish diplomat and dealer, Fredrik R. Martin (1868–1913), announced he had acquired several leaves in Istanbul. However, as mentioned above, one of the leaves he sold, now in Harvard, contains a Persian custom stamp. There is no other evidence to link the folios he sold to Istanbul or Persia or to suggest that the manuscript was broken up and dispersed as early as the sixteenth century.

While there was always a market in books, both domestic and international, the breaking apart of codices for sale and greater profit is known from

---

see, for example, M. Cohen (1996) and Whitfield and Sims-Williams (2004: 295, cat. 251).

103. "A Large Qur'an Leaf in Gold Kufic Script on Blue Vellum, North Africa or Near East, 9th–10th Century," in Sotheby's "Arts of the Islamic World 2015," Lot 62, www.sothebys.com/es/auctions/ecatalogue/2015/arts-islamic-world-l15220/lot.62.html. For the title of this section I am indebted to Doug Baude's video and artwork *Breaking the Codex* (altered book, box, collage, wooden stand, 12 x 12 x 3 in., 2010, http://dougbeube.com/art work/2933849_Re_Breaking_the_Codex.html).

104. The location of the binding of the Blue Qur'an is not known, if still extant, although Neumeier (2006: 16–17) notes that some loose pages inside a binding were offered for sale by Christie's in 1977 (Christie's sale, November 9, 1977, lot 66).

at least the seventeenth or eighteenth century through the case of a Christian Bible known now as the *Codex Auresh of Lorsch*. It was taken to Heidelberg from the Library of Lorsch just before the abbey's dissolution in 1563. It was stolen from here during the Thirty Years' War in 1622, when it was reported to have been broken in two and to have had the covers removed. The first half was sold to Bishop Ignác Batthyány (1741–98) and is in the library he founded in 1780, now in Romania, while the second half and the back cover are in the Vatican Library in Rome, and the front cover is in the Victoria and Albert Museum in London.

The history of the breakup of codices often is triggered by their no longer having a community to ensure their care. This might be a result of religious or political change. So the dissolution of the monasteries in many parts of the world meant that the contents of the monastery libraries no longer had a safe home or the community of monks to safeguard them. In some cases, there was an attempt to stop their destruction and dispersal. So, for example, in 1533 the king of England, Henry VIII (r. 1509–47), entrusted John Leland with a commission to visit and document the contents of libraries of religious houses of England.[105] In 1536 the king passed the first act for the dissolution of lesser monasteries, and Leland wrote to the chief minister, Thomas Cromwell, seeking help in rescuing their books, before, he said, they all disappeared to Germany: "The Germans perceive our desidiousness, and do send daily young scholars hither that spoileth [books], and cutteth them out of libraries, returning home and putting them abroad as monuments of their own country."[106] He was assisted in his endeavors by another bibliophile, John Bale, who, although he supported the dissolution, also lamented the unforeseen consequences for monastic libraries. He also compiled catalogs and did what he could to buy some of the books: "I have bene also at Norwyche, our second citye of name, and there all the library monuments are turned to the use of their grossers, candelmakers, sopesellers, and other worldly occupyers. . . . As much have I saved there and in certen other places in Northfolke and Southfolke concerning the authors names and titles of their workes, as I could, and as much wold I have done throughout the whole realm, yf I had been able to have borne the charges, as I am not."[107] The Royal Library was

105. Leland (2010).
106. Shrank (2004: 100). As Dagmar Riedel (2015) points out, the book dealers in Muslim societies also influenced and shaped this trade.
107. Graham and Watson (1998).

established to provide a home for many books, although not before others had already been dispersed.

The same situation is seen in nonreligious contexts, such as the end of the Republic of Venice, when its collections of manuscripts also became vulnerable.[108] In notable cases, such as the Cairo Geniza or the Dunhuang Library Cave, the community seems to have tried to provide a place of long-term storage, safe from destruction and dispersal.[109]

From the nineteenth century the desire to acquire old manuscripts became a fashion in the Western world, and American and European archaeologists, explorers, and others sought out collectors willing to sell. This led many to Egypt in search of early copies of the Bible. Charles Lang Freer (1854–1919), whose collection was later to form the Freer Gallery at the Smithsonian in Washington, D.C., summed up the element of competitiveness: "I am a little in doubt as to the wisdom of letting it be known ... that I anticipate visiting Egypt as one can never measure the competition that may spring up if it is known a real search is being made for rarities." Buyers' discoveries were reported in the press, inevitably raising both competition and prices.[110]

At this time many books were still purchased complete, and many remained so into the mid-nineteenth century. However, the market for individual folios, especially of illuminations, caused some to seek to safeguard their collections against fragmentation. In the 2015 Schoenberg Symposium on Manuscript Studies entitled "Picking Up the Pieces," Anne-Marie Eze discussed the case of Venetian manuscripts, which had started to be broken up for their illuminated frontispieces after the end of the Republic of Venice in 1797.[111] The American art historian Charles Eliot Norton (1827–1908) decided to give his collection of books to the recently opened Isabelle Stewart Gardner Museum in Boston to ensure their survival as complete books.[112]

108. Eze (2016).

109. Both these cases also bring up the issue of "sacred waste"—manuscripts, or fragments of manuscripts, no longer of use but of value because they contain text and therefore in need of being safeguarded. Also, while both endeavors were very successful in that the manuscripts remained hidden for a thousand years, the twentieth century has seen the discovery and the dispersal of both collections. See below for further discussion on the subsequent attempts at digital reunification.

110. For example, the *Times* of London reported the acquisition of twelve early Christian codices by Alfred Chester Beatty (November 17, 1931).

111. Eze (2016). The symposium is described at the Penn Libraries website at www.library.upenn.edu/exhibits/lectures/ljs_symposium8.html.

112. Eze (2016).

Other papers from the same conference showed the fate of codices coming onto the market: for example, the fifteenth-century Llangattock Breviary, which was sold as a complete codex of 513 folios at Christie's in 1958.[113] The purchasers, Goodspeeds of Boston, broke it apart and started selling individual folios on the market. In another case, William Randolph Hearst purchased the thirteenth-century Beauvais Missal from Sotheby's in 1926 and sold it in 1942 through Gimbel Brothers to the New York dealer Otto Ege, who then broke it up and started selling individual leaves.[114]

In other cases, the breakup was due to personal necessity. So, for example, Jens Kroger writes of an Islamic manuscript in the collection of the Sarre family.[115] Frederick Sarre (1865–1945) was founding director of the Museum of Islamic Art in Berlin between 1904 and 1931. Attempts were made during the Second World War to buy part of the collection from him, but he resisted because of the uncertain situation. Although surviving his death and the end of the war intact, the manuscript was then broken up and sold by his wife Maria (1875–1970) and his daughter Marie-Louise Sarre (1903–99) to finance their life in exile in Switzerland. Only in 1986 was the Museum of Islamic Art in Berlin able to purchase the fifty-four folios remaining with the family, with the colophon folio being gifted in 1988.

We will probably never know the reason for the breakup of the Blue Qur'an, but it had already happened by the early twentieth century. In his 1912 publication Martin gave the folios a provenance, the one mentioned above, that, although without any supporting evidence, was accepted and embellished by Thomas Arnold and Adolf Grohmann in their 1929 publication. Martin's folios were sold over the following years to the Museum of Fine Arts, Boston (1933), Sir Alfred Chester Beatty (before 1967; now in the Chester Beatty Library, Dublin), the Fogg Art Museum at Harvard University (1967), the Seattle Art Museum (1969), and Prince Sadruddin Aga Khan (1982).[116] The folio sold in 1933 fetched $85.[117]

In 1976 a Festival of Islam was held in London. Two leaves of the Blue Qur'an were on display, both from Tunisian collections. One was shown at the British Library, which attributed it to ninth-century Iran. The Hayward Gallery displayed the other, claiming that it was from tenth-century Tunisia.

113. Cashion (2016).
114. Davis (2015).
115. Kröger (2005).
116. Bloom (2015: 197).
117. Bloom (2015: 204). He notes that this is equivalent to $1,400 today.

Not only did this lead to the scholarly debate that continues today, but it also showcased the manuscript and undoubtedly created greater market interest. It also had the effect, argues Dagmar Riedel, of ending the acquisition of Islamic books and collections in bulk—and whole—by wealthy American individuals and institutions, as it "showcased manuscripts in Arabic script not as mere books, but as a cultural achievement of the Islamic civilization." In other words, a single folio was considered an art or cultural object in itself, rather than a page of text meaningless outside its context.

It is therefore not surprising that other isolated folios of the Blue Qur'an— their provenance usually unknown—started to appear and be sold, at increasingly higher prices, in Western auction houses. One folio was immediately placed for sale by Sotheby's, but it was in the early 1980s that folios began to appear regularly on the market. Since 1984, over thirty folios have been offered for sale, most by auction houses and many ending up in private collections.[118] Over this period the Middle East joined the market for Islamic books and works of art, especially with the establishment of new museums without foundation collections, such as the Museum of Islamic Art in Doha (founded in 2008). The museum has a folio of the Blue Qur'an.

The purchasing power of these new museums has pushed many other museums and libraries out of the market, especially public institutions. At the same time, some of these institutions have published guidelines stating they will not acquire detached folios.[119] The stated aim is to discourage the further breakup of works. However, such institutions form a small part of the market, and it is unlikely that many private museums or collectors will be dissuaded from the acquisition of single folios. It is the same conundrum as that posed by works of doubtful provenance on the market: Should public museums purchase them in order to provide a place where the material is conserved and accessible or refuse to do so in order not to support the looters? There is no solution, and the stand taken by these institutions is currently more of a moral stance than a realistic attempt to be a catalyst to change behavior.

118. See Bloom (2015: Appendix A), for a list by date of appearance up to 2012, although he omits the 2011 Sotheby's sale; see "A Large Qur'an Leaf in Gold Kufic Script on Blue Vellum, North Africa or Near East, 9th–10th Century," www.sothebys.com/en/auctions/ecatalogue/2011/arts-of-the-islamic-world-evening-sale-l11229/lot.2.html.

119. For example, the British Library states that "leaves and fragments from manuscripts broken-up in the last generation will not usually be acquired." British Library, "Western Manuscripts: Collection Development Strategy," n.d., accessed February 1, 2017, www.bl.uk/reshelp/bldept/manuscr/mancdp/.

The same institutions refusing to purchase single folios also often continue to display their own collections in this form, often with little information about their context as a "mere book," to quote Dagmar Riedel. Indeed, some have removed bindings in order to facilitate this. In 2012 three folios of the Blue Qur'an were on display in New York. Two leaves on loan from Boston were shown at the Metropolitan Museum of Art in their *Byzantium and Islam* exhibition, while a leaf held by Rose Trust, Dubai, was on display at the Rubin Museum. In her blog post on these exhibitions, Riedel noted the lack of any attempt in either to give the audience "information about the scholarly controversies triggered by the hermeneutic impossibility of making sense of a unique object." She also noted the differences in approach between the two exhibitions to the objects' materialities: the MMA made no attempt to show the Qur'an next to purple-dyed Byzantine manuscripts, also on display, and thus to create "a paratactic narrative in the course of which possibilities of causation are implied through sequence and context," whereas the Rubin created such a narrative by showing the Qur'an alongside blue-dyed Buddhist and other manuscripts.[120]

REUNIFYING THE CODEX

While the twentieth century can be characterized by the breakup of the codex, the twenty-first is becoming the century of digital reunification, as numerous projects have taken advantage of the potential for access of digitization and the Internet to try to counter the breakup and dispersal of the past.[121] These include projects to reunite archaeological collections, such as the International Dunhuang Project, but also those concentrating on a single codex, such as the Beauvais Missal.[122] Although many institutions were initially skeptical, the desire to join such projects is growing. It remains to be seen whether the Blue Qur'an will become the subject for such a project, but for now the known extant folios remain dispersed both actually and virtually.

120. Riedel (2013).
121. See Davis (2015).
122. See the websites for the International Dunhuang Project: The Silk Road Online (http://idp.bl.uk) and the Broken Books project (http://165.134.105.25/brokenBooks/home.html?demo=1).

EIGHT

A Byzantine Hunter Silk

ALTHOUGH SEVERAL SCHOLARS have tried to displace silk from its key role in trade assumed by the term *Silk Road* and have argued for the equal if not greater influence of other goods, the importance of silk is not so easily dismissed. The reason for this might have less to do with the actual rank of silk in terms of the economics or volume of trade goods—this has yet to be quantified—than with the stories that became attached to this fabric and the hunger to learn its secrets. Although China was the only culture with the knowledge of cultivating silk at the start of the Silk Road period, within a few centuries the technology had dispersed to other cultures along the trade routes. The piece under discussion here—which we shall call the "hunter silk"—was made in Byzantium (plate 7). The empire probably had its own silk production centers from the fourth century using imported thread, cultivation of its own silkworms from possibly as early as the fifth century, and sophisticated looms producing complex patterns as seen here by the eighth century.

This piece therefore has many stories to tell, not only of the diffusion of silk production, but of the cultural dialogues and influences seen in the design—here a medallion containing a hunting image, a motif found across the Silk Road. Both the technique and the motif have been subject to different interpretations by scholars, showing how our dialogue with objects from the past is often renewed and we can rarely assume that it has reached a conclusion. There is also the story of the changing functions and value of this silk as it traveled westwards, passing through the hands of emperors, taking on religious significance in a Christian setting and currently a museum artifact.

The hunter silk shows a pair of horsemen, separated by a tree, each poised

For places mentioned in this chapter see Map 1 in the color maps insert.

to spear a lion with their hunting dogs below. The composition is enclosed within a decorated medallion. Scholars have dated it variously from the eighth to the tenth century, on the basis of its weave and design.[1] It is fragmentary, measuring 73.5 centimeters high by 71 centimeters wide. The weave is a weft-faced compound twill—a samite—with Z-twisted warps, one binding and one main.[2] The wefts are untwisted and dyed blue, a reddish brown, yellow, and light blue.[3]

To understand the piece we first need to understand the "how," to place it within the story of the development of silk technology and its diffusion along the Silk Road in the first millennium, a story that is complex and remains full of gaps and uncertainties.

THE DEVELOPMENT AND TRANSMISSION
OF SERICULTURE

With the opening of routes across Central Asia, moriculture and sericulture—the skills of raising and harvesting mulberry trees (*Morus* sp.) for their leaves and of raising the pupae of the domestic silkworm—*Bombyx mori*—for the silk thread of their cocoons—inevitably started to spread out of China. Silk production had not been confined to China in this early period. India had wild silk production from as early as the mid-third millennium BC.[4] Fibers of wild silk have been found in Cyprus dating from 2000 BC.[5]

1. I am greatly indebted to the scholarship of Anna Muthesius for the original inspiration for this chapter. Many of the details about this textile come from Muthesius (1997: see esp. 68–69, 175). I am also indebted to Maximilien Durand, former director of the Textile Museum, Lyon, holder of the textile, and must thank him for offering his own insights; alerting me to recent scholarship, notably that of Sophie Desrosiers on the weave; showing me the textile and the original ledger book; and providing more information about the textile's acquisition. See Durand (2014) for a summary of scholarship and Brubacker and Haldon (2011: 225–26) for a recent discussion on the dating. All mistakes, misunderstandings, and omissions are my own.

2. See below, note 62, for a further discussion of the particularities of its technique.

3. What little analysis has been carried out on the dyes suggests the use of dyes derived from lichen and plants such as indigo, madder (alizarin and purpurin), and weld (apart from the famous and restricted purple that came from sea snails—see also chapter 7 above) (Muthesius 1997: 27–31).

4. Good, Kenoyer, and Meadow (2009).

5. At the site of Pyrgos-Mavroraki.

There is evidence for silk in the Bronze Age Aegean.[6] China also produced wild silk. But the only strong evidence for the specialist breeding and cultivation of domestic silkworms and the unreeling of the unbroken cocoons in the early period is from China, and current evidence suggests that it may have started as early as 2700 BC.[7]

As Muthesius points out, "The rearing of silk worms was and still is an immensely complex and sensitive occupation requiring a great deal of patience and skill."[8] By the time of the Silk Road, China had had long practice in refining the technology and was producing strong, sophisticated silks from the thread of the selectively bred *Bombyx mori* fed by the leaves of the white mulberry (*Morus alba*).[9] The silkworm larvae munched their way through prodigious quantities of leaves, increasing their weight up to ten thousand times in less than a month.[10] The leaves had to be finely shredded for the newly hatched worms, themselves little more than the size of a pinprick, and they were sometimes fed two times an hour for the first day and night. As they grew the leaves were presented in larger pieces and the number of feeds decreased. But this was still very labor intensive. The silkworm beds had to be cleared constantly of fecal remains and old leaves. The worms had to be checked for infection and kept warm and dry during this process—which lasted four or five weeks depending on the worms. Early Chinese records show that the rearing was the work of women and that both special rearing buildings and domestic farmhouses were used, with the worms placed on trays (figure 24).

Apart from the skills involved, silk rearing required a ready supply of fresh leaves and therefore plantations of healthy mulberries: any fungal or other infection would harm the delicate worms. Trees took three to six years to reach maturity. The trees are not particularly vulnerable, requiring a temperate climate and level, moist, light, and fertile soil. Leaves of the white mulberry are the preferred food of the *Bombyx* moth and produce the best silk.

6. Panagiotakopulu et al. (1997).

7. Good (2002). Recent finds from China push back the use of silk—although not necessarily sericulture—to before 6000 BC but remain tentative (Choi 2017).

8. Muthesius (1997: 5).

9. For a detailed account of moriculture and sericulture in China, see Needham and Kuhn (1988: 285–436).

10. For a time-lapse video showing worms eating and defecating, see *Silkworms Eating, Cuddling, and Spinning Timelapse*, YouTube, uploaded November 1, 2011, https://www.youtube.com/watch?v=UtHjDRVRM_Y.

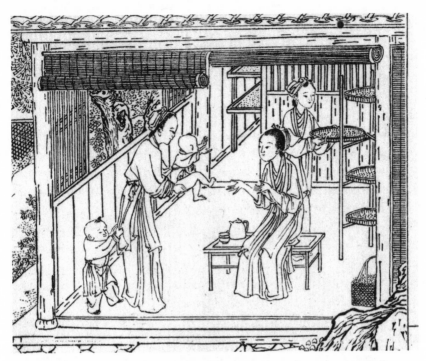

FIGURE 24. A seventeenth-century Chinese depiction of sericulture; the trays of silkworms can be seen in the background. From *Yuzhi gengzhi tu*, 1696.

This tree is indigenous to northern China, perhaps one reason why China took the lead in sericulture.[11] Chinese farmers also developed the skills of grafting white mulberries, so improving the crop.

The black mulberry (*Morus nigra L.*) is a distinct species. It was probably indigenous to the mountainous areas of West Asia but was cultivated from very early times throughout Central and West Asia and is reported to have reached Egypt by the middle of the second millennium BC. Black mulberry fruit was popular in Roman Europe, and it might have already spread as far as northern Europe by pre-Roman times. The spread of white mulberry in early times is not so well documented, and there continued to be a confusion about the trees well into modern times.[12] For example, it is possible that attempts to start a silk industry in Britain in the sixteenth and seventeenth centuries failed in large part because of such confusion—black mulberry being distrib-

11. Some sources suggest it was also indigenous further west to the Himalayas.
12. White mulberry, despite its name, also sometimes bears red or black fruits.

uted for cultivation rather than white mulberry.[13] However, there is evidence of white mulberry in Harappan sites of the Indus Valley Civilization dating before the third millennium BC, and in the early centuries AD in northwestern India and Kashmir.[14]

Once the silkworms had spun their cocoon—after three or four molts— they had to be killed by stifling or their further development had to be impeded by cold conditions so the moth did not emerge and break the cocoon. The dead worms could later be fried and eaten—still a delicacy in China today. The silk then had to be reeled, another skilled and delicate task. The cocoons were heated in a basin of water, and the ends of a small number of threads were picked out and unreeled together: the more threads, the heavier the silk thread and resulting fabric. The threads could be as long as nine hundred meters.[15] A slight twist was introduced into the thread at this point. However, the warp thread required a much greater twist, as many as two to three thousand twists per meter of thread, and a spindle wheel was needed to achieve this. The thread was twisted in one of two ways. The "S" twist is so called because the direction of the twist follows the central slant of the letter "S," while Z-twisted thread is twisted to follow the central slant of the letter "Z," that is, in the other direction. "S"-twisted threads are more typical of those produced in central China.[16] The silk thread was then ready, either for dyeing, sale or for weaving.

It is often stated that China considered silk technology as an industrial secret on which it wished to retain a monopoly. This has, however, been reasonably disputed by scholars such as M. G. Raschke, who points out that there are reports of Chinese immigrants taking sericulture to the Korean peninsula by the second century BC, of attempts to teach sericulture to the neighboring peoples in the Xiongnu confederation in the third century AD, and of the Jin court (265–420) presenting silkworms and a mulberry tree to its Xianbei neighbors.[17] Only remnants of the law code of the early period survive, and there is nothing mentioning silk in the extant sections on the materials that were forbidden for export.

13. The black mulberry trees, although hardier than the white mulberry and able to be grown in northern Europe, might also have suffered owing to the weather—Britain was experiencing a "Little Ice Age."

14. Asouti and Fuller (2008: 126).

15. Kuhn (1995: 78).

16. Zhao (2004: 70).

17. Raschke (1976: 622–23); Good (2002: 11).

China's opening of regular trade routes west from the first century BC could have been expected to lead to the greater diffusion of silk technology and the growth of markets for silk. This indeed appears to have been the trend from this time, with Zhao Feng arguing that Central Asian weavers had access to Chinese silks and tried to copy them. China had established garrison towns along the routes west into the Gobi and Taklamakan deserts of the Tarim basin and had resettled farmers from central China. Some of these would presumably have taken sericulture skills with them, even though it might have taken some time to establish trees in this desert environment.[18] The twentieth-century archaeologist, Aurel Stein (1862–1943), noted the desiccated remnants of mulberry trees at the first- to fourth-century site of Caḍota (Niya), and silk production in this region has been dated to the same period.[19] These oasis kingdoms were also home to Indians, who might have brought knowledge of their own silk-weaving skills.[20] Polychrome woven silk with a warp-faced compound tabby weave structure, called *jin*, had been produced in central China for as long as a millennium before this.[21] Its production required both skilled weavers and complex loom technology. In the early first millennium the local weavers in Central Asia did not have looms that were sophisticated enough to produce repeat patterns in the warp direction, so when they tried to replicate the Chinese *jin* they could produce only a limited pattern in the weft direction. Even though some of the designs on such

18. Silk in this region is often composed of broken threads. It has been suggested that this is because of the need to allow the moths to hatch to produce a new generation of silkworms: in central China where the silk moth was native this was not necessary. However, since one moth produces so many eggs, this seems unlikely. Another explanation is that Buddhist principles against killing any creature were responsible—seen today with the production of so-called Ahmisa or "peace" silk.

19. See, for example, Stein's Photo 392/26(178), which he has labeled "Row of Dead Mulberry Trees in Ancient Orchard" (British Library, http://idp.bl.uk). He does not note whether they are white or black mulberry, but we can assume the former if they came with settlers from China. Rashcke also notes this but makes the common mistake of confusing the silkworm-feeding mulberry (*Morus* sp.) with the mulberry whose bark is used for paper making (*Broussonetia papyrifera*)—a different family (although fibers from both families are found in paper). Zhao (2004: 70) suggests second to third centuries. Hill (2015: Appendix A) considers the story of the silk princess and suggests a first-century date for the arrival of sericulture in Khotan.

20. Rosemary Crill (2015: 143) suggests that at least one tapestry woven woolen fragment from Niya is Indian produced. A silk piece discussed below might also be Indian.

21. As Kuhn (1995: 79) points out, it was possible to produce warp-faced patterns because of the length of the silk threads obtained by reeling and the elasticity from twisting.

weaves, such as dragons, are typically Chinese, the weft-faced pattern and the Z twist of the warps distinguish these silks from those woven in China.[22]

Silks from China are found in the possessions of China's neighbors from much earlier: in the burials of the steppe at Pazyryk, now in Russia, and in Alagou (near Turfan) in the Tarim—dating to the fifth to third centuries BC. What is less certain, although often reported, is their existence further west in this early period. There was considerable excitement when silk was reported, for example, in an Egyptian burial of around 1000 BC, with news of the find reaching the press.[23] But this was later disputed and is no longer cited.[24] Other reputed finds have been similarly questioned: for example, in the Hallstatt burials in northern Europe dating between the eighth and sixth centuries BC, the silk found has now been identified as wild silk, not domestic reeled silk from China.[25]

If silk technology traveled along the land routes west from China and had reached the Tarim kingdoms by the first few centuries AD, then the next place to look for evidence of its production would be the neighboring Kushan Empire to the west (first to third centuries; see chapter 3). The Kushan Empire encompassed northern India and saw the growth and expansion of Buddhism into the Tarim. The importance of silks in Buddhism and the close relationship between Buddhism and trade have been well discussed elsewhere, and this would lead one to expect that silk was used in Kushan.[26] However, there are few remains of textiles in India or Kushan from this period, and so far few of the silks found in Central Asia have been identified as having been produced in India, so it is difficult to draw any firm conclusions either about the demand for silk or the development of silk technology in Kushan.

Evidence is also lacking for the role of silk in the Parthian Empire (ca. 250 BC–AD 224), which bordered Kushan to its west. The Parthians were known to be consumers of Chinese silk, but there is little evidence for them developing a silk industry themselves.[27] The textile evidence, which includes

22. See Zhao (2004: 70) for examples.

23. Lubec et al. (1993).

24. The sample was very small, and the preliminary identification was first changed to wild silk and then dropped altogether as a piece accidentally introduced into the excavation.

25. Wild (1984). See Good (2002) for a discussion of the original finding and subsequent discussion (36).

26. Liu (1996); Whitfield (2016).

27. Some sources suggest a silk-weaving industry using imported silk in the Achaemenid

very few excavated pieces, is of heavy cotton, linen, or wool.[28] There is one piece of a silk cord dating from the first century BC, probably imported.[29] However, evidence does exist that supports Parthian access to Chinese silks through their control of the land trade. The Romans sought to bypass the Parthians by transporting silk by sea through Indian ports.[30] The Parthian control of the trade was then challenged with the rise of the Kushan Empire. The Kushan, controlling the routes west from China to Parthia and south to the Indian ports, set their own gold standard and traded with the Romans through Indian ports. This might have been an impetus for the development of Parthian silk weaving, but there are no material remains to support this. To produce fine finished textiles, it was necessary to have developed a sophisticated weaving industry using looms that could be adapted for silk threads, which were much finer than other fibers. Skilled weavers were needed to operate the looms to produce the complex patterns being woven in China by this time. It probably remained more feasible and more cost-effective to continue to buy silk cloth from the Chinese. How much, if any, silk came to Parthia from India remains unknown.

However, moving further west from Parthia—to the lands of the ancient civilization of Mesopotamia around the Tigris and Euphrates Rivers (present-day Iraq and Syria)—we find evidence of second-century AD Chinese silk in tombs at Palmyra and third-century local compound weaves at Dura-Europos.[31] Although the latter might date from after the Parthians seized control of the city—it was part of the Roman Empire from AD 165—they suggest the existence of a weaving industry. Palmyra had been a thriving commercial center on the Silk Road from the end of the first century AD: an inscription dating to 137 mentions slaves, purple silk, and perfumes, while other sources give evidence of trade in silk, jade, muslin, ebony, incense, spices, ivory, gemstones, and glass.[32] Palmyran merchants sailed from Red Sea ports and had agents at Merv, east of the Caspian Sea.[33] It is not there-

---

period preceding the Parthians—"Kallixenos of Rhodes is said to have seen Persian silks embroidered with animals at a banquet given by Ptolemy Philadelphus" (Schmidt 1958: 51)—but nothing survives from this period. For an overview, see Thompson et al. ([1983] 2011).

28. From, for example, the Chehrabad Salt Mine. See Mouri et al. (2014).
29. Kawami (1992: n72).
30. Sen (2003: 161); Warmington (1928: 20).
31. Schmidt-Colinet and Stauffer (2000); Pfister (1934–40).
32. Ball (2002: 76).
33. Bryce (2014: 283).

fore surprising to find these examples of Chinese silk in elite tombs: they could have been obtained either through the seaports or through the merchants in Merv.

A great variety of textiles were found here, including tapestry weave pieces of Roman and Persian origin and silk weaves including tabby, damask, and *taquete*. There is also evidence of wool- and linen-weaving centers in this region. But wool and linen (and wild silk) produce much shorter threads than domestic silk, and their use resulted in very different looms being developed to produce, in general, weft-faced patterns.[34] And by the third century, just as in the Tarim kingdoms, textiles found in Dura-Europos suggest local weavers were trying to replicate Chinese silks. Textile historians' analysis of the Dura-Europos weaves suggests use of a drawloom but of a different type from that used in China—usually called a Western drawloom.

LOOM TECHNOLOGY

By this time looms had developed significantly from the simple hand loom, and their functioning, like that of many complex mechanical devices, is difficult to describe, even with images. But their development is inextricably linked with that of the diffusion of silk, and we cannot attempt to understand one without the other. First we need to return to China, since in China, unlike other weaving centers, looms were developed from very early times to take advantage of the extremely long, fine and strong silk threads produced from reeling. Their length meant that warp-faced patterns were possible, while the thinness meant that these could be extremely fine and complex.

A basic loom has threads held taut and running away from the weaver—the warp. The weaver threads the weft through the warps, one over and one under, producing the simplest weave, called a tabby. If the thread was woven two under, then it produced a twill weave. Looms were soon developed with devices enabling some of the warp threads to be raised so that an opening was created between the two sets of warp threads, called a shed (figure 25). The weaver sent a shuttle containing another thread, the weft, through the shed and ensured that the weft thread lay closely and tightly against the previous weft. The process was then repeated, but with another set of warp threads raised. Creating a pattern required some means of raising different sets of

34. Kuhn (1995: 80).

FIGURE 25. A simple Chinese treadle loom. From *Yuzhi gengzhi tu*, 1696.

warp threads. By the middle of the first millennium BC this was achieved in China by pattern rods.[35] Different sets of warps required for the pattern were threaded onto separate rods. Treadles operated lifting shafts to pull up the rods in the combinations required for the pattern, so allowing the weft thread to be pushed through the resulting opening. The width was constricted by the workability for the weaver, who had to insert the shuttle containing the weft and operate the treadles, and was usually about fifty centimeters at this time.[36] The length of a roll—or bolt—of silk was about nine hundred centimeters.[37]

To produce more complex patterns, more than one set or layer of warps

35. See Kuhn (1995) for a discussion of the loom in China.
36. Kuhn (1995: 80).
37. As noted above, a single cocoon might produce a single thread about this length.

and/or wefts were used, creating compound weaves. Weavers in China were able to produce *jin*—polychrome warp-faced compound tabby weaves—possibly as early as the eighth century BC.[38] In this period these were mainly woven with repeating small geometric patterns or animals.[39] *Jin* are commonly seen from the fifth century BC, and by the second century there were three major silk production centers in China. At this time the most common designs were of clouds and animals, sometimes with Chinese auspicious phrases woven into the silk. Many such Chinese-woven *jin* have been found in the Tarim. The complexities of producing these using a loom with treadles controlled by the weaver is reflected in a contemporary passage: "Huo Guang's second wife presented to Yan Chunyu 24 rolls of grape-patterned silk *jin* and 25 rolls of fine silk with a design of scattered flowers.... So Huo Guang invited her to come to their home, set up the loom and weave the cloth. The loom had 120 patterning devices and it took sixty days to make a bolt worth ten thousand cash."[40]

Discovery of a polychrome warp-faced compound tabby silk found in a grave in Noin-Ula in northern Mongolia has led to much scholarly discussion about the type of loom that would produce such a silk, with the conclusion that it was a type of pattern-rod loom of the heddle-rod type that could be lifted by the weaver, prefiguring the drawloom.[41] Three hundred and fifty pattern rods would have been needed, and these would have had to be lifted using the rods to create the pattern. This silk dates from the second half of the first century BC. The Chinese drawloom was probably invented in China not long afterward, although the first source we have is from the second century AD.[42] The drawloom had one or more assistants—replacing the treadles—to pull up the warps using drawing strings (figure 26).[43] They were

38. Zhao (2004: 67). "Brocade" is often used as a translation for the Chinese term *jin*, but it has a wider usage in general discussions of European textiles, so I have generally avoided its use here.

39. For a piece with dragons, phoenix, and dancers, see Kuhn (1995: 89) and Zhao (2004: 68, fig. 68).

40. Translated after Kuhn (1995: 91). Also see Bray (1997: 201–2). There are contemporary records from Niya of a pair of cloth trousers costing 400 cash (coins), one bolt of plain silk costing 600 cash, an ox costing 3,000 cash, and a female slave costing 20,000 cash (H. Wang 2004: 6–62).

41. Riboud (1977) and Kuhn (1995: 94–95).

42. Kuhn (1995: 95–97). For a further discussion see Usher (1988: 54–56, 261), and for a summary of opinions see Bray (1997: 191).

43. See Desrosiers (1994) for the problems with deciding what type of loom was used for complex weaves.

時女心眺郎曲雨盛

FIGURE 26. A Chinese drawloom. From *Yuzhi gengzhi tu*, 1696.

known later as drawboys or girls. A second-century Chinese poem entitled "Rhapsody on Women Weavers" describes the girls climbing on top of the loom to operate the strings.[44] But in this early period when the technology was still being developed and mastered, complex patterned silks probably had to be produced by the treadle loom and the pattern loom as well as the drawloom.[45]

By the third century AD, examples of weft-faced compound tabby weaves—called *taquete*—are found outside China, in the Tarim, Central Asia, and as far west as Dura-Europos in Syria. Mostly woven in wool or linen, they show complex patterns, but because of the shorter threads in

44. For an explanation and translation of some passages, see Kuhn (1995: 98–102). As Kuhn observes, the poet uses images taken from astronomy to describe the operation of the loom; see chapter 9 below for the importance of astronomy in Chinese culture.

45. Kuhn (1995: 102).

wool and linen different looms were developed than in China, and hence the patterns were generally on the weft. The designs of those in the Tarim show influences from its western neighbors rather than from China, with figures, grapevines, and rosettes, and Zhao suggests they were woven in Central Asia—Bactria or Gandhāra.[46] Among the Dura-Europos finds is a small fragment of silk *taquete* with a geometric pattern, the earliest known piece in West Asia.[47] It also suggests that the local weavers were copying Chinese woven silks. Whether the weavers who produced the silk *taquete* found in Dura-Europos were using locally produced thread or thread acquired from elsewhere is uncertain. Another Syrian *taquete*, but woven in wool, shows a hunting scene.[48] Zhao suggests that both were imitations of *jin* weaves, but with patterning in the weft rather than the warp direction. Many scholars believe that these complex-patterned weaves could have been woven only with a drawloom, but of a different type and origin from that invented in China because of the weft-faced pattern—hence, as mentioned above, often referred to as a "Western drawloom."[49]

So by the third century AD we see drawlooms being used in East, central, and West Asia to produce compound tabby weaves. Those in China have warp-faced patterns, while those from Central Asia westwards have weft-faced patterns. Patterns at this time are still mainly geometric, floral, or of small animals among clouds, still showing the primary influence to be China, but there are some larger designs, of hunting scenes for example. The influence of India is still uncertain.

In the late third century, the division of the administration of the Roman Empire into eastern and western parts started a process that would result in the separation of the eastern, Greek-speaking part and its establishment as the Byzantine Empire. Around 330 the capital, Byzantium, was moved to the site of present-day Istanbul by the emperor Constantine (hence

46. Zhao (2004: 71).

47. The site was abandoned in 256–57, giving an end date for the production of these silks. See Zhao (2004: 80, fig. 64).

48. Zhao (2004: 71, fig. 67).

49. For useful description and images, see Broudy (1979: 124–33). Muthesius concludes: "It seems reasonable to suggest that a form of draw loom was developed before the Arab conquests in Byzantine Syria (and perhaps also in Byzantine Egypt), quite independently from any draw loom invented in China. One would not expect the predominantly warp faced Chinese weaves to be woven on the same loom as the weft faced Eastern Mediterranean weaves. There is no evidence to suggest that China had a monopoly over draw loom manufacture, nor that looms were ever exported from there" (1997: 24, also n30).

Constantinople or Constantine's city). Only a few decades later Christianity became the official religion. The empire included most of the lands ringing the Mediterranean and Black Seas, encompassing the regions where there was earlier evidence of compound weaves imitating Chinese silks. The Byzantine Empire included provinces in North Africa and northern Arabia, thus controlling the northern Red Sea ports. They were allies with the Axumite kingdom—in present-day Ethiopia and Eritrea—who also sent merchants from the Red Sea (see chapter 3).

The popular account of the introduction of sericulture to Byzantium tells of Christian monks sent by Emperor Justinian I (r. 527–65) as envoys to the Chinese court in about 550. Like the Roman Empire, China had divided in the third century, and the northern part, including those areas bordering the Tarim and Central Asia, were ruled by Xianbei peoples from the northeastern steppe. Reportedly the Christian monks managed to acquire silkworm eggs that they brought back in hollow canes, enabling the start of Byzantine silk industry. However, there is evidence of mulberry plantations and sericulture in Byzantine Syria before this, by the fifth century.[50] We cannot know exactly how they reached there—or whether the plantations were of white or black mulberry—but given the demand for silk in Byzantium there was a strong economic imperative to master sericulture.[51] They might well have inherited the skilled weavers in the Mesopotamia and Syrian regions, evidenced by the textiles found at Dura-Europos. There is also evidence of weaving centers in North Africa: over 150,000 textiles have been found in tombs at Antinoopolis, some dating from the late third century.[52] Mostly linen and wool, they include pieces in the *taquete* compound weave, although there is no evidence of silk and the designs are seemingly more influenced by Roman and Coptic elements.

The situation was different in Sasania, the empire that in 224 had acquired from the Parthians the lands between Byzantium and Central Asia. Sasanian sources record that silk weaving had already began under Shapur II (r. 309–79), who had hired skillful weavers from Mesopotamia and Syria to set up

50. "The earliest documented Byzantine silkworms (most plausibly mulberry plantations as well) were located in fifth-century Byzantine Syria" (Muthesius 2002: 150). See also N. Oikonomides (1986).

51. Lady Maria Callcott (1842: 283), a nineteenth-century traveler to Syria, noted that white mulberry were more common than black and that they were grown for their leaves at the expense of the fruit.

52. Schrenk (2006).

weaving centers in Kūzestān.[53] And there is ample evidence of the Sasanians' access to silk through their ensuring control of the trade from China by both land and sea, previously threatened under the Parthians. By the mid-sixth century the Sasanians had a monopoly on the Chinese silk traded at Taprobane (Sri Lanka). The Byzantine emperor Justinian I asked his allies the Axumites to send their sea merchants to Taprobane to challenge this monopoly. He suggested that they undercut the Sasanians and buy all the silk themselves. He then intended that they would sell it on to him at a favorable price. The Axumite merchants were unsuccessful, however, and the Sasanians retained their hold on Chinese silk exported by sea.

The Sasanians also seem to have controlled the land transport of silk in this early period. Cosmas Indicopleustes, a sixth-century Alexandrian merchant who roamed as far as India (hence the name: "Cosmas, the Indian Navigator"), noted in 550 that Persia received most of its silk by land rather than by sea.[54] This was to be challenged. In 565 the Sogdian traders of the Central Asian cities of Bukhara and Samarkand approached the Sasanians, through the disposition of their Turkish neighbors, to propose that they travel through Sasania to trade silk directly with Byzantium. The Sasanians refused—and burned the silk the Sogdians had brought with them. After the failure of a second embassy—the delegates were poisoned—the Sogdians instead requested permission of the Turks to travel through their lands on the more northerly steppe route to Byzantium. The Turks agreed, and the embassy arrived at the court of Justin II around 568.[55] Direct trade was thereafter established between Sogdiana and Byzantium through this route. The Sogdians acquired much of their silk through the Turks, who had in turn been given it as payments by the Chinese for horses.[56] By this time the typical Chinese designs start to be replaced by figures and animals, sometimes enclosed inside roundels or frames and sometimes independent, showing influences coming into China from the Silk Road.[57]

53. Some scholars claim that this happened under Shapur I; for a discussion and references, see Thompson et al. ([1983] 2011).

54. Cosmas Indicopleustes (1897, vol. 2: 45–46).

55. The offer was accepted by Justin II, and in August 568 Zemarchus left Byzantium for Sogdia, events recorded by the Byzantine historian Menander the Guardsman (Blockley 1985).

56. See chapter 6.

57. Although, as Kuhn (1995: 89) notes, we see figures and animals on Chinese woven silks from as early as the period of the Warring States, and more realistic depictions of

Although the textual evidence, including the sources about Shapur II hiring weavers from Syria, suggests that the Sasanians had a silk-weaving industry, unfortunately there are few archaeological remains of any textiles, let alone silk.[58] Development of sericulture in Sasania is equally problematic but possibly started in about the sixth century on the borders of the Caspian Sea, then moved into central Iran. A report by the tenth-century traveler and geographer Eṣṭakrī suggests that silk was produced in most of the regions of the Iranian Plateau by his time. However, silkworm eggs continued to be brought from Merv.[59]

The Sasanian Empire fell to the armies of the Arab Caliphate, who moved eastward across Iran in the seventh century. They took over and developed the silk workshops, producing their own distinctive designs. This was also the time of a major development in silk weaving, the appearance of a weft-faced compound twill, the samite weave. This became the dominant weave in Byzantium and is used on our hunter silk. As Zhao explains: "Technically, it can be considered a development either from *taquete* . . . by changing the foundation weave from tabby to 2:1 twill, or from twill *jin* . . . by turning the warp and weft directions 90 degrees."[60] But with sericulture and silk-weaving centers by now established across North Africa and Asia, and trade, diplomatic, and other contacts continuing by land and sea, both technological developments and fashions in designs and motifs spread relatively fast. Byzantine samites typically have a paired main warp in contrast to samites woven in Central Asia, where the warps are in groups of three or four. Both use Z-twisted threads, in contrast to Chinese weaves, which have doubled or tripled S-twisted warps. Many of the samites, including some of the earliest found in the Tarim, are woven with designs, typically ascribed to the Sasanians, of animals contained inside roundels.

Reevaluation of some single main warp twill weaves previously dated to the sixth and seventh centuries and grouped together as "Alexandrian" silks, among them the Mozac hunter silk, led Muthesius to conclude that they had been woven in different centers of the eastern Mediterranean. Some, at

animals and figures from the Later Han probably also influenced by embroidery designs (104–10).

58. Finds include two from the Caucasus (Ierussalimskaya 1969, 1972; Riboud 1976). For finds in Susa and Fars, see Laiou (2002) and Lopez (1945).

59. Thompson at al. ([1983] 2011). Eilers ([1983] 2011) notes that the word for silk, *abrišam*, is a loanword from Iranian in Armenian *aprišum*, Syriac *'bryšwm*, and Arabic *ebrīsam*.

60. Zhao (2004: 73).

least, she argues, were woven in the Byzantine imperial workshops, and these workshops "may have played a significant role in the development of this type of silk."[61] Sophie Desrosiers's more recent reexamination of the piece has shown that it belongs to a small group of samites where the Z-twisted red warp thread is bound in a particular way.[62] Desrosiers agrees with Muthesius in seeing the hunter silk as a product of the Constantinople workshops but argues that this technique does not appear until the early ninth century and thus places its production later than Muthesius.

By the time of the hunter silk, therefore, we see sericulture and weaving across Asia—although not yet in Europe.[63] Although there were still markets for Chinese silk across Asia, the technology had become embedded elsewhere. The Byzantine court workshops with their paired-warp samites showing complex patterns challenged the influence of Chinese silks in Central Asia, with Central Asia weavers adapting their looms, patterns, and color schemes to emulate the Byzantine pieces, just as they had emulated Chinese *jin* a few centuries earlier.[64] The samite weave became widespread across West and Central Asia. The Byzantine imperial weavers were using sophisticated drawlooms, possibly with a figure harness, and silk reeled from the *Bombyx mori* silkworm. Given the sophistication and the design of the hunter silk, it is probable that it was made in these Byzantine imperial workshops.[65] Where the silk thread was produced is uncertain: it could have been local or imported. However, it was probably dyed locally. The color scheme is typical of Byzantine pieces, with bright red, blue and yellow.[66] Dye analysis has not been carried out on this piece.

61. Muthesius (1997: 74). See also Muthesius (2002: 156–58) for a discussion of Byzantine looms.

62. Desrosiers (2004: 20): "Mais il se distingue de cat. 104 et 105 par son tissage avec des passées paires à retour, un trait présent sur un autre exemple à fond bleu, le tissue de Mozac conservé à Lyon. Cette particularité se généralise, à partir du IXe–Xe siècle au moin, pour les samits tissés avec des chaines dans une proportion de 2/1."

63. Silk production was introduced to southern Spain under the rule of the Umayyad Caliphate in the eighth century and continued to about 1900. It started in southern Italy in the twelfth century and spread to the north by the fourteenth.

64. "What is of particular interest is how the looms of Central Asian weavers were adapted to cope with new patterns from Byzantium" (Muthesius 1997: 98).

65. "The Imperial Byzantine figure types that occur on pieces like the Mozac Hunter fabric would support the idea that imperial looms were used to weave this type of single main warp twill; and indeed, that the Imperial Byzantine workshop may have played a significant role in the development of this kind of silk" (Muthesius 1997: 74).

66. This was to be an influence on Central Asian–produced silks around this period,

Just as the technology had spread across Eurasia, so had motifs. The roundel pattern with pearls seen on the hunter silk is commonly cited as being of Sasanian origin, whether produced on Byzantine, Central Asian, or Chinese woven pieces. The design is found on Sasanian decorative art in other media, including metalwork and seals, and on some later wool textiles. It also is shown on clothing of images of Sasanians, especially the fourth-century stone reliefs at Tāq-e Bostān and Antinoopolis. But Matteo Compateri has observed that "the enigmatic pearl roundel pattern still represents one of the great problems of Sasanian art, especially in the field of textile production."[67] Carol Bromberg argues that its use by the Sasanians can be attested only in architectural decorative elements and not in textiles.[68] It is, however, widely used on textiles in Sogdiana, the Tarim, China, and Byzantium, and in Persia in the Islamic period.[69]

The enclosure inside the roundel of a hunting scene, rather than static single or paired animals, is also ascribed to Sasanians but becomes widespread.[70] Again it is a motif seen in decorative arts, including Sasanian and Central Asian metalware, rock art, and seals.[71] Hunting was widespread across the ancient world, but the hunter silk piece portrays what Thomas Allsen terms "political hunting," an activity that had as much to do with the display of royal power and diplomacy as with ensuring an additional source of protein. That is, it represented an investment of energy rather than a means of capturing energy.[72] The horsemen on the hunter silk are members of the imperial family, identified by their rich bejeweled civil costumes and the shape of their faces, resembling imperial portraits found on coins.[73] This is there-

---

with the traditional local tans and rusts replaced with the Byzantine red, blue, and green (Muthesius 1997: 51–52, n51). Also see Muthesius (2002: 158–60).

67. Compareti (2009).

68. Bromberg (1983: 252).

69. For its use in Sogdiana, see Compareti (2004, 2006a, 2006b); for use in China, see Meister (1970) and Zhao (1997).

70. "Textile Fragment with Hunting Scene," Metropolitan Museum of Art, www.metmuseum.org/collection/the-collection-online/search/451043.

71. See chapter 5 for a discussion of metalware and the hunt motif. See also Harper and Meyers (1981).

72. Allsen (2006: 9).

73. "The facial type of the Emperor comes closest to Imperial portraits on eighth century Byzantine coins, such as those of the Emperor Anastasius II (713–15). The same facial types

fore a depiction of the royal hunt. We can conclude that the image on the hunter silk symbolized imperial power, but of course the hunting motif also reflected the popularity of the hunt itself. By this time the royal hunt was also embedded in cultures across Eurasia.[74] As well as a symbol of royal power for domestic consumption, it was part of international diplomacy.[75]

While this is a common motif, Maximilien Durand claims that its particular representation, with a double representation of the emperor dressed in parade costume, is most similar to that seen in another silk, Gunther's Shroud (*Gunthertuch*), which is thought to depict the return of the Byzantine emperor John I Tzimiskes (r. 969–76) after his victory against the Rus in 971.[76] He argues that the Mozac piece probably celebrates either the double victories of the Byzantine emperor Nikephoros II Phokas (r. 963–69) against the Arab army in 965 or those of Emperor Basil II (r. 976–1025) against the Bulgars in 1017.[77] This would date the piece to the tenth or even eleventh century, later than previously suggested by either Muthesius (eighth century) or Desrosiers (ninth century). But as Durand remarks, this line of argument has been little followed.[78]

The animal being hunted, the lion, held a complex of symbolic meanings by this time, also shared across many Silk Road cultures. "As top predator, raider of livestock and foe with legendary strength, the lion has always been surrounded by myth."[79] It could represent the power of the king or of his strongest enemy, whether actual or spiritual. "Throughout four millennia, artists in Mesopotamia and Iran depicted quasi-religious connections between the sovereign of men and the fearless king of beasts—in the ancient

that inspired the weavers of the Sens 'Lion-Strangler' silk (M44, PL. 17A) and the Sens silk with a bust (M43, PL 18B), two of the paired main warp twills described in the last chapter, seem to have/been familiar to the weavers of the Mozac Hunter silk. These are oval faces with long, delicate noses, large eyes and small mouths" (Muthesius 1997: 74).

74. Allsen (2006: 266). But this participation was not always without some local opposition: the Chinese emperor Taizong (r. 627–40) had been criticized by his advisers for his participation, but he justified it because he realized the hunt's importance for his Iranian and Turkic neighbors (Marshak 2004: 47).

75. On the Byzantine use of silks for diplomacy, see Muthesius (1992).

76. Stephenson (2003: 62–65).

77. Durand (2014).

78. "Evidemment cette hypothèse a été peu suivé" (Durand 2014).

79. Ryken, Wilhoit, and Tremper Longman (2010: 30). For a discussion of the symbolism of the lion and the hunting theme in relation to art in the Greek world at the time of Alexander, see A. Cohen (2010).

Gilgamesh motif of Akkadian seals; the lion gateways of the Hittites; the Assyrian reliefs showing their kings in lion combats."[80] The Asiatic lion was found from southern Europe and the shores of the Mediterranean, into the Arabian Peninsula, eastwards across Persia and Central Asia, into India—although it had become extinct in Europe by the beginning of the first millennium AD. Lion thrones appear on Kushan coins and Sasanian coins and rock reliefs.[81] Although the lion was not found in the Tarim, East Asia, or Southeast Asia, it starts to be depicted at the beginning of the first millennium. This was probably through the intermediary of Buddhism, in which lions were a potent symbol as protectors of the *dharma*. They are depicted at the entrance to temples or flanking images of Buddha. Because they were symbols of chaos in North Africa and Mesopotamia, the killing of them was a symbol of political protection and of the defeat of chaos. In Christian times saints were depicted as hunters, destroying this power of chaos. "What appears initially as a secular, aristocratic image is infused with a sublimated religious and protective theme."[82] The Byzantines, with their close links to all these cultures, inherited this legacy of lion symbolism and undoubtedly adapted it to their own culture.[83]

The other parts of the scene on the hunter silk also bear some discussion. The importance of the horse in the cultures of the Silk Road is discussed in chapter 6, and I will not repeat that discussion here except to note the decorations on its tack, similar to the depiction from Khotan. In that case the horse's tail is tied. In this example, a ribbon is tied around the horses' tails: animals decorated with ribbons are seen on Sasanian metalware and stamp seals, although the ribbons are often tied around the neck. The hunting dog is ubiquitous across Eurasia. Hounds, especially the greyhound and saluki, are commonly depicted in images of royal hunts and falconry, although the two shown on the hunter silk do not seem to be of either of these breeds.[84] They possibly show a type of dog more related to those known in medieval Europe as Alaunt or Alans, praised for their ability to take on all kinds of prey. These are said to have been taken to Europe from the North Caucasus by the Alani.

80. Rosenfield (1967: 184).

81. Rosenfield (1967: 183–86); Harper (1978: 103–4, 107).

82. Ryder (2008).

83. Harper (1978: 139) notes the rareness of the lion-hunting scene on Sasanian silverware and argues that this might show it has a special significance, such as defeat of an enemy.

84. See Allsen (2006: 54–57) for a brief discussion of hunting dogs with references.

The Alani or Alans were a pastoralist people, many of whom migrated westwards as far as France, Spain, and North Africa in the fourth and early fifth centuries—hence the dog's European name.[85] Gaston de Foix's (1331–91) early fifteenth-century description of this hunting dog was translated by Edward of Norwich (ca. 1373–1415): "Alauntes will run gladly and bite the horse. Also they run at oxen and sheep, and swine, and at all other beasts, or at men or at other hounds. For men have seen alauntes slay their masters. In all manner of ways alauntes are treacherous and evil understanding, and more foolish and more harebrained than any other kind of hound."[86]

But what stands out about the design on the hunter silk are the stirrups. Stirrups are seen on depictions of horsemen from the fourth and fifth centuries on the eastern steppe and in the lands of China, Korea, and Japan (see chapter 6).[87] They are first mentioned in Byzantine texts in the *Strategikon* of Maurice, which some scholars date to the late sixth century. It has been suggested that their diffusion was with the Turkic Avars on the steppe.[88] But as Muthesius points out, despite this they are found on no other surviving silk showing a hunting scene.[89] They are equally rare on Sasanian metalware hunting scenes, the Pur-i Vahman plate being an exception.[90] Their rarity might have been due to the perpetuation of older forms for these hunter designs. There is also some evidence, discussed by Irfan Shahid, that the skilled rider might have not been considered to need a stirrup, either for stability or for mounting—he was expected to jump onto his horse.[91] Perhaps by this time the real world was starting to make its effect felt on these traditional designs, hence the appearance of the stirrup on this piece. This might also be a reason to believe in the later dating.

85. Bachrach (1973); Alemany (2000).
86. Edward of Norwich (2013: 117).
87. Dien (2000).
88. Hildinger (1997: 78).
89. Muthesius (1997: 68–69).
90. The State Hermitage Museum, S247. See State Hermitage Museum, "The Pur-i Vahman Plate: Silver Plate with Horse-Archer Hunting Lion and Boar," S247, http://warfare1.000webhostapp.com/Persia/StPetersburg-Dish_with_hunting_scene.htm. Harper discusses this and dates it to the late end of the Sasanian period because of the stirrup (P. Harper and Meyers 1981: 139–40). Bivar (1972: 290) argues that the stirrup is not seen in Iran before the Islamic period. See Shahid (1995: 575–78) for a review of the evidence. He concludes that the Byzantines learned the use of the stirrup around 600 following encounters with the Avars along the Danube.
91. Shahid (1995: 577).

The story of this silk now takes us from Asia into Europe, at this time on the fringes of the great trading network known as the Silk Road. Though Europe still had no silk production centers of its own, silk was nevertheless highly valued there, especially among the courts and clergy. It was therefore a perfect diplomatic gift, being light and portable. And it was even more so if the design reflected the power of the giver.[92] We do not known if this piece was intended for such purposes or whether, indeed, the purpose was decided in advance of its commission, but at the very least it was probably woven with the possibility that it would become a diplomatic gift.

Our first record of this piece is a source referring to the translation—rehousing—of the relics of Saint Austremoine from the church at Volvic, in the modern Puy de Domes in France, to the Abbey of Mozac, some four miles to its east.[93] The translation happened under the patronage of King Pepin, who, it is recorded, provided a piece of silk to wrap them, had the bundle marked with his royal seal, and traveled with them to their new home. The name Pepin in this record was originally believed to refer to the Carolingian king, Pepin the Short (r. 751–68), father of Charlemagne, and the date was

92. "A hierarchy of silken splendour was established across social, artistic, religious, economic and political boundaries. On one level silk was a decorative fabric socially exploited for its aesthetic qualities. On another level it was prized as a fabric fit for furnishing the House of God. Above all though, the Imperial house was intent to raise what was essentially a valuable economic asset to the heights of a powerful political weapon. Consequently silk was made to serve both as the prime Imperial ceremonial fabric and as the diplomatic cloth 'par excellence'" (Muthesius 1992: 101). Also see Cutler (2008).

93. Austremonius was, according to Gregory of Tours (ca. 538–94), one of seven bishops sent by the third-century pope Fabian from Rome to Gaul to preach. Stremonius, as he was called by Gregory, became bishop of Clermont and was successful in conversions. Later stories that he was beheaded are probably not true. He was buried in Issoire (Havey 1907; Gregory of Tours 1916, vol. 1: 30). Gregory reports that his cult started when a deacon, Cantius, saw a vision of angels around his tomb. His body—by now having taken on the mantle of saintly relics—was then translated to Volvic, west of Mozac, in the seventh century. There are records that his head was taken to St. Yvoine, north of Issoire, in the mid-ninth century and then was returned to Issoire in about 900 by Benedictine monks escaping a Norse invasion. The Church of Saint Austremoine, in Issoire, claims to hold the head today. The separate journey of the head would support the report that Austremoine was beheaded. But the division of the body of a saint was not unknown and indeed became common as the demand for relics increased (Snoek 1995: 22–23). After his interral at Mozac his saintly biography was written, and in this he was moved back in time to the first century to allow him to become one of the disciples of Jesus.

interpreted as February 1, 764. We know that in 757 a Byzantine imperial envoy was sent from the court of Constantine V (r. 741–75) in Constantinople to Pepin's court in Compiègne, a town north of Paris. Among the gifts carried was an organ, exciting enough to be noted by chroniclers.[94] There would certainly have been many other gifts, including textiles. Protracted negotiations were taking place at this time concerning a proposed marriage alliance between Constantine's son and Pepin's daughter.[95] The sources of this proposed alliance can be found in the seizure in 751 of Byzantine territory in southern Italy by the dukes of Lombard. They were also threatening papal territory in the region. Relations between the Byzantine and papal courts had seen deterioration from 726 because of the Byzantine policy of iconoclasm, whereby they periodically destroyed religious images of all sorts. Papal Rome protested: the first time there had been an open rebuke from the church to the empire. When the dukes of Lombard started their territorial encroachments, rather than working together, Constantine and the popes independently sought military help from Pepin. Pepin and his two sons were anointed by Pope Stephen in St. Denis in Paris in 754, and in 756 Pepin's army forced the Lombards to surrender their conquests. This papal favor was to continue with the coronation in 800 of Pepin's son, Charlemagne, in St. Peter's Church in Rome as the Roman emperor at the hands of Pope Leo III in 800.

However, as Maximilien Durand points out, the Pepin referred to in the document about the rehousing of Saint Austremoine's relics was more probably Pepin II of Aquitaine (838–64), and the date should be read as February 1, 847, or probably 848. Other textual evidence discussed by Durand supports this later date, as does the recent technical analysis of the silk by Desrosiers. For now, therefore, the weight of evidence suggests an early or mid-ninth-century origin for the silk. This leaves uncertain how Pepin II acquired the silk, although Durand suggests it was perhaps a gift from Emperor Theophilos (r. 829–42) to Louis the Pious (r. 814–40) in recognition of his help in the campaign against the Arabs. It would then have passed down to Louis's heir,

94. "Likely a steam organ, and used some of the same technology as the marvellous artificial singing bird in the palaces of al-Mam'un and al-Muqtadir a century later" (Truitt 2015: 22).

95. In this case, the marriage did not take place, but diplomatic marriages were as much part of the Eurasian political world as was the royal hunt. Constantine himself was married to a daughter of the Khazars in 720. Note that Muthesius (1997: 69) says the discussions between Pepin and Constantine V concerning the marriage did not begin until 765.

FIGURE 27. Mozac Abbey, 2016. Photograph by John Falconer.

Pepin I of Aquitaine (r. 797–838) and thence to his son, Pepin II.[96] The piece has been cut and stitched, suggesting it might have been made into a piece of clothing, but we do not know whether this was before or after Pepin's acquisition.

The abbey at Mozac was a much grander affair than Austremoine's original burial place in Issoire and the church at Volvic (figure 27). It had been founded in the sixth or seventh century by Calmin and his wife Namadie, both who also became sanctified.[97] The abbey was endowed, it is recorded, with relics of Saint Peter (Saint Pierre), to whom the church was dedicated: those of Calmin and his wife later joined them.

96. Durand (2014).

97. For a history of the abbey, see Gomot (1872). A twelfth-century shrine reliquary was later made to hold their remains. Thomas Dobrée (1810–95) was able to retire at twenty-eight and become an art collector. The reliquary was among the objects he acquired, and it became the inspiration for the palace he had built to house his not inconsiderable collection, which is now the museum (Aptel and Biotteau 1997).

A brief digression is perhaps useful here on the cult of relics across the Silk Road. By this time relics had become an integral part of medieval Christian belief, and in central and East Asia they were equally essential in the practice and ritual of Buddhism. In both communities they were interred at the heart of sacred structures—under the altar of Christian churches and in a chamber in the central core of the Buddhist stupa (discussed in chapter 4). In both religions, the relics pertained both to the life of their respective founders—Jesus and Śākyamuni—and to the lives of their disciples and saints/ monks.[98] Christian and Buddhist monasteries publicized their relics as the sites became places of pilgrimage and so increased the monasteries' revenue.[99] This demand for relics inevitably led both to a thriving trade and to thriving fraud. Augustine had attempted to control the trade in the fifth century, and Charlemagne (r. 800–814) (Pepin II's great-grandfather) would do the same, but to little avail.[100]

Just as in the Christian world, relics proliferated in Buddhism. As discussed in chapter 4, Buddhist relics were interred with the seven treasures of Buddhism: traditionally (although substitutions are seen in the case of the gemstones) gold, silver, lapis lazuli, crystal, agate, pearl, and carnelian. The relics said to be parts of the finger bones of the Buddha, found under the stupa of the Famen Temple near present-day Xian in China, for example, were in "Russian-doll" caskets of rock crystal, silver, and gold. Each casket was also wrapped in fine silk. In Christian churches reliquaries were also made of precious materials—rock crystal, gold, silver, ivory, gems, and enamel.[101] In the Carolingian period relics were wrapped first in linen, often several layers, before one or two outer wrappings of silk from the East—and especially from Byzantium.[102] The wrappings were secured with a tie. And in both traditions the powerful were often involved in the rituals: for exam-

98. Geary (1978).

99. "The possession of major relics seemed to enhance the prestige of ecclesiastical centers and helped to encourage the lucrative growth of pilgrimage" (Muthesius 1997: 119). Teter (2011: 108) cites the example of the Marian shrine at Altotting, which received revenue from pilgrimage of a sum equivalent to four thousand horses per year. For a discussion of Buddhist pilgrimage, see Galambos and van Schaik (2012: 35–59).

100. Teter (2011: 109).

101. For examples of reliquaries from Christian churches, see Boehm ([2001] 2011).

102. Liu (1996) discusses in more detail the use of silk in the Christian and Buddhist traditions. Also see Muthesius (2008: 119–20) for a summary of the use of silk to wrap Christian relics. The silks showed honor to the relics and absorbed sanctity through them (Muthesius 2008: 86). For silk as a status marker in Viking burials, see Vedeler (2014: 33).

ple, in 582 the Chinese emperor distributed the relics he had received from an Indian monk, sending thirty monks to carry them in great processions throughout the empire. The relics were divided by the emperor into thirty bottles made of red glass, each of which was placed inside a golden bottle, sealed with glue made of frankincense. Stupas were built in each of the thirty districts to receive the relics.[103]

Wrapping relics was only one of the many ways in which the Christian Church used silk. Others uses included ecclesiastical vestments, furnishings, hangings, the lining of metalwork, and the bindings of books. As discussed in chapter 4, Buddhist temples employed silk in similar ways. And in both religions leaders sometimes frowned upon monks or clerics acquiring or dressing in expensive silk. For example, Charlemagne disapproved of the practice, something he made sure was passed on to Archbishop Ethelhard of Canterbury (791–805) during his visit to England (the archbishop was warned in advance that Charlemagne did not wish to see the clergy of Ethelhard's entourage in silk).[104] But the frequent references and remains of silk garments suggest that silk continued to be widely used in this way.

Whether there was any cross-influence between the cult of relics in Buddhism and Christianity remains open to discussion. One obvious difference in practice was the accessibility to the general population of silk in East Asia. Whereas in Christian Europe kings and the elite gave churches small fragments of imported silk to wrap their relics, in Buddhist central and East Asia many pilgrims could probably afford to purchase fairly large pieces of locally produced silk to wrap reliquaries and to decorate temples and stupas. An early sixth-century Chinese pilgrim monk on his way to India, for example, notes that Buddhist statues and stupas in the southern Tarim kingdom of Khotan were adorned with tens of thousands of colored silk canopies and banners.[105]

To return to Austremoine's bones by now interred in the St. Mozac Abbey wrapped in a piece of the hunter silk given by King Pepin. There is no evidence to suggest that the relics were moved over the next few centuries. In

---

103. Liu (1996: 41–42).

104. Reported by the Monk of St. Gall—who also reports monks sewing silk onto their habits and describes the bishop dressed in silk and seated on a silk cushion (cited in Mutheusius 1980: n21). Also see Thomas (2012: 127).

105. Jenner (1981: 219–20); Beal (1884: lxxxvi; also discussed in chapter 6). The monk reads the Chinese inscriptions on the banners and finds that most of them date from the previous three decades.

1197 there was a new "recognition" of Saint Austremoine, and the relics were checked in their shrine by Bishop Robert of Clermont. He reported seeing the silk with Pepin's seal intact and, on cutting the tie (to avoid breaking the seal), also found the relics intact.[106] He re-placed them inside the silk. In the sixteenth century a wooden reliquary was made to house them, decorated by an Italian artist with paintings of the twelve apostles.

In 1790 during the French Revolution the abbey was dissolved and became the parish Church of Saint Peter. It is possible the relics were disturbed. When the reliquary was opened on October 24, 1839, it was found to contain several objects. These included four teeth in a glass vial contained in a porcelain vase, as well as several parcels of bones wrapped in linen with a parchment tie on which was written "Relics of Saint Austremoine." There was also a letter of Jean-Pierre Massillon (1663–1742), bishop of Clermont from 1717, concerning the disposition of relics. On January 29, 1852, the bones were listed by a vicar-general and a doctor as a right femur; a left femur; part of a right tibia and a left tibia; a large part of a pelvis; three vertebrae; a kneecap; the base of a skull; almost an entire head; two rib fragments; part of a heel bone; and several small pieces impossible to identify, but also including finger and toe joints.[107]

THE MUSEUM PIECE

We now reach the latest chapter in the story of this hunter silk, its removal from a sacred back to a secular setting and a return to the concentration on the silk itself. With the French secularization of the church initiated by the French Revolution, church property, such as St. Calmin's reliquary—mentioned above—started to be sold. This was not a new phenomenon. At various times, such as the Dissolution of the Monasteries from 1534 under Henry VIII in England and the Treaty of Westphalia in Germany in 1648, religious property was seized by the state and often passed or sold on.[108] The difference

106. *Liber miraculorum: Additamentum de reliquiis sancti Austremonii*, Acta Sanctorum [AS], November 1, 1887, 81; Durand (2014); Muthesius (1997: n52); Schorta (2016: 48); Gomot (1873–74: 47).

107. Gomot (1873–74: 220).

108. It had happened through history—the Chinese state seized much Buddhist metal statuary during the persecutions of Buddhism, melting it down to mint coins for their depleted treasury.

in the nineteenth century was that by this time there was a growing ideal of the "museum" as a site for the public appreciation of art and craft, so the materials were more likely to end up in public view.[109]

The piece was described by Hippolyte Gomot in his history of the church as having four hunters and four lions.[110] It seems that, possibly because of this publication, interest in the textile grew and the church was able to sell fragments, providing much-needed funds to help with its restoration. Two other pieces are known in the Borgelli Collection in Florence and in the Abegg-Stiftung in Riggisberg.[111]

Lyon was a center of silk and other textile production, and a museum to celebrate this industry was first proposed in 1797. A textile collection started to be amassed by the chamber of commerce over the next decades.[112] This was supplemented with material collected by the first French trade mission to China (1843–46). Many of the Lyon manufacturers attended the London Exhibition in 1850, and calls were renewed for a museum on their return. The chamber voted in favor in 1856. The resulting Museum of Art and Industry was opened on March 6, 1864. It was replaced with the Historical Museum of Textiles on August 6, 1891.

The museum had an active acquisition policy. Émile Guimet (1836–1918), founder in 1879 of the museum of his name in his birthplace of Lyon (it was handed over to the state and transferred to Paris in 1885), persuaded the Lyon Chamber of Commerce to sponsor excavations in Antinoopolis in Egypt.[113] The resulting finds went to the museum.[114] But the museum curators also sought acquisitions from local churches. In 1904 under the directorship of

---

109. Museums date back earlier, and the eighteenth century saw the foundation of many major museums, such as the Louvre, the British Museum, and the Prada. But they proliferated in the nineteenth century as private collectors sought to make their collections accessible to the public. See G. Lewis (2015).

110. Gomot (1873–74: 221–22): "l'ossement entier d'une jambe enveloppé dans un morceau d'étoffe très-ancienne sur laquelle sont dessinés quatre hommes d'armes à cheval et quatre lions."

111. Inventory numbers 2293 C and 1146 respectively. See Otavsky and Wardwell (2011: cat. 39) for the Abegg-Stiftung piece. Neither of these fits directly with the Lyon piece, suggesting there must have been more dispersed fragments.

112. The following information is summarized at the museum's website, www.mtmad.fr/fr/pages/topnavigation/musees_et_collections/mt_histoire_musee/mt-creation.aspx.

113. The Guimets, father and son, ran a factory in Lyon making synthetic ultramarine to replace the expensive lapis lazuli, a longtime Eurasian export from Bactria. See chapter 7.

114. Including the silk gaiter possibly showing a battle of the Axumites; see Whitfield (2015b: prol. and plate 1).

Raymond Jean-Marie Cox (1856–1921), the museum acquired the remains of the hunter silk from Mozac. But, by this time, the remaining piece showed only two hunters: the rest of the silk had presumably been dispersed to others. How the price for this piece was arrived at is not recorded, although a story has been handed down that it was agreed that the museum should pay the price of coins—the French louis—that could fit onto the silk. The acquisition register of the museum clearly records the purchase of this piece for eight thousand francs.[115] This was an enormous amount; the other entries on the page are for tens or, at most, a couple of hundred francs. The franc was linked to the gold standard, and this equated to 2,320 grams of gold, about US$100,000 today.

The hunter silk was classed as a historical artifact on January 20, 1909. It traveled to Paris for exhibitions in 1958 and 1992.[116] It seemed that its future was assured. But as history shows, there is no place of safekeeping. Like many museums worldwide, the Lyon Museum has been under threat from lack of funds. It continued to be supported by the Chamber of Commerce of Lyons, but in 2015 they announced that they could no longer support it and that the museum would close in 2016. By the time of the publication of this book, closure appeared to have been averted, but the news serves as a reminder that a later generation might have another chapter to write in the story of this wonderful textile.

115. Thanks to Maximilien Durand for this information. There is also correspondence relating to this purchase; see Durand (2014).
116. Musée Cernuschi (1958: cat. 254); Musée du Louvre (1992: cat. 132).

NINE

A Chinese Almanac

THOUSANDS OF TINY Chinese characters, diagrams, and drawings separated into three registers with different sections cover two panels of yellow-dyed paper, over three feet long and just under a foot high (plate 8). The document is printed, a technique invented in East Asia by the eighth century and at a level of sophistication by 877, the date of the production of this object.[1] This is an almanac, a guide for daily life, not only offering an annual calendar but marking lucky and unlucky days for tasks and events from marrying to washing hair to planting crops, as well as distributing exorcism methods, charms, *fengshui* advice, some farming events, astronomical data, astrological prognostications, and much more.[2]

We know one of the main reasons for the production of this almanac—the why. When woodblock printing was invented, two communities quickly realized its potential. The Buddhists, whose scriptures state that replicating the image or words of the Buddha is a great act of merit, exploited printing for their faith—although also undoubtedly profiting from sales of popular

For places mentioned in this chapter see Map 8 in the color maps insert.

1. I am very grateful to Alain Arrault for his invaluable comments on this chapter and his extensive research on this and other calendars and almanacs, which I have drawn on extensively (see esp. Arrault and Martzloff 2003). The date for our almanac was arrived at by Lionel Giles on the basis of three points in the text (L. Giles 1939: 1034; also see below). All mistakes, misunderstandings, and omissions are my own.

2. The term *almanac* is used advisedly. Arrault makes a clear distinction between the annual calendar and texts, such as this, that also include divinatory methods. However, I would argue that "day books"—*rishu*—which are found with the annual calendar from the third century BC mark the start of the almanac, which I define as a combination of a calendar and divinatory and other texts. This follows Wilkinson (2000: 172). See further notes below.

prayer sheets.[3] Private printers were primarily interested in monetary rather than religious gain. And one of the most popular types of book in China in this period —and up to the present—was the almanac.[4] There was certainly a market, and not only among the literate. Producing manuscript copies was a time-consuming and expensive business. Producing copies from woodblocks gave the potential for much cheaper almanacs, and private printers proliferated to take advantage of this opportunity.

Despite this popularity, the production of almanacs came with political risks, and to understand this object we first need to understand its relationship to the political authority of the time. But there is also the puzzle of how it survived: almanacs were ephemeral objects with a shelf life of a year—after which they were obsolete and discarded. How did this almanac survive into the following year, 878, let alone to the present? And, just as interestingly, how did it transform from a well-thumbed everyday object into a library treasure? I shall turn to these questions later.

CALENDARS, ALMANACS, AND POLITICAL POWER

Our almanac is an example of the ambiguity of literacy and power. The text of the almanac had authority, but the authority was not that of the rulers or officials. It represented an alternative authority—the natural order—that was more powerful than earthly rulers. Astral omenology—the correspondence of events in the sky and on earth—was central to Chinese political life and beliefs. Since ancient times in China, diviners and astronomers who could read the stars and predict unusual events such as eclipses or comets were under the exclusive control of the imperial court. This was vital, as such events might be used by political rivals to suggest evidence of the emperor being "out of tune" with the natural world and therefore not fit to rule. This was not an unfounded fear. The history of China is punctuated with rebel-

3. As Lionel Giles noted, "It can be imagined what a boon the invention of printing must have been to the Buddhist, seeing it enabled him to accumulate merit on a vast scale with comparatively little trouble or expense" (1939: 1031). Printing of complete sheets of text might well have been influenced by the production of stamps and stencils allowing production of multiple Buddha images long before this (McDermott 2006: 7–12). Also see Barrett (1997, 2001) for the development of printing in China.

4. We do not know the size of the market, but there is indirect evidence from the repeated legal prohibitions, at least for central and Southwest China, as discussed below.

lions by those professing to be carrying out "heaven's mandate."[5] Some of them were successful. At the end of the Later Han dynasty (AD 25–220), a group called the Yellow Turbans claimed the right to rebel, citing the famines and floods across the empire as a sign of the emperor having lost his mandate. Their uprising led to the fall of the dynasty. Shortly after this, in 267, there was an official ban on certain types of texts deemed to be heterodox, including *chen* predictive texts, discussed below.[6]

From early times the emperors' astronomers had calculated the calendar or "fixed the time" using a combination of solar days and lunar years, deciding when the year of an individual ruler would start, determining cyclical dates, and predicting cosmic events. While the solar calendar with its fixed seasons is most useful for farmers, giving the days for spring sowing, harvesting, and so on, the primary role of the mixed solar-lunar calendar, as found in China, was as a regulator of official rather than agricultural life.[7] The emperor produced a calendar as a sign of his right to rule.[8] An accurate calendar displayed the moral perfection of the ruler in that it showed he was in tune with events in the macro or cosmic sphere. The development of a new calendar without official sanction was therefore a revolutionary act.

The traditional date for the first publication of the imperial calendar is given as 2265 BC, although the earliest extant annual calendars date from the third century BC.[9] Made from woodslips, a traditional material for books in China before the invention of paper, four calendars for 213, 211, 210, and 209 BC were found in a tomb at Zhoujiatai.[10] These also incorporated "day books" (*rishu*), divinatory texts that gave auspicious and inauspicious days for certain activities, and sections on astrology and the magico-religious system.[11] Well-used copies of such texts are also found from the same period in

5. A term used by the Chinese classical philosopher Mencius/Mengzi. For a recent discussion of this, see Nuyen (2013).

6. Whitfield (1998: 9–10).

7. As Martzloff (2009: 64–66) notes, only three of the twenty-four points in the calendar specifically referred to farming events, while others were to astronomical and atmospheric phenomena (many of which, such as the weather, were also of course relevant to the farming calendar).

8. Eberhard (1957).

9. From Zhoujiatai (Arrault and Martzloff 2003: 85). Partial texts have also been found at the defensive walls north of Dunhuang in Northwest China dating from the first century.

10. Arrault and Martzloff (2003: 85).

11. See D. Harper (2016), Raphaels (2013: 203–12, 412–21). An international research project into such texts was started in 2013 based at the University of Erlangen; see

tombs of individuals ranging from low-level officials to the elite.[12] They were texts used by the tomb occupants in their lifetime, and their burial shows their importance to the deceased. They are, I would argue, the start of the process of syncretization of the annual calendar with astrological and other divination texts that together make up an almanac.[13]

One of the most complete calendars was written on silk, a more expensive writing material, and was discovered in the Mawangdui tomb in southern China dating from 129 BC.[14] This was during the Former Han dynasty (206 BC–AD 9), which had seized power from the Qin (221–206 BC) in the power vacuum after the death of the so-called First Emperor. During his reign— famed for his tomb guard of terracotta soldiers—there had been an infamous episode when books outside the Qin orthodoxy were ceremonially burned in 213 BC. These included the classic texts of the Confucian tradition. The texts were restored in the Han from oral transmissions, leading to the so-called New Texts (the "new" referring to their script or handwriting, which had been standardized in the Qin and was used to transcribe the orally transmitted texts). But other texts also started to be discovered in this period, some in the walls of the Confucian family house. They were in pre-Qin handwriting and thus became known as the "Old Texts."[15] There ensued a period of debate between proponents of the two traditions, with the New Text supporters arguing that the Old Texts had been forged to provide a classical justification for a certain contemporary political agenda.

Also popular in this period were the *chen* and *wei* texts, esoteric commentaries to the classics that interpreted the secret prophecies they claimed were part of the meaning of the original texts.[16] These covered the resonances

---

International Consortium for Research in the Humanities, "Research Project—Popular Culture and Books of Fate in Early China: The Daybook Manuscripts (*rishu*) of the Warring States, Qin, and Han Periods," last updated July 5, 2013, www.ikgf.uni-erlangen. de/research/research-projects/techniques-and-practices/popular-culture-and-books-of-fate-in-early-china.shtml.

12. The earliest is from 217 BC at Shuihudi. See also the bamboo slips Qin tombs at Jiudian, also in Hubei Province (Loewe and O'Shaughnessy 1999: 847–48; Wilkinson 2000: 173, 461).

13. Donald Harper (2016) uses the term *occult miscellanies*.

14. Wilkinson (2000: 794).

15. Nylan (1994: 83–145); Ess (1994: 146–70).

16. *Chen* consisted of predictions based on the esoteric commentaries on the classics, which constituted the *wei* texts. Their predictive power included the rise and fall of emperors. *Wei* is the term for the weft thread, while the orthodox Confucian texts were called *jing*, the warp. For further discussion, see Whitfield (1998: 10–11).

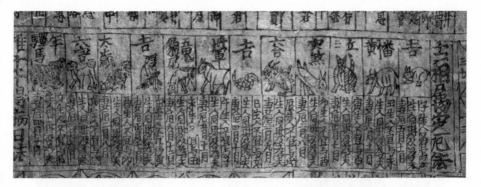

FIGURE 28. Detail of the almanac showing the animal zodiac. British Library, Or.8210/P.6 (detail).

of numbers, inauspicious and auspicious omens, relations between the sky and the earth, interpretation of stars and cloud formations, historical events, and the fall of dynasties. The Old-New Text debate was also concerned with whether the classics really fulfilled a role as prophetic texts.

The Han rulers lost power in AD 9 when the regent, Wang Mang, declared his own Xin dynasty. His reign was short-lived. The Han regained power in AD 25, but they had been forced east by rebels from Chang'an into Luoyang, a secondary capital along the Yellow River. This promoted a period of retrenchment not only in territory but also in thought as the Han rulers more strictly imposed a state orthodoxy. Many previously popular texts, such as day books, were deemed to fall outside the imperially imposed orthodoxy—there was a division into "inner" and "outer" texts. The "outer" texts were increasingly grouped together into popular digests that started to grow in size from this period. Their contents might include day books, fortunes based on the animals and the element of one's birth (figure 28), divination based on numerous different methods, talismans, and *fengshui* diagrams that showed the best alignment of various rooms and other parts of a home (figure 29).

The Han fell after the Yellow Turban rebellion, and their territory was split between various relatively short-lived kingdoms. During this period in 267 one such kingdom, the Jin (265–420), issued the first legal proscription on these popular prognostic texts. Anyone found with such esoteric books in their possession was subject to two years' imprisonment, and anyone studying such works was to be sentenced to death.[17] However, the regu-

17. Whitfield (1998: 11).

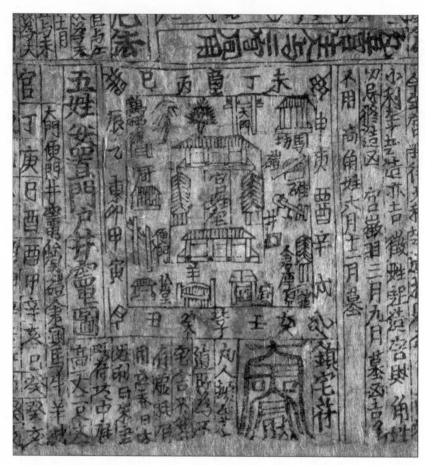

FIGURE 29. Detail of the almanac showing a *fengshui* diagram. British Library, Or.8210/P.6 (detail).

larity with which such decrees were promulgated in the centuries after this suggests that they were not effective and reflects the continuing popularity of such works.[18] A ban in 375 included the Daoist texts of the *Daodejing* and the *Zhuangzi*, along with works of divination and prophecy, and was also imposed by a non-Chinese ruler seeking to use orthodox Confucianism as a state ideology to legitimize his power. Article 110 of the Tang legal code, promulgated in 653, read: "All cases of possession of astronomical instruments, astronomical charts, charts and books of prognostication, military books, Qiyao Almanacs, the Methods of the Great Monad, or the Methods of the

18. For a survey of censorship ordinances in China, see An and Zheng (1992).

God of Thunder by private persons punish violators by two years of penal servitude."[19]

The imperial powers attempted to keep control of private almanacs' production and distribution, but in reality these abounded. In 835, an official from the southwest of China, in what is now Sichuan Province, sent a memorial to the emperor: "In all the provinces of Sichuan and Huainan, printed calendars are on sale in the markets. Every year, before the Imperial Observatory has submitted the new calendar for approval and had it officially promulgated, these printed calendars have flooded the empire. This violates the principle that the calendar is a gift of His Majesty."[20]

The ruling Tang power subsequently issued a decree stipulating that the private possession and private printing of almanacs by local administrations were forbidden. Until 1900 there were no known extant examples of printed almanacs from this period. They were well-thumbed objects but ephemeral, with a shelf life of a year.[21] Come the new year, the old almanac would become obsolete and presumably be discarded—perhaps recycled to line the soles of shoes, repair sacred manuscripts, or be used as "privy paper."[22] This changed in 1900 with the accidental discovery of a hidden library containing tens of thousands of documents near the Silk Road town of Dunhuang in the northwest of China, over a thousand miles from the center of Tang power. Most of these were Buddhist scriptures, whether copies from local monastery libraries or personal copies of deceased monks, and general sacred waste.[23] Among them were fragments from secular life, including the manuscript and printed almanacs discussed here. Many of the manuscript copies were locally produced—and from them and other documents we know much about the

19. Whitfield (1998). *Qiyao* almanacs are described as texts "dealing with the calendar, the Sun, the Moon, and the Five Planets."

20. Memorial by Feng Su, quoted in Tsien (1985: 151).

21. Although, as mentioned above, almanacs have been found in tombs, such as Mawangdui.

22. We can see sole-shaped patches cut out of old manuscripts. Many of the Dunhuang manuscripts had numerous repair patches, some of them originally parts of other manuscripts. The use by Confucians of old Buddhist manuscripts for toilet paper is mentioned by a Chinese monk Huiyuan (344–416), who makes clear his disgust at this sacrilege: "Their sins are as numerous as the grains of sand in the River Ganges, and many lives of repentance will not be sufficient to erase them. / Their bodies will sink for five hundred ages; they will always be condemned to be insects living in the night soil pit" (translated in Waley 1960: 122).

23. For a summing up of the various hypotheses concerning the function of the "library cave," see Galambos and van Schaik (2012: 18–28).

life of the local official astronomer.[24] This might explain why the almanacs were kept here, and thus survived, as discussed below.

However, the printed almanacs found at Dunhuang, of which three fragments are currently known in addition to ours, were almost certainly not printed locally. One is tentatively dated to the late ninth century. It was produced, so the large characters on its left tell us, "By the Da Family Printers of the East Market of Shangdu" (figure 30). "Shangdu" or "the Primary Capital," had been used to designate Chang'an since 762.[25] The East Market abutted the official buildings and the residences of the rich in Chang'an (the West Market was where traders came from the Silk Road and was in an area of churches of many faiths, inns, restaurants, and wine shops). The publication of the printer's name suggests the impunity with which printers treated the law, this almanac being printed and presumably sold under the noses of the officials who banned such production, and perhaps even to such officials and their families and servants. The motive is not hard to discern: profit.[26] The imperial order given to the Directorate of Astronomical Observation in 936 to compile and print almanacs for sale to the general public undoubtedly was an attempt to control the content of almanacs, but also a means of obtaining government revenue.

There must have been risks to private printers—and buyers—although the repeated ordinances (953, 958, 1071, 1080, 1202) and the very fact of the existence of this fragment suggest that they were not great: printers clearly continued producing these proscribed documents.[27] Apart from the single fragment known to be from the Chinese capital, the scant evidence from Dunhuang, our main source for this period, supports the evidence for printing in the southwest of China. Another almanac fragment bears the date 882 and the inscription "Family calendar of Fan Shang of Chengdu in Xichuan, province of Jiannan."[28] As well as the trade routes east and west from Dunhuang, there were well-traveled routes north and south, the last to

24. Zhai Fengda (883–996). See Teiser (1994: 102–21); also Whitfield (2015b, chap. 8).
25. British Library, Or.8210/P.12; Des Rotours (1947: 681). For a description of these printed almanacs, see Arrault and Martzloff (2003: 199–207).
26. In 936 the Directorate of Astronomical Observation received an imperial order to compile and print almanacs for sale to the general public.
27. Whitfield (1998: 14; 2001).
28. British Library Or.8210/P.10, dated "second year of Zhonghe" (L. Giles 1939: 1036–37).

FIGURE 30.
Fragment of privately
printed almanac from
the Chinese capital.
The British Library,
Or.8210/P.12.

the province of Shu—modern-day Sichuan.[29] The source of the third fragment is not known, but it is similar in content and organization to our almanac and is dated to 834.[30]

The fact that such texts were proscribed might not have been known by many people, especially those at Dunhuang on the frontier of China. This area was under only intermittent and then tenuous Chinese control from the mid-eighth century, when civil war in the heartland necessitated the withdrawal of troops from the borders and the Tibetans took Dunhuang in 786. They were to stay until 848, and although the Chinese family who expelled them professed loyalty to China the links with the capital and court remained intermittent. Dunhuang then came under increasing influence from a neighboring Turkic Uygur kingdom before becoming part of the Tangut kingdom from the mid-eleventh century.[31] Of course, this is not to say that most people purchasing or using almanacs, or those producing them, thought of them as subversive or had any intention of using them in this way. For most people at most times they were aids for everyday living, providing answers where none were forthcoming from the official or formal religious power structures.

Although almanacs consisted largely of text, we should not assume they were accessible only to the fully literate, a tiny elite. China was a culture accustomed to text, and it was part of everyday life, even for the partially or wholly illiterate. Valerie Hansen has shown how contracts were widely used, with parties signing their names with crosses or other marks.[32] These were part of a large community of the "functionally literate," possibly barely able to write but using text in their everyday lives and thereby "entangled in the webs created by writing."[33] Nor did the written word express only official

29. A manuscript copy of the Diamond Sutra, dated to 905, contains a note: "From the true printed text of the Guo family in Xichuan" (British Library, Or.8210/S.5534; see Giles 1940: 319). This is copied by an old man of eighty-two (Teiser 1994: 244).

30. In the Institute of Oriental Manuscripts in St. Petersburg, D.2880.

31. The date of the Tangut conquest is traditionally put at 1036, but see Russell-Smith (2005: 73) for a discussion concerning revisions to this date. Chinese astrological texts became popular among their neighboring cultures; see, for example, Matsui (2012) on Uygur almanacs.

32. She also shows the range of literacy in Dunhuang and Turfan (Hansen 1995: 11–12, 45, 63).

33. Moreland (2001: 84). Using *functionally literate* in the sense discussed by Beard for ancient Rome, "where many small traders, craftsmen and slaves must have needed some level of basic literacy and numeracy to function successfully in their jobs. . . . 'Functional literacy' of that sort gave even the 'middling' people some stake in what we would think of as high classical culture" (2015: 470). For a fuller discussion, see Beard (1991).

power, as in contracts. Texts were used, in John Moreland's words, "in the projection of, and resistance to, power, and they were used to create meaning in, and to structure, the routines of everyday life."[34] The written word also had power and meaning independent of its literal meaning. Quasi-writing, talismans, and charms were all expressions of the potentially subversive and private use of writing.[35] While use of official texts, such as contracts, tied the user to the official world above him, the use of talismanic writing linked him with the world below—that of spirits and demons.[36] "The act of writing itself" became a ritual activity.[37]

It would also be misleading to assume the existence of a distinction between science and superstition—in this case, between astronomy and astrology. This does not mean there was no distinction in China: the scholar-official class spoke out against superstition. But as Edward Schafer says, "For most early Chinese, even for the most advanced authorities on events in the sky, astronomy was indistinguishable from astrology. . . . There were certainly sceptics, but it appears that most men, even well-educated men, continued to believe that a predictable Jupiter remained an awful Jupiter."[38] The Dunhuang caves yielded another manuscript that reveals the rigor of Chinese astronomical observation as well as the broader boundaries of astrological belief.[39] This manuscript, now in the British Library, contains two texts—and a curious and crude drawing of the thunder god at the end. The first text is about divination based on cloud formation—nephelomancy. It is based on the Chinese belief that nothing is supernatural: everything is part of a linked natural order, and we can predict events in one part of this natural order from those displayed in others (the same reasoning lies behind astral omenology). The event predicted might be domestic or political: for example,

> Whenever a vapour is present inside someone's home and garden, and it is in the form of a leaping or crouching wolf or tiger, the family will certainly bear a son who will become a general and will be conferred a rank of nobility. This will happen within three years.[40]

34. Moreland (2001: 80).
35. See Mary Beard's (1991) criticism of William Harris's view of literacy in the Roman world.
36. Robson (2008: 128).
37. Robson (2008: 131), quoting Jonathan Smith.
38. Schafer (1977: 9).
39. British Library, Or.8210/S.3326.
40. This and following translations from Galambos (2009).

Or

Lü Buwei said that whenever you approach a mound on a plain and there is vapour in the shape of a thousand *zhang* long staff reaching high up into the sky, straight and vertical; if it is yellow, it is the colour of the Son of Heaven; blue, red, white and black all mean that there shall be tears and grief. Your servant Chunfeng says that such towns will inevitably produce dukes and knights. If its colour is greenish-blue it means illness; white means that a war will break out; black means that the towns will be flooded with robbers and thieves.

The author of the text, Li Chunfeng (602–70), makes clear that he considers its assertions to be based on and proven by observation.[41] He has not included any cloud formations that he has not tested and proved himself. He has consulted the observations of others, such as Lü Buwei, but he insists that for all entries "my own experiments showed them to be reliable, this is why I recorded them. I did not dare to include in this scroll the ones I have not tested for divination."

The second text on this manuscript is also based on observation, and the text was probably written by the same hand.[42] It is a complete representation of the Chinese sky, including 1,339 stars and groupings—asterisms—depicted in a succession of maps covering the full sky.[43] The twelve hour-angle maps are in quasi-cylindrical projection, and there is a circumpolar map in azimuthal projection. The quasi-cylindrical projection is close to that developed by the Flemish cartographer Geradus Mercator (1512–94) nine centuries later and used for mapping the earthly globe since. It is a remarkable object, being not only the earliest manuscript star chart from any civilization but also a highly accurate one.[44] And, like the cloud formations, it references the work of earlier observers of the sky, the three classical astronomers of China, Shi Shen, Gan De, and Wu Xian, who composed reference books describing the stars. The asterisms identified by each are distinguished by color—red, black, and white/yellow respectively—and labeled.

41. For the argument for Chunfeng as author, see Bonnet-Bidaud, Praderie, and Whitfield (2009).

42. Bonnet-Bidaud, Praderie, and Whitfield (2009).

43. The asterisms based on the Western tradition are called constellations and tend to be larger groups than those used in China. One that occurs in both systems is the Plough of the Western tradition, which is the Northern Ladle in the Chinese tradition.

44. Bonnet-Bidaud, Praderie, and Whitfield (2009) have studied the atlas in detail and shown its accuracy.

Although we would today recognize this second text as scientific, while consigning the cloud divination text to the realm of superstition, at its time the second text was also a tool for divination, and the author and others would almost certainly have considered both to be in the same category. Beside the equatorial region, the rest of the sky is divided in very numerous small asterisms (nearly three hundred), most associated with practical objects or persons of the Chinese Empire. These were used in astrological predictions from the time of the classical astronomers. The three distinct catalogs of these early astronomers were maintained through the Han period and were later combined by the imperial astronomer Chen Zhuo (220–80). The tradition of attributing each asterism (or Chinese constellation) to a different school survived because of the demands of astrological prediction. The accompanying texts to the left of each section describe the twelve divisions of the Chinese year and give associated astrological predictions. For example: "From the 8th degree of *Nü* to the 15th degree of *Wei*, associated with [the terrestrial branch] *zi*, is [the Jupiter station] *Xuan Xiao*. The colour of the North direction is black. When *Xu* [appears], [it will be] a bad harvest. At the 11th month, the spirit *yang* contracts, the spirit *yin* expands, the ten thousand beings [all creation] disappear into the darkness, there is no life, sky and Earth are without substance, the Sun [goes] into *Xuan Xiao*. This division corresponds to [the state of] *Qi*." But this does not stop the text also having scientific value, as Jean-Marc Bonnet-Bidaud, Françoise Praderie, and I point out: "These texts are mainly of astrological use but the scientific notation in degrees reveals that they are based on astronomical observations and have been produced with the attempt to be as precise as possible for this period."[45]

Just as in ancient Greece stories came to be associated with constellations, so in ancient China many of the asterisms had tales to tell. It is probable that many of these were widely known and some became the heart of festivals.[46] So while the population might not have had scientific training, many could probably recognize some of the stars of the sky.

This star chart, like our printed almanac, had subversive potential, and production of such documents was centrally controlled. Such control was

45. Bonnet-Bidaud, Praderie, and Whitfield (2009: 44).
46. One of the most famous, known since the Han dynasty in China, is that of the Cowherd and the Weaving Maid. The Qixi Festival, held on the seventh day of the seventh month, celebrates the annual meeting of these former lovers as a flock of magpies form a bridge across the Silver River (the Milky Way). See Schafer (1977: 143–47) for discussion of this, and his chap. 7 for other embodied stars.

probably more successful for astronomical knowledge than for almanacs, although a decree issued in 840 shows that there were leaks. The edict, which followed the appearance of several comets, among them Halley's, ordered officials engaged in astronomy and their subordinates to keep their business secret and not to talk to anyone, including others in government.[47] While we can reasonably hypothesize that the almanac, although not an officially sanctioned document, was produced for sale to anyone who would buy, the production of the star chart is far more uncertain.[48]

PAPER AND PRINTING

To return to the printed almanac, the "how" of the production is well understood. It is on paper, a material invented in China around the first century BC whose production was very refined by the ninth century. By this time too the knowledge of papermaking had spread westward along the trade routes to the Tarim and beyond to the Arab world. There were probably numerous centers of paper production, including in other areas of China, such as Sichuan, as well as Dunhuang and the Central Asian kingdom of Khotan. But fine paper, made from the long fibers of different mulberry trees often mixed with hemp, ramie, or other locally available fibers, was also regularly imported from China.[49] By this time paper was made by the laid-mold method (figure 31).[50] The fibers were pounded until macerated and were mixed with water to form a pulp. A sizing material, such as starch, was sometimes added. This helped keep the fibers floating and added to their bonding strength. It also acted as a filler in the finished paper. Rectangular molds were made of a wood or bamboo frame with a base of narrow bars on which was placed a screen made of fine strips of bamboo, reeds, or straw running verti-

47. Needham and Wang (1959: 193). The comet was named after Edmond Halley (1656–1742), who determined its periodicity in 1704, but it had been noted by Chinese astronomers from at least 240 BC and by Babylonians from at least the second century BC (Ridpath 1985).

48. Given its accuracy and the thinness and fine quality of the paper combined with the careless handwriting, one assumption is that the stars were traced from a master and that this was a working copy for a court astronomer. The question then arises about how it left the court and found its way to Dunhuang—but we will almost certainly never know the answer.

49. Analysis of paper from this period in Dunhuang shows that fibers of both the paper mulberry (*Broussonetia papyrifera*) and the silk mulberry (*Morus alba*) were often used.

50. Tsien (1985: 68); Drège (2002: 115–16).

蕩
料
入
簾

FIGURE 31. Woodblock showing one step in papermaking process. From *Tiangong kaiwu*, 1637.

cally and held in place with hemp or horsehair thread. The mold was lowered into the pulp, raised, and shaken to distribute the pulp evenly over the screen. Once the excess liquid had drained, the resulting sheet was turned out to dry. The pattern of the bamboo or reed and the string ties formed impressions on the paper called the laid and chain lines respectively. They can be seen when the paper is held up to the light. But by the sixth or seventh century Chinese papermakers added a fine silk cloth on top of the sieve that stopped the impression from being formed. Because of the maceration of the fibers from the pounding, it is often difficult to distinguish between different types even at a microscopic level.[51]

One side of the dry sheets was often beaten and polished to form a smooth surface—the recto—and to make it ready to receive text. Sometimes the paper was dyed. One of the most common dyes of the time was a yellow berberine-based dye made from the bark of the Amur cork tree (*Phellodendron amurense*) and called *huangbo*.[52] It not only colored the paper but also had water-repellent and insecticidal properties. Ink throughout this region was carbon—so-called Indian or Chinese—and was durable, noncorrosive, and nonsoluble. On manuscripts it was usually applied with a brush, although a wooden stylus was sometimes used instead, especially in the later period. Some of the finest manuscripts were prepared by scribes in scriptoria.[53]

For printing, a manuscript was first prepared on very thin paper by a scribe. A block was cut to the same size as a panel of paper using a hard wood. The paper was moistened and placed over the woodblock so that the written side faced down. The ink showed through the fine paper, and a skilled carver then cut out the areas in between the Chinese characters, leaving the characters in reverse and relief. The woodblock was then ready for printing. Ink was brushed over it so that the characters were inked, and a new panel of paper was placed on top and smoothed over with a dry brush so that the ink was transferred to the paper. This process could be repeated numerous times.

Although this technology might seem cumbersome and inflexible compared to movable type, for a nonalphabetic script such as Chinese it was, in fact, more efficient. A woodblock could be cut in less time than it would take to find and set movable type.[54] However, within a few centuries, wooden movable type was also used in the region for the Uygur script employed for the Old Turkic language.[55] The Uygur script was adopted from Sogdian script, which, in turn, had been based on the Aramaic consonantal alphabet.

51. See Cartwright, Duffy, and Wang (2014) for additional use of scanning electron microscopy to distinguish, for example, between silk and paper mulberry fibers in Chinese Ming-period paper money.

52. Gibbs and Seddon (1998).

53. Drège (1991).

54. See McDermott (2006: 14–24) for a discussion of the relative time and costs in the twentieth century.

55. Wooden movable type was found at Dunhuang by Paul Pelliot in 1908 and is now kept in the Guimet Museum. The Dunhuang Academy has also found more examples in its excavations of the northern caves.

Tradition tells of clay movable type invented for Chinese around AD 1000, but none survives. Interestingly, a visitor to the British Museum who saw the printed almanacs in the 1930s, Mr. Y. W. Wong, manager of the Commercial Press, Shanghai, suggested that both the almanac fragments from Sichuan were printed using clay blocks.[56] However, as far as I know he has been the only person to make this claim. We then find metal movable type used in Korea by the fourteenth century.[57]

The importance of the Southwest as a center of printing is shown by the fact that the Buddhist Canon was first printed here between 971 and 983 on imperial order. It required 130,000 woodblocks.[58] No woodblocks from this period are extant. The earliest set is that used to print the canon in the Korean peninsula in the thirteenth century under commission of the Goryeo dynasty (918–1392) and now at Haeinsa Monastery in South Korea. It consists of 81,258 woodblocks. The earliest extant printed text is believed to be a copy of the Dharani Sutra, probably dating from the early eighth century, certainly pre-751, when it was placed in a newly built stupa at Bulguksa, South Korea.[59] It was discovered in 1966.[60] The text was printed on a mulberry paper scroll 8 centimeters wide and 630 centimeters long. Another Dharani Sutra was printed in Japan around 770, and some copies are extent. They were printed on the command of Empress Shōtoku (r. 749–58) in a million copies, and each copy was stored in a tiny wooden stupa.[61]

Printing, like many other technologies, traveled across Eurasia, and in Europe, as in China, almanacs and religious texts were two of its main products. Astrology was as popular in Europe as in Asia, despite the censure of the Christian Church.[62] The German printer Johannes Gutenberg (ca. 1398–1468) printed an almanac before his famous Bible. In the sixteenth century booksellers stocking the almanac of the French astrologer Michel

56. L. Giles (1939: 1037). The use of clay movable type is traditionally said to have been invented around 1000, but examples survive only from much later.

57. M. Peterson (2010: 68).

58. Twitchett (1983: 35).

59. Tsien (1985: 149) dated it to pre-705 on the basis of forms of some Chinese characters being used only under the reign of Empress Wu Zetian (r. 680–704), while Pan Jixing (1997) has argued it was printed in Luoyang in China and sent to Korea.

60. Goodrich (1967). There have been more recent reports of earlier finds in China, but these were not verified at the time of going to press.

61. See chapter 4 above.

62. For example, in 1452 the Witchcraft Act made astrologers and the makers of almanacs open to prosecution for dabbling in occult powers.

de Nostradame (1503–66) were prosecuted, as his predictions were believed to be a threat to the power of Queen Elizabeth I of England and Ireland (r. 1558–1603). But they continued to be popular. Britain the two printed best sellers were the Bible and the almanac: in 1649, thirty thousand copies were made of one of the most popular annual almanacs, William Lilly's *Merlinus Angilicus*.[63] In 1775 a case was successfully brought in the English courts against the monopoly of the crown for the printing of almanacs.[64] Like those in China, European almanacs included all sorts of other information besides the calendar, much of it related to astrology, telling the future, and other popular beliefs.

To summarize, this almanac was produced by block printing on paper, and the impetus was probably profit: it was produced for sale. We do not know how many people bought copies, but effort and expense were involved in making the woodblocks that, if this were produced by a private printer, had to be covered by sales. We have no idea of the cost. The question now arises as to where the almanac was made. Was it produced in Dunhuang or taken there by a traveler? If produced in Dunhuang, were the paper and wood also local? And why are there not more copies of this or other printed almanacs in Dunhuang from this time?[65]

The calendar was first dated to 877 by Lionel Giles, so presumably it was made at the end of 876 for the new year.[66] At this time Dunhuang was ruled by the Zhang family, who in 848 had taken Dunhuang from the Tibetans after almost a century of rule. The region remained multilingual with Tibetan as a lingua franca.[67] Links with central China were renewed, with envoys from Dunhuang reaching the capital in 851.[68] But the ruling Tang dynasty was failing, subject to dissent and rebellions. We have printed prayer

63. See T. Miller (2001: 44). For an overview, see Capp (1979). Almanacs were not produced only by men. In seventh-century England, Sarah Jinner of London and Mary Holden of Sudbury were known for their prophetical and medical almanacs of seventeenth-century England (Weber 2003).

64. Arts and Humanities Research Council, "Stationers' Company v. Carnan, London (1775)," in "Primary Sources on Copyright (1450–1900)," archive edited by L. Bently and M. Kretschmer, accessed September 26, 2017, www.copyrighthistory.org/cam/tools/request/showRecord.php?id=record_uk_1775.

65. Apart from these examples, the other almanacs are all manuscript copies. See Arrault and Martzloff (2003) for a detailed review of those held in London and Paris.

66. This dating has been confirmed by others; see Arrault and Martzloff (2003: 203).

67. Takeuchi (2004a, 2004b).

68. Rong (2004: 57).

sheets and Buddhist sutras produced in Dunhuang in the tenth century sponsored by the Cao ruling family, who had taken power from the Zhang in 914. Some give the name of the woodblock carver, Lei Yanmei.[69] There is no example of local printing from before this. Also, as Alain Arrault points out, the calendar of our almanac was produced using methods different from those used for the manuscript calendars produced in Dunhuang. It is therefore most probable that our almanac was produced elsewhere. This would not be surprising. Dunhuang was a relatively small and remote outpost, and there is no evidence of printing in Tibet during the period of Tibetan control of the region.

So where was this almanac printed? As mentioned above, we have printed texts at Dunhuang from both the Chinese capital and the Southwest. The latter, however, are more predominant. There are also manuscript scrolls produced in the Southwest and brought to Dunhuang, such as a copy of the Diamond Sutra, mentioned above. A printed copy of the same sutra, dating to 868 and also discovered in the library cave, shows very sophisticated printing, and it is possible that it was also produced here. In further support, there is the 835 memorial from the official who speaks of the proliferation of printed almanacs in this region. So, while it will remain conjecture unless we get further evidence—for example, from analysis of the paper—our almanac may also have been produced in the Southwest.

How did the almanac find its way to Dunhuang? Perhaps with a traveler who carried it there in the year of its production. Or perhaps it was kept to be used as a template for later almanacs or for teaching. Or was it just kept as scrap paper? As with many historical objects, there are many uncertainties relating to its history, and we can only speculate to fill some of these gaps.

It was almost certainly originally made as an ephemeral production, useful for a year. After this, most almanacs were presumably discarded. We see paper reused, for example, to repair other texts that had a longer life. Paper was also used to line artifacts, such as sutra wrappers and soles of shoes. There were probably also many other reuses in everyday life—such as for cleaning or as toilet paper. Some clues to the survival of this almanac lie in the form in which it was found, not as an integral object but in two incomplete parts that had been reinforced and joined by being pasted onto other fragments of

69. For example, a prayer sheet in the British Library, Or.8210/P.9, dated 947 (L. Giles 1943: 149–50), and three copies of the Diamond Sutra dating to 950 (BnF, Pelliot chinois 4515 and 4516, and British Library, Or.8210/P.11).

paper. These backings contain writing, including the end of a contract with the names of the landlord and two witnesses. Two other parts both mention a man named Zhai. One has a line in black ink reading "written by Zhai, Group Head, Erudite/Doctor in the Prefectural School, and Vice-President of the Censorate, on the twenty-sixth day of the fourth month." The last character has been corrected in red, and there is a shorter line following, also in red, that reads: "For the attention of bhadanta Qu out of gratitude for his fatherly care." The second text consists of four lines reading: "Presented by city governor Zhai on the journey east."

Zhai is almost certainly Zhai Fengda (ca. 883–966), a local official charged with producing calendars in the early tenth century. Several of his calendars have been found at Dunhuang, but all are in manuscript form.[70] He could have used these fragments of text—pieces he had written as rough copies— to extend the life of a well-thumbed almanac, one that was made six years before he was born and that he acquired and then kept long beyond its original shelf life as a reference work. This does not explain how it survived from 877 to the date when Zhai found it, but we do know that Zhai was instructed in producing almanacs, and perhaps our almanac was first noticed and kept for reference by his teacher, who passed it on to his star pupil.

There is some evidence that the Dunhuang Library Cave contained the personal manuscript collections of monks, and it is possible that the collection of Zhai Fengda was also placed there on his death, just a few decades before the cave was closed and sealed.[71] One of the other items probably found in the same bundle as the almanac and therefore also possibly belonging to Zhai Fengda was a sheet containing stamps of Buddhist figures and Sanskrit *dhāraṇī*.[72] Although Zhai's almanacs survive only in manuscript form, it is possible that printed copies were produced but have long been lost or, more probably, that he was interested in using this technology for his calendars.

One of Zhai's manuscript calendars, probably for the year 956, was presented to the then-ruler of Dunhuang, Cao Yuanzhong (r. 944–74).[73] By this time printed texts were being produced at Dunhuang under Cao's patron-

---

70. See Teiser (1994) and Whitfield (2015b: chap. 8). These are not in the same hand, and several are probably copies, possibly made by pupils.

71. These findings are thanks to research done by Paschalia Terzi as an Erasmus Scholar at the British Library and will be the subject of a forthcoming article by Terzi and Whitfield.

72. British Library, IOL San 1446.

73. British Library Or.8210/S.95. Published in Whitfield and Sims-Williams (2004: cat. 160). See also Teiser (1994: 120–21).

age, as mentioned above. The copies of the Diamond Sutra were, interestingly, not in scroll format but in codex—more like a modern bound book. This was a form we see developing at this time in Dunhuang. The use of this format might show Cao's interest in changing technology. But it is also relatively small format, fourteen by ten centimeters, requiring a smaller woodblock and smaller sheet of paper than for printing a scroll (where each panel of paper was about thirty by fifty-six centimeters).[74] The paper is quite coarse, almost certainly of local production, and the printing is nowhere near the quality of the Diamond Sutra of 868. All this suggests that Dunhuang was developing printing technology at this time but that it was a long way behind central China.[75]

The adoption of a new technology is not a simple process. It requires both desire and skills, and the latter—and sometimes the former—often come from outside. It is possible that Lei Yanmei learned his skills as an apprentice in a center of printing, such as in the Southwest, and was brought to Dunhuang to take up his role as official woodblock maker under the patronage of Cao. Or he may have been local and trained by a woodblock printer from elsewhere. The prayer sheets were relatively simple affairs for printing, requiring only two blocks on a single sheet of paper. An almanac was far more complicated, and perhaps Zhai was hoping, by keeping examples of a printed almanac, to persuade Cao to commission Lei Yanmei to turn his skills to the calendars. But, of course, it is possible that Cao, like the rulers in central China, wished to restrict access to calendars and therefore did not want to encourage their printing and distribution. If only one copy was required for his office and a few others for distribution, there would be little point in going to the expense and effort of getting woodblocks cut.[76] The lack of printed almanacs might also suggest the lack of private printing in

74. Thanks to Xin Wen for his observations on this (pers. comm., September 2016, and forthcoming article). His work on the booklets suggests that their size was determined by making full use of a standard-size sheet of paper, as used for scrolls. But with writing on both sides and smaller margins, they proved more economical than scrolls.

75. However, it is not impossible that Dunhuang was ahead of central China in terms of producing the codex format and that this change from the scroll was driven, at least in part, by the shortage of paper.

76. Arrault and Martzloff (2003: 90) have pointed out a pre-900 Dunhuang account book in which 150 sheets of paper are requested for calendars. We have some evidence for the print runs of material in central China around this time: for example, several thousand copies of a biography of an alchemist and 140,000 copies of a print of Maitreya Stupa (Tsien 1985: 152, 255).

Dunhuang—or at least a stricter control by the authorities of their output.[77] The existence of material printed under the patronage of Cao along with the continued existence of manuscript almanacs might suggest this (but it might also suggest a limit to the skills and technology available).

Our printed almanac dated from eighty years before Zhai presented his calendar to the ruler but was kept and restored, probably by Zhai himself. The crudeness of the printing at this time and the lack of any evidence for other printed material produced in Dunhuang earlier suggests that the almanac was made not in Dunhuang but in an area where printing was already sophisticated by the eighth century, so central or Southwest China. How and when it came to Dunhuang will probably never be known, but it survived because of Zhai's interest. It was then placed in the library cave at the Mogao Buddhist Cave site southeast of the town, possibly on Zhai's death around 966, in a bundle containing his manuscripts and documents. This was only a few decades before the cave was sealed, and there it remained until the cave was discovered and reopened in 1900. Its progress since then is easier to track but takes us along the sometimes convoluted paths of European and imperial collection history.

THE JOURNEY WEST

The accidental discovery of the Dunhuang Library Cave in June 1900 by the self-appointed guardian and conservator Wang Yuanlu (ca. 1850–1931) has been often discussed.[78] What is less frequently mentioned is the fact that Wang and his workmen removed the contents from the cave at least three times in the years after its discovery, first "to search for valuables," then to remove the inscribed stone, and then to send the material for official safekeeping.[79] The contents were replaced by 1907 when the Hungarian-born but British-naturalized archaeologist Marc Aurel Stein (1862–1943) arrived on the second of four Central Asian expeditions. There is no indication that the contents were replaced in their original order, and, since there is no earlier

---

77. The general lack of printed contents from Dunhuang, apart from the Buddhist material sponsored by Cao, would support this, although, if profit is to be made, people are very quick to master new technologies.

78. For example, see Rong (2013: lecture 3). But also see Galambos and van Schaik (2012: 18–28) for alternative theories on the reasons for the sealing of the cave.

79. Stein (1912: 182); Wang Jiqing (2012: 3).

documentation of the cave we can only speculate as to its original arrangement. Wang originally showed Stein manuscripts that he brought to him from bundles at the top of the piles: "It was easy to recognize the special value of those bundles filled with miscellaneous texts, painted fabrics, ex-votos, papers of all sorts, which had evidently been stored away as no longer needed for use. By their irregular shape and fastening they could readily be distinguished from the uniform packets containing rolls of Buddhist texts in Chinese or Tibetan. Fortunately their very irregularity had caused the Tao-shi [Wang Yuanlu] to put them on top when he built up the all-like array of what I may call 'library bundles.'"[80]

Stein persuaded Wang to clear the cave for at least the fourth time and place the bundles in the corridor outside so that Stein and his Chinese assistant Jiang Xiaowan (1858–1922) could look through them for non-Chinese or non-Buddhist material. However, they had only a few days before they found that Wang had moved the bundles back into the cave, and they had to be content with what they had managed to select. A sum of money changed hands, later put to use by Wang to restore the guesthouse outside the library cave.[81]

The material was packed into twelve crates, which Stein originally planned to leave for safekeeping in the office of the magistrate—*yamen*—in Dunhuang town while he continued his explorations further east and to collect them on his return. However, he decided against this when he heard of local unrest and potential military intervention in the region. He therefore took the crates with him to the neighboring Anxi, where they were left at the *yamen*—a "room airy and easily watched." Large beams had been placed "on bricks to raise the precious cases well above the ground, and Ibrahim Beg was to see to it that once every week they were to carried out into the sun to prevent all possibility of damp attacking the contents."[82] A month after Stein's departure from Dunhuang the local populace rioted in protest at taxes and burned down the *yamen*.[83] Stein took advantage of the unrest and dispatched Jiang with four camels back to the library cave site, where Jiang obtained another 230 bundles containing three thousand rolls and deposited them with the others in Anxi. On Stein's return four months later he collected the crates. These were loaded onto four camels, and he set off on the

80. Stein (1912: 182–83).
81. Stein (1928: 356).
82. Stein (1912: 240).
83. Stein to P. S. Allen, October 14, 1907, MSS. Stein 4, Bodleian Library, Oxford University.

final leg of his expedition. In early November he sent these, and another four camel loads of finds, directly to Kashgar to remain under the safekeeping of the British consul there, George Macartney (1867–1945), while he continued on his expedition.

Stein was reunited with the finds on June 9, 1908, in Khotan—Macartney had sent them on. All the finds were repacked in Niaz Hakim Beg's garden for their journey. We do not know if the order of the crates in which they were originally packed was followed. If so, then the almanac, which was placed in crate 91, might have been in the batch acquired by Jiang on his revisit to Dunhuang. Stein does not mention the almanac in any of his publications on the expeditions. The crates were repacked very carefully, as they had a journey of "8,000 miles, including transport through high mountain ranges and across glacier passes, on camels, yak, and ponies, and subsequent travel by cart, rail, and steamer."[84] During the repacking Jiang prepared a slip catalog of about one-third of the Chinese Dunhuang material.[85] Ninety-three cases of material started back on August 1 under the care of Tila Bau to the glacier pass to Suget [Sanju] on the upper Kara kash to await Stein.[86] Stein rejoined the convoy of crates on September 27, but he was suffering from severe frostbite as a result of his enthusiasm for photography in the snow-covered Kunlun.[87] After four days making arrangements and settling accounts from his camp bed, he set off on September 30, carried on forced marches. He left R. B. Lal Singh in charge of the crates. Stein did not rejoin them until he arrived in London on steamer from Bombay (stopping in Italy to visit family) on January 20, 1909, where he learned they had arrived safely at the British Museum a few days before.[88] Having lain in its cliff vault for nine hundred years, within a decade the almanac had crossed to the other end of the Silk Road to find a new home in the vaults of the British Museum.

LIFE IN THE MUSEUM

The transition to the museum was not entirely smooth. Although the crates had been addressed by Stein to the care of the keeper of the Prints

84. Stein (1921: 1317).
85. Stein (1921: 1318).
86. Stein (1912: 438).
87. Stein (1912: 484).
88. Stein (1921: 1327).

and Drawing Department at the British Museum, the department did not agree to take them and initially redirected them to the India Office, then in Whitehall in central London.[89] Here they started to be checked and unpacked by Stein's assistants Fred Andrews (1866–1957), Hugh Evelyn-White (1874–1924), and Miss MacDonald. Stein continued to lobby the trustees of the museum—and anyone else he thought might help—to get working space in the museum. He considered the natural history branch of the museum in Kensington and the Ashmolean Museum in Oxford as alternatives if the British Museum did not agree. His persistence worked—as it usually did. The twenty-five boxes that had been unpacked in the India Office were repacked, and the material was transported to the Museum on August 5.[90] Andrews set about ordering glass cases for storage and securing tables on which to work.

In October 1909 Mr. White and Miss MacDonald were replaced by two new assistants, Mr. John Percival Droop (1882–1963) and Miss Lorimer (1883–1967).[91] By January 1910 they had unpacked thirty-seven crates.[92] Material had been sent to various scholars to identify and research, and other material was being conserved. This was in preparation for the division of the material and its acquisition into the museum collections. Stein's expedition had been jointly funded by the British Museum and the Government of India, and his collection was due to be split between the two: for example, the Chinese Dunhuang manuscripts went to the British Museum and most of the Tibetan Dunhuang manuscripts to the India Office Library.

The first exhibition of the material was in the Prints and Drawings Department of the museum in 1910 and included paintings from the Stein collection—but no manuscript material.[93] Further paintings and a few manuscripts were sent to the Indian Section of the Festival of Empire at Crystal Palace in North London in 1911, but these did not include the almanac.[94] By this time hundreds of Chinese scrolls from Dunhuang had been sent to

89. F. H. Andrews to Stein, December 6, 1908, MSS. Stein 37.

90. "At last things are settled for our transference to Bloomsbury on Thursday . . . cellars with 50 electric lights." Andrews to Stein, August 3, 1909, MSS. Stein 37/153. The list of cases is in MSS. Stein 37/155.

91. For an account of this period, especially Miss Lorimer's role, see H. Wang (1998).

92. MSS. Stein 37/155, but these were probably mainly nonmanuscript cases, as indicated by a later note from Lorimer (MSS. Stein 39/19).

93. Binyon (1910: 15–20).

94. Festival of Empire (1911: 14–26).

the French sinologist Paul Pelliot in 1910 for his catalog.[95] He had visited the museum in April to review the material, and Lionel Giles "ha[d] made a selection of the Chinese MSS. to show him."[96]

In 1913 a new department was established at the museum, Oriental Prints and Drawings, and Laurence Binyon (1868–1943), previously assistant keeper of prints and drawings, was put in charge. Arthur Waley (1889–1966), who was working in the Print Room, became his assistant. Binyon produced brief monthly reports for the trustees in which the paintings from Dunhuang are mentioned from August 1913: "2 paintings from the Stein Collection have been mounted as *kakemono*, and a third has been cleaned & specially repaired for mounting."[97] The paintings are thereafter mentioned most months—we know from Stein that the tightly compressed paintings were being unfolded under "Sir Sidney Colvin's kind supervision."[98] It is only in the report in May 1914 that Binyon first reports work on the manuscripts: "200 Chinese scrolls have been examined & numbered." Thereafter there are "about 500" in June, 60 in July, and 550 in August, and in September "the sorting and listing of the Chinese rolls in the Stein Collection has been continued."[99]

There was a major exhibition in 1914 in the newly built northern galleries

95. For the manuscripts sent to Pelliot, see F. Wood (2012). Pelliot had visited the library cave in 1908 and had acquired another large cache of manuscripts—now in the Bibliothèque nationale de France. Over a fortnight in 1910 Pelliot surveyed Stein's collection in the British Museum and estimated there to be nine thousand manuscripts. To facilitate Pelliot's cataloguing work, two crates containing 440 manuscripts were sent from the British Museum to 59 Boulevard Edgar Quinet in Paris, where Pelliot signed a receipt for them on January 13, 1911. No list of the manuscripts survives other than the simple description on the packing list: "15 bundles of mss., numbered 1–233, except no. 55 (Brahmi) and 213 (a painting), and 14 bundles of mss. numbered 234–443, except no. 237 (not found)" (F. Wood 2012: 1). Pelliot was due to finish the catalog within one year. Denison Ross carried some material back from Paris by hand for inclusion in the British Museum exhibition in 1913 (F. Wood 2012: 3). On March 7, 1913, the keeper of Oriental Manuscripts and Printed Books at the Museum, Lionel Barnett, wrote to Pelliot, "Our friend Ross has returned home with the mss. And the notes" (Wood 2012: 3).

96. MSS. Stein 39/24. Lionel Giles (1875–1958) was an assistant keeper at the museum.

97. Laurence Binyon, monthly report, May 6, 1914, British Museum Oriental Department (ORIS), 1913–26, Asia Dept. Archives. A *kakemono* is a hanging Japanese scroll.

98. Sydney Colvin (1845–1927) was keeper in the Department of Prints and Drawings at the British Museum from 1884 to 1912.

99. Laurence Binyon, monthly report, September 1, 1914, British Museum Oriental Department (ORIS), 1913–26, Asia Dept. Archives.

of the museum, opened by the British king and queen, and an almanac was included, but not ours.[100]

We can assume that the almanac remained in the British Museum for all this time, while other manuscripts and paintings were on display or sent to scholars worldwide, as there are no records to suggest otherwise. By the time of the First World War, pressure was increasing on Andrews and Lorimer to finish sorting the material and for the distribution between the museum and the India Office to be made.[101] There was a fear that an incendiary bomb might hit the museum, and while the collections from Prints and Drawings were moved by train to the National Library of Wales in Aberystwyth between February and May many of the antiquities and coins were moved to a new section of the London underground railway between Holborn and Oxford Street.[102] However, the Stein material remained in London.[103]

By the end of the First World War it was clear that Pelliot was not going to produce the promised catalog, and scrolls still remaining with him in Paris were returned to London. The task of cataloguing the Chinese Dunhuang manuscripts and printed documents was instead assigned to Lionel Giles. Giles became keeper of Oriental Manuscripts and Printed Books in 1936 and prepared a series of articles on dated manuscripts among the Chinese scrolls. They were published in the *Bulletin of the School of Oriental and African Studies* between 1935 and 1943. The article on ninth-century documents appeared in 1939. In it Giles described the almanac, giving the reasons for dating it to 877 and noting the mention of Zhai on the backing paper.[104]

During the Second World War the almanac was probably included in the forty boxes of scrolls from the Stein collection sent in 1939 with other manu-

---

100. British Museum (1914).

101. See Lorimer to Stein, January 30, 1918: "The P&D Dept. is being cleared entirely. . . . The I.O. are accordingly proposing to take away their share of the things now, i.e. as soon as possible after Feb. 28th—and to house them at the I.O. until they can be taken to India. . . . The Museum Dept will take charge of their own share and put them in safety with the rest of their goods" (MSS. Stein 44/84-8).

102. Kavanagh (1994: 30–32).

103. On August 20, 1918, Lionel Barnett, keeper of Oriental Printed Books and Manuscripts, wrote to Stein, then in his Kashmiri summer mountain retreat, from Aberwrystwth: "I am . . . like you . . . on the top of a hill. . . . For the present (i.e. for some years to come) the mss. That are to revert to our Department will be kept in their present home, all together in glass cases" (MSS. Stein 65). See Morgan (2012: 1).

104. L. Giles (1939).

scripts from the museum's collection to Aberystwyth. However, the above-ground building was thought to be unsafe, and a tunnel was built into the hillside. This was completed in 1940. Four boxes of Stein scrolls were moved into the tunnel: it is not clear if the almanac was among them. With the end of the war, the material from the tunnel was moved in May 1945 back into the library building. It was sent back to London a year later, in May 1946.[105]

As Joyce Morgan has noted, the manuscript of Giles's catalog, completed before the manuscripts went to Wales and his retirement in 1940, was misplaced during this period but fortunately rediscovered in 1946.[106] However, it was not published until 1957. His catalog entry on the almanac repeats the information in the former article.

Several visitors came to see the collection over this period, but I have found no mention of the almanac in the archives or in published work.[107] Nor is the almanac mentioned by Joseph Needham and Wang Ling in their section on astronomy for *Science and Civilisation in China*, published in 1959, although they mention other documents from Dunhuang.[108]

Around this time the almanac was microfilmed, along with the rest of the Chinese Dunhuang scrolls in the British Museum, and the images show it with its tenth-century backing. Sometime after this it was sent for conservation, but unfortunately there are no extant records of this work. This would suggest that it was noted as an important document. There were over six thousand scrolls from Dunhuang in the museum, many of which had fragmentary beginnings and ends, stress cracks from the silk ties, tears, and other damage from handling before they were placed in the library cave. The conservation of all of these would involve decades of specialist conservation time. But Stein's was only one among many collections competing for limited conservation time. The curator had to make selections, and although no records are extant from this time it is clear that such decisions were often prompted by scholarly interest.

Once the collection had been catalogued and microfilmed it became more accessible to scholars. Copies of the microfilm were sent to Japan and were carefully studied by Fujieda Akira. He recognized the importance of this piece and published an article on it in 1973.[109] But it was conserved before

105. For a full account, see Morgan (2012).
106. Morgan (2012:5).
107. They included the Chinese scholars Hu Shi and Xiang Da.
108. Needham and Wang (1959).
109. Fujieda (1973). For later studies, see Arrault and Matzloff (2003) and note 116 below.

this. It might simply be that all the printed and dated texts in the collection were deemed to be important and thus priorities for conservation.[110]

A library, whether personal, private, or public, has a remit of preserving its collections. The demands on libraries are complex, as they have an objective to rival that of preservation—namely access. Books are kept to be consulted. And one of the main threats to preservation is handling. Resolving this tension is an ongoing issue. So just as in Zhai's library, where he ensured the preservation of the almanac—by then probably frayed and fragile because of constant handling—by reinforcing it with a backing of other paper, so the British Museum and, more recently, the British Library have been faced with similar decisions about what to do with the almanac.

Most objects are not like an insect caught in a drop of amber, preserved in a frozen moment of time. They change as they are used, and these changes—whether the backing on our almanac or the collectors' seals added to Chinese paintings—are important parts of their history. However, in some cases conservators have sought to return objects as closely as possible to their "original" condition, before any messy entanglement with nature or people. In other cases, they have not considered—or have little knowledge of—the original condition or materials, and they have used familiar practices and materials, whether appropriate or not. Our almanac has been subject to both types of conservation.[111]

First, when the almanac received repairs in the British Museum in the 1950s or early 1960s, a relatively thick Western paper was used to supplement the lining that already existed. At this time both Kraft and manila papers were used for lining.[112] This was a method much favored at the time, thought to provide support to the delicate and often fractured original paper.[113] The lining of Chinese and Japanese painting scrolls, albeit with very different and more sympathetic materials, was also seen as an example to follow.

Although this attempt at preservation was done in good faith, it was later

110. Two-thirds of the dated documents were conserved in this period, supporting this hypothesis.

111. See Barnard and Wood (2004) for a brief survey of conservation of this material.

112. The former was produced by a highly alkaline process, invented in 1884, that produced paper notably stronger than other methods of the time, hence the name Kraft, after the German for "strength." The brown color is a natural side effect of the process. Manila, originally made of old Manila hemp ropes used on ship, hence the name, was by this time produced from wood fibers.

113. Although there were some who realized the issues, such as Lionel Giles; see note 114 below.

understood that the linings created their own damage. Simply rolling up a scroll means that the lining paper has to travel further than the original and therefore introduces stresses on the original. If the papers are very different in weight and type, then these stresses are exacerbated.[114] Much of the conservation on the Dunhuang material from the late twentieth century has been concerned with removing these linings before they do further damage.[115]

In 1973 the British Library was established as the National Library of Great Britain and Ireland, and the manuscripts and printed books in the British Museum—including the almanac and other Chinese Dunhuang material in the Department of Oriental Manuscripts and Printed Books (OMPB)—became part of the British Library collection. They retained their museum registration numbers, prefixed with "Or." for "Oriental." In 1981 the former OMPB collections were moved to new premises in Store Street, just off Oxford Street in central London. Cupboards were designed and built to house the Dunhuang scrolls—remaining in use today. In 1982 the India Office Library and Records—the collections of the department established in 1858 and charged with the administration of British India—were also moved on loan to the administration of the British Library. The Store Street collections were moved into the India Office Library building on Blackfriars Road over the end of 1990 and the beginning of 1991. The India Office archives included manuscripts found in the library cave, such as IOL San 1446, a single sheet containing stamps of Buddhist images and Sanskrit texts. This sheet was probably stored in the same bundle as the almanac in the library cave. In 1997 the collections were moved into the storage basements of the purpose-built British Library at St. Pancras, where they remain today.

By this time, Chinese scholars had published on the almanac, and one was to produce a complete transcription in 2001.[116] The almanac was deemed a conservation priority and was conserved again in 2002, with the work car-

114. The inappropriateness of heavy linings was noted by Lionel Giles in a 1939 article, in relation to the 868 printed Diamond Sutra: "Many years ago, before the Stein Collection had been taken over by the Department of Oriental Printed Books and MSS, it was mounted on unnecessarily stiff paper, which shows a tendency to crack" (1939: 1031). However, the practice continued until 1968, as an internal note dated February 19, 1981 states ("The rolls most in need of support were backed in the bindery until about 1968. Acidic paper was used, and will have to be removed"). This was prompted by a report made in 1979 on the conservation by two Japanese scholars, Watanabe Akiyoshi and Masuda Katsuhiko.

115. There is also the question of the chemical composition of the lining paper and possible migration into the original.

116. Huang (1992); Deng (1996, 2001); Arrault and Martzloff (2003).

ried out in the British Library Oriental Conservation Studio. The stresses imposed by using inappropriate backings were by now well understood, and, thanks to Peter Lawson, head of the British Library Oriental Conservation Studio, connections had been made with colleagues in China and Japan. Materials closer to the original, such as Japanese *kozo* paper and starch paste, were being used rather than Western papers and glue.[117] At this point, the attempt was made to return the almanac to an "original" condition. The 1950s backing was removed, and extensive repairs were carried out on the fractured original paper using toned *kozo* paper and wheat starch paste. The tenth-century linings at the beginning and end were also removed. One fragment that was attached to the back of the calendar was identified as part of the missing second month, so it was also positioned in its original place. The lining and reconstructed almanac, now in several pieces, were encapsulated in large clear plastic sheets made of polyethylene terephthalate (PET, usually known by various trade names—Mylar, Melinex, Secal).[118] These sheets were secured inside a folder. The newly conserved almanac was digitized in May 2002 in the studios of the International Dunhuang Project as part of a project funded by the Andrew W. Mellon Foundation, and images of the almanac became freely available online.[119]

In 2004 the almanac was placed on public display in the British Library exhibition *The Silk Road: Trade, Travel, War and Faith*.[120] It was displayed again in the British Library Treasures Gallery from 2014 to 2015.

117. Indeed, the conservator who worked on this, Kumiko Matsuoka, was Japanese and had trained there before coming to London.

118. For a discussion of PET for encapsulation, see Cope (1999).

119. International Dunhuang Project, Or.8210/P.6, http://idp.bl.uk/database/oo_loader.a4d?pm=Or.8210/P.6.

120. Whitfield and Sims-Williams (2004: 302–3, cat. 264.).

TEN

The Unknown Slave

UNLIKE THE OTHER CHAPTERS in this book, this one does not focus on a single object that survives today. That is because the object in question—the slave—is an animate one and has long died and decayed. There are no examples in museums—except perhaps represented by models in the dioramas that were so popular from the late nineteenth century.[1] While some slaves were buried with their master and their corpses might survive, we know little or nothing of their lives. So why include this chapter in a book on material culture? Because slaves, like silks, were Silk Road goods, to be bought, used, and sold for profit, and many were transported long distances by land and sea to trade in foreign markets.[2] While no slaves from this time survive to tell their story, they have left traces in art, archaeology, and texts.[3] From these we can see that slavery is found throughout the Silk Road, not particular to any culture, place, or period. Its importance to the Silk Road economy probably rivaled that of the silk, horses, or other goods discussed here. Yet slaves rarely have a central if any role in the Silk Road histories that are told today. This chapter uses these traces to tell something of their stories across the Silk Road.[4] As in the other chapters, I will address the issues

For places mentioned in this chapter see Map 1 in the color maps insert.

1. See Quinn (2006); Halloran (2009: esp. chap. 3).
2. And, as Ian Hodder (2012: 9) notes, human beings are also things: the relationship between a human and a silver ewer is one of interdependence or entanglement between two things, just as is that between a master and his slave.
3. And in the gene pool, as Cameron (2011: 169) points out.
4. I do not aim here to give a comprehensive account of the institution of slavery in any one culture but rather to give snapshots of the practices of slavery across time and cultures and, where available, to give the experience of individual slaves. This is a very broad-brush

of how and why—although the when and where are hardly relevant since, as the *Macmillan Encyclopedia of World Slavery* has noted: "With the exception of marriage, the family and religion, slavery is perhaps the most ubiquitous social institution in human history."[5]

In this chapter, unlike many of the others, most of the evidence for our knowledge of the object is textual and includes extant legal codes. We have to be cautious while taking written legal codes as indicative of practices, for as David Wyatt has pointed out in his discussion of slaves in medieval Britain and Ireland, "The legal norms of a given society might not reflect actual social and cultural practices that were not enshrined in the law codes."[6] However, they do show something of the situation, even if in some cases they describe an ideal probably not often realized in practice. From Sasanian Iran (224–651), for example, we have a Pahlavi compilation of law cases collected in the sixth century that includes a chapter on slavery. Although only part is extant, the discussion of slavery in other chapters helps supplement the picture.[7] There is also an extant text on slavery among the Christian communities of Iran.[8] From China the legal code of the Tang period (618–907) classes people into three groups, with slaves belonging to the lowest, the inferior. Their punishments are harsher than those for the higher groups.

We also have many literary sources and primary documents to supplement our understanding. Slaves commonly appear in contemporary stories, for example, in *One Thousand and One Nights*; they are used by al-Khwārizmī in his mathematical puzzles; and they are mentioned in passing in many of the tales recounted by the Arab shipmaster Buzurg ibn Shahriyār.[9] We have original contracts for slaves in any number of languages: Gāndhārī, Chinese, Sogdian, Hebrew, Arabic, Latin. Other contemporary authors, such as Ibn

---

picture and must inevitably be skewed and selective. References are given throughout to more detailed and scholarly discussions. Volume 2 of the *Cambridge World History of Slavery* will cover much of the period and places of the Silk Road. Rome is considered a major slave-owning society, but much has been written on this, and I tell the story with only occasional reference to Roman practices for comparison.

5. Finkelman and Miller (1998: viii). Where exceptions are found to this they are noted.

6. Wyatt (2009: 43).

7. *Mādayān ī hazār dādestān,* a compilation of law cases collected by Farroxmard ī Wahrāmān in the sixth century A.D. But only part of the chapter on slaves (*Mādayān,* pt. 1, 1.1–17) has been included (Macuch 2008).

8. The law book of Īšōʿboxt—extant in a Syriac translation of the Persian original. See Macuch (2008).

9. Starr (2013: 169); Buzurg ibn Shahriyār (1928).

Rusta (fl. tenth century) and Ibn Khurradādhbih (ca. 820–912), discuss slave trade routes. And we have surviving images, for example, showing domestic slaves in the Roman Empire and one from the thirteenth century showing the slave market at Zabid in the Yemen.[10] From all these we can piece together a picture that, although far from complete, gives an idea of the practices of slavery across Afro-Eurasia at the time of the Silk Road.

BECOMING A SLAVE

How did someone become a slave to be used and traded on the Silk Road? There were several processes, whether stated formally, as in the various legal codes, or happening in practice, sometimes in contravention of the law. Some slaves were born into the condition. Some children, born to free but poor parents, were sold either by their parents or after being abandoned or abducted. In some cases people sold themselves into slavery to redeem a debt. Slavery was also imposed as a legal punishment for various crimes. But the largest number of slaves was made up of those that were taken as prisoners of war or in raids, by land or sea.

When was a child born into slavery? This depended upon the law of the time. For example, what we know of the legal code of the Sasanians suggests that in the early years of Sasanian rule the child took the status of the father: that is, it became a slave if the father was a slave, but a child born of a slave woman and free man—and such cases were undoubtedly not uncommon— remained free. But the law changed, probably around the early fifth century, and the child inherited the status of the mother.[11]

In Arabic society the child also took the status of the mother. However, if this meant they were born into slavery the father could choose to recognize and liberate the child.[12] Such was the case with the Arabic poet of the pre-Islamic period ʿAntara, whose parents were an Arab father from the ʿAbs tribe and an Ethiopian slave woman.[13] An account tells how he gained his freedom: "The ʿAbs pursued and fought then and ʿAntara, who was present, was

10. See Rose (2008) for the former. For the latter, see Yaḥā ibn Maḥmūd al-Wāsiṭī, *al-Maqāmāt al-ḥarīriyah*. [The assemblies of Al-Hariri], Bibliothèque nationale de France, MS Arabe 5847, fol. 105r.

11. Macuch (2008).

12. B. Lewis (1990: 24).

13. B. Lewis (1990: 24).

called on by his father to charge. "'Antara is a slave,' he replied, 'he does not know how to charge, only to milk camels and bind their udders.' 'Charge!' cried his father, 'and you are free.' And 'Antara charged."[14]

However, later Islamic law gave children the status of their father.[15] In China, relationships between free women and male slaves were forbidden— although this is not to say they did not happen. Certainly men took slaves as concubines. The child inherited the status of its father.[16]

Who could be sold? Under classical Roman law a father was allowed to sell his children into slavery, but if they were sold three times then he no longer retained his power over them—his *patria potestas* (the power of a father). A law passed in 294 attempted to stop this practice but without success.[17] A constitution of 322 sought to end the practice of the sale of children due to poverty by releasing the families from their debts.[18]

The law in Han dynasty China (206 BC–AD 220) also prohibited families from selling children or other relatives: "Those who sell their children shall be punished for one year. [Those who sell] relatives of the same surname, who are their superiors or elders within the five grades of mourning, shall die. Those who sell their near relatives, or their concubines, or their sons' wives, shall be banished."[19] But the fact that this law was promulgated suggests that the practice existed. A few centuries later we have the account of a Chinese official exiled to the south of China, near present-day Guizhou. He noted that it was common for local children to be sold to their debtors by poor parents or abducted and sold into slavery. As magistrate of the district, he set about ensuring an end to this practice, passing a law to allow the parents to work off their debts.[20] He also passed an edict allowing slaves to be freed and is recorded as having redeemed several children with his own funds when families were too poor to do so.[21]

Nevertheless, families faced with poverty, famine, and other straitened circumstances continued to find a market for their children along the Silk

14. Quoted in B. Lewis (1990: 24).
15. Perry (2014: 4).
16. Johnson (1997: art. 191, 169–72).
17. Rotman and Todd (2009: 174).
18. Rotman and Todd (2009: 175).
19. W. Martin (1968).
20. Liu Zongyuan (773–819). His essay "Tong Ou Ji zhuan" [The story of the child Ou Ji] tells of an eleven-year-old boy who manages to defeat his kidnappers and escape this fate.
21. Schafer (1967: 104).

Road. The Chinese emperor Xuanzong notes that the peoples of the far south were oppressed by taxes and forced to sell their sons and daughters, so that "men and women become wares and wealth, along with horn and ivory."[22] A Byzantine law of 1095 spoke of the practice of Bulgar families selling their children in times of famine. But the law also determined that anyone who could prove that he was born of free parents would also be deemed free.[23]

A surviving loan contract from Dura Europos is between two Parthians, one of noble birth and one a peasant. The latter agrees to serve as a slave to the former in payment of the interest on the loan.[24] In Sasanian law this practice continued: a person could be given as security for a loan or debt and kept effectively as a slave for this period. If the debt was not discharged, then the person could be kept as a slave.[25] It is not clear whether this was always a "voluntary" action or whether the debtor sometimes offered someone in his family, such as a child, as surety. In Roman law, legislation of Justinian had banned creditors from taking children of their debtors into slavery as payment for a loan. But, again, the fact that the law was promulgated showed that this situation was not uncommon, and we cannot know if the law was effective.

In China, from the time of the Jin dynasty (265–420), the law gave exemptions from tax and military service to individuals who became slaves to elite families.[26] The families were allowed a fixed number of exempt slaves. For the highest officials, this was set at forty households.[27] But there were also many cases of men selling their wives and children because of poverty. One recorded case tells of a man selling two children, a daughter and a son, in order to raise funds to pay for his father's funeral.[28]

If a person committed a crime in China, then his punishment might often extend to family members. In the most severe cases, all members of his extended family might be executed, but a lesser sentence might be given, such as their enslavement. They became government slaves, not under private ownership. Both male and female slaves were used as slave labor. The men were

22. Schafer (1963: 45).
23. Rotman and Todd (2009: 175–76).
24. Shaki ([1992] 2011).
25. Macuch (2008).
26. Wang Yu-t'ung (1953: 310).
27. Wang Yu-t'ung (1953: 311).
28. Wang Yu-t'ung (1953: 313–14).

assigned to a labor camp in the capital named the "Division of Servitude." Younger men were often castrated to serve as court eunuchs—as in several Silk Road societies. The women were placed the supervision of an official and given forced labor, although often comparatively light tasks such as rice husking. Some might also become maids or consorts in the imperial palace. They were at the mercy of the government, which could keep them or which might present them as gifts to favored generals or civil officials.[29] Although the practice was illegal, cases are recorded of influential families seizing government-owned slaves for themselves.[30]

We know of many such gifts. For example, General Yu Luoba was rewarded with forty slaves by the emperor of the Western Wei (535–57) after a major victory, while some years later the general Yu Jin received a thousand slaves from the emperor of the Northern Zhou (557–81) for his capture of the city of Jiangling in 554. The official Xu Boyang (516–81) was rewarded with a gift of slaves after composing a poem on a pleasure trip to the mountains with his colleagues and boss.[31] When in 601 Yang Su (544–606) became one of the vice-directors of the Secretariat he was given a hundred fine horses, two hundred mares, and one hundred slaves and maidservants.[32] Luo Fahe was presented with two hundred slaves by the emperor for his magic power, and Wang Yu captured the empress's favor and was rewarded with several hundred slaves.[33]

While all the above situations forced people into slavery, across Eurasia the greatest number of slaves were from battle or abduction: by land, sea, or river. This is reflected in a commonly used word for "slave" in Middle Persian sources, namely *anšahrīg*—"foreigner." The numbers given are sometimes staggering. Chinese histories record that more than one hundred thousand prisoners were taken captive when the Northern Zhou took Jiangling in 554.[34] This was only one of hundreds of battles in the expansion of northern dynasties in China into the South and Southwest resulting in the acquisition of vast numbers of slaves.[35] One account gives more detail on the logistics of dealing with so many enslaved peoples. It concerns the southward invasion

29. Wang Yu-t'ung (1953: 308–10).
30. Wang Yu-t'ung (1953: 312).
31. Knechtges and Chang (2010–14: 1679).
32. Knechtges and Chang (2010–14: 1832).
33. Wang Yu-t'ung (1953: 315).
34. Wang Yu-t'ung (1953: 298).
35. See table in Wang Yu-t'ung (1953: 303–5).

of the Northern Wei dynasty (386–535) in 468. The captured people were divided according to their status. Socially prominent captured households were not enslaved but forcibly relocated north to an area designated for their settlement and under the jurisdiction of a new province. Although not slaves, the histories give many tales of their hardship: for example, of one man who endured ten years of forced labor in order to support his aging parents before dying himself. Others joined the army or monastic institutions to ensure their survival. However, it was worse for the ordinary population, who all became government slaves.

The Chinese were also expanding their territory into areas of different peoples and cultures who were often not considered equal to the Chinese. A major source of slaves during the Jin dynasty was the Liao peoples who lived in what is now northern Sichuan. The local governors were periodically ordered to raid the area and capture more slaves. The profitability of this trade is suggested by the histories when they record that groups of businessmen specialized in the Liao slave trade.[36] During the Tang period (618–907), the peoples of the South were, in Edward Schafer's words, "systematically enslaved" and usually described as hardly human.[37] To the far south, in what is now Vietnam, the girls were prized as "sleek of buttery flesh."[38]

The Chinese were also subject to enslavement when their territories were attacked, both on the border regions and in more distant battlefields. The many battles between the Chinese and the Tibetans resulted in numerous prisoners of war. Tibetan sources tell us that when first captured by the Tibetans all prisoners were kept in a large pit. The more important were questioned and sometimes tortured before being tattooed and assigned duties. Literate prisoners were appointed as interpreters and advisers and were tattooed on the arm, while ordinary prisoners received face tattoos.[39] Escapes were not uncommon, but those who were recaptured were flogged with a leather whip. The bodies of high-ranking prisoners on both sides who died

36. Wang Yu-t'ung (1953: 308).
37. Schafer (1967: 57).
38. Schafer (1967: 56).
39. Sperling (1979: 22–24); Demiéville (1952: 197–98). For an overview of the similar use of tattooing in the Chinese army, see C. Reed (2000: 19–24). Also see Zhu (2016: 642) on the government tattooing of enslaved captives, men and women. For tattooing of slaves working in Parthian mines, see Perikhanian (2008: 635).

in captivity were returned in coffins under the conditions of various treaties between the two empires.

Exchanges of live prisoners were arranged between the Byzantines and Arabs. In one such exchange in 845 in Constantinople the Arab prisoners considerably outnumbered the Byzantine ones. It is reported that, to even out the numbers, the Caliph al-Wāthiq (r. 842–47) ordered Byzantine slaves for sale in Baghdad and Raqqa to be ransomed and also brought Byzantine women from his personal harem.[40]

Prisoners of war legally became the property of the captor in most societies, and these might include men, women, and children. The Byzantine *Prochiros Nomos* (870–79) cited older legislation that "according the law of war, the conquered belong to the conquerors."[41]

Even in times of peace, local populations were not safe, especially if they lived on the borderlands, on navigable rivers, or by the coast. Seemingly friendly merchants might harbor ulterior motives, as a tale recounted by a tenth-century shipmaster makes clear. This tells of an Arab merchant who sailed to the east coast of Africa (reachable from the Gulf by the northwestern monsoons) for trade with the local king. After their business was successfully concluded, the king, as a courtesy, went to see him off. The story continues: "I thought to myself, that young king would fetch at least thirty *dinars*, if he were auctioned in the marketplace at Oman, and his seven attendants a hundred and sixty *dinars*." The unsuspecting king and his entourage were taken prisoner and added to the existing cargo of two hundred slaves.[42]

During the Samanid dynasty (819–999) in Central Asia the neighboring Turkic-controlled lands were a constant source of slave soldiers, as discussed below. In 893 a single raid acquired ten to fifteen thousand captives. Apart from men for the army, these included the wife of a Turkic chief.[43] The Samanids were continuing a practice started by the Arab armies when they expanded into the lands of the Caucasus and Transoxania. Here they could acquire large numbers of slaves, Turks from the Central Asian steppe and Slavs from the traders from the north. Although in these early centuries they continued to acquire slaves from unconverted regions of Iran, such as Daylam

40. Al-Ṭabarī (1989: 39–40).
41. Rotman and Todd (2009: 26).
42. Buzurg ibn Shahriyār (1928: 43). The story goes on to say how the merchant returned later to the same place and had an audience with the same king who had escaped.
43. Starr (2013: n29).

and Ḡūr, as well as from Africa and Byzantium, by the time of the Samanids most were Turks or Africans.[44] In tenth-century Transoxania, Muslim girls were seized in raids by the Ghuzz, who sold them on in neighboring non-Muslim lands to Chinese, Indian, and Byzantine merchants.

Raids by sea and river were also prevalent. The North Sea was subject to frequent raids by peoples of Scandinavia then variously known as peoples of the North, Varangians, and Rus, but now more popularly known as Vikings.[45] Those settled in eastern Europe moved down the Dneiper and Volga Rivers into Central Asia. They also traveled down the coasts of France and Spain and into the western Mediterranean and North Africa. The eastern Mediterranean was home to both Byzantine and Arab pirates. Indian pirates roamed the Red Sea, the Gulf, and the Indian Ocean. We also have reports of piracy on many rivers, from the Danube, the Tigris, the Indus, and more. Some pirates attacked merchant ships, killing their crews and stealing their goods. These would have often included slaves. Others made raids on the land for people and livestock. All were marketable.[46]

The Vikings perhaps provide the model in the West for piracy, but their exploits were no more than those of many other seafaring peoples of the time. Their raids from the late eighth century were not only about acquiring marketable goods—including people to be sold as slaves—but also about their need for labor for their own expansions into new territories and their battles against increasingly belligerent Christian neighbors.[47] The lands they reached were considerable. They traveled across the North Sea to the coast of Britain and Ireland, the islands to the north, and thence Iceland, Greenland, and the mainland of North America. These settlers included slaves, both men and women. The use of slaves in this expansion is shown in the Saga of Eric the Red, whose journey is precipitated by his slaves, who accidentally destroy the farm of his neighbor Eyjolf the Foul by causing a landslide. Eyjolf kills the slaves and is then killed himself by Eric the Red. His kinsmen

44. B. Lewis (1990: 23).

45. There has been much discussion about these names: I use them advisedly.

46. As Desmond Keenan notes: "For the slave raiders, slaves were a valuable currency. You could sell them to buy wine and other luxury goods. There was always a market for them. There was always an unending supply of them, if only you were stronger than your neighbour. . . . For the Irish, slave-raiding was a lucrative extension to the cattle-raiding" (2004: 152).

47. The Vikings attacked Constantinople in 860, and although they were repelled, deals were made to prevent further attacks and some Vikings were recruited as Byzantine bodyguards (Lynch and Adamo 2014: 122).

demand that Eric be banished, and he departs for Oxney Island in Iceland, thus starting his journeys westward that would possibly take him as far as North America.[48]

The *Annals of Ulster* records numerous raids by "heathens" on the coasts of Britain and Ireland over the ninth and tenth centuries, including the seizure of a large number of women in a raid near Dublin in 821.[49] In 850–51 many Viking ships overwintered on the Thames estuary in Britain, and over this same period the Vikings made raids up the French river valleys to Rouen, Nantes, Bordeaux, Paris, and other Frankish cities.[50] Sometimes they did not even need to raid: in 845 their planned attack on Paris was diverted by payment of 7,000 pounds of silver.[51]

They also traveled by ship and land down from their settlements in northeastern Europe, where the peoples they raided and enslaved were known in history as Slavs—giving us the modern English word for slaves.[52] They raided settlements as they traveled down the river routes, often selling on the slaves to the Bulgar and Khazar kingdoms and receiving Islamic silver coins (dirhams) in return. Many hundreds of thousands of these coins have been found in coin hoards along these routes and in their settlement areas.[53] These slaves were sent to the market of Baghdad, while others were traded in the markets of Prague and Constantinople.[54] The trade was described by several Islamic writers, including Ibn Rusta in the tenth century: "The Rus . . . raid the Saqaliba, sailing in their ships until they come upon them, take them captive and sell them in Khazaria and in Bulgar. They have no cultivated fields and they live by pillaging the land of the Saqaliba. . . . They earn their living by trading in sable, grey squirrel and other furs. They sell them for silver coins which they set in belts and wear round their waists. . . . They

48. Sephton (1880).

49. *Annals of Ulster* (2000), Year U821.3. "Étar was plundered by the heathens, and they carried off a great number of women into captivity." But note that the Irish also engaged in raids for slaves and cattle. See, for example, years U951.3, U1012.2. and see note 46 above. Note that by the late tenth century the Viking rulers in Ireland were subjected to a series of defeats by the Irish, who also took prisoners of war to be enslaved.

50. Lynch and Adamo (2014: 122).

51. Sawyer (2001).

52. For a discussion of the issue around defining the ethnicity of the Slavs, see Curta (2001: 227–29).

53. A recent count suggests 800,000 dirhams (Jankowiak 2012).

54. Slave markets are discussed below.

treat their slaves well and dress them suitably, because for them they are an article of trade."[55]

Pirates have been known to have been active in the Mediterranean since at least the second millennium BC.[56] And at the time of the Silk Road, as well as the Vikings, the Byzantines and Arabs made raids on each other's coastal settlements and sometimes even further inland. In 768 the Byzantine emperor Constantine V (r. 741–75) ransomed prisoners taken by "Slavic pirates" with 2,500 silk robes.[57] In 855 Byzantine raiders took as prisoners men from the al-Zuṭṭ peoples from northwestern India who had been settled in Ayn Zarba (Anazarbus) by the Arabs only twenty years before.[58] The women and livestock were also seized. This was despite the repair of the city's defenses in 796 and again only a few years before the raids.[59] Between 942 and 943 the Byzantines raided Diyarbakir, across the border on the banks of the Tigris. They continued their raids up to Erzurum, a region in what is now the Northeast of Turkey that had long been under dispute between the Byzantines and Arabs.

In 988 the Arab geographer Ibn Ḥawqal wrote of the raids: "In our time, the Byzantines were relentless in attempting raids on the coast of Syria and the beaches of Egypt. They drove off the ships of the coastal residents along all the coasts and captured them everywhere. No hope, no aid was procured from the Muslims, and no one cared." Al Muqaddasī, another tenth-century Arab geographer, recorded that Byzantine ships often took Arab prisoners to guard stations at Gaza and Jaffa, where they were exchanged or ransomed. And it was not only Muslims who paid the ransom to secure the release of the pirates' captives. Documents in the Cairo Geniza tell of Byzantine pirates also raiding Byzantine Jewish settlements in the Levant. While some captives were sold on in Byzantine slave markets, others were redeemed by local Jewish communities.

The Arabs were active in the Mediterranean from the early ninth century, seizing people for enslavement and ransom from Sicily, southern Italy, the Greek islands and mainland, the Peloponnese, and the Aegean coast.[60]

---

55. Jankowiak (2012: 4).
56. Called the sea people and mentioned on the Obelisk in Byblos.
57. Thomas (2012: 129).
58. Rotman and Todd (2009: 49).
59. Canard (2012).
60. Rotman and Todd (2009: 47).

After capturing Crete in 826 they used it as a base for further raids in the eastern Mediterranean.

The seas of the Indian Ocean and the South China Sea were also home to pirates. Pliny the Elder (ca. 23–79) notes that merchant ships traveling the Red Sea and Indian Ocean routes had to carry companies of archers on board to dispel attacks. We know from Arab and Chinese sources of the slave trade of the island of Kish in the Gulf. They report how they sent expeditions to acquire slaves from the Zanzibar coast in East Africa and sent trading parties to the Arab port of Basra near the mouth of the Shatt al-Arab River into the Gulf.

In the sixth and seventh centuries Chinese pirates seized women from the Koguryo and Silla kingdoms of the Korean peninsula and sold them in markets in eastern China. They were in great demand as maids, concubines, and entertainers, although an attempt was made to ban the trade in 692.[61] In the eighth century pirates based on the large island of Hainan in the South China Sea regularly plundered ships to gain their cargos, including Persian slaves. Jianzhen, a Buddhist monk stranded on the island in 748, reports that their numbers were so great one could walk the length and breadth of the island and find them in all the villages.[62]

Once captured, the raiders had to turn their captives into profit, and for that they needed to take them somewhere to sell.

TRADING SLAVES

Slave markets were found across the whole of the Silk Road, from Dublin on the shores of the Atlantic to Shandong on the Pacific. And while much of the trade was by private merchants, government also profited by imposing taxes both on the movement and on the sale of slaves.[63] As with many other "things" traded along the Silk Road, there was both local and regional trade, as well as trade over longer distances.

Dublin, for example, probably the largest slave market in western Europe, was convenient for the Irish, Vikings, and others who had seized captives in

61. Schafer (1963: 44); Wilbur (1943b: 92); Lee (1997: 51–52).
62. Bingheimer (2004: 146).
63. Numerous documents record the sale and cost of slaves at different times and different places. I do not cite them here, as they are fairly meaningless without more context.

raids and battles. Shandong, in eastern China, was specifically for selling on slaves captured from the Korean peninsula. But one of the most extensive trading networks, certainly by the ninth and tenth centuries, was that in Slavs, captured by the Rus in northern Europe and sold at the capital of the Bulgars, Bulgar, and the capital of the Khazars, Khamlij (Atil). Ibn Faḍlān visited Khamlij in 922 and wrote:

> I saw the Rusiya, when they came hither on their trading voyages and had encamped by the river Itil. . . . With them, there are fair maidens who are destined for sale to the merchant, and they may have intercourse with their girl while their comrades look on. . . . When their boats arrive come to this anchorage, each one of them goes ashore... and prostrates himself before [the great image], Then he says: "Oh my lord, I have come from a far country and have with me so many slave girls for such a price, and so many sable skins. . . . I wish that thou shouldst provide me with a merchants who has many *dinars* and *dirhams* and who would buy from me at the price I desire."[64]

Marek Jankowiak argues that by the ninth and tenth centuries there was another distinct system also dealing in Slav slaves. Jewish merchants bought slaves at the market in Prague for sale to the Spanish, making payment, he argues, in small pieces of cloth that had an exchange rate for silver.[65] He cites the travelogue of Ibrahim ibn Ya'qub, a merchant from Tortosa, who noted the trade when he traveled to Prague in the 960s. He also cites Ibn Ḥawqal, who writes on Saqaliba—the land of the Slavs. "The country [of the Saqaliba] is long and wide. . . . Half of their country . . . is raided by the Khurasanis [Khorezm] who take prisoners from it, while its northern half is raided by the Andalusians who buy them in Galicia, in France, in Lombardy and in Calabria so as to make them eunuchs, and thereafter they ferry them over to Egypt and Africa. All the Saqaliba eunuchs in the world come from Andalusia. . . . They are castrated near this country. The operation is performed by Jewish merchants."[66]

Ibn Khurradādhbih (ca. 820–912) records a wider network, extending

64. Ibn Faḍlan (2005: 63–65).
65. Jankowiak (2012) argues that, after furs and gold, "slaves were the third major commodity redistributed through Andalusi markets" (Constable 1996: 203). The use of cloth as money is well attested at the eastern end of the Silk Road, where rolls of silk were a common form of payment. See H. Wang (2004).
66. Jankowiak (2012). Also quoted in La Puente (2017: 127–28), who expresses skepticism about the accuracy of this report.

from western Europe through to Africa, Arabia, India, and China, run by Jewish merchants whom he refers to as Radhanites.[67] It is worth quoting in full as one of the few detailed and extant itineraries:

> These merchants speak Arabic, Persian, Greek, Latin, Frankish, Andalusian and Slavic. They journey from west to east, from east to west, traveling by land and by sea. From the west they export eunuchs, young girls and boys, brocade, beaver pelts, marten and other furs and also swords.
>
> They set sail from Firanj [France] on the western sea and then head for Farama [Pelusium] in Egypt. There they transfer their merchandise to the backs of camels and travel to Qulzum [Clysma, Suez] on the Red Sea, a distance of 25 farsakhs. They sail down the Red Sea to al-Jar, the port of Medina, and to Jeddah, the port of Mecca. Then they continue on to Sindh, India and China.
>
> They return from China with musk, aloe wood, camphor, cinnamon and other eastern products, docking again at Qulzum, then proceed to Farama, from where they again set sail on the western sea. . . .
>
> These different journeys can also be made by land. The merchants that start from Spain or France go to Sus al-Aksa [near Tangier] and then to Tangier, whence they walk to Kairouan and the capital of Egypt. Thence they go to ar-Ramiah, visit Damascus, al-Kufa, Baghdad, and al-Basra, cross Ahvez, Fars, Kerman, Sindh, Hind, and arrive in China.
>
> Sometimes, also, they take the route behind Rome and, passing through the country of the Slavs, arrive at Khamlij, the capital of the Khazars. They embark on the Jorjan Sea [Caspian], arrive at Balkh, betake themselves from there across the Oxus, and continue their journey toward Yurt, Toghuzghuz [Turkic lands in Central Asia], and from there to China.[68]

It was not only the merchants who profited from the slaves: the governments of the lands they passed through or ports of embarkation and the markets they sold at often imposed taxes or monopolies. For example, although there was a slave market at Constantinople—in the Valley of the Lamentations—several contemporary sources note that merchants often avoided it because of the high taxes and that ships docked instead at Antioch.[69] In eighth-century Khanfu (present-day Guangzhou in southern China), all goods coming into the port were controlled by the government

---

67. The term *Radhanites*—Arabic *al-Rādhāniyya*—is found in only a few sources, some of which might derive from this one, and its scope is not clear. See Pellat (2012).

68. Adler (1987: 2–3).

69. Rotman and Todd (2009: 68–80).

office of "the commissioner for commercial argosies," which purchased all imports desired by the government.[70]

Turkic male slaves for the caliphate's army were taken from the borders of the steppe in Central Asia to Nishapur, which sent thousand of slaves westward to Baghdad each year.[71] Male slaves could be transported across the Amu Darya only with a government-issued license, costing from seventy to one hundred dirhams.[72]

SLAVES FOR WHAT?

Slaves were put to many uses. Slaves from childhood onwards were used as household servants.[73] They were used for labor—agricultural, construction, and mining.[74] Women were often used for as entertainers—dancers and musicians—and, inevitably, sex was a large motive for the slave trade. Some boys and young men were castrated: the Arab, Chinese, and Byzantine courts all had eunuchs. Some slaves were in the ownership of monastic institutions to help with general duties.[75] Others acted as private guards for rich owners—

70. Schafer (1963: 23). See p. 24 for further discussion, also citing an Arab source who reported that his compatriots had to surrender one-third of their cargo to imperial warehouses on arrival in China.

71. Starr (2013: 197).

72. Barthold (1968: 239). Duties were levied elsewhere on slaves. For example, La Vaissière (2005: 165) cites a document dating from 648 where a certain Mi Xunzhi of Beshbaliq requests a trading permit take two slaves to the market at Turfan—a boy of fifteen and a girl of twelve—as well as an eight-year-old camel and fifteen sheep. This was a comparatively short journey, south across the Tianshan.

73. A satirical piece written in China in 59 BC enumerates all the duties for a recalcitrant domestic servant (Wilbur 1943b: 82/382).

74. See, for example, Yaacov's (2012: 138) discussion of slave labor on olive estates in ninth- to tenth-century Tunisia; La Vaissière's (2005: 281) account of a governor of Merv who took captive Sogdian nobles to Medina and used them as agricultural laborers; the discovery in Samanid mines of manacles probably used on Turk and Slav slaves (Starr 2013: 233n30); and Cicero's mention, in a letter to Atticus, of a runaway slave who said he had worked in the mines of the Parthian king and who, in proof of his story, showed a mark branded on his body (Perikhanian 2008: 63). On industrial slaves in Han-period China, see Wilbur (1943a).

75. For Buddhism, see Schopen (1994). The entwinement of slavery and religion is an interesting topic. As Bernard Lewis (1990) points out in his discussion of slavery in the Middle East, the concept of slavery was accepted in religious texts: the Old and New Testaments and the Qur'an. The Essene community was possibly unique in rejecting slavery: it was found in all other communities of the region, whether Jewish, Christian, or pagan

and some as spies.[76] And a large number were used as soldiers. In a Chinese poem, a bridegroom dreams of the slaves he will have by becoming rich:

> Chinese slaves to take charge of treasury and barn.
> Foreign slaves to take care of my cattle and sheep.
> Strong-legged slaves to run by my saddle and stirrup when I ride,
> Powerful slaves to till the fields with might and main,
> Handsome slaves to play the harp and hand the wine;
> Slim-waisted slaves to sing me songs and dance;
> Dwarfs to hold the candle by my dining couch.[77]

There is no space here to discuss all of these roles, so I look very briefly at two: female slaves used for sex and male slaves as soldiers.[78]

Slavery for Sex

Slave girls and young women were found across the Silk Road.[79] They realized high prices because, as well as other duties, they could be used for sex. Like most slaves, they had little say in their lives. For example, a contract from the first- to fourth-century Taklamakan kingdom of Caḍota records the purchase by a scribe of a female slave for payment of two camels and two

---

(Lewis 1990: 5). Slavery had no religious boundaries; it was also found in Zoroastrian Iran, Islamic Arabia, and the Hindu, Confucian, and Buddhist East.

76. "The Sogdian merchants often bought slaves (*chakar*) and formed guards or even private armies to guard their homes while they were traveling" (Frye 2012: 195–96n81, citing Findley 2005: 45). On spies, see Barthold (1968: 221–22). According to the author of *Tarikhi Khayrat*, "'Amr bought young slaves, trained them in his own service and then gave them to his nobles; these slaves reported to him all the actions of their masters. Nor were they deterred by fear of the latter, as in 'Amr's reign not one noble dared beat a slave without the permission of the sovereign."

77. Waley (1960: 162): translation of a poem from a manuscript found at the Silk Road town of Dunhuang.

78. Slaves for domestic and military use were probably the most common among most societies for much of the period in question. As Perry notes: "In contrast to the major slave-systems in the early modern Atlantic, that of the Islamic world was not associated primarily with large-scale agricultural production. Even though slaves in ninth-century Iraq and tenth-century Ifriqiyah were used heavily in agricultural projects, the majority of slaves in the Islamic empire at any given time served primarily as domestic servants and slave soldiers" (2014: 3–4).

79. "The scale of captive-taking is startling. Captives, especially captive women, were present in societies of almost every socio-political level from bands to states and in societies on every continent" (Cameron 2011: 169). For a detailed study of female slaves based on the Geniza records, see Perry (2014).

carpets. The contract states that he may "beat her, bind her, sell her, give her to others as a present, exchange her, pledge her . . . do whatsoever he pleases with her."[80] A twelfth-century document from the Cairo Geniza records the case of a Jewish merchant in a Red Sea port who made his slave pregnant but, after she had given birth to a son, took her to the port of Berbera (present-day Somalia) and abandoned them both.[81] However, as Catherine Cameron points out, such slaves, although on the lowest rungs of society, often still left a cultural and, of course, a genetic legacy.[82]

While the vast majority of these female slaves remained illiterate and forgotten to history, a portion were trained to become entertainers to be rented out by their owners, both men and women. They ranged from what Lisa Nielson in her several discussions of the Islamic tradition calls musical concubines at the bottom to elite courtesans at the top.[83] The same differentiation could be made in any number of cultures of the Silk Road.[84] The elite of these slaves were highly educated and literate, some leaving their own legacy of poetry. Their achievements were also recorded in poems and writings of male admirers. Two such works in the Islamic tradition are the "Epistle on the Singing Girls," by Jāḥiẓ (776–869), and "Wahid, the Singing Slave-Girl of ʿAmhamah," by Ibn al-Rūmī (836–96), which contains the lines "She is blamed because when she sings / The free-born become enslaved by her."[85] The best among them were said to know as many as four thousand songs and to be well educated in the traditional sciences and the Qurʾan.[86]

The exploitation of slaves for sex was commonplace among men, but there are also cases recorded of women taking advantage.[87] For example, *One*

---

80. Whitfield and Sims-Williams (2004: 174).

81. Perry (2014: 1).

82. Cameron (2011, 2016) discusses this. She points out, for example, that "captives had the potential to be important agents in the transmission of cultural practices. Kristiansen and Larsson (2005) urge us to consider how alien cultural practices are assimilated and given new meaning" (2011: 187).

Lenski (2008) documents the role of captives in the spread of Christianity during the Germanic tribes "in the first few centuries AD."

83. Nielson (2017). See the other papers in this collection (Gordon and Hain 2017) for detailed discussion of this tradition.

84. For example, see Dauphin (1996) for Byzantium, and see Zhang Bangwei (2016: 174–77) for China.

85. Line 29 of "Wahid." See Motoyoshi (2001).

86. Motoyoshi (2001: 9).

87. And there are cases of homosexual activities, for example, in Rome; see Verstraete (1980).

Thousand and One Nights tells of the king returning early from a trip to find his wife in bed with a male slave, thus precipitating the events that would lead to the telling of the tales.[88] And a tenth-century poetess from Balkh, Balkhi Rabia, wrote of her love for a Turkic male slave:[89]

> My prayer to God is this:
> That you be bound in love with someone
> Unmoving as stick and stone
>
> For only having suffered love's agony
> Of pain and separation
> Shall you come to feel and value
> My love for you.

She suffered for her love: she was killed by her brother.

In another case, we are told of male prisoners of war in China being apportioned among the local widows. But this was exceptional: most enslaved prisoners of war were assigned military duty for their masters.[90]

Slaves for War

Slaves were used in armies across the Silk Road, but the Arab Caliphate took this to extremes as the number of volunteers dwindled under the Umayyad Caliphate (661–750). They captured and purchased large numbers of male slaves—mainly Turks—to man their armies.[91] These armies of *mamluk*—foreign military slaves—first appeared in North Africa, then spread to Spain and Egypt and thence to West Asia.[92] Although many were manumitted and most converted, manumission became less common as their numbers grew, and conversion was often only a formality.[93]

Nizam al-Mulk (1018–92), a Persian scholar and high official in the Seljuk Empire (1037–1194), described the potential career path for a Turkish slave:

88. Shahriyar's wife before he married Scheherazade, teller of the tales. Made distrustful of all women, Shahriyar takes a new wife every night and has her killed before morning. Scheherazade, with her tales, postpones her own death.
89. Starr (2013: 226n5, xvii).
90. Schafer (1963: 42).
91. Crone (1980). Although black slaves were used in the armies of the Aghlabids and Fatimids (Lev 2012: 138).
92. Crone (1980: 75).
93. Crone (1980: 79).

During the first year the slave served on foot in the capacity of a groom, and not even in secret, under pain of punishment, did he dare mount a horse. At this period he wore garments of Zandaniji cloth.[94] After a year the hajib, in agreement with the commander of the tent, gave him a Turkish horse with plain harness. In the third year he received a long sword; in the fifth a better saddle, a snaffle ornamented with stars, richer clothing, and a club; in the sixth year parade dress; in the seventh the rank of "Commander of the Tent," which he shared with three other men. . . . He gradually rose to the following grades, Khayl-bashr (section commander) and Hajib. At the head of the whole court establishment was the chief hajib, one of the first dignitaries in the kingdom.[95]

As this passage suggests, although the vast majority of the Turkic soldiers undoubtedly remained in the lower ranks, there was a possibility of advancement. Nizam al-Mulk also noted:

One obedient slave is better
than three hundred sons;
for the latter desire their father's death
the former, his master's glory.[96]

Such was the case with John Axouch, a Turk captured at the Siege of Nicaea in 1097 and presented to the Byzantine emperor Alexios I Komnenos (r. 1081–1118). John gained the trust of the emperor's heir, John Komnenos. On the ascendancy to the throne of the heir (John II Komnenos, r. 1118–43), the former slave was appointed commander in chief of the Byzantine army.[97] Another prominent example is the case of Sebüktigin (ca. 942–97), founder of the Ghaznavid Empire (977–1186). He was born in what is now Kyrghyzstan, taken prisoner at the age of twelve, sold as a slave, and then bought by Alptigin, the chamberlain of the Samanids.[98]

While John Axouch and Sebüktigin were inevitably rare among the hundreds of thousands taken as slaves who remained so, there were several other ways to escape from slavery.

94. There is an ongoing debate about the type of cloth this signifies, whether cotton or a fine silk, but in this case it would probably be expected to be the former. See Marshak (2006) and Dode (2016) for discussions and bibliographies.

95. Barthold (1968: 227).

96. Findley (2005: 67).This idea is somewhat like that of the Chinese Tang emperor who believed that foreign generals would be less likely to rebel against him. However, this was proved a misjudgment when Rokhsan (An Lushan) did just that.

97. Kazhdan (2005: Axouch).

98. Bosworth (2012).

While most slaves died as slaves, some escaped. Many enslaved POWs must have been attempted to escape back to their homeland , although we hear of only a few. For example, in about 839 a Chinese official captured by the Tibetans spent six years in captivity before making his escape. Although he returned to China—where he wrote of his experiences—he lost part of his foot to frostbite, presumably while crossing the high mountain passes from the Tibetan Plateau.[99]

Salufa, the East African king mentioned above who was enslaved by merchants, was able to escape. He was sold at Oman and taken to Basra by his owner. Sold again, he was taken to Baghdad, where he became a Muslim and studied the Qur'an. Wishing to make the pilgrimage to Mecca, he managed to escape and join a group of pilgrims. After this he joined a caravan to Cairo and from there made his way up the Nile back to his homeland. His people had also converted in his absence.[100]

He was fortunate: the authorities had an obligation to return slaves. The 969 Arab-Byzantine treaty of Aleppo stated that Arabs were to return slaves, whether Christian or Muslim. It suggests that attempted escapes were not uncommon:

> If a Muslim or Christian slave, man or woman, flees to a country other than the territories designated, so long as a slave remains in those territories, the Muslims must not hide the slave but must denounce him or her. The slave's owner will pay a price of thirty Greek dinars for a man, twenty for a woman, and fifteen for a young boy or girl; if the owner does not have the means to purchase the slave, the emir will charge the owner a duty of three dinars and will remit the slave to the owner.[101]

In other cases, slaves were redeemed by their countrymen or coreligionists. We hear of Byzantine Jews abducted by Arabs and taken to Egypt, where they were purchased by both Arabs and Christians. They were then redeemed by local Jewish communities. In some cases, poorer communities had to seek help, especially from the richer community in Al-Fustat in Egypt.[102] In

---

99. Sperling (1979: 22–24); Demiéville (1952: 197–98). For an overview of the similar use of tattooing by the Chinese army, see C. Reed (2000: 19–24).

100. Devic and Quennell (1928).

101. Rotman and Todd (2009: 55).

102. Rotman and Todd (2009: 51–52).

another case, two Spanish Jews on their way to the Levant were abducted and sold as slaves in Ramla before they were also redeemed by the local Jewish community.[103]

Many must have tried to escape, and many presumably failed and were duly punished. But there was also the possibility of manumission, a legal route to freedom. In the Islamic world there was a legal term for a manumitted slave who remained in a special relationship with his former owner.[104] The voluntary act of manumission was considered an act of creation—the freed slave remaining a "creature" or "son" of his former owner.

We hear of several cases of manumitted slaves remaining in a relationship with their former owners. So, for example, the fourth-century historian Rufinis tells of the children Frumentius and Edesius, who accompanied their uncle from their homeland in the Levant to the Axum Empire in East Africa. The entire crew, apart from the two boys, were slain when they made port on the Red Sea. The boys were taken to the king of Axum as slaves and rose to positions of trust. He freed them shortly before their deaths. They remained at the court and helped the young prince. Frumentius is known in Ethiopia for his part in the spread of Christianity.[105]

The Chinese Tang law code acknowledged manumission. According to the Household Statutes: "All cases of manumission of personal retainers, female personal retainers, or slaves as commoners ... will be permitted. In all cases the person manumitted will receive a certificate ... from the head of the household. The eldest son and those younger than he jointly sign it . . . and the name is put in the correct place in the household register."[106]

Another example is Andrew of Constantinople (d. 936), a slave of the bodyguard Theognostus. During a siege of the city he claimed to have a vision of Mary surrounded by saints, and after this the attackers retreated. His master released him from slavery, and he thereafter lived as a "Fool for Christ" and became revered as a saint in the Eastern Orthodox Church.[107]

Examples of the emancipation of slaves are also found throughout this period. There were benevolent rulers or local officials, such as Liu Zongyuan, mentioned above, who freed slaves when he served as a magistrate in South China. But in many cases emancipation was linked to religious conver-

103. Rotman and Todd (2009: 53).
104. Forand (1971).
105. Trimingham (2013: 38–39).
106. Johnson (1997: 133).
107. Harris (2017: 93).

sion and also sometimes had a demographic motive. So, for example, in the Byzantine Empire, Arab captives who converted to Christianity, married, and remained in the territory were emancipated.[108] A law of asylum promulgated under Justinian (r. 527–65) offered slaves the opportunity to join religious life as a member of the clergy and gave the church the right to end their slave status. But this was only while they remained members of the clergy. If they left, they were returned back to slave status.[109]

Under Byzantine law, Jews—as well as other non-Christians, such as Samaritans—were not allowed to purchase Christian slaves, but they could keep slaves if these had been obtained by other means, such as inheritance.[110]

In Zoroastrian Iran, if slaves owned by non-Zoroastrians converted to Zoroastrianism, then they had the right to leave their owner and become free after appropriate compensation had been paid. One textual source even suggests that a loan might be granted, probably by a Zoroastrian institution, to slaves to buy their freedom.[111]

Bernard Lewis notes that while the Qur'an continued the tradition of the Old and New Testaments in countenancing slavery the legislation developed had far-reaching effects: the presumption of freedom and a ban on enslavement of free persons except in strictly defined situations.[112] Later Muslim jurists rejected the enslavement of free Muslims "of whatever race or origin."[113] Protection was also afforded to the Jewish and Christian communities living under their jurisdiction.

We see, therefore, that religion—as well as ethnicity—sometimes formed a way of defining the "other." "Others" could legitimately be enslaved, while coreligionists were entitled to their freedom. In the Islamic Caliphate, as conversions grew, this reduced the pool of available slaves. So while Berbers were sold on the African Mediterranean coast, under Arab control from the seventh century onwards, as this population converted they were no longer

---

108. Rotman and Todd (2009: 41).
109. Rotman and Todd (2009: 144).
110. Rotman and Todd (2009: 66–67).
111. A slave converted to Zoroastrianism could leave his infidel owner and become a "subject of the king of kings," i.e., a free citizen, after having compensated his previous master. An important passage in the Ērbadestān indicates that a loan (abām) was even granted (probably by a religious institution) to the slave for this purpose (ed. Kotwal and Boyd 1980: 12v, secs. 11–15).
112. B. Lewis (1990: 5).
113. B. Lewis (1990: 55).

available as slaves and the slave merchants had to go further afield. This led to a growth in slaves brought from sub-Saharan Africa.[114]

Sadly, there was no route out of slavery for most: they were forced to keep this status until their deaths and sometimes even passed it on, unwillingly, to their children.

114. Lev (2012: 138) discusses this development in Aghlabid Tunisia.

Abel-Rémusat, Jean Pierre. 1820. *Histoire de la ville de Khotan, tirée des annales de la Chine et traduite du chinois suivie de recherches sur la substance minérale appelée par les Chinois "ierre de Iu," et sur le jaspe des anciens.* Paris: Doublet.

Adler, Elkan. 1987. *Jewish Travellers in the Middle Ages.* New York: Dover Publications.

Alemany, Agustí. 2000. *Sources on the Alans: A Critical Compilation.* Leiden: Brill.

Allsen, Thomas T. 2006. *The Royal Hunt in Eurasian History.* Philadelphia: University of Pennsylvania Press.

Alram, Michael. 1986. *Nomina propria Iranica in nummis: Materialgrundlagen zu den iranischen Personennamen auf antiken Münzen.* Iranisches Personennamenbuch 4. Vienna: Verlag der Osterreichischen Akademie der Wissenschaften.

———. 2016. *Das Antlitz des Fremden: Die Münzprägung der Hunnen und Westtürken in Zentralasien und Indien.* Vienna: Austrian Academy of Science.

An Jiayao. 2004. "The Art of Glass along the Silk Road." In Watt et al. 2004: 57–66.

Annals of Ulster. 2000. CELT: The Corpus of Electronic Texts. https://celt.ucc.ie/published/T100001A/index.html.

An Pingqiu and Zheng Peiheng. 1992. 中国禁书大观 *Zhongguo jinshu daguan.* Shanghai: Shanghai wenhua chubanshe.

Aptel, Claire, and Nathalie Biotteau. 1997. *Thomas Dobrée, 1810-1895: Un homme, un musée.* Exh. cat. Nantes: Musée Dobrée and Somogy.

Arnold, Thomas W., and Adolf Grohman. 1929. *The Islamic Book: A Contribution to Its Art and History from the VII–XVIII Century.* Paris: Pegasus Press.

Arrault, Alain, and J.-C. Martzloff. 2003. "Les calendriers." In *Divination et société dans la Chine medieval,* edited by Marc Kalinowski, 86–211. Paris: Bibliothèque nationale de France.

Aruz, Joan, Ann Farkas, Andrei Alekseev, and Elena Korolkova, eds. 2000. *The Golden Deer of Eurasia: Scythian and Sarmatian Treasures from the Russian Steppes.* Exh. cat. New York: Metropolitan Museum of Art.

Aruz, Joan, and Elizabeth Valtz Fino, eds. 2012. *Afghanistan: Forging Civilizations along the Silk Road.* New York: Metropolitan Museum of Art.

Asouti, Eeleni, and Dorian Q. Fuller. 2008. *Trees and Woodlands of South India: Archaeological Perspectives*. Walnut Creek, CA: Left Coast Press.

Bachrach, Bernard S. 1973. *A History of the Alans in the West, from Their First Appearance in the Sources of Classical Antiquity through the Early Middle Ages*. Minneapolis: University of Minnesota Press.

Bagnall, Roger S., et al. 2012. *The Encyclopedia of Ancient History*. London: Wiley-Blackwell.

Bagnera, Alessandra. 2006. "Preliminary Note on the Islamic Settlement of Udegram, Swat: The Islamic Graveyard (11th–13th Century A.D.)." *East and West* 56 (1–3): 205–28.

Balfour-Paul, Jenny. 1998. *Indigo*. London: British Museum Press.

Ball, Warwick. 2002. *Rome in the East: The Transformation of an Empire*. London: Routledge.

Baranov, Vladimir. n.d. "II. Materials and Techniques of Manuscript Production. 1. Parchment." In *Medieval Manuscript Manual*. Central European University, Department of Medieval Studies. http://web.ceu.hu/medstud/manual/MMM/parchment.html.

Barnard, Mark, and Frances Wood. 2004. "A Short History of the Conservation of the Dunhuang Manuscripts in London." In *The Silk Road: Trade, Travel, War and Faith*, exh. cat., edited by Susan Whitfield and Ursula Sims-Williams, 97–104. London: British Library; Chicago: Serindia.

Barrett, T. H. 1997. "The Feng-tao k'o and Printing on Paper in Seventh-Century China." *Bulletin of the School of Oriental and African Studies* 60 (3): 538–40.

———. 2001. "Woodblock Dyeing and Printing Technology in China, c. 700 A.D.: The Innovations of Ms. Liu and Other Evidence." *Bulletin of the School of Oriental and African Studies* 64 (2): 240–47.

Barthold, V. V. 1968. *Turkestan Down to the Mongol Invasion*. 3rd ed. London: Luzac.

Bass, G. F. 1987. "Oldest Known Shipwreck Reveals Splendors of the Bronze Age." *National Geographic*, December: 696–733.

Basu, M. K., S. K. Basu, and R. V. Lele. 1974. "4000 Year Old Faience Bangles from Punjab." *Central Glass and Ceramic Research Institute Bulletin* 21 (4): 85–90.

Bazin, Louis, György Hazai, and Hans Robert Roemer, eds. 2000. *Philologiae et Historiae Turcicae Fundamenta*. Vol. 1. Berlin: Klaus Schwarz.

Beal, Samuel, trans. 1884. *Si-Yu-Ki: Buddhist Records of the Western World, Translated from the Chinese of Hiuen Tsiang (A.D. 629)*. London: K. Paul, Trench, Trübner.

Beard, Mary. 1991. "Writing and Religion: Ancient Literacy and the Function of the Written Word in the Roman Religion." In *Literacy in the Roman World*, edited by Mary Beard, Alan K. Bowman, and Mireille Corbier, 35–58. *Journal of Roman Archaeology*, suppl. 3. Ann Arbor, MI: n.p.

———. 2015. *SPQR: A History of Ancient Rome*. London: W. W. Norton.

Beer, Robert. 2015. *The Handbook of Tibetan Buddhist Symbols*. Kindle ed. Boulder, CO: Shambhala Publications.

Behrendt, Kurt A. 2004. *The Buddhist Architecture of Gandhara*. Handbook of Oriental Studies, sec. 2, South Asia, vol. 17. Leiden: Brill.

Beit-Arié, Malachi. 1993. *Hebrew Manuscripts of East and West: Towards a Comparative Codicology*. Panizzi Lectures, 1992. London: British Library.

———. 2009. "The Script and Book Craft in the Hebrew Medieval Codex." In *Crossing Borders: Hebrew Manuscripts as a Meeting-Place of Cultures*, edited by Piet van Bixel and Sabine Arndt, 21–34. Oxford: Bodleian Library.

Bellina, Bérénice. 1997. *Cultural Exchange between India and Southeast Asia: Production and Distribution of Hard Stone Ornaments, c. VI BCE–VI CE*. Paris: Editions de la Maison des Sciences de l'homme.

Bellina, Bérénice, and Ian Glover. 2004. "The Archaeology of Early Contact with India and the Mediterranean World, from the Fourth Century BC to the Fourth Century AD." In *Southeast Asia: From Prehistory to History*, edited by Ian C. Glover and Peter Bellwood, 68–89. London: Routledge/Curzon Press.

Benjamin, Craig. 2007. *The Yuezhi: Origin, Migration and the Conquest of Northern Bactria*. Turnhout: Brepols.

Bernard, Paul. 1981. "Problèmes d'histoire coloniale greques à travers l'urbanisme d'une cité hellénistique d'Asie Centrale." In *150 Jahre Deutsches Archäologisches Institut, 1829–1979*, edited by Deutsches Archäologisches Institut, 108–20. Mainz: P. von Zabern.

Bernard, Paul, Roland Besenval, and Philippe Marquis. 2006. "Du 'mirage bactrien' aux réalitiés archéologiques: Nouvelles fouilles de la Délégation archéologique française en Afghanistan (DAFA) à Bactres (2004–2005)." *CRAI* 150:1175–1248.

Bernshtam, Aleksander N. 1951. *Ocherk istorii gunnov*. Leningrad: Izd-vo. Leningradskogo gos. universiteta.

Berrada, Khalid. 2006. *Metaphors of Lights and Darkness in the Holy Quran: A Conceptual Approach*. https://www.flbenmsik.ma/data/bassamat/basamat1/Berrada.pdf.

Berzina, S. I. 1984. "Kushana Coins in Axum." *Information Bulletin of the International Association for the Study of the Cultures of Central Asia* 7:57–64.

Bhattacharya-Haesner, Chhaya. 2003. *Central Asian Temple Banners in the Turfan Collection of the Museum für Indische Kunst*. Berlin: Reimar.

Biggam, C. P. 2002. "Knowledge of Whelk Dyes and Pigments in Anglo-Saxon England." In *Anglo-Saxon England 35*, edited by Malcolm Goddena and Simon Keynes, 23–57. Cambridge: Cambridge University Press.

Bingheimer, Marcus. 2004. "Translation of the Tōdaiwajō tōseiden 唐大和上東征傳 (Part 2)." *Indian International Journal of Buddhist Studies* 5:142–81.

Binyon, R. L. 1910. *Guide to an Exhibition of Chinese and Japanese Paintings (Fourth to Nineteenth Century AD) in the Print and Drawing Gallery*. London: British Museum, Department of Prints and Drawings.

Biran, Michael. [2004] 2012. "Ilak-Khanids." In *Encyclopaedia Iranica Online*. Last updated March 27. www.iranicaonline.org/articles/ilak-khanids.

Bivar, A. D. H. 1972. "Cavalry Equipment and Tactics on the Euphrates Frontier." *Dumbarton Oaks Papers* 26:273–91.

———. [2003] 2012. "Hephthalites." In *Encyclopaedia Iranica Online*. Last updated March 22. www.iranicaonline.org/articles/hephthalites.

Blair, Sheila S., and Jonathan M. Bloom. 1994. *The Art and Architecture of Islam, 1250–1800*. New Haven, CT: Yale University Press.

Blockley, R. C., trans. 1985. *The History of Menander the Guardsman*. Liverpool: Francis Cairns.

Bloom, Jonathan M. 2001. *Paper before Print: The History and Impact of Paper in the Islamic World*. New Haven, CT: Yale University Press.

———. 2015. "The Blue Koran Revisited." *Journal of Islamic Manuscripts* 6 (2–3): 196–218.

Bloom, Jonathan M., and Sheila Blair. 2011. "Introduction: Color in Islamic Art and Culture." In *Diverse Are Their Hues: Color in Islamic Art and Culture*, edited by Jonathan M. Bloom and Sheila S. Blair, 1–52. New Haven, CT: Yale University Press.

Boardman, John. 2012. "Tillya Tepe: Echoes of Greece and China." In Aruz and Fino 2012: 102–11.

Boehm, Barbara Drake. [2001] 2011. "Relics and Reliquaries in Medieval Christianity." Heilbrunn Timeline of Art History, April. Metropolitan Museum of Art. www.metmuseum.org/toah/hd/relc/hd_relc.htm.

Boesken Kanold, Inge. 2005. "The Purple Fermentation Vat: Dyeing or Painting Parchment with *Murex trunculus*." In *Dyes in History and Archaeology 20: Including Papers Presented at the 20th Meeting, Held at the Instituut Collectiie Nederland, Amsterdam, the Netherlands, 1–2 November 2001*, edited by J. Kirkby 150–54. London: Archetype.

Bonnet-Bidaud, Jean-Marc, Françoise Praderie, and Susan Whitfield. 2009. "The Dunhuang Sky: A Comprehensive Study of the Oldest Known Star Atlas." *Journal of Astronomical History and Heritage* 12:39–59. http://idp.bl.uk/education/astronomy_researchers/index.a4d.

Borell, Brigitte. 2010. "Trade and Glass Vessels along the Maritime Silk Road." In *Glass along the Silk Road from 200 BC to 1000 AD*, edited by Bettina Zorn and Alexandra Hilger, 127–42. Darmstadt: Betz-Druck.

———. 2011. "Han Period Glass Vessels in the Early Tongking Gulf Region." In *The Tongking Gulf through History*, edited by Nola Cooke, Li Tana, and James A. Anderson, 53–66. Philadelphia: University of Pennsylvania Press.

Borovka, Gregory. 1928. *Scythian Art*. Translated by V. G. Childe. London: Ernest Benn.

Bosworth, C. E. 2012. "Maḥmūd b. Sebüktigin." In *Encyclopaedia Iranica Online*. Last updated December 21. www.iranicaonline.org/articles/mahmud-b-sebuktegin.

Bracey, Robert. 2009. "The Coinage of Wima Kadphises." *Gandharan Studies* 3:25–75.

———. 2012. "The Mint Cities of the Kushan Empire." In *The City and the Coin in the Ancient and Early Medieval Worlds*, edited by Fernando López Sánchez, 117–29. Oxford: Archaeopress.

Braghin, Cecilia, ed. 2002. *Chinese Glass: Archaeological Studies on the Uses and*

Social Context of Glass Artefacts from the Warring States to the Northern Song Period. Orientalia Venetiana 14. Florence: Leo S. Olschki.

Bray, Francesca. 1997. *Technology and Gender: Fabrics of Power in Late Imperial China*. Berkeley: University of California Press.

Brill, Robert H. 1991–92. "Some Thoughts on the Origins of the Chinese Word 'Boli.'" *Silk Road Art and Archaeology* 2:129–36.

———. 1995. "Scientific Research in Early Asian Glass." In *Proceedings of XVII International Congress on Glass*, vol. 1, *Invited Lectures*, 270–79. Beijing: Chinese Ceramic Society.

———. 1999. *Chemical Analyses of Early Glasses*. Vol. 2. *Table of Analyses*. Corning, NY: Corning Museum of Glass.

Brill, Robert H., and J. H. Martin, eds. 1991. *Scientific Research in Early Chinese Glass: Proceedings of the Archaeometry of Glass Sessions of the 1984 International Symposium on Glass. Beijing, September 7, 1984*. Corning, NY: Corning Museum of Glass.

Brill, Robert H., S. S. C. Tong, and D. Dohrenwend. 1991. "Chemical Analyses of Some Early Chinese Glasses." In Brill and Martin 1991: 31–58.

Brindley, Erica Fox. 2015. *Ancient China and the Yue*. Cambridge: Cambridge University Press.

British Museum. 1914. *Guide to an Exhibition of Paintings, Manuscripts and Other Archaeological Objects Collected by Sir Aurel Stein K.C.I.E. in Chinese Turkestan*. London: Trustees of the British Museum.

Bromberg, Carol A. 1983. "Sasanian Stucco Influence: Sorrento and East-West." *Orientalia Lovaniensia Periodica* 14:247–67.

Brosseder, Ursula. 2011. "Belt Plaques as an Indicator of East-West Relations in the Eurasian Steppe at the Turn of the Millennia." In Brosseder and Miller 2011: 349–424.

Brosseder, Ursula, and Bryan K. Miller, eds. 2011. *Xiongnu Archaeology: Multidisciplinary Perspectives of the First Steppe Empire in Inner Asia*. Bonn: Vor und Frühgeschichtliche Archäologie Rheniische Freidrich-Wilhelms-Universität.

Broudy, Eric. 1979. *The Book of Looms: A History of the Handloom from Ancient Times to the Present*. Lebanon, NH: University Press of New England.

Brown, Michelle P., ed. 2006. *In the Beginning: Bibles before the Year 1000*. Washington, DC: Smithsonian Books.

Brubaker, Leslie, and John Haldon. 2011. "Byzantium in the Iconoclast Era, c.680–850." *English Historical Review* 127 (528): 1182–84.

Bryce, Trevor. 2014. *Ancient Syria: A Three Thousand Year History*. Oxford: Oxford University Press.

Buck, Bruce. A. 1982. "Ancient Technology in Contemporary Surgery." *Western Journal of Medicine* 136 (3): 265–69.

Bunker, Emma C. 1983. "Sources of Foreign Elements in the Culture of Eastern Zhou." In *The Great Bronze Age of China: A Symposium*, edited by George Kuwayama, 84–93. Seattle: University of Washington Press.

———. 1988. "Lost Wax and Lost Textile: An Unusual Ancient Technique for Casting Gold Belt Plaques." In *The Beginning of the Use of Metals and Alloys*, edited by Robert Maddin, 222–27. Cambridge, MA: MIT Press.

———. 1997. *Ancient Bronzes of the Eastern Eurasian Steppes from the Arthur M. Sackler Collections*. New York: Arthur M. Sackler Foundation.

Bunker, Emma C., Bruce Chatwin, and Ann R. Farkas. 1970. *"Animal Style": Art from East to West*. New York: Asia Society.

Bunker, Emma C., James C. Y. Watt, and Zhixin Sun. 2002. *Nomadic Art from the Eastern Eurasian Steppes: The Eugene V. Thaw and Other New York Collections*. New York: Metropolitan Museum of Art.

Burrow, Thomas. 1940. *A Translation of the Kharosthi Documents from Chinese Turkestan*. London: Royal Asiatic Society.

Buzurg ibn Shahriyār. 1928. *The Book of the Marvels of India*. Translated by Devic, L. Marcel and Peter Quennell. London: Routledge & Sons.

Callcott, Maria. 1842. *A Scripture Herbal*. London: Longman, Brown, Green, & Longmans.

Callieri, Pierfrancesco. 1996. "Hephthalites in Margiana? New Evidence from the Buddhist Relics in Merv." In *La Perse e l'Asie centrale da Alessandro al X secolo*, 391–400. Atti dei convvegni Lincei 127. Rome: Academia Nazionale dei Lincei.

———, ed. 2006. *Architetti, capomastri, artigiani: L'organizzazione dei cantieri e della produzione artistica nell'Asia ellenistica: Studi offerti a Domenico Faccenna nel suo ottantesimo compleanno*. Rome: Istituto italiano per l'Africa e l'Oriente.

———. 2007. "Barikot: An Indo-Greek Urban Center in Gandhara." In Srinivasan 2007: 133–64.

Cameron, Catherine M. 2011. "Captives and Cultural Change: Implications for Archaeology." *Current Anthropology* 52 (2): 169–209.

———. 2016. *Captives: How Stolen People Changed the World*. Lincoln: University of Nebraska Press.

Canard, M. 2012. "Ayn Zarba." In *The Encyclopaedia of Islam*, 2nd ed., edited by P. Bearman, Th. Bianquis, C. E. Bosworth, E. van Donzel, and W. P. Heinrichs. http://brillonline.nl/entries/encyclopaedia-of-islam-2/ayn-zarba-SIM_0917?s.num=89&s.rows=50&s.start=80.

Canby, Sheila. 2012. "The Qur'an." *Islamic Arts and Architecture*, April 3. http://islamic-arts.org/2012/the-qur%E2%80%99an/.

Capp, Bernard. 1979. *English Almanacs, 1500–1800: Astrology and the Popular Press*. Ithaca, NY: Cornell University Press.

Cardon, Dominique. 2007. *Natural Dyes: Sources, Tradition, Technology and Science*. London: Archetype Publications.

Carlà, Filippo. 2012. "Horses, Greece and Rome." In *The Encyclopedia of Ancient History*. Wiley Online Library. DOI: 10.1002/9781444338386.wbeah06166.

Carter, M. L. 1974. "Royal, Festal Themes in Sasanian Silverware and Their Central Asian Parallels." *Acta Iranica* 1:171–202.

Cartwright, Caroline R., Christina M. Duffy, and Helen Wang. 2014. "Microscopical Examination of Fibres Used in Ming Dynasty Paper Money." *British Museum Technical Research Bulletin* 8:105–16.

Cashion, Debra Taylor. 2016. "Broken Books." *Manuscript Studies: A Journal of the Schoenberg Institute for Manuscript Studies* 1 (2): 342–52.

Casselman, Karen Diadick, and Takako Terada. 2012. "The Politics of Purple: Dyes from Shellfish and Lichens." Paper 666, Symposium Proceedings of the Textile Society of America. http://digitalcommons.unl.edu/cgi/viewcontent.cgi?article =1665&context=tsaconf.

Chakrabarti, D. K. 1995. "Buddhist Sites across South Asia as Influenced by Political and Economic Forces." *World Archaeology* 27:185–202.

Chang, Claudia. 2008. "Mobility and Sedentism of the Iron Age Agropastoralists of Southeast Kazakhstan." In *The Archaeology of Mobility: Old World and New World Nomadism*, edited by Hans Barnard and Willeke Wendrich, 329–42. Los Angeles: Cotsen Institute of Archaeology, University of California, Los Angeles.

Chang, Claudia, Norbert Benecke, Fedor P. Grigoriev, and Perry Tourtellotte. 2003. "Iron Age Society and Chronology in South-East Kazakhstan." *Antiquity* 73 (296): 298–312.

Chavannes, Édouard. 1903a. *Documents sur les Tou-Kiue (Turcs) occidentaux recueillis et commentés par E. Chavannes*. Paris: Librairie d'Amérique et d'Orient Adrien Maisonneuve.

———. 1903b. "Le voyage de Song Yun dans l'Udyana et le Gandhara." *Bulletin de l'École Française d'Extrême Orient* 3:379–441.

———. 1907. "Chinese Inscriptions and Records." Appendix A in *Serindia: Detailed Report of Explorations in Central Asia and Westernmost China*, edited by Marc Aurel Stein, 1329–39. Oxford: Oxford University Press.

Chavannes, Édouard, and Sylvain Lévi. 1895. "L'itinéraire d'Ou-k'ong (751–90)." *Journal Asiatique*, n.s., 6 (9): 341–84.

Chin, Tamara T. 2010. "Familiarizing the Foreigner: Sima Qian's Ethnography and Han-Xiongnu Marriage Diplomacy." *Harvard Journal of Asiatic Studies* 70 (2): 311–54.

———. 2013. "The Invention of the Silk Road, 1877." *Critical Inquiry* 40 (1): 194–219.

Chittick, Neville. 1974. "Excavations at Aksum 1973–74: A Preliminary Report." *Azania* 9:159–205.

Choi, Charles Q. 2017. "Oldest Evidence of Silk Found in 8,500-Year-Old Tombs." *LiveScience*, January 10. https://www.livescience.com/57437-oldest-evidence-of-silk-found-china.html.

Christian, David. 1994. "Inner Eurasia as a Unit of World History." *Journal of World History* 5 (2): 173–211.

———. 1998. *A History of Russia, Central Asia and Mongolia*. Vol. 1. *Inner Eurasia from Prehistory to the Mongol Empire*. Oxford: Blackwell.

Cline, E. H. 1994. *Sailing the Wine-Dark Sea: International Trade and the Late Bronze Age Aegean*. Oxford: Tempus Reparatum.

Cohen, Ada. 2010. *Art in the Era of Alexander the Great: Paradigms of Manhood and Their Cultural Traditions*. Cambridge: Cambridge University Press.

Cohen, Monique, ed. 1996. *Sérinde, Terre de Bouddha*. Paris: Réunion des Musées Nationaux.

Colledge, Malcolm A. R. 1986. *The Parthian Period*. Leiden: E. J. Brill.

Compareti, M. 2004. "The Sasanian and the Sogdian 'Pearl Roundel' Design: Remarks on an Iranian Decorative Pattern." *Study of Art History* 6:259–72.

———. 2006a. "The Role of the Sogdian Colonies in the Diffusion of the Pearl Roundel Designs." In *Ērān ud Anērān: Studies Presented to Boris Maršak on the Occasion of His 70th Birthday*, edited by M. Compareti, P. Raffetta, and G. Scarcia, 149–74. Venice: Cafoscarina.

———. 2006b. "Textile Patterns in Sogdian Painting: The Sasanian and the Local Components." In *Ancient and Mediaeval Culture of the Bukhara Oasis*, edited by C. Silvi Antonini and D. K. Mirzaahmedov, 60–68. Samarkand: Institute of Archaeology of the Academy of Sciences of the Republic of Uzbekstan; Rome: Rome University.

———. 2009. "Sasanian Textiles." In *Encyclopaedia Iranica Online*. Last updated December 15. www.iranicaonline.org/articles/sasanian-textiles.

———. 2012. "Classical Elements in Sogdian Art: Aesop's Fables Represented in the Mural Paintings at Panjikant." *Iranica Antiqua* 47:303–16.

Constable, Olivia Remie. 1996. *Trade and Traders in Muslim Spain: The Commercial Realignment of the Iberian Peninsula, 900–1500*. Cambridge: Cambridge University Press.

Cope, Barry. 1999. "Transparent Plastic Film Materials for Document Conservation." *IDP [International Dunhuang Project] News* 14. http://idp.bl.uk/archives/news14/idpnews_14.a4d#3.

Cosmas Indicopleustes. 1897. *Christian Topography*. Translated by Father Montfaucon. www.tertullian.org/fathers/cosmas_00_2_intro.htm.

Cowell, E. B., ed. Robert Chalmer, W. H. D. Rouse, H. T. Francis, and R. A. Neil, trans. 1895. *The Jataka*. 6 vols. Cambridge: Cambridge University Press. http://sacred-texts.com/bud/j1/index.htm.

Craddock, Paul T. 2009. *Scientific Investigation of Copies, Fakes and Forgeries*. London: Routledge.

Creel, H. G. 1965. "The Role of the Horse in Chinese History." *American Historical Review* 70 (3): 647–72.

Cribb, Joe. 1984. "The Sino-Kharosthi Coins of Khotan: Their Attribution and Relevance to Kushan Chronology: Part 1." *Numismatic Chronicle* 144:128–52.

———. 1985. "The Sino-Kharosthi Coins of Khotan: Their Attribution and Relevance to Kushan Chronology: Part 2." *Numismatic Chronicle* 145:136–49.

———. 1997. "Siva Images on Kushan and Kushano-Sassanian Coins." *Silk Road Art and Archaeology* 6:11–66.

———. 2009. "Money as Metaphor: 4a." *Numismatic Chronicle* 169:461–529.

Crill, Rosemary. 2015. *The Fabric of India*. London: Victoria and Albert Museum.

Crone, Patricia. 1980. *Slaves on Horses: The Evolution of the Islamic Polity*. Cambridge: Cambridge University Press.

Curci, Meliora di. 2003. "The History and Technology of Parchment Making." Society for Creative Anachronism. https://www.sca.org.au/scribe/articles/parchment.htm.

Curta, Florin. 2001. *The Making of the Slavs: History and Archaeology of the Lower Danube Region c.500–700.* Cambridge: Cambridge University Press.

Cutler, Anthony. 2008. "Significant Gifts: Patterns of Exchange in Late Antique, Byzantine and Early Islamic Diplomacy." *Journal of Medieval and Early Modern Studies* 38:79–101.

Dani, A. H., B. A. Litvinsky, and M. H. Zamir Safi. 1996. "Eastern Kushans, Kidarities in Gandhara and Kashmir, and Later Hephthalites." In Litvinsky, Zhang Guang-da, and Samghabadi 1996: 163–84.

Dauphin, Claudine. 1996. "Brothels, Baths and Babes: Prostitution in the Byzantine Holy Land." *Classics Ireland* 3:47–72.

Davis, Lisa Fagin. 2015. "Hangest's Codex, Duschnes' Knife: The Beauvais Missal as a Case Study in Digital Surrogacy." Paper presented at the Eighth Annual Schoenberg Symposium for Manuscript Studies, Philadelphia, November 12–14. In YouTube video of the symposium at https://www.youtube.com/playlist?list=PL8e3GREuozuC5qTU-lr-V4-ZQiatChYpR.

Davydova, Anthonyna, and Sergey Miniaev. 2008. *The Xiongnu Decorative Bronzes.* St. Petersburg: GAMAS.

Deane, H. A. 1896. "Note on Udyāna and Gandhāra." *Journal of the Royal Asiatic Society* 28 (4): 655–77.

Debaine-Francfort, Corinne, and Abduressul Idriss, eds. 2001. *Keriya, mémoires d'un fleuve: Archéologie et civilisation des oasis du Taklamakan.* Paris: Findakly.

Dehejia, Vidya. 1992. "The Collective and Popular Basis of Early Buddhist Patronage: Sacred Monuments, 100 BC–AD 250." In *The Powers of Arts: Patronage in Indian Culture,* edited by Barbara Stoler Miller, 35–45. Delhi: Oxford University Press.

Demiéville, Paul. 1952. *Le Concile de Lhasa: Une controverse sur le quiétisme entre bouddhistes de l'Inde et de la Chine au VIIIe siècle de l'ère chrétienne.* Paris: Presses universitaires de France.

Deng Wenkuan 鄧文寬. 1996. *Dunhuang tianwen lifa wenxie jijiao* 敦煌天文曆法文獻輯校. Nanjing: Jiangsu guji chubanshe.

———. 2001. "Dunhuang ben *Tang Qianfu sinian dingyou sui (877 nian) juzhu liri 'zazhan' bulu*" 敦煌本唐乾符四年丁酉歲 (877年) 具注曆日雜占補錄. In *Dunhuangxue yu Zhongguo shi yanjiu lunji: Jinian Sun Xiushen xiansheng shishi yi zhounian* 敦煌学与中国史研究论集: 纪念孙修身先生逝世一周年, edited by Duan Wenjie and Masahiro Mogi 段文杰. 茂木雅博, 135–45. Lanzhou: Gansu remin chubanshe.

Déroche, Francoise. 2006. "Written Transmission." In *The Blackwell Companion to the Qur'an,* edited by Andrew Rippin, 172–86. Oxford: Wiley-Blackwell.

Desrosiers, Sophie. 1994. "La soierie méditeranénne." *Revue du Musée des Arts et Métiers* 7:51–58.

———. 2004. *Soieries et autres textiles de l'antiquité au XVIe siècle.* Paris: Reunion des Musées Nationaux.

Des Rotours, Robert, trans. 1947. *Traité des Fonctionnaires et Traité de l'Armée, traduits de la Nouvelle Histoire des T'ang (chap. XLVI–L).* Leiden: Brill.

Di Cosmo, Nicola. 1994. "Ancient Inner Asian Nomads: Their Economic Basis and Its Significance in Chinese History." *Journal of Asian Studies* 53 (4): 1092–1126.

———. 1996. "Ancient Xinjiang between Central Asia and China." *Anthropology and Archeology of Eurasia* 34 (4): 87-101.

———. 1999. "The Northern Frontier in Pre-Imperial China." In *Cambridge History of Ancient China*, edited by Michael Loewe and Edward L. Shaughnessy, 885–966. Cambridge: Cambridge University Press.

———. 2002. *Ancient China and Its Enemies: The Rise of Nomadic Power in East Asian History*. Cambridge: Cambridge University Press.

———. 2013. "Aristocratic Elites in the Xiongnu Empire as Seen from Historical and Archeological Evidence." In *Nomad Aristocrats in a World of Empires*, edited by Jürgen Paul, 23–53. Wiesbaden: Reichert.

Dien, Albert. 1991. "A New Look at the Xianbei and Their Impact on Chinese Culture." In *Ancient Mortuary Traditions of China: Papers on Chinese Ceramic Funerary Sculptures*, edited by George Kuwayama, 40–59. Los Angeles: Los Angeles County Museum of Art.

———. 2000. "The Stirrup and Its Effect on Chinese History." Silk Road Foundation. http://silkroadfoundation.org/artl/stirrup.shtml.

Diringer, David. 1982. *The Book before Printing: Ancient, Medieval and Oriental*. New York: Dover Publications.

Dode, Zvezdana. 2016. " 'Zandaniji Silks.' The Story of a Myth." *The Silk Road* 14: 213–222. Available at http://www.silkroadfoundation.org/newsletter/vol14/Dode_SR14_2016_213_222.pdf.

Dowman, Keith, trans. 1973. *Legend of the Great Stupa*. Berkeley: Dharma Press. www.sacred-texts.com/bud/tib/stupa.htm.

Drège, Jean-Paul. 1991. *Les bibliothèques en Chine au temps des manuscrits (jusqu'au Xe siècle)*. Publications de l'École française d'Extrême-Orient 156. Paris: École française d'Extrême-Orient.

———. 2002. "Dunhuang Papers: Preliminary Morphological Analysis of Dated Chinese Manuscripts." In *Dunhuang Manuscript Forgeries*, edited by Susan Whitfield, 115–79. London: British Library. Introduction downloadable at http://idp.bl.uk/downloads/Forgeries.pdf.

Dreibholz, Ursula. 1997. "Some Aspects of Bookbindings from the Great Mosque of Sana'a, Yemen." In *Scribes et manuscrits du Moyen-Orient*, edited by François Déroche and Francis Richards, 15–34. Paris: Bibliothèque nationale de France.

Dubin, Lois Sherr. 2009. *The History of Beads: From 100,000 BC to the Present*. Rev. ed. New York: Abrams.

Durand, Maximilien. 2014. "Suaire de saint Austremoine, dit aussi 'Suaire de Mozac.'" Description for online catalog, Musée des Tissus / Musée des Arts Decoratifs de Lyon (MTMAD). www.mtmad.fr.

During Caspers, E. C. L. 1979. "Sumer, Coastal Arabia and the Indus Valley in the Protoliterate and Early Dynastic Eras." *Journal of the Economic and Social History of the Orient* 22 (2): 121–35.

Easthaugh, Nicholas, Valentine Walsh, Tracey Chaplin, and Ruth Siddall. 2007. *Pigment Compendium: A Dictionary of Historical Pigments*. London: Routledge.

Easton, D. F., J. D. Hawkins, A. G. Sherratt, and E. S. Sherratt. 2002. "Troy in Recent Perspective." *Anatolian Studies* 52:75–109.

Eberhard, Wolfram. 1957. "The Political Function of Astronomy and Astronomers in Han China." In *Chinese Thought and Institutions*, edited by John K. Fairbank, 33–70. Chicago: University of Chicago Press.

Eck, Diana L. 2013. *India: A Sacred Geography*. London: Three Rivers Press.

Edward of Norwich. 2013. *The Master of Game*. Edited by William A. Baillie-Grohman and F. N. Baillie-Grohman. Philadelphia: University of Pennsylvannia Press.

Eilers, W. [1983] 2011. "Abrīšam: i. Etymology." In *Encyclopaedia Iranica Online*. Last updated July 19. www.iranicaonline.org/articles/abrisam-silk-index.

Emmerick, Ronald F. 1967. *Tibetan Texts Concerning Khotan*. Oxford: Oxford University Press.

———. 1968. *The Book of Zambasta: A Khotanese Poem on Buddhism*. Oxford: Oxford University Press.

———. 1983. "Buddhism among Iranian Peoples." In *The Cambridge History of Iran*, Vol. 3(2), *The Seleucid, Parthian and Sasanian Periods*, edited by Ehsan Yarshater, 949–64. Cambridge: Cambridge University Press.

Emmerick, Ronald F., and Oktor Skjærvø. 1990. "Buddhism: iii. Buddhist Literature in Khotanese and Tumshuqese." In *Encyclopaedia Iranica Online*. www.iranicaonline.org/articles/buddhism-iii.

Enoki, Kazuo. 1959. "On the Nationality of the Ephtalites." *Memoirs of the Research Department of the Toyo Bunko* 18:1–58.

Erdenebaatar, Diimaazhav, Tömör-Ochir Iderkhangai, Baatar Galbadrakh, Enkh-baiar Minzhiddorzh, and Samdanzhamts Orgilbaiar. 2011. "Excavations of Satellite Burial 30, Tomb 1 Complex, Gol Mod 2 Necropolis." In Brosseder and Miller 2011: 303–13.

Erickson, Susan M. 2010. "Han Dynasty Tomb Structures and Contents." In Nylan and Loewe 2010: 13–82.

Erickson, Susan M., Yi Song-mi, and Michael Nylan. 2010. "The Archaeology of the Outlying Lands." In Nylan and Loewe 2010: 135–68.

Erkes, Eduard. 1940. "Das Pferd im alten China." *T'oung Pao* 36:26–63.

Errington, Elizabeth. 2000. "Numismatic Evidence for Dating the Buddhist Remains of Gandhara." *Silk Road Art and Archaeology* 6:191–216.

Esin, Emil. 1965. "The Horse in Turkic Art." *Central Asiatic Journal* 10:167–227.

Ess, Hans Van. 1994. "The Old Text/New Text Controversy: Has the 20th Century Got It Wrong?" *T'oung Pao* 80:146–70.

Ettinghausen, Richard. 1967–68. "A Persian Treasure." *Arts in Virginia* 8:29–41.

Evans, Helen C., and Brandie Ratliff, eds. 2012. *Byzantium and Islam: Age of Transition*. New York: Metropolitan Museum of Art.

Eze, Anne-Marie. 2016. "'Safe from Destruction by Fire': Isabelle Stewart Gardner's

Venetian Manuscripts." *Manuscript Studies: A Journal for the Schoenberg Institute for Manuscript Studies* 1 (2): 189–215.

Faccenna, C., L. Olivieri, S. Lorenzoni, and E. Lorenzoni Zanettin. 1993. "Geoarcheology of the Swat Valley (N.W.F.P. Pakistan) in the Charbag-Barikot Stretch: Preliminary Note." *East and West* 41 (1–4): 257–70.

Faccenna, Domenico. 2007. "The Artistic Center of Butkara I and Saidu Sharif I in the Pre-Kusana Period." In Srinivasan 2007: 165–200.

Faccenna, Domenico, and Piero Spagnesi. 2014. *Buddhist Architecture in the Swat Valley, Pakistan: Stupas, Viharas, a Dwelling Unit.* Lahore: Sang-e-Meel Publications.

Falk, Harry. 2006. *Aśokan Sites and Artefacts: A Source-Book with Bibliography.* Mainz: P. von. Zabern.

———. 2009. "Making Wine in Gandhara under Buddhist Monastic Supervision." *Bulletin of the Asia Institute* 23:65–78.

———. 2012. "Ancient Indian Eras: An Overview." *Bulletin of the Asia Institute* 21:131–45.

———. 2014a. "Kushan Dynasty iii. Chronology of the Kushans." In *Encyclopaedia Iranica.* December 8. www.iranicaonline.org/articles/kushan-03-chronology.

———. 2014b. "Owners' Graffiti on Pottery from Tissamaharama." *Zeitschrift für Archäologie außereuropäischer Kulturen* 6:45–94.

———. 2015. *Across the Ocean: Nine Essays on Indo-Mediterranean Trade.* Leiden: Brill.

Fan Shimin and Zhou Baozhong. 1991. "Some Glass in the Museum of Chinese History." In Brill and Martin 1991: 193–200.

Fedorko, Motrja P. 2000. "Museum Exhibitions: Comparing the Two Scythian Shows in NYC." *Ukranian Weekly,* December 17. www.ukrweekly.com/old/archive/2000/510025.shtml.

Ferreira, Ester S. B., Alison N. Hulme, Hamish McNab, and Anita Quye. 2004. "The Natural Constituents of Historical Textile Dyes." *Chemical Society Reviews* 33:329–36.

Festival of Empire. 1911. *Indian Court, Festival of Empire, 1911: Guide Book and Catalogue.* London: Bemrose & Sons.

Fiddyment, Sarah, et al. 2015. "The Animal Origin of Thirteenth-Century Uterine Vellum Revealed Using Non-invasive Peptide Fingerprinting." *PNAS* 112 (49): 15066–71. www.pnas.org/content/112/49/15066.short.

Findley, Carter V. 2005. *The Turks in World History.* Oxford: Oxford University Press.

Finkelman, Paul, and Joseph Calder Miller. 1998. *Macmillan Encyclopedia of World Slavery.* Vol. 2. New York: Macmillan Reference USA.

Finneran, Niall. 2007. *The Archaeology of Ethiopia.* London: Routledge.

Firdausi. 1915. *The Sháhnáma of Firdausi.* Vol. 7. Translated by Arthur George Warner and Edmond Warner. London: Kegan Paul, Trench, Trübner. https://ia801500.us.archive.org/21/items/in.ernet.dli.2015.82395/2015.82395.The-Shahnama-Of-Firdausi-7.pdf.

Forand, Paul G. 1971. "The Relation of the Slave and the Client to the Master or Patron in Medieval Islam." *International Journal of Middle East Studies* 2 (1): 59–66.

Forêt, Philippe. 2013. "Climate Change: A Challenge to the Geographers of Central Asia." *Perspectives*, no. 9. http://rfiea.fr/en/articles/climate-change-challenge-geographers-colonial-asia.

Foucher, Alfred. 1942–47. *La vieille route de l'Inde de Bactres à Taxila: Mémoires de la Délégation archéologique française en Afghanistan*. Paris: Éditions d'art et d'histoire.

Frachetti, Michael D. 2011. "Seeds for the Soul: East/West Diffusion of Domesticated Grains." Lecture presented at the Silk Road Symposium, Penn Museum, Philadelphia, March 2011. https://www.penn.museum/collections/videos/video/999.

Frachetti, Michael D., Robert N. Spengler III, Gayle J. Fritz, and Alexei N. Mar'yashev. 2010. "Earliest Direct Evidence for Broomcorn Millet and Wheat in the Central Eurasian Steppe Region." *Antiquity* 84:993–1010.

Francis, Peter. 2002. *Asia's Maritime Bead Trade: 300 B. C. to the Present*. Honolulu: University of Hawaii Press.

Fraser, Marcus, and Will Kwiatkowski. 2006. *Ink and Gold: Islamic Calligraphy*. London: Sam Fogg.

Frumkin, Grégoire. 1970. *Archaeology in Soviet Central Asia*. Leiden: Brill.

Frye, Richard N. 2012. *The Heritage of Central Asia*. Princeton, NJ: Markus Wiener.

Fujieda, Akira. 1973. "Tonko rekijitsu fu." *Tōhō Gakuhō* 45:377–441.

Fussman, Gérard. 1986. "Symbolism of the Buddhist Stūpa." *Journal of the International Association of Buddhist Studies* 9 (2): 37–93.

Galambos, Imre, trans. 2009. *Translation of the Dunhuang Star Chart (Or.8210/S.3326)*. London: IDP. http://idp.bl.uk/database/oo_cat.a4d?shortref=Galambos_2009.

Galambos, Imre, and Sam van Schaik. 2012. *Manuscripts and Travellers: The Sino-Tibetan Documents of a Tenth-Century Buddhist Pilgrim*. Studies in Manuscript Cultures 2. Berlin: De Gruyter.

Gamble, Harry Y. 2006. "Bible and Book." In Brown 2006: 15–36.

Gan Fuxi. 2009a. "Origin and Evolution of Ancient Chinese Glass." In Gan, Brill, and Tian 2009: 1–40.

———. 2009b. "The Silk Road and Ancient Chinese Glass." In Gan, Brill, and Tian 2009: 41–108.

Gan Fuxi, Robert H. Brill, and Tian Shouyun, eds. 2009. *Ancient Chinese Glass Research along the Silk Road*. Singapore: World Scientific Publishing.

Gan Fuxi, H. Cheng, Y. Hu, H. Ma, and D. Gu. 2009. "Study on the Most Early Glass Eye-Beads in China Unearthed from Xu Jialing Tomb in Xuchuan of Henan Province, China." *Science in China Series E: Technological Sciences* 52 (4): 922–27.

Geary, Patrick J. 1978. *Furta Sacra: Thefts of Relics in the Central Middle Ages*. Princeton, NJ: Princeton University Press.

Geertz, Clifford. 1973. "Thick Description: Towards an Interpretative Theory of Culture." In *Selected Essays*, 3–20. New York: Basic Books. www.sociosite.net/topics/texts/Geertz_Think_Description.php.

George, Alain. 2009. "Calligraphy, Colour and Light in the Blue Qur'an." *Journal of Qur'anic Studies* 11 (1): 75–125.

———. 2010. *The Rise of Islamic Calligraphy*. London: Saqi.

Gernet, Jacques. 1995. *Buddhism in Chinese Society*. Translated by Franciscus Verellen. New York: Columbia University Press.

Gibbs, Peter J., and Kenneth R. Seddon. 1998. *Berberine and Huangbo: Ancient Chinese Colorants and Dyes*. London: British Library.

Giles, Herbert A., trans. 1923. *The Travels of Fa-hsien (399–414 AD), or Record of the Buddhistic Kingdoms*. Cambridge: Cambridge University Press.

Giles, Lionel. 1939. "Dated Chinese Manuscripts in the Stein Collection, IV, Ninth Century." *Bulletin of the School of Oriental and African Studies* 9 (4): 1023–46.

———. 1940. "Dated Chinese Manuscripts in the Stein Collection, V, Tenth Century." *Bulletin of the School of Oriental and African Studies* 10 (2): 317–44.

———. 1943. "Dated Chinese Manuscripts in the Stein Collection, VI, Tenth Century." *Bulletin of the School of Oriental and African Studies* 11 (1): 148–73.

Gledhill, John, and Henrike Donner. 2017. *World Anthropologies in Practice: Situated Perspectives, Global Knowledge*. London: Bloomsbury.

Glover, Ian. 2004. *Southeast Asia: From Prehistory to History*. London: Psychology Press.

Göbl, Robert. 1957. "Die Münzprägung der Kusan von Vima Kadphises bis Bahram IV." In *Finanzgeschichte der Spätantike*, edited by Franz Altheim and Ruth Stiehl, 173–256. Frankfurt: V. Klostermann.

———. 1967. *Dokumente zur Geschichte der iranischen Hunnen in Baktrien und Indien*. 4 vols. Wiesbaden: Harrassowitz.

———. 1970. "Der Kusanische Goldmünzschatz von Debra Damo (Aithiopien) 1940 (Vima Kadphises bis Vasudeva I)." *Central Asiatic Journal* 14 (1): 241–52.

———. 1984. *System und Chronologie der Münzprägung des Kušānreiches*. Vienna: Verlag der Österreichischen Akademie der Wissenschaften.

Goldin, Paul R. 2011. "Steppe Nomads as a Philosophical Problem in Classical China." In *Mapping Mongolia: Situating Mongolia in the World from Geologic Time to the Present*, edited by Paul L. W. Sabloff, 220–46. Philadelphia: University of Pennsylvania Press.

Gommans, Josh J. L. 1995. *The Rise of the Indo-Afghan Empire c.1710–1780*. Leiden: Brill.

Gomot, M. Hippolyte. 1872. *Histoire de l'Abbaye Royale de Mozat*. Paris: Libraire de la Société des Bibliophiles Français.

———. 1873–74. *Monuments historiques de l'Auvergne: Abbaye royale de Mozat (de l'ordre de Saint Benoit)*. Riom: G. Leboyer.

Good, Irene L. 2002. "The Archaeology of Early Silk." In *Silk Roads, Other Roads: Proceedings of the Eighth Biennial Symposium of the Textile Society of America,*

September 26–28, 2002, Northampton, Massachusetts, 7–15. http://digitalcom
mons.unl.edu/tsaconf/388/.

Good, Irene L., J. M. Kenoyer, and R. H. Meadow. 2009. "New Evidence for Early
Silk in the Indus Civilization." *Archaeometry,* prepublished online, January 21.

Goodrich, L. Carrington. 1967. "Printing: A New Discovery." *Journal of the Hong
Kong Branch of the Royal Asiatic Society* 7:39–41.

Gordon, Matthew S., and Kathryn A. Hain, eds. 2017. *Concubines and Courtesans:
Women and Slavery in Islamic History.* Oxford: Oxford University Press.

Graham, Timothy, and Andrew G. Watson. 1998. *The Recovery of the Past in Early
Elizabethan England: Documents by John Bale and John Joscelyn from the Circle of
Matthew Parker.* Cambridge Bibliographical Society Monograph 13. Cambridge:
Cambridge Bibliographical Society.

Gregory of Tours. 1916. *History of the Franks.* Translated by Earnest Brehaut. New
York: Columbia University Press. http://sourcebooks.fordham.edu/halsall/
basis/gregory-hist.asp.

Grenet, Frantz. 2002. "Regional Interaction in Central Asia and Northwest India
in the Kidarite and Hephthalite Periods." *Proceedings of the British Academy*
116:203–24.

Grenet, Frantz, and Zhang Guangda. 1996. "The Last Refuge of the Sogdian Religion: Dunhuang in the Ninth and Tenth Centuries." *Bulletin of the Asia Institute*
10:175–86.

Grousset, René. 1948. *De la Grèce a la Chine.* Monaco: Les Documents d'Art.

Guinta, R. 2006. "A Selection of Islamic Coins from the Excavations of Udegram,
Swat." *East and West* 56 (1–3): 237–62.

Gulácsi, Zsuzsanna. 2005. *Mediaeval Manichaean Book Art: A Codicological Study
of Iranian and Turkic Illuminated Book Fragments from 8th–11th Century East
Central Asia.* Leiden: Brill.

———. 2011. "Searching for Mani's Picture-Book in Textual and Pictorial Sources."
Transcultural Studies 1:233–62. http://heiup.uni-heidelberg.de/journals/index.
php/transcultural/article/view/6173/2966.

———. 2015. *Mani's Pictures: The Didactic Images of the Manichaeans from Sasanian
Mesopotamia to Uygur Central Asia and Tang-Ming China.* Leiden: Brill.

Halloran, Vivian Nun. 2009. *Exhibiting Slavery: The Caribbean Postmodern Novel
as Museum.* Charlottesville: University of Virginia Press.

Hansen, Valerie. 1993. "Gods on Walls: A Case of Indian Influence on Chinese Lay
Religion?" In *Religion and Society in T'ang and Sung China,* edited by Patricia
Buckley Ebrey and Peter Gregory, 75–113. Honolulu: University of Hawaii Press.

———. 1995. *Negotiating Daily Life in Traditional China: How Ordinary People
Used Contracts, 600–1400.* New Haven, CT: Yale University Press.

Harper, Donald. 2016. "Occult Miscellanies in Medieval China." In *One-Volume
Libraries: Composite and Multiple Text Manuscripts,* edited by Michael Fredrich
and Cosmia Schwarke, 305–54. Berlin: Walter de Gruyter.

Harper, Prudence Oliver. 1971. "Sources of Certain Female Representations in Sasanian Art." In *Atti del Convegno Internazionale sul tema: La Persia nel Medioevo*, 503–15. Rome: Roma Accademia Nazionale dei Lincei.

———. 1995. *Assyrian Origins: Discoveries at Ashur on the Tigris: Antiquities in the Vorderasiatisches Museum*. New York: Metropolitan Museum of Art.

Harper, Prudence Oliver, and Pieter Meyers. 1981. *Silver Vessels of the Sasanian Period I. Royal Imagery*. New York: Metropolitan Museum of Art.

Harper, Prudence Oliver, Melanie Snedcof, Holly Pittman, and Tobia Frankel. 1975. *From the Lands of the Scythians: Ancient Treasures from the Museums of the USSR, 3000 B.C.–100 B.C.* New York: Metropolitan Museum of Art.

Harris, Jonathan. 2017. *Constantinople: Capital of Byzantium*. London: Bloomsbury.

Harvey, Karen. 2009. *History and Material Culture: A Student's Guide to Approaching Alternative Sources*. New York: Routledge.

Hatke, George. 2013. *Aksum and Nubia: Warfare, Commerce, and Political Fictions in Ancient Northeast Africa*. New York: New York University Press.

Hauptmann, Andreas, Robert Madding, and Michael Prange. 2002. "On the Structure and Composition of Copper and Tin Ingots Excavated from the Shipwreck of Uluburun." *Bulletin of the American Schools of Oriental Research* 328:1–30.

Havey, F. 1907. "St. Austremonius." In *The Catholic Encyclopedia*. New York: Robert Appleton. Accessed June 13, 2015, New Advent. www.newadvent.org/cathen/02121a.htm.

Henderson, Julian. 1995. "Archaeotechnology: The Analysis of Ancient Glass Part I: Materials, Properties and Early European Glass." *Journal of Materials* 47 (11): 62–68.

———. 2013a. *Ancient Glass: An Interdisciplinary Exploration*. Cambridge: Cambridge University Press.

———. 2013b. *The Science and Archaeology of Materials: An Investigation of Inorganic Materials*. London: Routledge.

Henze, Paul B. 2000. *Layers of Time: A History of Ethiopia*. London: Hurst.

Herdan, Innes, trans. 1973. *The Three Hundred T'ang Poems*. Taipei: Far East Book.

Herrmann, Georgina. 1997. "Early and Medieval Merv: A Tale of Three Cities." *Proceedings of the British Academy* 94:1–43.

Hickman, J. 2012. "Bactrian Gold: Workshop Traditions at Tillya Tepe." In Fino 2012: 78–87.

Hicks, Dan, and Mary Carolyn Beaudry. 2010. *Oxford Handbook of Material Culture Studies*. Oxford: Oxford University Press.

Hiebert, Fredrik, and Pierre Cambon, eds. 2007. *Afghanistan: Hidden Treasures from the National Museum, Kabul*. Washington, DC: National Geographic.

Hildinger, Erik. 1997. *Warriors of the Steppe: A Military History of Central Asia, 500 B.C. to A.D. 1700*. Boston: DaCapo Press.

Hill, John E. 1988. "Notes on the Dating of Khotanese History." *Indo-Iranian Journal* 31:179–90.

———, trans. 2009. *Through the Jade Gate to Rome: A Study of the Silk Routes during the Later Han Dynasty 1st to 2nd Centuries CE: An Annotated Translation of the Chronicle on the "Western Regions" in the Hou Hanshu*. Charleston, SC: Booksurge. Earlier edition (2003) online at https://depts.washington.edu/silkroad/texts/hhshu/hou_han_shu.html.

———. 2015. *Through the Jade Gate to Rome: A Study of the Silk Routes during the later Han Dynasty 1st to 2nd Centuries CE*. 2 vols. Updated, expanded ed. CreateSpace Independent Publishing Platform.

Hirst, K. Kris. 2017. "Stable Isotope Analysis in Archaeology: A Plain English Introduction." June 17. http://archaeology.about.com/od/stableisotopes/qt/dummies.htm.

Hobbs, Lindsey. n.d. "The Islamic Codex." Ultimate History Project. http://ultimatehistoryproject.com/the-islamic-codex.html.

Hodder, Ian. 2012. *Entangled: An Archaeology of the Relationships between Humans and Things*. London: Wiley-Blackwell.

Hodges, Henry. 1992. *Technology in the Ancient World*. 2nd ed. New York: Barnes and Noble.

Hoffman, Eva R. 2007. "Pathways of Portability: Islamic and Christian Interchange from the Tenth to the Twelfth Century." In *Late Antique and Medieval Art of the Mediterranean World*, edited by Eva R. Hoffman, 317–49. Oxford: Blackwell.

Holcombe, Charles. 1999. "Trade-Buddhism: Maritime Trade, Immigration, and the Buddhist Landfall in Early Japan." *Journal of the American Oriental Society* 119 (2): 280–89.

Holloway, April. 1014. "New Study Reveal [*sic*] Origins of Elongated Skulls in the Carpathian Basin." *Ancient Origins*, April 6. www.ancient-origins.net/news-evolution-human-origins/new-study-reveal-origins-elongated-skulls-carpathian-basin-001530#ixzz3gH7nZdNv.

Holt, Frank L. 1988. *Alexander the Great and Bactria: The Formation of a Greek Frontier*. Leiden: Brill Archive.

———. 2012. "Coins: The Great Guides of the Historian." In Aruz and Fino 2012: 30–53.

Hopkirk, Peter. 2006. *Foreign Devils of the Silk Road: The Search for the Lost Treasure of Central Asia*. London: John Murray.

Huang Yilong 黄一農. 1992. Dunhuang ben juzhu liri xintan 敦煌本具注历日新探.*Xin Shixue* 新史学 3 (4): 1–56.

Hughes, Richard W. 2013. "The Rubies and Spinels of Afghanistan: A Brief History." Updated March 7. www.ruby-sapphire.com/afghanistan-ruby-spinel.htm.

Huntingdon, Ellsworth. 1906. "The Rivers of Chinese Turkestan and the Desiccation of Asia." *Geographical Journal* 28 (4): 352–67.

———. 1907. *The Pulse of Asia: A Journey in Central Asia Illustrating the Geographical Basis of History*. Boston: Houghton Mifflin.

Ibn al-Nadim. 1872. *Kitab al-Fihrist*. Edited by Gustav Flügel. Leipzig: F. C. W. Vogel.

Ibn Faḍlān. 2005. *Ibn Fadlan's Journey to Russia: A Tenth-Century Traveller from Baghdad to the Volga River*. Edited and translated by Richard Frye. Princeton, NJ: Markus Weiner.

Ibn Ḥawqal. 2014. *Kitāb Ṣūrat al-arḍ*. Edited by M. J. de Goeje. Leiden: Brill.

Ierussalimskaya, Anna. 1969. "The 'Chelyabinsk' Fabric, a Post-Sasanian Silk." *Trudy Gosudarstvennogo Ermitazha* 10:99–100.

———. 1972. "A Newly Discovered Silk with the Sēnmurw Pattern." *Soobshcheniya Gosudarstvennogo Ermitazha* 24:11–15.

Ilyasov, Jangar. 2003. "Covered Tails and 'Flying' Tassels." *Iranica Antiqua* 13:259–325.

Ingram, R. S. 2005. "Faience and Glass Beads from the Late Bronze Age Shipwreck at Uluburun." MA thesis, Texas A&M University.

Iori, E. 2016. "The Early-Historic Urban Area at Mingora in the Light of Domenico Faccenna's Excavations at Barama-I (Swat)." *Frontier Archaeology* 7:99–112.

Irvine, A. K., Otto F. A. Meinardus, and Sefu Metaferia. 1975. "Zä-Mika'él 'Arägawi." In *The Dictionary of Ethiopian Biography*, vol. 1, *From Early Times to the End of the Zagwé Dynasty c. 1270 AD*, edited by Michael Belaynesh, S. Chojnacki, and Richard Pankhurst. Addis Ababa: Institute of Ethiopian Studies. Reprinted by the Dictionary of African Christian Biography, https://dacb.org/stories/ethiopia/za-mikael-aragawi/.

Jackson, C. M., and P. T. Nicholson. 2010. "The Provenance of Some Glass Ingots from the Ukuburun Shipwreck." *Journal of Archaeological Science* 37:295–301.

Jackson-Tal, Ruth E. 2004. "The Late Hellenistic Glass Industry in Syro-Palestine: A Reappraisal." *Journal of Glass Studies* 46:11–32.

Jacobson, Esther. 1995. *The Art of the Scythians: The Interpretation of Cultures at the Edge of the Hellenic World*. Leiden: Brill.

———. 1999. "Early Nomadic Sources for Scythian Art." In *Scythian Gold: Treasures from Ancient Ukraine*, exh. cat., edited by Ellen D. Reeder and Esther Jacobson, 59–69. New York: Harry N. Abrams.

Jankowiak, Marek. 2012. "Dirhams for Slaves: Investigating the Slavic Slave Trade in the Tenth Century." Paper presented at the Medieval Seminar, All Souls, Oxford, February. https://www.academia.edu/1764468/Dirhams_for_slaves._Investigating_the_Slavic_slave_trade_in_the_tenth_century.

Japanese National Commission to UNESCO. 1957. *Research in Japan in History of Eastern and Western Cultural Contacts: Its Development and Present Situation*. Tokyo: UNESCO.

Jenner, W. J. 1981. *Memories of Lo-yang: Yang Hsuan-chih and the Lost Capital (493–534)*. Oxford: Clarendon Press.

Jennings, S. 2000. "Late Hellenistic and Early Roman Cast Glass from the Souks Excavations (BEY 006), Beirut, Lebanon." *Journal of Glass Studies* 42:41–60.

Jing Zhichun 荆志淳, Xu Guangde 徐廣德, He Yulin 何毓靈, and Tang Jigen 唐際根. 2007. "Mu wushisi chutu yuqi de dizhikaoguxue yanjiu" 出土玉器的地质考古学研究. M54. In *Anyang Yinxu Huanyuanzhuang dongdi Shangdai muzang* 安阳殷墟花园庄东地商代墓葬, edited by Institute of Archaeology, Chinese Academy of Social Sciences, 345–87. Beijing: Science Press.

Job of Edessa. 1935. *The Book of Treasures by Job of Edessa: Encyclopedia of Philosophical and Natural Sciences as Taught in Baghdad about A.A. 817*. Translated by Alphonse Mingana. Cambridge: W. Heffer and Sons.

Johnson, Wallace, trans. 1997. *The T'ang Code*. Vol. 2. *Specific Articles*. Princeton, NJ: Princeton University Press.

Jones, Sian. 1996. *The Archaeology of Ethnicity*. London: Routledge.

Joshua the Stylite. 1882. *The Chronicle of Joshua the Stylite: Composed in Syriac A.D. 507*. Edited and translated by W. Wright. Cambridge: Cambridge University Press. https://archive.org/details/chronicleofjoshuoojosh.

Juliano, Annette L. 1985. "Possible Origins of the Chinese Mirror." *Source: Notes in the History of Art* 4 (2–3): 36–45.

Juliano, Annette L., and Judith A. Lerner. 2001. *Monks and Merchants: Silk Road Treasures from Northwest China*. Exh. cat. New York: Harry N. Abrams and Asia Society.

Karttunen, Klaus. 1989. *India in Early Greek Literature*. Studia Orientalia 65. Helsinki: Finnish Oriental Society.

———. 2014. "India and World Trade: From the Beginnings to the Hellenistic Age." In *Melammu: The Ancient World in an Age of Globalization*, edited by Markham J. Geller, 329–40. Edition Open Access. http://edition-open-access.de/proceedings/7/17/index.html.

Kavanagh, Gaynor. 1994. *Museums and the First World War: A Social History*. Leicester: University of Leicester.

Kawami, Trudy S. 1992. "Archaeological Evidence for Textiles in Pre-Islamic Iran." *Iranian Studies* 25 (1–2): 7–18.

Kazhdan, Alexander P. ed. 2005. *The Oxford Dictionary of Byzantium*. Online ed. Oxford: Oxford University Press.

Keenan, Desmond. 2004. *The True Origins of Irish Society*. Bloomington, IN: Xlibris.

Kellens, J. [1987] 2011. "Avesta: i. Survey of the History and Contents of the Book." In *Encyclopaedia Iranica Online*. Last updated August 17. www.iranicaonline.org/articles/avesta-holy-book.

Kempe, D. R. C. 1986. "Gandhara Sculptural Schists: Proposed Source." *Journal of Archaeological Science* 13 (1): 79–88.

Kenoyer, Jonathan M. 1998. *Ancient Cities of the Indus Valley Civilization*. Oxford: Oxford University Press.

Kerr, Rose, Joseph Needham, and Nigel Wood. 2004. *Science and Civilisation in China*. Vol. 5. *Chemistry and Chemical Technology*. Part 12. *Ceramic Technology*. Cambridge: Cambridge University Press.

Kessler, Adam T. 1993. *Empires beyond the Great Wall: The Heritage of Genghis Khan*. Exh. cat. Los Angeles: Natural History Museum of Los Angeles County.

Kessler, Herbert L. 2006. "The Book as Icon." In Brown 2006: 77–103.

Khan, F. A. 1968. "Conservation. Excavated Remains at Swat (1) Amlokdara Stupa." *Pakistan Archaeology* 5:227–28.

Kim, Hyun Jin. 2016. *The Huns*. London: Routledge.

King, Matthew. 2015. "Buddhism in Central Asia." *Oxford Bibliographies*. www.oxfordbibliographies.com/view/document/obo-9780195393521/obo-9780195393521-0211.xml. DOI: 10.1093/obo/9780195393521-0211.

Kinoshita Hiromi. 2009. "Foreign Glass Excavated in China." In *Byzantine Trade, 4th–12th Centuries: The Archaeology of Local, Regional and International Exchange: Papers on the Thirty-Eighth Spring Symposium of Byzantine Studies, St. John's College, University of Oxford March 2004*, edited by Maria Mudell Mango, 253–62. Farnham: Ashgate.

Knechtges, David, and Taiping Chang, eds. 2010–14. *Ancient and Early Medieval Chinese Literature: A Reference Guide*. 4 vols. Leiden: E. J. Brill.

Kotwal, F. M., and J. W. Boyd, eds. 1980. Ērbadīstān ud Nirangistān: Facsimile Edition of the Manuscript TD. Cambridge, MA: Harvard University Press.

Kowalski, Kurt, and Herbert Zimiles. 2006. "The Relations between Children's Conceptual Functioning with Color and Color Term Acquisition." *Journal of Experimental Child Psychology* 94 (4): 301/21.

Kowatli, I., H. H. Curvers, B. Stuart, Y. Sablerolles, J. Henderson, and P. Reynolds. 2008. "A Pottery and Glassmaking Site in Beirut (015)." *Bulletin de Archéologie et d'Architecture Libanaises* 10:103–20.

Kristiansen, Kristian, and Thomas B. Larsson. 2005. *The Rise of Bronze Age Society: Travels, Transmissions and Transformations*. Cambridge: Cambridge University Press.

Kröger, Jens. 2005. "Ernst Herzfeld and Friedrich Sarre." In *Ernst Herzfeld and the Development of Near Eastern Studies, 1900-1950*, edited by Ann Clyburn Gunter and Stefan R. Hauser, 49–54. Leiden: Brill.

Kroll, J. L. 2010. "The Han-Xiongnu Heqin Treaty (200–135 B.C.) in the Light of Chinese Political and Diplomatic Traditions." *Bulletin of the Museum of Far Eastern Antiquities* 78:109–24.

Kuehn, Sara. 2011. *The Dragon in Medieval East Christian and Islamic Art*. Leiden: Brill.

Kuhn, Dieter. 1995. "Silk Weaving in Ancient China: From Geometric Figures to Patterns of Pictorial Likeness." *Chinese Science* 12:77–114.

Kumamoto, Hiroshi. 2009. "Khotan: ii. History in the Pre-Islamic Period." In *Encyclopaedia Iranica Online*. Last updated April 20. www.iranicaonline.org/articles/khotan-i-pre-islamic-history.

Kurbanov, Aydogdy. 2010. "The Hephthalites: Archaeological and Historical Analysis." PhD diss., Free University of Berlin.

Kurlansky, Mark. 2002. *Salt: A World History*. London: Jonathan Cape.

Kuwayama, Shoshin. 1991. "L'inscription du Gaṇeśa de Gardez et la chronologie des Turki-Śāhis." *Journal Asiatique* 279:267–87.

———. 1992. "The Hephthalites in Tokharistan and Northwest India." *Zinbun, Annals of the Institute for Research in the Humanities, Kyoto University* 24:25–77.

———. 2006. "Swāt, Udyāna, and Gandhāra: Some Issues Related to Chinese Accounts." In Callieri 2006:59–77.

Laiou, Angeliki E., ed. 2002. *The Economic History of Byzantium: From the Seventh through the Fifteenth Century*. Washington, DC: Dumbarton Oaks Research Library and Collection.

Lal, B. B. 1987. "Glass Technology in Early India." In *Archaeometry of Glass: Proceed-*

ings of the Archaeometry Session of the XIV International Congress on Glass, edited by H. C. Bhardwaj, 44–56. New Delhi: Indian Ceramic Society.

Lam, Raymond. 2013. "Kuāna Emperors and Indian Buddhism: Political, Economic and Cultural Factors Responsible for the Spread of Buddhism through Eurasia." *South Asia: Journal of South Asian Studies* 36 (3). DOI: dx.doi.org/10.1080/0885 6401.2013.777497.

Lankton, J. W., and L. Dussubieux. 2006. "Early Glass in Asian Maritime Trade: A Review and an Interpretation of Compositional Analyses." *Journal of Glass Studies* 48:121–44.

Lapatain, Kenneth, ed. 2014. *The Berthouville Silver Treasure and Roman Luxury.* Los Angeles: Getty Publications.

La Puente, Cristina de. 2012. "The Ethnic Origins of Female Slaves in al-Andalus." In Roper and Hain 2012: 124–42.

Laugu, Nurdin, 2007. "The Roles of Mosque Libraries through History." *Al-Jami'ah* 45 (1): 91–118.

La Vaissière, Etienne de. 2005. *Sogdian Traders: A History.* Translated by James Ward. Leiden: Brill.

———. 2007. "Is There a Nationality of the Hephthalites?" *Bulletin of the Asia Institute* 17:119–32.

———. 2009. *"Huns et Xiongnu." Central Asiatic Journal 49: 3–26.*

———. 2014. "The Steppe World and the Rise of the Huns." In *The Cambridge Companion to the Age of Attila*, edited by M. Maas, 175–92. Cambridge: Cambridge University Press.

Lee, Kenneth B. 1997. *Korea and East Asia: The Story of a Phoenix.* Westport, CT: Greenwood.

Leidy, Denise Patry. 2012. "Links, Missing and Otherwise: Tillya Tepe and East Asia." In Aruz and Fino 2012: 112–21.

Leland, John. 2010. *De viris illustribus/On Famous Men.* Edited and translated by James P. Carley. British Writers of the Middle Ages and the Early Modern Period 1. Toronto: Pontifical Institute of Medieval Studies; Oxford: Bodleian Library.

Lenski, Noel. 2008. "Slavery between Rome and the Barbarians." In *Rome and the Barbarians: The Birth of a New World*, edited by Jean-Jacques Aillagon, 228–31. Rome: Skira.

Lenz, Timothy. 2003. *A New Version of the Gāndhārī Dharmapada and a Collection of Previous-Birth Stories: British Library Kharoṣṭhī Fragments 16 + 25.* Seattle: University of Washington Press.

Leriche, P., and F. Grenet. [1988] 2011. *"Bactria."* In *Encyclopaedia Iranica Online.* Last updated August 19. www.iranicaonline.org/articles/bactria.

Lerner, Judith, and Nicholas Sims-Williams. 2011. *Seals, Sealings and Tokens from Bactria to Gandhara (4th to 8th Century CE).* Vienna: Verlag der Österreichischen Akademie der Wissenschaften.

Lev, Yaacov. 2012. "Mediterranean Encounters: The Fatamids and Europe, Tenth to Twelfth Centuries." In *Shipping, Trade and Crusade in the Medieval Mediterra-*

nean: *Studies in Honour of John Pryor*, edited by Ruthy Gertwagen and Elizabeth Jeffreys, 131–56. London: Ashgate.

Lewis, Bernard. 1990. *Race and Slavery in the Middle East: An Historical Enquiry.* Oxford: Oxford University Press.

Lewis, Geoffrey D. 2015. "The History of Museums." In *Encyclopædia Britannica Online.* August 15. www.britannica.com/topic/history-398827.

Li, Q. H., S. Liu, H. X. Zhao, F. X. Gan, and P. Zhang. 2014. "Characterization of Some Ancient Glass Beads Unearthed from the Kizil Reservoir and Wanquan Cemeteries in Xinjiang, China." *Archaeometry* 56 (4): 601–24.

Li Jaang [Li Zhang]. 2011. "Long-Distance Interactions as Reflected in the Earliest Chinese Bronze Mirrors." In *The Lloyd Cotsen Study Collection of Chinese Bronze Mirrors*, vol. 2, *Studies*, edited by Lothar von Falkenhausen, 34–49. Los Angeles: UCLA Cotsen Institute of Archaeology Press.

Lin, James C. S. 2012. *The Search for Immortality: Tomb Treasures of Han China.* Exh. cat. New Haven, CT: Yale University Press.

Linduff, Katheryn M. 2008. "The Gender of Luxury and Power among the Xiongnu in Eastern Eurasia." In Linduff and Rubinson 2008: 175–212.

———. 2009. "Production of Signature Artifacts for the Nomad Market in the State of Qin During the Late Warring States Period in China (4th-3rd Century BCE." In *Metallurgy and Civilisation: Eurasia and Beyond*, edited by J. Mei and Th. Rehren, 90–96. London: Archetype.

Linduff, Katheryn M., and Karen S. Rubinson, eds. 2008. *Are All Warriors Male? Gender Roles on the Ancient Eurasian Steppe.* Lanham, MD: AltaMira Press/ Roman and Littlefield.

Lin Shen-Yu. 2010. "Pehar: A Historical Survey." *Revue d'Etudes Tibétaines* 19:5-26.

Li Qinghui, Yongchun Xu, Ping Zhang, Fuxi Gan, and Huansheng Sheng. 2009. "Chemical Composition Analyses of Early Glasses of Different Historical Periods Found in Xinjiang, China." In Gan, Brill, and Tian 2009: 331–57.

Litvinsky, B. A. 1996. "The Hephthalite Empire." In Litvinsky, Zhang Guang-da, and Samghabadi 1996: 135–62.

Litvinsky, B. A., Zhang Guang-da, and R. Sharani Samghabadi, eds. 1996. *History of Civilizations of Central Asia.* Vol. 3. *The Crossroads of Civilizations: A.D. 250 to 750.* Paris: UNESCO.

Liu Xinru. 1994. *Ancient India and Ancient China: Trade and Religious Exchanges*, AD *1–600.* Delhi: Oxford University Press.

———. 1996. *Silk and Religion: An Exploration of Material Life and the Thought of People*, AD *600–1200.* Delhi: Oxford University Press.

———. 2001. "Migration and Settlement of the Yuezhi-Kushan. Interaction and Interdependence of Nomadic and Sedentary Societies." *Journal of World History* 12 (2): 261–92.

Loewe, Michael. 2004. "Guangzhou: The Evidence of the Standard Histories from the Shi ji to the Chen shu, a Preliminary Survey." In *Guangdong: Archaeology and Early Texts (Zhou-Tang)*, edited by S. Mülle, Thomas O. Höllmann, and Putao Gui, 51–80. Wiesbaden: Harrassowitz.

Loewe, Michael, and Edward O'Shaughnessy. 1999. *The Cambridge History of Ancient China: From the Origins of Civilisation to 221 BC*. Cambridge: Cambridge University Press.

Lopez, R. S. 1945. "Silk Industry in the Byzantine Empire." *Speculum* 20 (1): 1–42.

———. 1978. *Byzantium and the World around It*. London: Variorum Reprints.

Lubar, Steven, and W. David Kinger, eds. 1995. *History from Things: Essays on Material Culture*. Washington, DC: Smithsonian Books.

Lubec, G., J. Holaubek, C. Feldl, B. Lubec, and E. Strouhal. 1993. "Use of Silk in Ancient Egypt." *Nature*, March 4. www.silkroadfoundation.org/artl/egyptsilk .shtml.

Lukšić, Tugomir. 1996. *Put svile: Muzej Mimara: 8. rujna 1996.–8. siječnja 1997.* Zagreb: Muzejsko-galerijski centar.

Lullo, Sheri. 2004. "Glass in Early China: A Substitute for Luxury?" In *Silk Road Exchange in China*, Sino-Platonic Papers 142, edited by Kateryn Linduff, 17–26. Philadelphia: University of Pennsylvania Press. http://sino-platonic.org/com plete/spp142_silk_road_china.pdf.

Luttwak, E. N. 1976. *The Grand Strategy of the Roman Empire: From the First Century A.D. to the Third*. Baltimore: John Hopkins University Press.

Lynch, Joseph H., and Phillip C. Adamo. 2014. *The Medieval Church: A Brief History*. London: Routledge.

Maas, Michel. 2014. *The Cambridge Companion to the Age of Attila*. Cambridge: Cambridge University Press.

MacGregor, Neil. 2011. *History of the World in a Hundred Objects*. London: British Museum.

Macuch, Maria. 1981. *Das sasanidische Rechtsbuch "Mātakdān-i Hazār Dādistān."* Vol. 2. Wiesbaden: Steiner.

Maggi, Mauro, and Anna Filigenzi. 2008. "Pelliot tibétain 2222: A Dunhuang Painting with a Khotanese Inscription." *Journal of Inner Asian Art and Archaeology* 3:83–89.

Mairs, Rachel. 2013. "The Hellenistic Far East: From the Oikoumene to the Community." In *Shifting Social Imaginaries in the Hellenistic Period: Narrations, Practices and Images*, edited by Eftychia Stavrianopoulou, 365–85. Leiden: Brill.

Mallory, J. P., and Douglas Q. Adams, eds. 1997. *The Encyclopedia of Indo-European Culture*. Oxford: Taylor & Francis.

Marshak, Boris I. 2002. *Legends, Tales and Fables in the Art of Sogdiana*. New York: Bibliotheca Persica.

———. 2004. "Central Asian Metalwork in China." In Watt et al. 2004: 47–65.

———. 2006. "The So-Called Zandanījī Silks: Comparisons with the Art of Sogdia." In *Central Asian Textiles and Their Contexts in the Early Middle Ages*, edited by Regula Schorta, 49–60. Riggisberg: Abegg-Stiftung.

Marshak, Boris I., and Anazawa Wakou. 1989. "Some Notes on the Tomb of Li Xian and His Wife under the Northern Zhou Dynasty at Guyuan, Ningxia and Its Gold-Gilt Silver Ewer with Greek Mythological Scenes Unearthed There." *Cultura Antiqua* 41 (1): 54–57.

Marshall, John H. 1951. *Taxila: An Illustrated Account of Archaeological Excavations, Carried Out at Taxila under the Orders of the Government of India between the Years 1913 and 1934.* 3 vols. Cambridge: Cambridge University Press.

Martin, Frederik Robert. 1912. *Miniature Painting and Painters of Persia, India and Turkey from the 8th to the 18th Century.* 2 vols. Paris: Vever.

Martin, Wilbur C. 1968. "Slavery during China in the Former Han Dynasty, 206 B.C.–A.D. 25." PhD thesis, Columbia University.

Martzloff, J.-C. 2009. *Le calendrier chinois: Structure et calculs (104 av. J.C. –1644).* Paris: Champion.

Marzo, Flavio. n.d. "'Islamic-Style' Binding: A Misleading Term Ripe for Further Research." Accessed October 3, 2017. https://www.qdl.qa/en/'islamic-style'-bind ing-misleading-term-ripe-further-research.

Matsui Dai. 2012. "Uyghur Divination Fragments from Dunhuang." In *Dunhuang Studies: Prospects and Problems for the Coming Second Century of Research*, edited by I. Popova and Liu Yi, 154–66. St. Petersburg: Institute of Oriental Manuscripts.

McCarthy, B. 2008. "Faience in Ancient South Asia." In *Encyclopedia of the History of Science, Technology, and Medicine in Non-Western Cultures*, edited by Helaine Selin, 915–17. Heidelberg: Springer Science and Business Media.

McCarthy, B., and Pamela B. Vandiver. 1991. "Ancient High Strength Ceramics: Fritted Faience Bracelet Manufacture at Harappa (Pakistan), c. 2300–1800 BC." In *Materials Issues in Art and Archaeology II,* edited by Pamela B. Vandiver, James Druzik, and George Seagon Wheeler, 495–510. Pittsburgh, PA: Materials Research Society.

McDermott, Joseph P. 2006. *A Social History of the Chinese Book: Books and Literati Culture in Late Imperial China.* Hong Kong: Hong Kong University Press.

McGrail, Seán. 2001. *Boats of the World: From the Stone Age to Medieval Times.* Oxford: Oxford University Press.

McHugh, Feldore. 1999. *Theoretical and Quantitative Approaches to the Study of Mortuary Practice.* British Archaeological Reports, International Series 785. Oxford: Archaeopress.

McIntosh, Jane. 2008. *The Ancient Indus Valley: New Perspectives.* Santa Barbara, CA: ABC-CLIO.

McNair, W. W. 1884. "A Visit to Kafiristan." *Proceedings of the Royal Geographical Society* 6 (1): 1–18.

Meister, M. W. 1970. "The Pearl Roundel in Chinese Textile Design." *Ars Orientalis* 8:255–67.

Michon, Daniel. 2015. *Archaeology and Religion in Early Northwest India: History, Theory, Practice.* London: Routledge.

Miller, Naomi F., Robert N. Spengler, and Michael Frachetti. 2016. "Millet Cultivation across Eurasia: Origins, Spread, and the Influence of Seasonal Climate." *Holocene* 26 (10). DOI: 10.1177/0959683616641742.

Miller, Timothy C. 2001. "Almanacs: Britain and the United States." In Jones 2001: 43–45.

Millward, James A. 2007. *Eurasian Crossroads: A History of Xinjiang.* New York: Columbia University Press.

Miniaev, Sergey. 2015. "Is'mennye Istočniki O Rannej Istorii Sjunn." Apxeo *Arheologičeskie vesti* 21:304–27.

———. 2016. "Production of Bronze Wares among the Xiongnu." Translated by Jargalan Burentogtock and Daniel Waugh. *Silk Road* 14:147–65. www.silkroad foundation.org/newsletter/vol14/Miniaev_SR14_2016_147_165.pdf.

Mintz, Sidney. 1985. *Sweetness and Power: The Place of Sugar in Modern History.* London: Penguin.

Mirsky, Jeanette. 1998. *Sir Aurel Stein: Archaeological Explorer.* Chicago: University of Chicago Press.

Molnar, M., I. Jason, L. Szucs, and L. Szathmary. 2014. "Artificially Deformed Crania from the Hun-Germanic Period (5th–6th Century AD) in Northeastern Hungary: Historical and Morphological Analysis." *Neurosurgical Focus* 36 (4): 1–9. DOI: 10.3171/2014.1.FOCUS13466.

Momigliano, Arnaldo. 1979. *Alien Wisdom: The Limits of Hellenization.* Cambridge: Cambridge University Press.

Moorcroft, Williams. 1886. *Observations on the Breeding of Horses within the Provinces under the Bengal Establishment.* Simla: Government Central Branch Press.

Moorey, P. R. S. 1994. *Ancient Mesopotamian Materials and Industries: The Archaeological Evidence.* Oxford: Clarendon Press.

———. 2001. "The Mobility of Artisans and Opportunities for Technology Transfer between Western Asia and Egypt in the Late Bronze Age." In *The Social Context of Technological Change: Egypt and the Near East, 1650 –1550 BC,* edited by A. J. Shortland, 1–14. Oxford: Oxbow Books.

Mordini, Antonio. 1967. "Gold Kushana Coins in the Convent of Dabra Dammo." *Journal of the Numismatic Society of India* 29:19–25.

Moreland, John. 1991. "Methods and Theory in Medieval Archaeology in the 1990s." *Archaeologica Medievale* 18:7–42.

———. 2001. *Archaeology and Text.* London: Bloomsbury Academic.

Morgan, Joyce. 2012. "The Stein Collection and World War II." In H. Wang 2012: 1–6.

Motoyoshi Akiko. 2001. "Sensibility and Synaesthesia: Ibn al-Rumi's Singing Slave Girl." *Journal of Arabic Literature* 32 (1): 1–29.

Mouri, Chika, Abolfazi Aali, Xian Zhang, and Richard Laursen. 2014. "Analysis of Dyes in Textiles from the Chehrabad Salt Mine." *Heritage Science* 2:20. https://doi.org/10.1186/s40494-014-0020-3.

Muhly, James D. 2011. "Archaeometry and Shipwrecks: A Review Article." *Expedition* 53 (1): 26–44. https://www.penn.museum/sites/expedition/archaeometry-and-shipwrecks/.

Munger, Jeffrey, and Alice Cooney Frelinghuysen. 2003. "East and West: Chinese Export Porcelain." Heilbrunn Timeline of Art History, October, Metropolitan Museum of Art. www.metmuseum.org/toah/hd/ewpor/hd_ewpor.htm.

Munro-Hay, Stuart. 1991. *Aksum: An African Civilisation of Late Antiquity.* Edinburgh: Edinburgh University Press.

———. 2002. *Ethiopia, the Unknown Land: A Cultural and Historical Guide.* London: I. B. Tauris.

Musée Cernuschi. 1958. *Orient-Occident: Recontres et influences durant cinquante siècles d'art.* Paris: Editions des Musées Nationaux.

Musée du Louvre. 1992. *Byzance: L'art Byzantin dans le collection publiques françaises.* Paris: Réunion des Musées Nationaux.

Muthesius, Anna. 1980. "Eastern Silks in Western Shrines and Treasuries before 1200." PhD diss., Courtauld Institute.

———. 1992. *Silk, Power and Diplomacy in Byzantium: Textiles in Daily Life: Proceedings of the Third Biennial Symposium of the Textile Society of America, September 24–26, 1992.* Earlsville, MD: Textile Society of America. http://digital commons.unl.edu/cgi/viewcontent.cgi?article=1579&context=tsaconf.

———. 1997. *Byzantine Silk Weaving, AD 400 to AD 1200.* Vienna: Fassbaender.

———. 2002. "Essential Processes, Looms, and Technical Aspects of the Production of Silk Textiles." In *The Economic History of Byzantium: From the Seventh through the Fifteenth Century,* edited by Angeliki E. Laiou, 147–68. Washington, DC: Dumbarton Oaks Research Library and Collection.

———. 2008. *Studies in Byzantine, Islamic and Near East Silk Weaving.* London: Pindar.

Nattier, Jan. 1991. *Once upon a Future Time: Studies in a Buddhist Prophecy of Decline.* Fremont, CA: Asian Humanities Press.

Needham, Joseph, and Dieter Kuhn. 1988. *Science and Civilisation in China.* Vol. 5. *Chemistry and Chemical Technology: Spinning and Reeling.* Cambridge: Cambridge University Press.

Needham, Joseph, and Ling Wang. 1959. *Science and Civilisation in China.* Vol. 3. *Mathematics and the Sciences of the Heavens and the Earth: Section 20: Astronomy.* Cambridge: Cambridge University Press.

Needham, Joseph, Ling Wang, and Gwei Djen Lu. 1971. *Science and Civilisation in China.* Vol. 4(3). *Civil Engineering and Nautics.* Cambridge: Cambridge University Press.

Neelis, Jason. 2013. *Early Buddhist Transmission and Trade Networks: Mobility and Exchange within and beyond the Northwestern Borderlands of South Asia.* Leiden: Brill.

———. n.d. "Buddhism and Trade." University of Washington, *Art of the Silk Road,* virtual exhibit for *Silk Road Seattle.* https://depts.washington.edu/silkroad/exhibit/religion/buddhism/buddhism.html.

Nees, Lawrence. 2011. "Blue behind Gold: The Inscription of the Dome of the Rock and Its Relatives." In *Diverse Are Their Hues: Color in Islamic Art and Culture,* edited by Jonathan M. Bloom and Sheila S. Blair, 152–73. New Haven, CT: Yale University Press.

Neumeier, Emily. 2006. "Early Koranic Manuscripts: The Blue Koran Debate."

April. https://www.researchgate.net/publication/291602722_Early_Koranic _Manuscripts_The_Blue_Koran_Debate.

Nickel, Lukas. 2012. "The Nanyue Silver Box." *Arts of Asia* 42 (3): 98–107.

———. 2013. "The First Emperor and Sculpture in China." *Bulletin of the School of Oriental and African Studies* 76 (3): 413–47.

Nielson, Lisa. 2017. "Visibility and Performance: Courtesans in the Early Islamicate Courts (661–950 CE)." In *Concubines and Courtesans: Women and Slavery in Islamic History*, edited by Matthew S. Gordon and Kathryn A. Hain, 75–99. Oxford: Oxford University Press.

Nikolaev, N. 2005. *Les Huns/De Hunnen*. Brussels: Mercator.

Nuyen, A. T. 2013. "The 'Mandate of Heaven': Mencius and the Divine Command Theory of Political Legitimacy." *Philosophy East and West.* 63 (2): 113–26.

Nylan, Michael. 1994. "The Chin wen/Ku wen Controversy in Han Times." *T'oung Pao* 80:83–145.

Nylan, Michael, and Michael Loewe, eds. 2010. *China's Early Empires: A Reappraisal*. Cambridge: Cambridge University Press.

Ohta, Alison. 2012. "Covering the Book: Bindings of the Mamluk Period, 1250–1516 CE." PhD diss., University of London.

Oikonomides, Nicolas. 1986. "Silk Trade and Production in Byzantium from the Sixth to the Ninth Century: The Seals of Kommerkiarioi." *Dumbarton Oaks Papers* 40:35–53.

Oikonomou, A., J, Henderson, M. Gnade, S. Chenery, and N. Zacharias. 2016. "An Archaeometric Study of Hellenistic Glass Vessels: Evidence for Multiple Sources." *Archaeological and Anthropological Sciences*, prepublished online May 16. doi: 10.1007/s12520-016-0336-x.

Olivieri, Luca M. 1996. "Notes on the Problematic Sequence of Alexander's Itinerary in Swat: A Geo-Historical Approach." *East and West* 46 (1–2): 45–78.

———. 2003. *The Survey of Bir-kot Hill: Architectural Comparisons and Photographic Documentation*. Bir-kot-ghwanai Interim Reports 1, IsIAO Reports and Memories Series. Rome: IsIAO.

———. 2012. "When and Why the Ancient Town of Barikot Was Abandoned? A Preliminary Note Based on the Last Archaeological Data." *Pakistan Heritage* 4:109–20.

———. 2014. *The Last Phases of the Urban Site of bir-Kot-Ghwandai (Barikot): The Buddhist Sites of Gumbat and Amluk-Dara (Barikot)*. Lahore: Sang-e-Meel Publications.

———. 2015a. "'Frontier Archaeology': Sir Aurel Stein, Swat and the Indian Aornos." *South Asian Studies* 31 (1): 58–70.

———. 2015b. *Talking Stones: Painted Rock Shelters of the Swat Valley*. Lahore: Sang-e-Meel Publications.

———. 2016. "The Graveyard and the Buddhist Shrine at Saidu Sharif I (Swat, Pakistan): Fresh Chronological and Stratigraphic Evidence." *Journal of Ancient History* 76 (3): 559–78.

Olivieri, Luca M., and M. Vidale. 2006. "Archaeology and Settlement History in a Test Area of the Swat Valley: Preliminary Report on the AMSV Project (1st Phase)." *East and West* 54 (1–3): 73–150.

Otavsky, Karel, and Anne E. Wardwell, eds. 2011. *Mittelalterliche Textilien II: Zwischen Europa und China*. Riggisberg: Abegg-Stiftung.

Othwa, Najwa. [2002] 2010. "Kairouan: Capital of Political Power and Learning in the Ifriqiya." Muslim Heritage. Updated. www.muslimheritage.com/article/kairouan-capital-political-power-and-learning-ifriqiya.

Pagès-Camagna, Sandrine. 1998. "Pigments bleus et vert égyptiens en question: Vocabulaire et analyses." In *La couleur dans la peinture et l'emaillage de l'Egypte ancienne*, edited by Sylvie Colinart and Michel Menu, 163–75. Bari: Edipuglia.

Panagiotakopulu, E., P. C. Buckland, P. M. Day, C. Doumas, A. Sarpaki, and P. Skidmore. 1997. "A Lepidopterous Cocoon from Thera and Evidence for Silk in the Aegean Bronze Age." *Antiquity* 71:420–29.

Pan Jixing. 1997. "On the Origin of Printing in the Light of New Archaeological Discoveries." *Chinese Science Bulletin* 42 (12): 976–81.

Paynter, Sarah. 2009. "Links between Glazes and Glass in Mid-2nd Millennium BC Mesopotamia and Egypt." In *From Mine to Microscope: Advances in the Study of Ancient Technology*, edited by Andrew J. Shortland, Ian C. Freestone, and Thilo Rehren, 93–108. Oxford: Oxbow Books.

Pedersen, Johannes. 1984. *The Arabic Book*. Princeton, NJ: Princeton University Press.

Pellat, Ch. [2012] 2017. "al-Rādhāniyya." In Encyclopaedia of Islam, 2nd ed., edited by P. Bearman, Th. Bianquis, C. E. Bosworth, E. van Donzel, and W. P. Heinrichs. Accessed October 21, 2017. http://dx.doi.org/10.1163/1573-3912_islam_SIM_6168.

Perikhanian, Anahit. 2008. "Iranian Society and Law." In *The Cambridge History of Iran*, vol. 3(2), *The Seleucid, Parthian, and Sasanid Periods*, edited by Ehsan Yarshater, 625–80. Cambridge: Cambridge University Press.

Perry, Craig. 2014. "The Daily Life of Slavery and Global Reach of Slavery in Medieval Egypt, 969–1250 CE." PhD diss., Emory University.

Peterson, Mark. 2010. *A Brief History of Korea*. New York: InfoBase.

Peterson, Sara. 2017. "Roses, Poppies and Narcissi: plant iconography at Tillya-tepe and connected cultures across the ancient world." PhD diss. University of London.

Pfister, P. 1934–40. *Textiles de Palmyre découverts par le Service des Antiquités du Haut-Commissariat de la République française dans la Nécropole de Palmyre*. 3 vols. Paris: Éditions d'art et d'histoire.

Phillipson, David W. 1998. *Ancient Ethiopia: Aksum: Its Antecedents and Successors*. London: British Museum Press.

———. 2012. *Foundations of an African Civilisation: Aksum and the Northern Horn, 1000 BC –AD 1300*. Martlesham: Boydell and Brewer.

Pines, Yuri. 2012a. "Beasts or Humans: Pre-Imperial Origins of the 'Sino-Barbarian' Dichotomy." In *Mongols, Turks and Others: Eurasian Nomads and the Sedentary World*, edited by Reuven Amitai and Michal Biran, 59–102. Leiden: Brill.

————. 2012b. *The Everlasting Empire: The Political Culture of Ancient China and Its Imperial Legacy*. Princeton, NJ: Princeton University Press.

Piotrovsky, Boris. 1973–74. "From the Lands of Scythians: Ancient Treasures from the Museum of the USSR 3000 B.C.–100 B.C." *Metropolitan Museum of Art Bulletin* 32 (5).

Pliny the Elder. 1855. *Natural History*. Translated by John Bostock. London: Taylor & Francis. www.perseus.tufts.edu/hopper/text?doc=Perseus:text:1999.02.0137.

Pohl, Walter. 2002. *Die Awaren: Ein Steppenvolk in Mitteleuropa*. Munich: C. H. Beck.

Porter, Cheryl. 2008. "The Identification of Purple in Manuscripts." In *Dyes in History and Archaeology 21, Including Papers Presented at the 21st Meeting, Held at Avignon and Lauris, France, 10–13 October 2002*, edited by Jo Kirby, 59–64. London: Archetype Productions.

————. 2018. "The Materiality of the Blue Quran: A Physical and Technological Study." In *The Aghlabids and Their Neighbours*, edited by Claire D. Anderson, Corisande Fenwick, and Mariam Rosser-Owen, 575–86. Leiden: Brill.

Priscus. 2014. *The Fragmentary History of Priscus: Attila, the Huns and the Roman Empire, AD 430–476*. Translated by John Given. Merchantville, NJ: Evolution Publishing.

Procopius. 1961. *History of the Wars*. Edited and translated by H. B. Dewing. London: Heinemann6666. https://en.wikisource.org/wiki/History_of_the_Wars.

Psarras, Sophia-Karin. 2003. "Han and Xiongnu: A Reexamination of Cultural and Political Relations (I)." *Monumenta Serica: Journal of Oriental Studies* 51:55–236.

Pulak, Cemal. 1998. "The Uluburun Shipwreck: An Overview." *International Journal of Nautical Archaeology* 27 (3): 188–224.

Pulleyblank, E. G. 2000a. "The Hsiung-nu." In Bazin, Hazai, and Roemer 2000: 52–75.

————. 2000b. "The Nomads in China and Central Asia in the Post-Han Period." In Bazin, Hazai, and Roemer 2000: 76–94.

Quinn, Stephen Christopher. 2006. *Windows on Nature: The Great Habitat Dioramas of the American Museum of Natural History*. New York: Abrams.

al-Rammah, M. 1995. "The Ancient Library of Kairaouan and Its Methods of Conservation." In *The Conservation and Preservation of Islamic Manuscripts: Proceedings of the Third Conference of Al-Furqān Islamic Heritage Foundation*, 29–47. London: Al-Furqān Islamic Heritage Foundation.

Raphaels, Lisa. 2013. *Divination and Prediction in Early China and Ancient Greece*. Cambridge: Cambridge University Press.

Raschke, M. G. 1976. "New Studies in Roman Commerce with the East." In *Aufstieg und Niedergang der Romischen Welt*, pt. 2, *Principat*, vol. 92, 604–1233. Berlin: Walter de Gruyter.

Rawson, Jessica. 1992. *The British Museum Book of Chinese Art*. London: Trustees of the British Museum.

————. 2002. *Chinese Jade from the Neolithic to the Qing*. Chicago: ArtMedia Resources.

————. 2010. "Carnelian Beads, Animal Figures and Exotic Vessels: Traces of Contact between the Chinese States and Inner Asia, c. 1000–650 BC." In *Archäologie in China*, vol. 1, *Bridging Eurasia*, edited by Mayke Wagner and Wang Wei, 1–42. Berlin: Deutsches Archaeologisches Institut.

Ray, Himanshu Prabha. 1994. *The Winds of Change: Buddhism and the Maritime Links of Early South Asia*. New Delhi: Oxford University Press.

Reade, Julian. 2013. *The Indian Ocean in Antiquity*. London: Kegan Paul.

Reader, Ian. 1991. "Letters to the Gods: The Form and Meaning of *Ema*." *Japanese Journal of Religious Studies* 18 (1): 23–50.

Reed, Carrie E. 2000. *Early Chinese Tattoo*. Sino-Platonic Papers 103. Philadelphia: Department of Asian and Middle Eastern Studies, University of Pennsylvania.

Reed, Ronald. 1975. *The Nature and Making of Parchment*. Leeds: Elmete Press.

Reeder, Ellen D., and Esther Jacobson. 1999. *Scythian Gold: Treasures from Ancient Ukraine*. Exh. cat. New York: Harry N. Abrams.

Reynolds, Douglas. 2012. *Turkey, Greece, and the Borders of Europe: Images of Nations in the West German Press, 1950–1975*. Berlin: Frank and Timme.

Rhys Davids, T. W., trans. 1890–94. *The Questions of King Milinda, Parts 1 and II*. Sacred Books of the East 35 and 36. Oxford: Oxford University Press.

Riboud, Krishna. 1976. "A Newly Excavated Caftan from the Northern Caucasus." *Textile Museum Journal* 4 (3): 21–42.

————. 1977. "A Detailed Study of the Figured Silk with Birds, Rocks and Trees from the Han Dynasty." *Bulletin de Liaison* 45:51–60.

Ridpath, Ian. 1985. *A Comet Called Halley*. Cambridge: Cambridge University Press.

Riedel, Dagmar. 2013. "The Anxiety of Influence: Framing the Blue Quran." *Islamic Books* blog, May 13. https://researchblogs.cul.columbia.edu/islamicbooks/2013/05/10/bquran/

————. 2015. "Buying by the Box: Islamic Manuscripts and American Collectors, 1865–1976." Paper presented at the Schoenberg Symposium on Manuscript Studies, Philadelphia, November 12–14. https://www.academia.edu/14971932/.

Rienjang, Wannaporn. 2012. "Aurel Stein's Work in the North-West Frontier Province, Pakistan." In H. Wang 2012: 1–10. .

Roberts, Colin H., and T. C. Skeat. 1983. *The Birth of the Codex*. Oxford: Oxford University Press.

Robson, James. 2008. "Signs of Power: Talismanic Writing in Chinese Buddhism." *History of Religions* 48 (2): 130–69.

Rockwell, Peter. 2006. "Gandharan Stoneworking in the Swat Valley." In Callieri 2006: 157–80.

Rong Xinjiang. 2004. "Official Life at Dunhuang in the Tenth Century: The Case of Cao Yuanzhong." In Whitfield and Sims Williams 2004: 57–62.

————. 2013. *Eighteen Lectures on Dunhuang*. Translated by Imre Galambos. Leiden: Brill.

Roper, Geoffrey. 2010. "The History of the Book in the Muslim World." In *The*

Oxford Companion to the Book, edited by Michael F. Suarez and H. R. Woodhyusen, 321–39. Oxford: Oxford University Press.

Rose, Marice E. 2008. "The Construction of Mistress and Slave Relationships in Late Antique Art." *Women's Art Journal* 29 (2): 41–49.

Rosenfield, John M. 1967. *The Dynastic Arts of the Kushans*. Berkeley: University of California Press.

———. 2011. "Prologue: Some Debating Points on Gandhāran Buddhism and Kuṣāṇa History." In *Gandhāran Buddhism: Archaeology, Art and Texts*, edited by Kurt Behrendt and Pia Brancaccio, 9–38. Vancouver: UBC Press.

Rosenthal-Heginbottom, Renate. 2013. "Roman and Late Antique Hoards of Silver Tableware as Status Symbols." In *Hoards and Genizot as Chapters in History: Catalogue No. 33*, Spring 2013, 41–48. Haifa: Hecht Museum, University of Haifa.

Rotman, Youval, and Jane Marie Todd. 2009. *Byzantine Slavery and the Mediterranean World*. Cambridge, MA: Harvard University Press.

Rotroff, Susan I. 2007. "Material Culture." in *The Cambridge Companion to the Hellenistic World*, edited by Glenn R. Bugh, 136–57. Cambridge: Cambridge University Press.

Rowland, Benjamin. 1977. *The Art and Architecture of India*. New York: Penguin.

Rtveladze, Edward V. 1993. "Coins of the Yuezhi Rulers of Northern Bactria." *Silk Road Art and Archaeology* 3:81–96.

Rubinson, Karen S. 1985. "Mirrors on the Fringe: Some Notes." *Source: Notes in the History of Art* 4 (2–3): 46–50.

———. 2008. "Tillya Tepe: Aspects of Gender and Cultural Identity." In Linduff and Rubinson 2008: 51–66.

Russell-Smith, Lilla. 2005. *Uyghur Patronage in Dunhuang: Regional Art Centres on the Northern Silk Road in the Tenth and Eleventh Century*. Leiden: Brill.

Ryan, John C., and Alan Thein Durning. 1997. *Stuff: The Secret Life of Everyday Things*. Seattle: Northwest Environment Watch.

Ryder, Edmund C. 2008. "Popular Religion: Magical Uses of Imagery in Byzantine Art." In Heilbrunn Timeline of Art History, Metropolitan Museum of Art. www.metmuseum.org/toah/hd/popu/hd_popu.htm.

Ryken, Leland, James C. Wilhoit, and Tremper Longman III, eds. 2010. *Dictionary of Biblical Imagery*. Westmont, IL: InterVarsity Press.

Salles, J.-F. 1996. "Achaemenid and Hellenistic Trade in the Indian Ocean." In *The Indian Ocean in Antiquity*, edited by Julian Reade, 251–67. London: Kegan Paul International in association with British Museum.

Salomon, Richard. 1999. *Ancient Buddhist Scrolls from Gandhāra: The British Library Kharoṣṭhī Fragments*. Seattle: University of Washington Press.

Salomon, Richard, and Gregory Schopen. 1984. "The Indravarman (Avaca) Casket Inscription Reconsidered: Further Evidence for Canonical Passage in Buddhist Inscriptions." *Journal of the International Association of Buddhist Studies* 7 (1): 107–23.

Sandberg, Gosta. 1989. *Indigo Textiles: Technique and History*. Asheville, NC: Lark Books.

Sarianidi, Victor I. 1985. *The Golden Hoard of Bactria: From the Tillya-Tepe Excavations in Northern Afghanistan.* New York: Harry N. Abrams.

———. 1990. "The Golden Hoard of Bactria." *National Geographic*, March, 50–75.

———. 1990–92. "Tilya Tepe: The Burial of a Noble Warrior." *Persica* 14:103–30.

Sawyer, Peter. 2001. *The Oxford Illustrated History of the Vikings.* Oxford: Oxford University Press.

Schafer, Edward H. 1961. "Languages of Ancient Khotan." *Archiv Orientalní* 29:35–52.

———. 1963. *The Golden Peaches of Samarkand.* Berkeley: University of California Press.

——— 1967. *The Vermilion Bird: T'ang Images of the South.* Berkeley: University of California Press.

———. 1977. *Pacing the Void: T'ang Approaches to the Stars.* Berkeley: University of California Press.

Schimmel, Annemarie. 1984. *Calligraphy and Islamic Culture.* New York: New York University Press.

Schlütz, Frank, and Frank Lehmkuhl. 2007. "Climatic Change in the Russian Altai, Southern Siberia, Based on Palynological and Geomorphological Results, with Implications for Climatic Teleconnections and Human History since the Middle Holocene." *Vegetation History of Archaeobotany* 16:101–18.

Schmidt, Henirich Jakob. 1958. *Alte Seidenstoffe: Ein Hanbuch für Sammler und Liebhaber.* Leipzig: Klinkhardt und Biermann.

Schmidt-Colinet, Andreas, and Annemarie Stauffer. 2000. *Die Textilien aus Palmyra, Neue und Alte Funde.* Mainz: P. von Zabern.

Schoeler, Gregor. 2006. *The Oral and the Written in Early Islam.* Translated by Uwe Vagelpohl. London: Routledge.

Schopen, Gregory. 1994. "The Monastic Ownership of Servants or Slaves: Local or Legal Factors in the Redactional History of the Two Vinayas." *Journal of the International Association of Buddhist Studies* 17 (2): 145–73.

———. 1997. *Bones, Stones, and Buddhist Monks: Collected Papers on the Archaeology, Epigraphy, and Texts of Monastic Buddhism in India.* Honolulu: University of Hawaii Press.

———. 2006a. "The Buddhist 'Monastery' and the Indian Garden: Aesthetics, Assimilations, and the Siting of Monastic Establishments." *Journal of the American Oriental Society* 126 (4): 487–505.

———. 2006b. "On Monks and Menial Laborers: Some Monastic Accounts of Building Buddhist Monasteries." In Callieri 2006: 225–45.

Schopphoff, Claudia. 2009. *Der Gürtel: Funktion und Symbolik eines Kleidungsstückes in Antike und Mittelalter.* Pictura et Poesis 27. Cologne: Böhlau.

Schorta, Regula. 2016. "Central Asian Silks in the East and the West during the Second Half of the First Millennium." In *Oriental Silks in Medieval Europe*, edited by Juliane von Fircks and Regula Schorta, 47–63. Riggisberg: Abegg-Stiftung.

Schrenk, Sabine. 2006. "Silks from Antinoopolis." In *Central Asian Textiles and*

Their Contexts in the Early Middle Ages, edited by Regula Schorta, 23–34. Riggisberg: Abegg-Stiftung.

Seland, Eivind Heldaas. 2013. "Ancient Afghanistan and the Indian Ocean: Maritime Links of the Kushan Empire ca. 500–200 CE." *Journal of Indian Ocean Archaeology* 9:66–74.

Sen, Tansen. 2003. *Buddhism, Diplomacy, and Trade: The Realignment of Sino-Indian Relations, 600–1400*. Honolulu: University of Hawaii Press.

Senior, R. C. 2008. "The Final Nail in the Coffin of Azes II." *Journal of the Oriental Numismatic Society* 197:25–27.

Sephton, J. 1880. *Eirik the Red's Saga: A Translation Read before the Literary and Philosophical Society of Liverpool, January 12, 1880*. Liverpool: Marples. http://sagadb.org/eiriks_saga_rauda.en.

Shaanxi sheng kaogu yanjiusuo 陝西省考古研究所 [Shaanxi Institute of Archaeology]. 2005. *Tang Li Xian mu fajue baogao* 唐李憲幕發掘報告. Beijing: Kexue.

Shabuh, Ibrahim. 1956. "Sijil qadim li-Maktabat Jami' al-Qayrawan." *Majallat Ma'had al-Makhtutat al-'Arabiya* 2:339–72.

Shahbazi, A. Sh. [1987] 2011. "Asb 'horse': i. In Pre-Islamic Iran." In *Encyclopaedia Iranica Online*. Last updated April 16. www.iranicaonline.org/articles/asb-horse-equus-cabullus-av.

Shahid, Irfan. 1995. *Byzantium and the Arabs in the Sixth Century*. Washington, DC: Dumbarton Oaks.

Shaki, Mansour. [1992] 2011. "Contracts: ii. In the Parthian and Sasanian Periods." In *Encyclopaedia Iranica Online*. Last updated October 28. www.iranicaonline.org/articles/contracts-legally-enforceable-undertakings-between-two-or-more-consenting-parties#pt2.

Shelach-Lavi, Gideon. 2014. "Steppe-Land Interactions and Their Effects on Chinese Cultures during Second and Early First Millennia BC." In *Nomads as Agents of Cultural Change: The Mongols and Their Eurasian Predecessors*, edited by Amitai Reuven and Michal Biran, 10–31. Honolulu: University of Hawaii Press.

Shen Congwen 沈从文. 2012. *Zhongguo gudai fushi yanjiu* 中国古代服饰研究. Shanghai: Shanghai Bookstores Publications.

Shen Hsueh-man. 2000. "Buddhist Relic Deposits from Tang (618–907) to Northern Song (960–1127) and Liao (907–1125)." PhD diss., Oxford University.

———. 2002. "Luxury or Necessity: Glassware in Śarīra Relic Pagodas of the Tang and Northern Song Periods." In *Chinese Glass: Archaeological Studies on the Uses and Social Context of Glass Artefacts from the Warring States to the Northern Song Period*, Orientalia Venetiana 14, edited by Cecilia Braghin, 71–110. Florence: Leo S. Olschki.

Shepherd, D. G. 1964. "Sasanian Art in Cleveland." *Bulletin of the Cleveland Museum of Art* 51 (4): 82–92.

Shimada, Akira. 2012. *Early Buddhist Architecture in Context: The Great Stupa at Amaravati (ca. 300 BCE–300 CE)*. Leiden: Brill.

Shrank, Cathy. 2004. *Writing the Nation in Reformation England, 1530–1580*. Oxford: Oxford University Press.

Silk, Jonathan A. 2008. *Managing Monks: Administrators and Administrative Roles in Indian Buddhist Monasticism.* Oxford: Oxford University Press.

Sima Qian. 1993. *Shiji.* Translated by Burton Watson as *Records of the Grand Historian of China: Han Dynasty II,* rev. ed. New York: Columbia University Press.

Sims-Williams, Nicholas. 2000. *Bactrian Documents from Northern Afghanistan.* Vol. 1. *Legal and Economic Documents.* Oxford: Oxford University Press.

———. 2007. "Bactrian Letters from the Sasanian and Hephthalite Periods." In *Proceedings of the 5th Conference of the Societas Iranologica Europæa Held in Ravenna, 6–11 October 2003,* edited by Antonio Panaino and Andrea Piras, 701–13. Milan: Mimesis.

Sinor, Denis. 1972. "Horse and Pasture in Inner Asian History." *Oriens Extremus* 19:171–84.

———. 1990. *The Cambridge History of Early Inner Asia.* Cambridge: Cambridge University Press.

Skeat, T. C. 1994. "The Origin of the Christian Codex." *Zeitschrift für Papyrologie und Epigraphik* 102:263–68.

Skjærvø, Oktor. 2012. 'The Zoroastrian Oral Tradition as Reflected in the Texts." In *The Tranmission of the Avesta,* edited by A. Cantera, 2–48. Wiesbaden: Harrassowitz.

Smith, C. S. 1981. *A Search for Structure.* Cambridge, MA: MIT Press.

Snodgrass, Adrian. 1991. *The Symbolism of the Stupa.* Ithaca, NY: Cornell University Press.

Snoek, Godefridus J. C. 1995. *Medieval Piety from Relics to the Eucharist: A Process of Mutual Interaction.* Leiden: Brill.

So, Jenny F., and Emma C. Bunker. 1995. *Traders and Raiders on China's Northern Frontier.* Exh. cat. Seattle: University of Washington Press.

Sperling, Elliot. 1979. "A Captivity in Ninth-Century Tibet." *Tibet Journal* 4 (4): 17–67.

Splitstoser, Jeffrey C., Tom D. Dillehay, Jan Wouters, and Ana Claro. 2016. "Early Pre-Hispanic Use of Indigo Blue in Peru." *Science Advances* 2 (9). DOI: 10.1126/sciadv.1501623.

Spooner, D. B. 1908–9. "Excavations at Shāh-ji-Dherī." *Annual Report of the Archaeological Survey of India,* 38–59.

Stanley, Tim. 1995. *The Qur'an and Calligraphy: A Selection of Fine Manuscript Material.* Catalogue 1213. London: Bernard Quarich.

Starr, S. Frederick. 2013. *Lost Enlightenment: Central Asia's Golden Age from the Arab Conquest to Tamerlane.* Princeton, NJ: Princeton University Press.

Stein, Marc Aurel. 1904. *Sand-Buried Ruins of Khotan.* London: Hurst and Blackett.

———. 1907. *Ancient Khotan.* Oxford: Clarendon Press.

———. 1912. *Ruins of Desert Cathay: Personal Narrative of Explorations in Central Asia and Westernmost China.* London: Macmillan.

———. 1921. *Serindia: Detailed Report of Explorations in Central Asia and Westernmost China.* Oxford: Oxford University Press.

———. 1928. *Innermost Asia.* Oxford: Clarendon Press.

————. 1929. *On Alexander's Track to the Indus: Personal Narrative of Explorations on the North-West Frontier of India*. London: Macmillan. http://archive.org/stream/onalexanderstraco35425mbp/onalexanderstraco35425mbp_djvu.txt.

————. 1930. *An Archaeological Tour in Upper Swat and Adjacent Hill Tracts*. Memoirs of the Archaeological Survey of India 42. Calcutta: Archaeological Survey of India.

Stephenson, Paul. 2003. *The Legend of Basil the Bulgar-Slayer*. Cambridge: Cambridge University Press.

Strong, John. 2004. *Relics of the Buddha*. Princeton, NJ: Princeton University Press.

Al-Ṭabarī. 1989. *The History of al-Tabari*. Vol. 34. *Incipient Decline*. Translated and annotated by Joel L. Kraemer. Albany: State University of New York Press.

Taddesse Tamrat. 1972. *Church and State in Ethiopia, 1270–1527*. Oxford: Clarendon Press.

Takeuchi Tsuguhito. 2004a. "Sociolinguistic Implications of the Use of Tibetan in East Turkestan from the End of Tibetan Domination through the Tangut Period (9th–12th c.)." In *Turfan Revisited: The First Century of Research into the Arts and Cultures of the Silk Road*, edited by Desmond Durkin-Meisterernst, Simone-Christiane Raschmann, Jens Wilkens, Marianne Yaldiz, and Peter Zieme, 341–48. Berlin: Dietrich Reimer.

————. 2004b. "The Tibetan Military System and Its Activities from Khotan to Lop Nor." In Whitfield and Sims Williams 2004: 50–56.

Tallet, Pierre. 2012. *Ayn Sukhna and Wadi el-Jarf: Two Newly Discovered Pharaonic Harbours on the Suez Gulf*. British Museum Studies in Ancient Egypt and Sudan 18. London: British Museum.

Teiser, Stephen F. 1994. *The Scripture of the Ten Kings and the Making of Purgatory in Medieval China*. Studies in East Asian Buddhism 9. Honolulu: University of Hawaii Press.

Teter, Magda. 2011. *Sinners on Trial*. Cambridge, MA: Harvard University Press.

Thiel, J. H. 1966. *Eudoxus of Cyzicus: A Chapter in the History of the Sea-Route to India and the Route around the Cape in Ancient Times*. Historische Studien 23. Groningen: J. B. Wolters.

Thierry, Francois. 2005. "Yuezhi and Kouchans: Pièges et dangers des sources chinoises." In *Afghanistan: Ancien carrefour entre l'est et l'ouest*, edited by Osmund Boperachchi and Marie-Francoise Boussac, 421–539. Turnhout: Brepols.

Thomas, Thelma K. 2012. "'Ornaments of Excellence' from 'the Miserable Gains of Commerce': Luxury Art and Byzantine Culture." In *Byzantium and Islam: Age of Transition*, edited by Helen C. Evans and Brandie Ratliff, 124–33. New York: Metropolitan Museum of Art.

Thompson, D., et al. [1983] 2011. "Abrīšam: iii. Silk Textiles in Iran." In *Encyclopaedia Iranica Online*. Last updated July 19. www.iranicaonline.org/articles/abrisam-silk-index.

Tian Guangjin 田广金 and Guo Suxin 郭素新. 1986. *E'erduosi shi qing tong qi* 鄂尔多斯式青銅器. Beijing: Wenwu.

Timperman, Ilse. 2017. "Early Niche Graves in the Turfan Basin and Inner Eurasia." PhD diss., University of London.

Ting, Joseph S. P., ed. 2006. *The Maritime Silk Route: 2000 Years of Trade on the South China Sea*. Hong Kong: Urban Council.

Tomber, Roberta. 2008. *Indo-Roman Trade: From Pots to Pepper*. London: Duckworth.

Tosi, Maurizio. 1974. "The Lapis Trade across the Iranian Plateau in the 3rd Millennium BC." In *Gururājamañjarikā: Studi in onore di Guiseppe Tucci*, 3–22. Naples: Istituto Universitario Orientale.

Touati, Houari. "Scribes and Commissioners of the Early Qur'anic Codices." Paper presented at the International Conference on Patronage and the Sacred Book in the Medieval Mediterranean, October 18–19. Abstract at Centro de Ciencias Humanas y Sociales, Consejo Superior de Investigaciones Científicas, 2010, www.congresos.cchs.csic.es/patronage_and_the_sacred_book/Abstracts.

Trainor, Kevin. 1997. *Relics, Ritual and Representation in Buddhism: Rematerializing the Sri Lankan Theravada Tradition*. Cambridge: Cambridge University Press.

Treister, Michael Yu. 2001. *Hammering Techniques in Greek and Roman Jewellery and Toreutics*. Leiden: Brill.

Tretiakov, P. N., and A. L. Mongait, eds. 1961. *Contributions to the Ancient History of the U.S.S.R. with Special Reference to Transcaucasia*. Cambridge, MA: Peabody Museum.

Trever, Camilla. 1967. "A propos des temples de la déesse Anahita en Iran sassanide." *Iranica Antiqua* 7:121–34.

Trimingham, J. Spencer. 2013. *Islam in Ethiopia*. London: Routledge.

Trousdale, William. 1968. "The Crenelated Mane: Survival of an Ancient Tradition in Afghanistan." *East and West* 18 (1–2): 169–77.

Trowbridge, M. I. 1930. *Philological Studies in Ancient Glass*. University of Illinois Studies in Language and Literature 13, nos. 3–4. Urbana: University of Illinois.

Truitt, E. R. 2015. *Medieval Robots: Mechanism, Magic, Nature, and Art*. Philadelphia: University of Pennsylvania Press.

Tsien Tsuen-Hsuin. 1985. *Science and Civilisation in China*. Vol. 5. *Chemistry and Chemical Technology*. Part 1. *Paper and Printing*. Cambridge: Cambridge University Press.

Tucci, Guiseppe. 1940. *Travels of Tibetan Pilgrims in the Swat Valley*. Calcutta: Greater India Society.

———. 1949. *Tibetan Painted Scrolls*. Rome: La Libreria dello Stato.

———. 1958. "Preliminary Report on an Archaeological Survey in Swat." *East and West* 9 (4): 279–328.

Twitchett, Denis, ed. 1983. *Printing and Publishing in Medieval China*. New York: Frederic C. Beil.

Usher, Abbott Payson. 1988. *A History of Mechanical Inventions*. Rev. ed. New York: Dover.

van Giffen, Astrid. n.d. "Weathered Archaeological Glass." Accessed September

16, 2017. Corning Museum of Glass. www.cmog.org/article/weathered-archae ological-glass.

van Schaik, Sam. 2011. *Tibet: A History*. New Haven, CT: Yale University Press.

Vasil'e v, K.V. 1961. "Rezenzia na: Gumilev L. Hunnu. Sredinnaja Asia v drevnie vremena." *Vestnik Drevney Istorii* 2:120–24.

Vaziri, Mostafa. 2012. *Buddhism in Iran: An Anthropological Approach to Traces and Influences*. New York: Palgrave Macmillan.

Vedeler, Marianne. 2014. *Silk for the Vikings*. Oxford: Oxbow Books.

Verstraete, B. C. 1980. "Slavery and the Social Dynamics of Male Homosexual Relations in Ancient Rome." *Journal of Homosexuality* 5 (3): 227–36.

Vnouček, Jiří. 2018. "Learning the History of Manuscripts with the Help of Visual Assessment of the Parchment: The Differences in Animals and Processes Employed in the Preparation of Parchment." PhD diss., University of York.

Vondrovec, Klaus. 2014. *Coinage of the Iranian Huns and Their Successors from Bactria to Gandhara (4th to 8th Century CE)*. Vienna: Verlag der Österreichischen Akademie der Wissenschaften.

Von le Coq, Albert. 1913. *Chotscho: Facsimile-Wiedergaben der Wichtigeren Funde der Ersten Königlich Preussischen Expedition nach Turfan in Ost-Turkistan*. Berlin: Dietrich Reimer.

Von Simson, Otto. 1988. *The Gothic Cathedral: Origins of Gothic Architecture and the Medieval Concept of Order*. Princeton, NJ: Princeton University Press.

Wagner, Mayke, Xinhua Wu, Pavel Tarasov, Ailijiang Aisha, Christopher Bronk Ramsey, Michael Schultz, Tyede Schmidt-Schultz, and Julia Gresky. 2011. "Carbon-Dated Archaeological Record of Early First Millennium B.C. Mounted Pastoralists in the Kunlun Mountains, China." *PNAS* 108 (38): 15733–38. www .pnas.org/content/108/38/15733.full.pdf.

Waldron, Arthur. 1990. *The Great Wall of China: From History to Myth*. Cambridge: Cambridge University Press.

Waley, Arthur, trans. 1960. *Ballads and Stories from Tun-Huang: An Anthology*. London: George Allen and Unwin.

Walker, Annabel. 1998. *Aurel Stein: Pioneer of the Silk Road*. London: John Murray.

Walter, Mariko Namba. 2014. *Buddhism in Central Asian History*. In *The Wiley Companion to East and Inner Asian Buddhism*, edited by Mario Poceski, 21–39. Malden, MA: Wiley Blackwell.

Wang, Helen. 1998. "Stein's Recording Angel: Miss F. M. G. Lorimer." *Journal of the Royal Asiatic Society*, 3rd ser., 8 (2): 207–28.

———. 2004. *Money on the Silk Road: The Evidence from Eastern Central Asia to c. AD 800*. London: British Museum.

———, ed. 2012. *Sir Aurel Stein: Colleagues and Collections*. British Museum Research Publication 194. London: British Museum.

Wang Binghua 王炳华. 1993. "Xi Han yiqian Xinjiang he Zhongyuan diqu lishi guanxi kaoxu" 西汉以前新疆和中原地区历史关系考索. In *Sichou zhi lu kaogu yanjiu* 丝绸之路考古研究. Urumqi: Xinjiang renmin chubanshe.

Wang Bo and Lu Lipeng. 2009. "Glass Artifacts Unearthed from the Tombs at the Zhagunluke and Sampula Cemeteries in Xinjiang." In *Ancient Chinese Glass Research along the Silk Road*, edited by Gan Fuxi, Robert H. Brill, and Tian Shouyun, 229–330. Singapore: World Scientific Publishing.

Wang Jiqing. 2012. "Aurel Stein's Dealings with Wang Yuanlu and Chinese Officials in Dunhuang in 1907." In H. Wang 2012: 1–6.

Wang Yu-t'ung. 1953. "Slaves and Other Comparable Social Groups during the Northern Dynasties (386–618)." *Harvard Journal of Asiatic Studies* 16 (3–4): 293–364.

Ward, Gerald W. R. 2008. *The Grove Encyclopedia of Materials and Techniques in Art*. Oxford: Oxford University Press.

Warmington, E. H. 1928. *The Commerce between the Roman Empire and India*. Cambridge: Cambridge University Press.

Watt, James C. Y., An Jiayao, Angela F. Howard, Boris I. Marshak, Su Bai, and Zhao Feng, eds. 2004. *Dawn of a Golden Age, 200–750 AD*. Exh. cat. New York: Metropolitan Museum of Art. www.metmuseum.org/research/metpublications/ China_Dawn_of_a_Golden_Age_200_750_AD.

Waugh, Daniel C .2007. "Richtofen's 'Silk Roads': Toward the Archaeology of a Concept." *Silk Road* 5 (1): 1–10. silkroadfoundation.org/newsletter/vol5num1/ srjournal_v5n1.pdf.

Weber, A. S. 2003. "Women's Early Modern Medical Almanacs in Historical Context." *English Literary Renaissance* 33 (3): 358–402.

West, V. 2009. "Letters from Antonio Mordini." *Journal of the Oriental Numismatic Society* 200:5–9.

West FitzHugh, Elisabeth, and Lynda A. Zycherman, 1992. "A Purple Barium Copper Silicate Pigment from Early China." *Studies in Conservation* 37 (3): 145–54.

Whitehouse, David. 1989. "Begram: The Periplus and Gandharan Art." *Journal of Roman Archaeology* 2:93–100.

Whitfield, Susan. 1998. "Under the Censor's Eye: Printed Almanacs and Censorship in Ninth-Century China." *British Library Quarterly* 24 (1): 4–22.

———. 2001. "Almanacs: China." In *Censorship: A World Encyclopedia,* edited by Derek Jones, 43. Chicago: Fitzroy Dearborn.

———. 2008. "The Perils of Dichotomous Thinking: Ebb and Flow Rather Than East and West." In *Marco Polo and the Encounter of East and West*, edited by Suzanne Akbari and Amilcare A. Iannucci. Toronto: University of Toronto Press. https://www.academia.edu/2645165/The_Perils_of_Dichotomous_Thinking _Ebb_and_flow_rather_than_east_and_west.

———. 2009. *La Route de la Soie: Un voyage à travers la vie et la mort*. Exh. cat. Brussels: Mercator.

———. 2015a. "Creating a Codicology of Central Asian Manuscripts." In *From Mulberry Leaves to Silk Scrolls: New Approaches to the Study of Asian Manuscript Traditions,* edited by Justin Thomas McDaniel and Lynn Ransom, 207–30. Philadelphia: University of Pennsylvania Press.

———. 2015b. *Life along the Silk Road*. 2nd ed. Oakland: University of California Press.

———. 2016. "Dunhuang and Its Network of Patronage and Trade." In *Cave Temples of Dunhuang: Buddhist Art on China's Silk Road*, edited by Neville Agnew, Marcia Reed, and Tevvy Ball, 59–76. Los Angeles: Getty Conservation Institute and Getty Research Institute.

———. 2018a. "Buddhist Rock Cut Architecture and Stupas across Central Asia and into China." In *Cambridge World History of Religious Architecture*, edited by Richard Etlin. Cambridge: Cambridge University Press

———. 2018b. "The Expanding Silk Road." *Bulletin of the Museum of Far Eastern Antiquities* 81.

———. 2018c. "On the Silk Road: Trade in the Tarim?" In *Trade and Civilization*, edited by Kristian Kristiansen, Thomas Lindkvist, and Janken Myrdal, 299–331. Cambridge: Cambridge University Press.

Whitfield, Susan, and Ursula Sims-Williams, eds. 2004. *The Silk Road: Trade, Travel, War and Faith*. Exh. cat. London: British Library and Serindia. Online exhibition at http://idp.bl.uk/education/silk_road/index.a4d.

Wietzmann, Kurt. 1943. "Three 'Bactrian' Silver Vessels with Illustrations from Euripides." *Art Bulletin* 25 (4): 289–324.

Wilbur, Clarence Martin. 1943a. "Industrial Slavery during China in the Former Han Dynasty (206 B.C.–A.D. 25)." *Journal of Economic History* 3 (1): 56–69.

———. 1943b. *Slavery in China during the Former Han Dynasty, 206 B.C.–A.D. 25*. Anthropological Series, Field Museum of Natural History, Vol. 34. Chicago: Field Museum of Natural History.

Wild, J. P. 1984. "Some Early Silk Finds in Northwestern Europe." *Textile Museum Journal* 23:17–19, 22.

Wilkinson, Endymion. 2000. *Chinese History: A Manual*. Cambridge, MA: Harvard University Asia Center.

Williams, Joanna. 1973. "The Iconography of Khotanese Painting." *East and West* 23 (1–2): 109–54.

Williams, Tim. 2014. *The Silk Roads: An ICOMOS Thematic Study*. Paris: ICOMOS.

Wolters, Jochem. 1998. *Die Granulation: Geschichte und Technik einer alten Goldschmiedekunst*. Munich: Callwey.

Wood, Frances. 2012. "A Tentative Listing of the Stein Manuscripts in Paris, 1911–19." In H. Wang 2012: 1–6.

Wood, Marilee. 2016. "Glass Beads from Pre-European Contact Sub-Saharan Africa: Peter Francis's Work Revisited and Updated." *Archaeological Research in Asia* 6:65–80.

Woodford, Susan. 2003. *The Trojan War in Ancient Art*. Ithaca, NY: Cornell University Press.

Wu Hung. 2002. "A Case of Cultural Interaction: House-shaped Sarcophagi of the Northern Dynasties." *Orientations* 33.5: 34–41.

Wu Zhuo. 1989. "Notes on the Silver Ewer from the Tomb of Li Xian." *Bulletin of the Asia Institute* 3:61–70.

Wyatt, David. 2009. *Slaves and Warriors in Medieval Britain and Ireland, 800–1200.* Leiden: Brill.

Xigoupan. Yikezhao Meng wen wu gong zuo zhan 伊克昭盟文物工作站, and Nei Menggu wen wu gong zuo dui 内蒙古文物工作队. 1980. "Xigoupan Xiongnu mu" 西沟畔匈奴墓. *Wenwu* 文物 7:1–10.

Yaacov, Lew. 2012. "A Mediterranean Encounter: The Fatimids and Europe, Tenth to Twelfth Century." In *Shipping, Trade and Crusade in the Medieval Mediterranean: Studies in Honour of John Pryor,* edited by Ruthy Gertwagen and Elizabeth Jeffreys, 131–56. London: Ashgate.

Yamazaki, Gen'ichi. 1990. "The Legend of the Foundation of Khotan." *Memoirs of the Research Department of the Toyo Bunko* 47:55–80.

Yang Han-Sung, Jan Yun-Hua, Iida Shotaro, and Lawrence W. Preston, eds. and trans. 1984. *The Hye Ch'o Diary: Memoir of the Pilgrimage to the Five Regions of China.* Berkeley, CA: Asian Humanities Press; Seoul: Po Chin Chai.

Yetts, W. Perceval. 1926. "Discoveries of the Kozlov Expedition." *Burlington Magazine for Connoisseurs* 48 (277): 168–85.

Zhang Bangwei. 2016. "Women: Han Women Living in the Territory of Song." In *A Social History of Middle-Period China,* edited by Zhu Ruixin, Zhang Bangwei, Liu Fusheng, Cai Chongbang, and Wang Zengyu, 171–203. Cambridge: Cambridge University Press.

Zhang, L. [L. Jaang]. 2011. "Long-Distance Interactions as Reflected in the Earliest Chinese Bronze Mirrors." In *The Lloyd Cotsen Study Collection of Chinese Bronze Mirrors,* vol. 2, Studies, edited by Lothar von Falkenhausen, 34–49. Los Angeles: UCLA Cotsen Institute of Archaeology Press.

Zhang Qingjie, Chang Hongxia, Zhang Xingmin, and Li Aiguo. 2002. "The Yu Hong Tomb of the Sui Dynasty in Taiyuan." Translated by Victor Mair. *Chinese Archaeology* 2:258–68.

Zhao Feng. 1997. "Silk Roundels from the Sui to the Tang." *HALI* 92:81–85.

———. 2004. "The Evolution of Textiles along the Silk Road." In Watt et al. 2004: 67–77.

Zhu Ruixin. 2016. "Chinese Character Tattoos, Pattern Tattoos, and Flower Pinning." In *A Social History of Middle-Period China,* edited by Zhu Ruixin, Zhang Bangwei, Liu Fusheng, Cai Chongbang, and Wang Zengyu, 639–48. Cambridge: Cambridge University Press.

Zieme, Peter, Christiane Reck, Nicholas Sims-Williams, Desmond Durkin-Meisterernst, and Matteo Compareti. n.d. "Aesop's Fables in Central Asia." Turfanforschung project. www.vitterhetsakad.se/pdf/uai/Turfan.pdf.

Zürcher, Eric. 1959. *The Buddhist Conquest of China.* Leiden: Brill.

———. 1968. "The Yuezhi and Kaniska in Chinese Sources." In *Papers on the Date of Kaniska: Submitted to the Conference on the Date of Kaniska, London 20–22 April, 1960,* edited by A. L. Balsham, 346–90. Leiden: E. J. Brill.

INDEX

313

almanac, vii, ix, 7, 165, 219–49, *plate8*. *See also* calendar

almonds, 38

al-Muqaddasī. *See* Muqaddasī, al-

aloeswood, 263

Alptigin (fl. 963), 268

Altai, 4, 20, 157

Altaic languages, 133. *See also* Turkic (Old Turkic) language

Altotting, 214n99

aluminum, 35, 43

al-Wāthiq. *See* Wāthiq, al-

al-Zuṭṭ. *See* Zuṭṭ, al-

amber, 16, 18, 38, 247

American Museum of Natural History, New York, 31n95

amethyst, 98

Amharic, 77

Amluk Dara Khwar, 89

Amluk Dara stupa, vii, viii, 3, 6, 74n71, 81–110, 90*fig*.13, 108*fig*.14, *plate3*

amorphous material, viii, 36*fig*.4, 47

Amsterdam, 32n

Amu Darya (Oxus River), 59, 60, 61, 112, 118, 121, 128, 161, 263, 264. *See also* Transoxania

Amur cork tree (*Phellodendron amurense*), 180n81, 234

Anahita, 130

Anastasius II (713–715), 207n73

Anazarbus (Ayn Zarba), 260

Anazawa Wakou, 130, 131

Andalusia, 262, 263

Andijan, 152

Andrew of Constantinople (d. 936), 270

Andrews, Fred (1866–1957), 243, 245

An Lushan 安禄山 (ca. 703–757), 268n96

Annals of Ulster, 259

'Antara (525–608), 252–53

antelope, 26, 106

anthropology, 2n2, 10, 12, 21n52, 181

antimony, 38

Antinoe. *See* Antinoopolis

Antinoopolis, 203, 207, 217

Antioch, 263

Anxi, 61, 241

Anyang, 27

Aornos, 81, 82–83

Aphrodite, 126, 129, 131

apiculture, 78, 96

Apollo, 86n20, 128

Appaloosan horse, 162n97

apple, 5, 126, 131, 163

apricot, 163

aquamarine, 98

Aquitaine, 212, 213

Arab Caliphate, 179, 202n49, 205, 206n63, 208, 212, 232, 257, 258, 260–61, 264, 265n78, 267–68, 269, 271. *See also* Abbasid Caliphate; Fatimid Caliphate; Umayyad Caliphate

Arabia, 52, 66, 72, 73, 203, 209, 261, 262–63, 265n75. *See also* Basra; Mecca; Medina; Yemen

Arabian Sea, 52n79

Arabic, xiii, 7, 76, 113, 164, 165n2, 170, 176, 181, 188, 205n59, 251, 252, 261, 263

Arabic literature, 77, 113, 170, 176, 181, 252, 260, 261

Arabs, 77, 170n33, 232, 251, 252, 257, 258, 259, 260–61, 264, 264n70, 269, 271

Aramaic, 169, 170, 234–35

archaeology, xi, xiii, 1, 2, 6, 7, 8, 10–11, 12, 13, 16–33, 34, 35, 37–39, 40, 43–44, 48, 49–56, 58n7, 60–61, 62, 66–67, 72, 74, 75–76, 78–80, 81n1, 85, 86, 88–98, 100– 109, 111, 113–15, 121, 122–23, 125, 128–29, 132, 135, 136, 137–38, 139, 144, 146–52, 153–54, 155–56, 157, 159, 163, 186, 189, 195, 196n24, 197, 205, 217, 234n55, 240–42, 250; historical, 2, 3, 6, 7, 13n17, 29, 58n7, 60–61, 62, 72, 74, 101, 113–15, 128–29, 138, 250; maritime, 38–39, 52–54

archery, 16, 35, 58n6, 60, 113, 154, 158, 210n90, 261

architecture, 2, 6, 12n13, 14, 15, 28, 32–33, 57, 74–76, 77, 81, 83–95, 97, 98, 99–102, 103n90, 104, 105, 106–7, 109, 127, 139, 141–42, 149, 152, 192, 183, 207, 213n97, 215, 226, 235, 244, 246, 248

Ardashir I (r. 224–242), 70

Ardoxsho, 69

Arikamedu, 51, 52

Ark of the Covenant, 76

Armah (r. 614–631), 76

barley, 78. *See also* agriculture

Barnard, Paul, 128

Barnett, Lionel (1871–1960), 244n95, 245n103

Basagra, 37n15

Basil II (r. 976–1025), 208

Basmils, 162

Basra, 261, 269

Batthyány, Bishop Ignác (1741–1798), 185

Bayt al-Ḥikma, 178

Bazira (Beira) 92n42. *See also* Barikot

beads, 11, 16n36, 18, 28, 36–39, 43, 44–45, 46, 47n68, 48–52, 54–55, 63, 74, 98; faience, 39; glass, 36–39, 43, 44–45, 46, 47n68, 48–52, 54–55, 74; gold, 18, 98; Indo-Pacific, 43, 74; stone, 11, 16n36, 37, 52

Beauvais Missal, 187, 189

beaver, 263

Begash, 10

Behrendt, Karl, 85

Beijing, 16, 32n101, 133

Beijing World Art Museum, 32n101

Beira (Bazira), 92n42. *See also* Barikot

Beirut, 40

Beishi 北史, 48, 120n39, 132

Beit-Arié, Malachi, 167

Bellina, Bérénice, 52

belt, viii, 19*fig.*3, 20–28, 49, 50, 55, 130, 131, 142, 259

Belus River, 39, 42

Benedictine monks, 211n93

Berbera, 266

berberine, 180n81

Berbers, 271

Berlin, 187

Berthouville Treasure, 125n54

beryl, 46

Berzina, S. I., 79

Beshbaliq, 264n72

Bezymianny (nameless) mound, 115n20

Bhamala stupa, 146

Bhaṭa Hor Turks, 154–55

Bhutan, 110

Bible, 165–66, 173, 180, 235, 236, 264n75, 271; printed, 235, 236

Bibliothèque nationale de France, Paris, 165n7, 244n95

biliuli 碧琉璃, 53

Binyon, Laurence (1868–1943), 244

birchbark, 86, 168

Black Sea, 21, 32n99, 203

Bloom, Jonathan, 176, 177–78, 181, 183, 184

Blue Qu'ran, 3, 7, 164–89, *plate*6

boar, 21, 210n90

bodhisattvas, 101, 132

Bombay, 242

Bombyx mori, 191, 192, 206. *See also* sericulture; silkworms

Bonnet-Bidaud, Jean-Marc, 231

book burning, 222

book dealers, 185–86

book formats, 165–66, 173*fig.*22, 177*fig.*23, 215, 221, 239. *See also* manuscripts: codex, pothi, scroll, woodslip

Book of Zambasta, viii, 145*fig.*18

Bordeaux, 259

Borell, Brigitte, 35, 42, 50*fig.*5, 51

Borgelli Collection, Florence, 217

Bosshard, Walter (1892–1975), 148n40

Boston, 175, 176n62, 186, 187, 189

Bracey, Robert, 57n1, 64, 65, 67–68

Braghin, Cecilia, 34n1, 47–48

Brahmi script, 83n7, 142, 144–45

brass, 73

Brill, Robert, 45

Britain, 87, 152, 193, 240, 251, 258, 259. *See also* England; Wales

British Library, London, 187, 188n119, 229, 247–49

British Museum, London, 122, 148n42, 152, 217n109, 234, 242–47

brocade. *See jin*

Broken Books Project, 189n122

Bromberg, Carol, 207

bronze, 11, 16, 21n50, 23, 26, 45, 49, 55, 72, 73, 123, 157, 192

Bronze Age, 157, 192

Brooklyn Museum of Art, New York, 32n99

Broussonetia papyrifera, 195n19. *See also* mulberry, paper

Brussels, 33, 34, 136n89

Bucephala, 71

Buddha, 63, 68, 84, 86, 95, 98, 100, 101, 106, 145, 148–49, 154, 161, 168, 214; on coins,

ceramics *(continued)*
126; Indian, 52; Mesopotamian, 44, 128; porcelain, 44, 126; rouletted ware, 52; Seleucid, 128; stoneware, 44
Chagatai khanate (1225–1680s), 106–7
Chalcedon, 75
chalk, 171
Chang'an, 16n33,91, 133, 134, 136, 223, 226, 237. *See also* Xian
chariot, horse-drawn, 11, 157, 158
Charlemagne (747–814), 180, 211, 212, 214, 215
Charsadda, 82
chattra, 84, 88, 89, 91, 98, 106, 107
Chehrabad Salt Mine, 197n28
Chengdu, 226
Chennai, 53
Chen Zhuo 陳卓 (220–280), 231
Chester Beatty, Alfred (1875–1968), 186n110, 187
Chester Beatty Library, Dublin, 187
Chilek bowl, 122*fig.*16
Chin, Tamara, 12
China, 4, 5, 6, 7, 8, 9–16, 18, 20–21, 22–28, 30–33, 34–35, 41–51, 52, 54, 56, 58–59, 61, 63, 70, 73, 89, 91, 96, 102, 104–5, 111, 112, 114, 120, 123, 127, 132–36, 137, 138, 140–45, 148, 153, 155–56, 158–60, 161, 169, 190, 191–97, 209–14, 217, 220–49, 251, 253, 254, 255, 261, 262, 263–64, 267, 269 , 270; steppe and, 11–15, 20, 120, 133, 203. *See also heqin*
Chinese, language and script, xiii, 23, 133, 150, 219, 234, 241, 242, 243, 244, 245, 251
Chini-Bagh, 151
Chira River, 147, 148
chiton, 126–27, 129–30
Chittick, Neville (1924–1984), 79
Christian, David, 58, 62
Christianity, 7, 27, 57, 74–77, 87, 121, 137, 165–66, 179–80, 190, 203, 209, 211–18, 235, 258, 264n74, 266n82, 269, 270, 271; Arabic, 271; Armenian, 7; Axumite, 74–78, 165n5, 270; Baptist, 169; Benedictine, 211n93; books, 165–66, 179–80; Coptic, 75; Eastern Church, 75, 270; Indian, 75; Iranian, 251; Malamkara,

75; monasticism, 7, 57, 75–76, 77–78, 166n10, 185–86, 211, 214, 216–17; relics, 211–16
Christie's, 184n104, 187
chrysography, 175–76
Chu kingdom, 22, 24
Chu valley, 59
Cicero, Marcus Tullius (106–43 BC), 264n74
cinnabar (vermilion), 153
cinnamon, 263
Clermont, 211n93, 216
climate change, 4, 147
clothing, 13, 22, 55n94, 96, 98, 99, 101, 126–27, 129–30, 131, 132, 134, 142, 143, 144n27, 155, 158, 174, 179, 200n40, 207, 208, 213, 215, 217n114
Clysma (Qulzum), 263
cobalt, 37, 38, 39
Coca Cola, 1n2
codex. *See* manuscripts, codex
Codex Aureus of Lorsch, 185
Codex Purpureus Petropolitanus, 180n82
Codex Sinaiticus, 166
Cohen, Ada, 22
coins, viii, 6–7, 28, 57–80, 84, 86, 87, 100, 101, 102n84, 106, 113, 115–17, 118, 119, 121–23, 128, 139–40, 147, 151, 157n72, 161n91, 174, 200n40, 207, 209, 216n108, 218, 245, 259, 269; Alkhan-Huns, viii, 115, 116*fig.*15, 116n22, 122; Arabic, 76; Axumite, 73–74, 76; Bactrian, 113, 128, 140n14; brass, 73; bronze, 74, 139; Byzantine, 207; Chinese 28, 139, 140, 147, 151, 200n40, 216n108; copper, 64, 147, 151; French, 218; Ghaznavid, 105; gold, 64–70, 73, 76, 79, 174; Greek, 64, 128, 269; Hephthalite, 100, 113, 115–17, 118, 121–23, 140n14; Hindu Shahi, 100; Indo-Greek, 85, 86; Indo-Parthian, 140; Indo-Scythian, 86, 140; Islamic, 259; Khwarezmid, 106; Kidarite, 100, 101, 102n84, 119; Kushan, viii, 6–7, 57–80, 66*fig.*7, 67*fig.*8, 68*fig.*9, 69*fig.*10, 70*fig.*11, 86, 87, 128, 139, 140, 209; Kushano-Sasanian, 100; minting, 63, 65, 105, 106, 113, 116n22, 119, 121–23, 140, 216n108; Roman, 63, 64, 66, 72n64, 73, 76, 174; Sasanian, 100, 116n22, 117, 121, 122,

dog, 19, 191, 209–10, *plate7*
Doha, 188
Dome of the Rock, Jerusalem, 181, 183
Domoko, 154
donkey, 151n50
dragons, 16, 17n39, 25, 26–27, 101, 196, 200n39; elongated, 26–27; lupine, 26–27
drawloom. *See* looms, drawlooms
drinking, 40, 45n55, 50, 54, 59. *See also* wine
Droop, John Percival (1882–1963), 243
Dubai, 189
Dublin, 187, 259, 261–62
Du Fu 杜甫 (721–770), 161n96
Dunhuang, 28, 59, 134, 142, 144, 145, 152, 154, 183n102, 186, 221n9, 225–27, 232, 234n55, 236–41, 243–46, 265n77; library cave 144, 145, 183n102, 186, 225–41, 244n95, 246, 248
Duomo, Florence, 87n25
Dura Europos, 197, 198, 200, 201, 202, 203, 254
Durand, Maximilien, 191n1, 208, 212
dyes, 7, 65, 171–75, 177, 179–80, 183, 189, 191, 194, 206, 219, 234. *See also huangbo*; indigo; lichen; murex sea snails; Tyrian purple; ultramarine
Dyrestuy cemetery, 21n50

earthquakes, 100, 104, 106, 110
East Africa, 7, 72, 80, 87, 165, 257, 261, 269, 270. *See also* Eritrea; Ethiopia; Somalia; Sudan
East Asia, vii, viii, 7, 8, 9, 43, 62, 142, 162, 168, 176n64, 183, 209, 214, 215, 219. *See also* China; Japan; Korea
Eastern Han. *See* Former (Western) Han
Eastern Wei (534–550), 134
ebony, 38, 181, 197
Edesius (fl. 4th century), 270
Edna, 75, 76
Edward of Norwich (ca. 1373–1415), 210
Ege, Otto (1888–1951), 187
Eggala, Tigray, 75
Egypt, 19, 21, 26, 35, 36, 39, 45, 46, 52, 71, 72, 76, 82, 107, 172, 186, 193, 202n49, 217, 260, 262, 263, 267, 269

Egyptian blue (pigment), 36, 46
Egyptian empire, 26, 196
Ejin River/Etsin-gol, 20
elephants, 3, 53, 74, 118, 144. *See also* ivory
Elizabeth I (r. 1558–1603), 236
Elkhasaites, 169
Ely Cathedral, 91
ema 絵馬, 153
embalming, 39
emeralds, 121n46, 141–42
enamel, 214
Encyclopedia Iranica, xiii
Encyclopedia of Islam, xiii
Endere, 139n10
Endybis (t. ca. 270–300), 73
engineering, 178
England, 185, 215, 236
"Epistle on the Singing Girls," 266
Epitoma historiarum Philippicarum, 112n4
Eragrostis tef, 73
Eric the Red (950–ca. 1003), 258–59
Eridu, 37
Eritrea, 72, 80, 203
Erlitou culture (ca. 1900–1500 BC), 20. *See also* Shang (Yin) dynasty
Erzurum, 260
Esin, Emil, 155
Essenes, 264n75
Eṣṭakrī (10th century), 205
Ethelhard of Canterbury (791–805), 215
Ethiopia, 7, 57, 72, 76, 203, 252, 270, *plate2*. *See also* Axumite kingdom
Etruscan, 22, 127
Eudoxus of Cyzicus, 52
Eugene V. Thaw Collection, 32n100
eunuchs, 255, 262, 263, 264
Euphrates River, 197. *See also* Mesopotamia
Euripides (480–406 BC), 129
Europalia Festival (Belgium), 32n101
Europe, 4n15, 5, 10, 39, 45, 54, 91, 114, 115, 157, 166, 172, 193, 196, 200n38, 206, 209, 210, 211, 215, 235, 240, 258. *See also* England; France; Greece; Italy; Spain; Sweden; Switzerland; Wales
Evelyn-White, Hugh (1874–1924), 243
exhibitions, 8, 31–33, 129n69, 136, 218, 243–45, 249

Ghuzz, 258

Giles, Lionel (1875–1958), 219n1, 220n3, 236, 244, 245, 246, 248n114

Gilgamesh, 209

Gilgit, 71, 145

Gilgit River, 82

Gimbel Brothers, 187

glair (egg white), 176n61

glass, vii, viii, 2, 3, 5–6, 8, 16, 18, 24, 25n73,74, 30, 34–56, 65, 72, 74, 136, 160n87, 197, 214, 216, 243, *plate*1b; analysis of, 35, 41–42, 51, 54; in Buddhism, 5–6, 46, 47, 56, 214–15; Central Asia, 43–44; China, 5–6, 8, 24, 35, 41, 43–47, 52, 53–54, 56; Christianity, 216; Egyptian, 36, 37, 39, 40, 46; Europe, 39; Harappan, 36, 37–38; Hellenistic, 5, 8, 30, 34–56; Islamic, 45n55; lead-barium 45, 49, 51; materials, 35–45; Mesopotamia, 36–38; mosaic, 50n76; Mycenean, 39; potash-lime, 43, 44–45, 51, 52, 55; production, 5, 35–43, 54; Roman, 8, 24, 34–35, 50–51, 56, 72, 74; Sasanian, 54, 136; soda-lime, 37, 43, 51n77, 52, 55, 62; Southeast Asian, 43, 44, 52; structure of 35–36, 36*fig.*4; substitute for gemstone, 25n73, 36, 37, 45–47, 50n76, 52; trade in, 38–39, 42, 43–44, 47n68, 48, 50n76, 52–55, 72, 74, 197; Vietnam, 24, 35, 43, 47; volcanic, 35; weathering, 34, 37, 55–56; West Asia, 39–42, 43, 47, 54. *See also* beads

glazes, 36, 44, 47, 128

goad, 68

goat, 78, 166, 171

Gobi Desert, 58, 132–33, 154, 195

Godescalc, 180

gods, 1n2, 44n51, 63, 64n34, 67, 68, 69, 75, 87, 94, 99, 102, 125, 126–27, 128, 130, 153, 161, 225, 229; Chinese, 44n51, 225, 229; Greco-Roman, 68, 69n57, 130; Greek, 63, 67n50, 125, 126–27, 128, 130, 131; Indian, 63, 67, 68, 69n57, 81, 94, 99; Iranian, 68, 69, 130; Kushan, 63, 64n34, 67; Shinto, 153; sun, 161; Swat, 94n51; Tibetan, 94n51

Gods Must be Crazy, The (film), 1n2

Gog and Magog, 15n31

Gogdara, 94

Gola Dhora. *See* Bagasra

gold, 7, 17, 18, 19, 20, 21, 23, 24, 26, 28, 38, 40, 49, 53, 57, 64, 65–68, 80, 97, 98, 101, 111, 121–23, 125, 135, 141, 147n38, 164, 174, 177, 179, 180–83, 188n118, 214, 218; sources of, 65–67, 121–23; techniques, 17, 18, 19n43, 23, 24; trade in, 53, 65; writing in, 164, 175–76, 177, 180, 182, 183

Golden Deer of Eurasia: Scythian and Samaritan Treasures from the Russian Steppe, The (exhibition), 32

Goldin, Paul, 12, 13

Gol Mod, 2, 24

Gomot, Hippolyte, 217

Gondophares, 61n

Goryeo dynasty (918–1392), 235

Goths, 15n

graffiti, rock cut. *See* Shatial

Gragn. *See* Aḥmad ibn Ibrāhīm al-Ghāzī

grain, 14, 63, 65; as money, 63; trade, 65. *See also* barley, millet, wheat

granite, 74, 89, 94

granulation, 17, 18, 19n43

grapes, 96–98, 106, 135, 200, 202

Great Wall, 12n13, 15n30. *See also* limes

Greco-Bactrians (256–125 BC), 112, 128, 129, 130

Greece, 22, 23n64, 39, 40, 52, 111, 130, 158, 208n79, 231, 260. *See also* Hellenism

Greek gods. *See* Aphrodite; Athena; Dionysus; Hera; Heracles; Hermes

Greek language, 65, 67, 68, 72, 73, 86, 127, 128, 129, 170, 202, 263

Greeks, 15, 18, 22, 135n85

Greek script, 67, 69, 112, 128, 129

Greenland, 258

Gregory of Tours (ca. 538–594), 211n93

Grenet, Frantz, 102–3

greyhound, 209. *See also* saluki

griffin, 22n55

Grohmann, Adolf (1877–1977), 187

Guangdong province, 49

Guangxi province, 49

Guangzhou, 48, 49, 51, 53, 55, 263

Guan Zhong 管仲 (ca. 720–645 BC), 28

Guanzi, 管子, 28

Gucci, 55n92

marble, 25, 27
Mardan, 83
Margiana, 20, 128
Margilan, 152
maritime trade. *See* trade, maritime
marriage, political, 9, 14, 29, 117, 128, 144, 212, 251, 252. *See also heqin*
Marshak, Boris (1933–2016), 130, 131, 132
marten, 263
Martin, Fredrik R. (1868–1913), 184, 187
Martore, F., 90*fig*.13
Mary (mother of Jesus), 214n99, 270
Mashad, 179
Massillon, Jean-Pierre (1663–1742), 216
mathematics, 158n77, 251
Matsuoka, Kumiko, 249n117
Mattéwos, 75
Maurya empire (322–180 BC), 62, 83, 84, 85
Mawangdui, 222, 225n21
McHugh, Feldore, 29
McNair, W. W., 92n43
Mecca, 263, 269
medicine, 3, 7, 106, 178, 238n63
Medina, 263, 264n74
Mediterranean, 39, 40, 50n76, 52, 83, 127, 178, 202n49, 203, 205, 209, 258, 260–66, 271
mekku-stone, 39
Mellon, Andrew W. Foundation, 249
Meluḫḫa, 52n79
Menander I (r. ca. 160–130 BC), 62, 86
Menander Protector (fl. 6th century), 118, 120, 204n55
Mencius, 221n5
Menelaus of Sparta, 125–26, 131*fig*.17, 132, *plate*4
Menelik I (r. ca. 950 BC), 76
Mercator, Geradus (1512–1594), 230
merchants, 38–39, 48, 71, 72, 74, 80, 85, 92, 95, 103, 134, 142, 197–98, 203–4, 257, 258, 261, 262–63, 265n76, 266, 269, 272; Arab, 251, 257, 261, 262; Axumite, 203, 204; Bactrian, 71, 103; Buddhism and, 85, 95, 103, 142; Byzantine, 258; Central Asian, 48; Chinese, 258, 261; Egyptian, 72, 204; Greek, 72; Indian, 258; Jewish 262–63, 266; Palmyran, 197–98; Parthia, 71, 204; Persian, 71; Phoenician,

39; Rus, 262; Sasanian, 204; Sogdian, 71, 103, 265n76; Syro-Palestinan, 38–39. *See also* trade
mercury gilding, 23, 124
Merlinus Angilicus, 236
Merv, 103, 112, 152, 197–98, 205, 264n74
Mesopotamia, 11, 19, 36–38, 44, 45, 52, 128, 129, 157, 169, 197, 203, 208, 209
metalwares, 3, 111–36, 121, 127, 207, 209, 210, 215, 216, *plate*4. *See also* bronze; gold; silver
metalworking, 18, 36, 121–25; casting, 123, 127; granulation, 17, 18; hammering, 18, 124, 127, 129; lost-wax, lost-textile, 23, 124–25; repoussé, 124, 129
meteorite, 35
Metropolitan Museum of Art, New York, 32, 86n20, 125, 130, 136n89, 176n62, 189, 207n70
mica, 44
mice, 28
Michon, Daniel, 63–64
Middle East, 172, 188, 264n74. *See also* Levant; West Asia
Middle Persian, 71, 112n3, 139, 169, 255
Miiro. *See* Mithra
Milinda Panha (The questions of Milanda), 62, 86. *See also* Menander I
Milky Way, 231n46
millet, 10, 78. *See also* agriculture
mills, 96
Millward, James, 61
mines, 122–24, 138, 256n39, 264
Mingora, 62, 85, 109
Miniaev, Sergey, 9n1, 12
mints, 65, 113, 116n22, 119, 121, 122, 140n14
mirrors, 11, 20–21, 27
Mitanni kingdom (ca. 1500–1300 BC), 38
Mithra (Miiro), 68*fig*.9, 69, 161n92
Mi Xunzhi 米巡職 (fl. 648), 264n72
Modu (r. 209–174 BC), 13, 59
Mogao caves, 144, 154, 240. *See also* Dunhuang
Moh scale, 25n76, 47
molasses, 99
monastery, 7, 57, 62–63, 75–76, 77–78, 80, 87, 90, 92–98, 100, 101, 102, 104, 141, 143, 144, 149, 151, 163, 165, 166n10, 185–

neuroscience, 181

New York, 23, 31–32, 129, 136n89, 176n62, 187, 189

Niaz Hakim Beg (fl. 1666–1908), 242

Nicaea, 70, 268; Seige of, 268

Nickel, Lukas, 49–50

Nielson, Lisa, 266

Nikephoros II Phokas, (r. 963–969), 208

Nile River, 73, 269

Nimrud, 21

Nine Saints, 75–76

Ningxia province, 13n19, 132

nirvāṇa, 83, 85

Nishapur, 265

Niya. *See* Caḍota

Nizam al-Mulk (1018–1092), 267

Noin-Ula, 23n60, 27, 200

nomadism. *See* pastoralism

Norfolk, 185

Normans, 87

Norse, 211n93. *See also* Rus

North Africa, vii, 39, 40, 41, 165, 172, 177, 181, 183, 188n118, 203, 205, 209, 210, 258, 267. *See also* Egypt; Tunisia

North America, 31, 32, 259

Northern Dynasties (386–581), 48

Northern Wei (383–535), 70, 102, 120, 132, 133, 135, 255

Northern Zhou (557–581), 134, 135n81, 255

North Sea, 258

Norton, Charles Eliot (1827–1908), 186

Norwich, 185, 210

Nostradame, Michel de (1503–1566), 235–36

Nuwa 女媧, 44n51

obelisk, 21

obsidian, 35, 63

Ockham's razor, 177

Oḍḍiyāna, 82n4. *See* Udyāna

Odysseus, 126

Odyssey, 125–26

Oesho. *See* Wesho

Oguz Turks, 162

Ohta, Alison, 164n1, 176

oilpresses, for lamps, 96

Old/New Text debate, 222–23

Old Turdi, 147

oleaster, 163

olives, 264n74

Olivieri, Luca, 81n1, 89, 90, 91, 94, 95–96, 100, 107–8, 109

Oman, 52n79, 257, 269

Omsk, 26

onager, 124

One Thousand and One Nights, 251, 266–67

oracle bones, 11

orchil. *See* lichen

Ordos, 13, 16, 20, 21, 24, 28, 31, 133

Ordos Museum, 31

organ, 212

Orgyan Pa, 106. *See also* Padmasambhava

Osh, 152

ostrich eggs, 38

Ottoman empire (ca. 1299–1922), 184

Outer Eurasia, 9, 58, 60, 158. *See also* Eurasia

oxen. *See* cattle

Oxford, 243

Oxney Island, 259

Oxus. *See* Amu Darya

Oxyartes, 127

Pachomius (ca. 292–348), 75–76

Pacific Ocean, 261

Padmasambhava (Guru Rinpoche) (fl. 8th century), 98–99, 106

Pahlavi, 251

paintings, 2, 90, 94, 95, 121, 125, 126, 144, 146, 148–50, 152–54, 163, 243, 244

Pakistan, 64n32, 90, 109

Pali, 86

Paliputra, 83

palm bark/leaves, for manuscripts, 165n4, 168

Palmyra, 197

Pamir Mountains, 138, 139, 140, 141, 146, 161n93

Pangoraria stupa, 91

Panshjr valley, 121

Pantheon, Rome, 89n31, 91

Panyu, 49. *See also* Guangzhou

papal court, 166n44, 212

paper, ix, 8, 141, 142, 149–51, 154, 167n17, 168, 176n64, 177, 179n81, 183, 195n19, 219, 221, 225, 232–34, 235, 236, 237–38, 239–40, 245, 247–49; Arab, 177,

232–40, 247–49; Chinese, 8, 142, 151, 167n17, 168, 179n81, 183, 219, 221, 232–34; conservation, 245, 247–49; Japanese, 167n17, 249; making, 141, 142, 195n19, 232–34, 233fig.31; materials of, 8, 167n17, 232, 234n51, 235; Tibetan, 168, 183n100

papyrus, 166, 171n35, 176n64

parchment, viii, 8, 164, 165n4, 166–67, 169–71, 172fig.21, 173–75, 176n61, 178, 179–80, 216; dyeing, 173–75, 179–80. *See also* vellum

Paris, 32, 180n83, 212, 218, 259

Paris of Troy, 5, 125-31

parrot, 93

Parthian Empire (247 BC–AD 224), 15, 50n76, 61, 70, 196–97, 203, 204, 254, 256n39, 264n74; silk in, 196–97; slavery in, 254, 256n39, 264n74

Parthian language, 71, 169

Parthians, 15n31, 66, 128

particle-induced X-ray emission (PIXE), 41

Pashto, 81, 89

pastoralism/nomadic-pastoralism, 4, 10–15, 19, 24, 49, 58–61, 67, 80, 114, 119–20, 155

Patna, 83

Pazyryk, 196

peacock, 93, 181

pearls, 53, 98n72, 214

Pekar, 154–55

Pelius, 161

Pella, 22

Pelliot, Paul (1878–1945), 234n55, 244

Peloponnese, 260

Pelusium (Farama), 263

Penjikent, 71, 130n76

Penn Library, 186n111

pens, 175, 234

Pepin I of Aquitaine (r. 797–838), 213

Pepin II of Aquitaine (r. 838–864), 211–12, 213, 214, 215–16

Pepin the Short (r. 751–768), 211–12

Pergamum, 171n35

Periplus of the Erythraean Sea, 72, 73

Peroz I (r. 459–484), 116–17, 122

Persepolis, 21, 124

Persia, 15, 73, 82, 111, 112, 113, 128, 158, 160, 179n80, 184, 197n27, 198; silk, 197n27,

198, 207, 209. *See also* Achaemenid Empire; Iran; Parthian Empire; Sasanian Empire

Persian, xiii, 113, 151, 162, 251n8, 263. *See also* Middle Persian

persimmon, 81

Peru, 172n43

Peshawar, 70, 82, 92, 97, 105, 106, 146

Peshawar Museum, 97n70

Petra, 170

petroglyphs, 52, 82, 95–96, 97, 207, 209

Pharro, 69

pheasant, 93

Phellodendron amurense. *See* Amur cork tree

Phillipson, David, 79

Phoenicians, 39, 71, 173

phoenix, 200n39

pigments, 36, 37n10, 44, 46, 152–53, 181, 217n113; synthetic, 36, 37n10, 44, 46, 217. *See also* Egyptian blue; Han blue/purple; lapis lazuli; lead white; murex sea snails; ultramarine

pilgrimage, 81, 92, 94, 98, 106, 133, 142, 143, 214. *See also* Faxian; Hyecho; Songyun; Xuanzang

Pines, Yuri, 15

pirates, 258, 260–61

Pirmat-Baba-Tepe, 115n20

Pir Sar (Aornus), 82–83, 103

plant ash, 35, 36, 37, 38, 39

plastic, structure of, 36

platera, 24

Pliny the Elder (ca. 23–79), 39, 50n76, 66, 171n35, 261

poetry, 53, 117, 125–26, 145, 161n96, 170, 180, 181, 201, 252, 255, 265, 266–67. *See also* "Epistle on the Singing Girls"; *Iliad; Odyssey;* "Rhapsody on Women Weavers"; *Shahnameh;* "Wahid, the Singing Slave-Girl of 'Amhamah"

Pokrovka 2 cemetery, 23

polo, 158, 160

pomegranate, 38

Pompei, 125

Pondicherry, 52

poplar, 149, 152

porcelain, 44, 216. *See also* ceramics

Porter, Cheryl, 164n1, 174–76
Portugal, 77–78
Poseidon, 161
potash. *See* potassium
potassium, 41, 43, 44, 45, 51
potassium oxide, 44
pothi. *See* manuscript, pothi
pottery. *See* ceramics
Prada, 217n109
Praderie, Françoise, 231
Prague, 259, 262
Prajñāpāramitāsūtra, 141
Prākrit, 68, 83, 86, 139n10, 140
printing, vii, ix, 7, 165, 172*fig*.21, 219–
    40, 233*fig*.31, 244n95, 245, 247, 248,
    *plate*8; Buddhism, 219–20, 228n29, 235,
    248n114; China, 219–40; Dunhuang,
    226, 236–40; Europe, 235–36; Japan,
    235; Korea, 235; moveable type, 234–35;
    Tibet, 237; Uygur, 234–35; woodblock,
    ix, 172*fig*.21, 219–37, 233*fig*.31, 239–40
prisoners of war, 252, 255–57, 259, 260, 267,
    268, 269
Prochiros Nomos (870–879), 257
Procopius of Caesurea (ca. 500–560), 113,
    115n20, 120, 121
Ptolemy, Claudius (ca. 100–170), 112n3
Ptolemy VIII Euergetes II (r. 145–116 BC),
    52
Ptolemy Philadelphus (r. 285–246 BC),
    197n27
pumice, 171
Punjab, 43
Pur-i Vahman, 210
Purpura lapillus, 174. *See also* murex sea
    snails
purpurin, 191n3
Pushkalāvatī (Charsadda), 82
pustaka, 168. *See also* manuscript, pothi
Puta, 61
Puy de Domes, 211
Pyrgos-Mavroraki, 191n5
pyrite, 181

Qaiqaniah Turks, 162
Qianying, 151
Qijia culture (ca. 2200–1700 BC), 20
Qilian Mountains, 20, 59

Qin dynasty (221–206 BC), 12, 13, 14, 28,
    48–49, 158, 222
Qinshihuangdi (r. 246–210 BC), 48, 127,
    158, 222
Qixi Festival, 231n46
quartz, 18, 26, 41, 47
Qur'an, 3, 7, 164–89, 264n75, 266, 269, 271,
    *plate*6

Radhanites, 263. *See also* merchants, Jewish
radiocarbon dating, 75n76, 169, 170n32
Rakush, 162
Rāma, 81, 145. See also *Rāmāyana*
Raman spectroscopy, 176n62
Rāmāyana, 81n2, 82, 145
Ramla, 270
Raqqa, 257
Raqqada National Museum of Islamic Art,
    178
Raschke, M. G. 194
Rawak, 146, 148, 151
Rawak stupa, 146, 148
Rawson, Jessica, 11
Reader, Ian, 153
Rea Sea, 52, 54, 71, 72, 166n13, 197, 203, 258,
    263, 266, 271
reeds, 149, 175, 232
relics. *See* Buddhism, relics; Christianity,
    relics
religion. *See* Avesta; Buddhism; Christian-
    ity; Daoism; gods; Hinduism; Islam;
    Judaism; Manicheanism; Shinto; Vedic
    culture; Zoroastrianism
"Rhapsody on Women Weavers," 201
Riedel, Dagmar, 188, 189
Riggisburg, 217
Rigveda, 82
rishu 日書 (day books), 219, 221–22
Rob (Ruy), 120n41
Robert of Clermont (1256–1317), 211n93,
    216
rock crystal, rock paintings, 95–96, 97, 207
Rockwell, Peter, 94
Rokhsan. *See* An Lushan
Roman empire, 5, 8, 15, 24, 50n76, 61, 63,
    64, 66, 73, 112, 115, 135n85, 169, 181, 193,
    197, 202, 228n33, 252; literacy in, 228n33;